FODOR'S

NEW EDITION

BED & BREAKFASTS AND COUNTRY INNS

NEW ENGLAND

DELIGHTFUL
PLACES TO
STAY AND GREAT
THINGS TO DO
WHEN YOU
GET THERE

ISBN 0-679-02563-4

Second Edition

Fodor's Bed & Breakfasts and Country Inns

Editors: Jillian L. Magalaner, Scott McNeely
Creative Director: Fabrizio La Rocca
Cartographer: David Lindroth
Illustrators: Alida Beck
Design: Fabrizio La Rocca and Tigist Getachew

Special Sales

Fodor's Travel Publications are available at special discounts for bulk purchases for sales promotions or premiums. Special editions, including personalized covers, excerpts of existing guides, and corporate imprints, can be created in large quantities for special needs. For more information, contact your local bookseller or write to Special Marketing, Fodor's Travel Publications, 201 East 50th St., New York, NY 10022. Inquiries from Canada should be directed to your local Canadian bookseller or sent to Random House of Canada, Ltd., Marketing Dept., 1265 Aerowood Drive, Mississanga, Ontario L4W 1B9. Inquiries from the United Kingdom should be sent to Fodor's Travel Publications, 20 Vauxhall Bridge Rd., London, England SW1V 2SA.

MANUFACTURED IN THE UNITED STATES OF AMERICA
10 9 8 7 6 5 4 3 2 1

Contributors

Nigel Fisher, *editor of the monthly travel publication,* Voyager International, *revised the chapter on Rhode Island. He currently lives in New England.*

Mary H. Frakes, *who wrote our Vermont chapter, is a restaurant columnist for the* Boston Phoenix. *She also writes on travel, business, and contemporary arts and crafts.*

Candice Gianetti, *who wrote the Cape Cod, Martha's Vineyard, and Nantucket sections of the Massachusetts chapter, is the author of Fodor's* Cape Cod. *She lives year-round on the Cape.*

Deborah Kovacs, *who wrote the Rhode Island chapter and the section on Southeastern Massachusetts, is the author of 12 children's books. She lives in South Dartmouth, Massachusetts.*

David Laskin, *who lives on Long Island, wrote our Maine chapter. His work has appeared in* The New York Times *and* Travel & Leisure. *In 1990 he published the book* Eastern Islands: Accessible Islands of the East Coast.

Betty Lowry *lives in Massachusetts, is the author of our New Hampshire chapter, and has written extensively on New England, the Caribbean, and Europe for publications throughout the United States.*

Anne Merewood, *a transplanted Englishwoman who lives in Boston, is the author of two travel guides to Greece and writes frequently on health and travel for American magazines. She wrote about the Massachusetts North Shore, Pioneer Valley, and Berkshires for this book.*

Hilary Nangle, *who lives in Round Pond, Maine, divides her time between travel and sports writing and working as an associate editor for* Gourmet News. *She revised the Maine chapter.*

Arthur S. Rosenblatt, *who lives in Connecticut, is the author of 16 books for children and a frequent contributor to* Food & Wine *and* Poets and Writers.

Andrew Collins, *who has edited and contributed to numerous Fodor's guides, revised the Connecticut chapter.*

Contents

Foreword

While every care has been taken to ensure the accuracy of the information in this guide, the passage of time will always bring change, and, consequently, the publisher cannot accept responsibility for errors that may occur.

All prices and listings are based on information available to us at press time. Details may change, however, and the prudent traveler will avoid inconvenience by calling ahead.

Fodor's wants to hear about your travel experiences, both pleasant and unpleasant. When an inn or B&B fails to live up to its billing, let us know and we will investigate the complaint and revise our entries where the facts warrant it.

Send your letters to the editors of Fodor's Travel Publications, 201 E. 50th Street, New York, NY 10022.

Introduction

Fodor's Bed & Breakfasts and Country Inns *is a complete weekend planner that tells you not just where to stay but how to enjoy yourself when you get there. We describe the B&Bs and country inns, of course, but we also help you organize trips around them, with information on everything from parks to beaches to antiques stores—as well as nightlife and memorable places to dine. We also include names and addresses of B&B reservation services, should properties we recommend be full or should you be inspired to go in search of additional places on your own. Reviews are divided by state, and, within each state, by region.*

All inns are not created equal, and age in itself is no guarantee of good taste, quality, or charm. We therefore avoid the directory approach, preferring instead to discriminate—recommending the very best for travelers with different interests, budgets, and sensibilities.

It's a sad commentary on other B&B guides today that we feel obliged to tell you our reviewers visited every property in person, and that it is they, not the innkeepers, who wrote the reviews. No one paid a fee or promised to sell or promote the book, in order to be included in it. Fodor's has no stake in anything but the truth: A dark room with peeling wallpaper is not called quaint or atmospheric, it's called run-down; a gutted 18th-century barn with motel units at either end is called a gutted 18th-century barn with motel units at either end, not a historic inn.

Is there a difference between a B&B and a country inn? Not really, not any more; the public has blurred the distinction—hence our decision to include both in the title. There was a time when the B&B experience meant an extra room in someone's home, often with paper-thin walls and a shared bathroom full of bobby pins and used cottonballs. But no longer; Laura Ashley has come to town with her matching prints, and some B&Bs are as elegant as the country's most venerable inns. The only distinction that seems to hold is that a B&B was built as a private home and an inn was built for paying guests. Most B&Bs, but not all, serve breakfast, and some serve dinner, too; most inns have full-service restaurants. B&Bs tend to be run by their owners, creating a homey, family feeling (which can be anathema to those who relish privacy), while inns are often run by managers; but the reverse is true, too. B&Bs can cost more than inns, or less. B&Bs tend to be smaller, with fewer rooms, but not always. The truth is that many B&Bs are called so only to circumvent local zoning laws.

What all places in this guide—B&Bs or country inns—offer is the promise of a unique experience. Each is one of a kind, and each exudes a sense of time and place. All are destinations in themselves—not just places to put your head at night, but an integral part of a wonderful weekend escape.

So trust us, the way you'd trust a knowledgeable, well-traveled friend. And have a wonderful weekend!

***

A word about the service material in this guide:

A second address in parentheses is a mailing address that differs from the actual address of the property. A double room is for two people, regardless of the size or type of beds; if you're looking for twin beds or a king- or queen-size bed, be sure to ask.

Rates are for two in the high season, and include breakfast; ask about special packages and off-season discounts. Mandatory state taxes are extra. Most places leave tipping to the discretion of the visitor, but some add a service charge to the bill; if the issue concerns you, inquire when you make your reservation, not when you check out.

What we call a restaurant serves meals other than breakfast and is usually open to the general public. Inns listed as MAP (Modified American Plan) require guests to pay for two meals, usually breakfast and dinner. The requirement is usually enforced during the high season, but an inn may waive it if it is otherwise unable to fill all its rooms.

B&Bs don't have phones or TVs in rooms unless otherwise noted. Pools and bicycles are free; "bike rentals" are not. Properties are open year-round, unless otherwise noted. On the following pages is a chart that will help you quickly select an inn that suits your needs.

Michael Spring
Editorial Director

New England

CANADA
QUEBEC
NEW YORK
VERMONT
NEW HAMPSHIRE
MASSACHUSETTS
CONNECTICUT
RHODE ISLAND
Stratton
Rangeley
Mooselookmeguntic Lake
Newport
Colebrook
Enosburg Falls
St. Albans
Orleans
Barton
Island Pond
North Stratford
Errol
Wilton
Rumford
Lake Champlain
Morrisville
Hardwick
Lydonville
Groveton
Lancaster
Berlin
Newry
Bethel
Burlington
St. Johnsbury
Littleton
Gorham
Winthrop
S. Paris
Montpelier
Barre
Twin Mtn.
Woodsville
Mechanic Falls
Auburn
Vergennes
Middlebury
Lincoln
Bartlett
North Conway
Bridgton
Fryeburg
Conway
Randolph
Brandon
Connecticut River
Tamworth
Sebago Lake
Brunswick
Ossipee
Westbrook
Portland
Rutland
Woodstock
Lebanon
Meredith
Lake Winnipesaukee
Bristol
Biddeford
Sanford
Wallingford
Poultney
Ludlow
Laconia
Claremont
Kennebunkport
Springfield
Rochester
Manchester
Concord
Dover
Kittery
Arlington
Portsmouth
Keene
Bennington
Wilmington
Brattleboro
Milford
Nashua
Amesbury
Haverhill
Newburyport
Lawrence
Williamstown
Lowell
Gloucester
Athol
Fitchburg
Danvers
Beverly
Greenfield
Gardner
Leominster
Salem
Lexington
Pittsfield
Cambridge
Amherst
Northampton
Marlborough
Stockbridge
Boston
Worcester
Braintree
Sandisfield
Chicopee
Springfield
Brockton
Provincetown
Canaan
Lakeville
Winsted
Windsor Locks
Putnam
Bridgewater
Plymouth
Providence
Taunton
Cape Cod
Torrington
Manchester
Hartford
Willimantic
Warwick
Fall River
Kent
New Britain
New Milford
Bristol
Bristol
New Bedford
Hyannis
Waterbury
Meriden
Middletown
Falmouth
Newport
Norwich
Oak Bluffs
Wallingford
Danbury
Mystic
Westerly
Wakefield
Martha's Vineyard
New Haven
New London
Block Island Sound
Block Island
Long Island Sound
Bridgeport
Norwalk
Stamford
Long Island
91
89
93
7
95
1
90
495
84
395
195

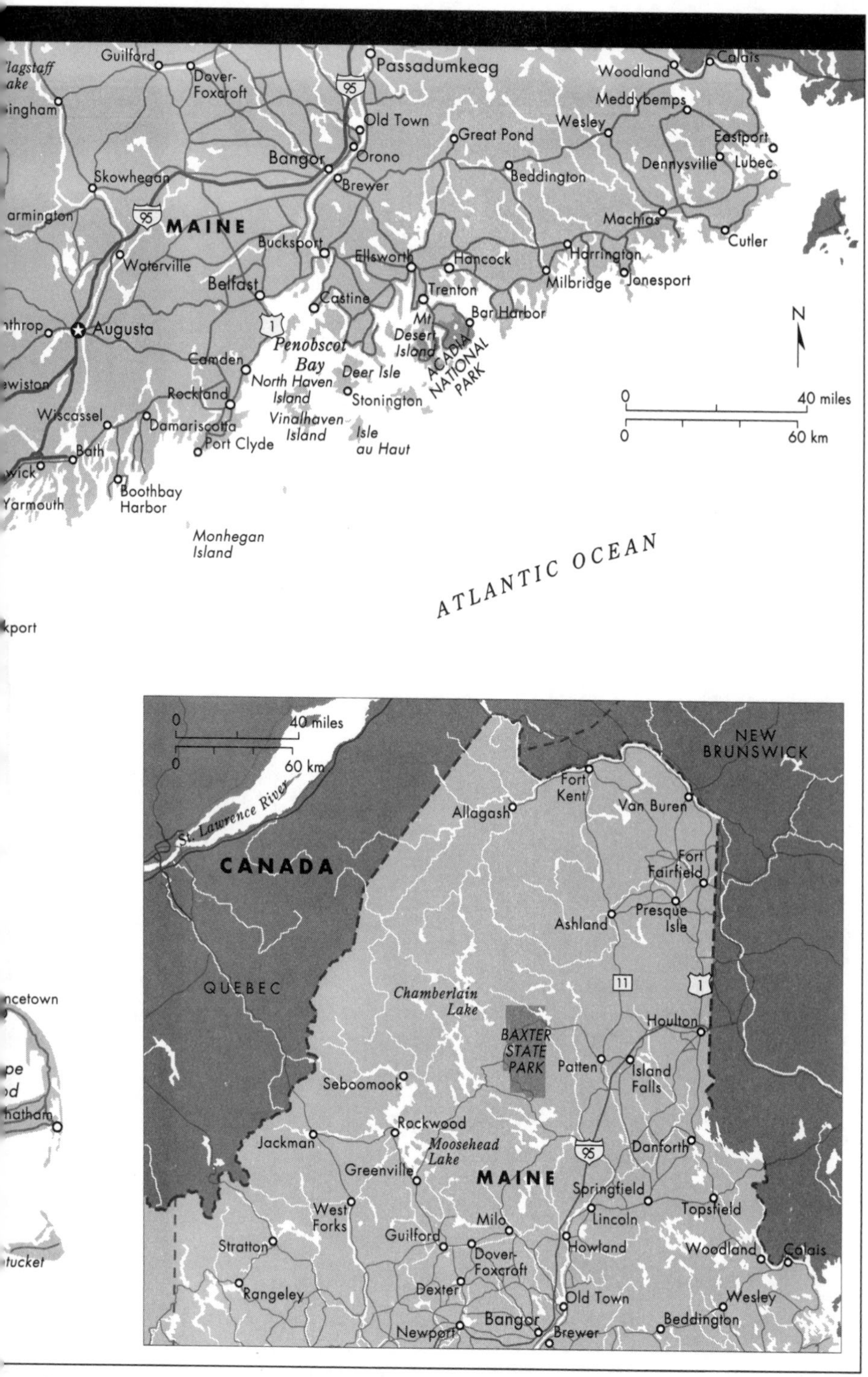
Guilford
Dover-Foxcroft
Passadumkeag
Woodland
Calais
Meddybemps
Old Town
Wesley
Great Pond
Eastport
Bangor
Orono
Dennysville
Lubec
Skowhegan
Brewer
Beddington
MAINE
Machias
Cutler
Bucksport
Ellsworth
Hancock
Harrington
Waterville
Milbridge
Jonesport
Belfast
Trenton
Castine
Bar Harbor
Augusta
Mt Desert Island
ACADIA NATIONAL PARK
Penobscot Bay
Camden
Deer Isle
North Haven Island
Rockland
Stonington
Wiscassel
Damariscotta
Vinalhaven Island
Isle au Haut
Port Clyde
Bath
Boothbay Harbor
Yarmouth
Monhegan Island
ATLANTIC OCEAN
N
0
40 miles
60 km
NEW BRUNSWICK
Fort Kent
St. Lawrence River
Allagash
Van Buren
CANADA
Fort Fairfield
Presque Isle
Ashland
QUEBEC
Chamberlain Lake
Houlton
BAXTER STATE PARK
Patten
Island Falls
Seboomook
Rockwood
Jackman
Moosehead Lake
Danforth
Greenville
MAINE
Springfield
West Forks
Lincoln
Topsfield
Milo
Guilford
Stratton
Howland
Woodland
Dover-Foxcroft
Dexter
Rangeley
Old Town
Wesley
Bangor
Beddington
Newport
Brewer

Special Features at a Glance

Name of Property	*Accessible for Disabled*	*Antiques*	*On the Water*	*Good Value*	*Car Not Necessary*	*Full Meal Service*	*Historic Building*
CONNECTICUT							
Antiques & Accommodations		✓					✓
Barney House		✓		✓			✓
Bee & Thistle Inn		✓	✓	✓		✓	✓
Bishopsgate Inn		✓		✓			✓
Boulders Inn		✓	✓	✓		✓	
Captain Stannard House		✓		✓			✓
Cobble Hill Farm		✓		✓			✓
Copper Beech Inn	✓	✓				✓	✓
The Country Goose		✓		✓			✓
The Elms	✓			✓	✓	✓	✓
The Greenwoods Gate		✓					✓
Griswold Inn		✓				✓	✓
Harbor House Inn			✓	✓			
Harbour Inne & Cottage			✓	✓	✓		
Highland Farm		✓					✓
The Homestead Inn (Greenwich)		✓		✓		✓	✓
The Homestead Inn (New Milford)		✓		✓			✓
Hopkins Inn			✓	✓		✓	✓
The Inn at Chapel West	✓	✓			✓		
The Inn at Lake Waramaug			✓			✓	✓
The Inn at Longshore			✓			✓	✓
Ivoryton Inn	✓					✓	✓
Lasbury's Guest House			✓	✓	✓		✓
Manor House		✓		✓			✓

	Romantic Hideaway	*Luxurious*	*Pets Allowed*	*No Smoking Indoors*	*Good Place for Families*	*Near Arts Festivals*	*Beach Nearby*	*Cross-Country Ski Trail*	*Golf Within 5 Miles*	*Fitness Facilities*	*Good Biking Terrain*	*Skiing*	*Horseback Riding*	*Tennis*	*Swimming on Premises*	*Conference Facilities*
	✓	✓		✓			✓		✓		✓					
					✓			✓	✓		✓				✓	✓
	✓	✓		✓		✓	✓		✓		✓					
	✓				✓				✓		✓					
	✓				✓		✓	✓	✓		✓	✓		✓	✓	✓
				✓			✓		✓		✓					
				✓	✓		✓	✓	✓		✓	✓		✓	✓	
	✓	✓							✓		✓					
	✓			✓		✓		✓	✓		✓	✓				
					✓	✓		✓	✓		✓					✓
	✓	✓		✓		✓		✓	✓		✓	✓	✓			
	✓				✓		✓		✓		✓					✓
							✓		✓		✓					
			✓		✓	✓	✓		✓							
								✓	✓		✓	✓				
	✓	✓					✓		✓		✓					
			✓		✓				✓					✓		
	✓						✓		✓		✓	✓				
	✓	✓				✓			✓							✓
				✓	✓		✓		✓	✓	✓	✓		✓	✓	✓
	✓	✓			✓	✓	✓		✓		✓			✓	✓	✓
					✓				✓		✓			✓		
					✓	✓	✓		✓		✓					
	✓	✓				✓		✓	✓			✓	✓			

Name of Property	*Accessible for Disabled*	*Antiques*	*On the Water*	*Good Value*	*Car Not Necessary*	*Full Meal Service*	*Historic Building*
The Maples Inn		✓					✓
The Mayflower Inn	✓	✓				✓	
Old Riverton Inn			✓			✓	✓
Old Lyme Inn	✓	✓				✓	✓
The Palmer Inn		✓					✓
Randall's Ordinary	✓	✓				✓	✓
Red Brook Inn		✓					✓
Riverwind		✓		✓			✓
Roger Sherman Inn		✓		✓		✓	✓
Silvermine Tavern		✓	✓	✓		✓	✓
Simsbury 1820 House	✓	✓		✓		✓	✓
The Stanton House Inn				✓			✓
Stonehenge	✓	✓				✓	
Talcott House		✓	✓	✓			
Toll Gate Hill Inn & Restaurant	✓	✓				✓	✓
Tucker Hill Inn				✓			
Under Mountain Inn		✓		✓		✓	✓
Wake Robin Inn	✓	✓				✓	✓
West Lane Inn	✓	✓					✓
The Whaler's Inn	✓		✓	✓	✓	✓	
The White Hart						✓	✓
Yesterday's Yankee B&B					✓		✓
The Curtis House				✓		✓	✓

	Romantic Hideaway	*Luxurious*	*Pets Allowed*	*No Smoking Indoors*	*Good Place for Families*	*Near Arts Festivals*	*Beach Nearby*	*Cross-Country Ski Trail*	*Golf Within 5 Miles*	*Fitness Facilities*	*Good Biking Terrain*	*Skiing*	*Horseback Riding*	*Tennis*	*Swimming on Premises*	*Conference Facilities*
	✓	✓			✓	✓			✓		✓					
	✓	✓		✓				✓	✓	✓	✓	✓		✓	✓	✓
			✓		✓		✓	✓	✓		✓	✓				✓
		✓	✓		✓	✓	✓		✓		✓					✓
	✓						✓		✓		✓					
	✓						✓		✓							✓
	✓	✓		✓		✓	✓		✓							
	✓	✓							✓		✓					
						✓			✓		✓					✓
	✓					✓	✓		✓		✓					
	✓	✓	✓			✓		✓	✓		✓	✓				✓
				✓	✓		✓		✓							
	✓	✓							✓		✓				✓	✓
	✓				✓		✓		✓		✓				✓	
	✓		✓					✓	✓		✓	✓	✓			
				✓				✓	✓		✓	✓				
	✓			✓		✓	✓	✓	✓		✓	✓	✓			
			✓		✓	✓		✓	✓	✓		✓	✓	✓	✓	✓
					✓	✓			✓		✓					✓
					✓	✓	✓		✓		✓					
	✓	✓			✓	✓		✓	✓		✓	✓	✓			✓
	✓					✓		✓	✓		✓	✓	✓			
			✓		✓				✓		✓	✓				

Name of Property	*Accessible for Disabled*	*Antiques*	*On the Water*	*Good Value*	*Car Not Necessary*	*Full Meal Service*	*Historic Building*
MAINE							
Blue Hill Inn		✓				✓	
The Bradley Inn				✓		✓	
Brannon-Bunker Inn		✓		✓			
Breezemere Farm			✓				
The Briar Rose		✓		✓			
Broad Bay Inn and Gallery		✓					
Bufflehead Cove			✓	✓			
The Camden Maine Stay		✓		✓			✓
The Captain Jefferds Inn		✓					✓
The Captain Lord Mansion		✓					✓
The Castine Inn						✓	✓
Claremont Hotel			✓	✓		✓	✓
Cleftstone Manor		✓					✓
Country Club Inn							
The Craignair Inn			✓	✓		✓	✓
The Crocker House Inn				✓		✓	
Dockside Guest Quarters			✓	✓		✓	
The East Wind Inn & Meeting House			✓	✓		✓	
Edgecomb-Coles House		✓					
Eggemoggin Inn			✓	✓			
Fairhaven Inn			✓	✓			
The Green Heron				✓			
Holbrook House		✓					
Homeport Inn		✓	✓	✓			✓

	Romantic Hideaway	Luxurious	Pets Allowed	No Smoking Indoors	Good Place for Families	Near Arts Festivals	Beach Nearby	Cross-Country Ski Trail	Golf Within 5 Miles	Fitness Facilities	Good Biking Terrain	Skiing	Horseback Riding	Tennis	Swimming on Premises	Conference Facilities
				✓							✓					
							✓				✓					
				✓				✓			✓					
				✓	✓		✓	✓			✓			✓	✓	
				✓			✓		✓		✓					
											✓					
	✓			✓			✓	✓	✓		✓					
				✓			✓	✓	✓		✓	✓				
	✓	✓	✓				✓		✓		✓					
	✓	✓					✓		✓		✓					
							✓		✓		✓					
	✓				✓	✓	✓		✓		✓			✓		
	✓	✓					✓		✓		✓					
	✓		✓		✓			✓	✓							
					✓			✓			✓					
			✓								✓					
							✓		✓		✓					
											✓					✓
	✓	✓					✓	✓	✓		✓					
					✓		✓				✓					
	✓				✓			✓	✓		✓					
					✓	✓	✓		✓		✓					
	✓					✓	✓		✓		✓					
	✓	✓									✓					

Name of Property	Accessible for Disabled	Antiques	On the Water	Good Value	Car Not Necessary	Full Meal Service	Historic Building
Inn at Canoe Point		✓	✓				
The Inn at Harbor Head		✓	✓				✓
Inn at Long Lake		✓		✓			
The Inn at Southwest							
The Isaac Randall House		✓					
The Island House		✓		✓			✓
The John Peters Inn		✓	✓				✓
Kedarburn Inn		✓				✓	
The Kingsleigh Inn							
Lake House							
Le Domaine						✓	
Londonderry Inn				✓			
The Lookout			✓	✓		✓	
The Maine Stay Inn and Cottages							✓
Manor House Inn		✓					
Mill Pond Inn			✓	✓			
Mira Monte							
Moorings Inn			✓	✓			
The Newcastle Inn		✓	✓			✓	
The Noble House			✓				
Norumbega		✓					✓
Old Fort Inn		✓					
181 Main Street		✓					
The Pentagoet		✓				✓	
Penury Hall Bed 'n Breakfast				✓			

	Romantic Hideaway	Luxurious	Pets Allowed	No Smoking Indoors	Good Place for Families	Near Arts Festivals	Beach Nearby	Cross-Country Ski Trail	Golf Within 5 Miles	Fitness Facilities	Good Biking Terrain	Skiing	Horseback Riding	Tennis	Swimming on Premises	Conference Facilities
	✓	✓				✓	✓		✓		✓				✓	
	✓			✓			✓		✓		✓					
							✓		✓		✓	✓				
				✓		✓			✓		✓					
	✓	✓			✓				✓							
						✓			✓		✓					
	✓	✓									✓					
	✓		✓		✓		✓		✓		✓	✓				
	✓					✓	✓		✓		✓					
	✓						✓		✓							
	✓															
											✓					
					✓		✓				✓					
					✓		✓		✓		✓					
	✓					✓	✓		✓		✓					
	✓										✓				✓	
						✓	✓		✓		✓					
					✓	✓	✓		✓		✓					
	✓			✓							✓					
	✓								✓			✓				
	✓	✓					✓		✓		✓	✓				
	✓	✓					✓		✓		✓					
				✓					✓						✓	
	✓	✓					✓		✓		✓					
						✓	✓				✓					✓

Name of Property	*Accessible for Disabled*	*Antiques*	*On the Water*	*Good Value*	*Car Not Necessary*	*Full Meal Service*	*Historic Building*
Pilgrim's Inn		✓	✓			✓	✓
The Pomegranate Inn		✓			✓		
Sebago Lake Lodge & Cottages			✓				
The Squire Tarbox Inn		✓				✓	
The Waterford Inne		✓		✓		✓	
Westways			✓			✓	
The White Barn Inn						✓	
Whitehall Inn		✓				✓	✓
Windward House		✓		✓			
York Harbor Inn		✓				✓	✓
MASSACHUSETTS							
A Cambridge House Bed-and-Breakfast	✓	✓			✓		
Addison Choate Inn	✓	✓		✓	✓		✓
Admiral Benbow Inn		✓					✓
Aldworth Manor		✓					
Allen House		✓	✓	✓	✓	✓	✓
The Allen House	✓	✓		✓			✓
Amelia Payson Guest House	✓			✓	✓		
Apple Tree Inn		✓				✓	✓
Ashley Manor		✓					✓
Augustus Snow House		✓				✓	✓
Bacon Barn Inn		✓		✓			✓
Bay Beach			✓				
The Bayberry		✓					

	Romantic Hideaway	*Luxurious*	*Pets Allowed*	*No Smoking Indoors*	*Good Place for Families*	*Near Arts Festivals*	*Beach Nearby*	*Cross-Country Ski Trail*	*Golf Within 5 Miles*	*Fitness Facilities*	*Good Biking Terrain*	*Skiing*	*Horseback Riding*	*Tennis*	*Swimming on Premises*	*Conference Facilities*
	✓	✓				✓	✓				✓					
	✓	✓				✓			✓							
			✓		✓		✓		✓						✓	
	✓	✓						✓			✓					
			✓		✓		✓	✓			✓	✓				
	✓	✓			✓		✓	✓	✓		✓	✓		✓	✓	
	✓	✓					✓		✓		✓					
							✓		✓		✓					
	✓	✓		✓			✓		✓		✓	✓				
	✓						✓		✓		✓					✓
					✓											
		✓		✓			✓								✓	
				✓			✓		✓		✓					
	✓	✓		✓			✓		✓		✓					
	✓			✓	✓		✓				✓					
		✓		✓												
				✓	✓											
	✓	✓		✓		✓		✓	✓		✓	✓	✓	✓	✓	✓
	✓	✓		✓			✓		✓		✓			✓		
	✓	✓					✓		✓							✓
	✓			✓			✓		✓		✓					
	✓	✓		✓			✓		✓	✓	✓				✓	
				✓					✓		✓					

Name of Property	*Accessible for Disabled*	*Antiques*	*On the Water*	*Good Value*	*Car Not Necessary*	*Full Meal Service*	*Historic Building*
Beach Plum Inn and Cottages						✓	
Beacon Hill Bed and Breakfast					✓		
Beacon Inns	✓			✓	✓		
Beechwood		✓					✓
The Bertram Inn	✓	✓		✓	✓		
Blantyre	✓	✓					✓
Breakfast at Tiasquam	✓						
Brewster Farmhouse Inn							
Brook Farm Inn	✓	✓		✓			
The Candlelight Inn		✓				✓	✓
Captain Dexter House		✓			✓		✓
Captain Freeman Inn		✓		✓			✓
Captain's House Inn		✓					✓
Centerboard Guest House		✓			✓		✓
Century House					✓		✓
Charlotte Inn		✓			✓	✓	✓
Chatham Bars Inn			✓			✓	✓
Clark Currier Inn	✓	✓		✓	✓		✓
Cliffwood Inn		✓					✓
Colonel Ebenezer Crafts Inn & the Publick House	✓	✓				✓	✓
Corner House		✓		✓	✓		✓
Daggett House		✓	✓		✓	✓	✓
Dalton House	✓			✓			
Deerfield Inn		✓				✓	✓
Durant Sail Loft Inn	✓	✓	✓			✓	✓

Romantic Hideaway	Luxurious	Pets Allowed	No Smoking Indoors	Good Place for Families	Near Arts Festivals	Beach Nearby	Cross-Country Ski Trail	Golf Within 5 Miles	Fitness Facilities	Good Biking Terrain	Skiing	Horseback Riding	Tennis	Swimming on Premises	Conference Facilities
✓		✓				✓				✓			✓		
			✓												
		✓		✓											
✓						✓		✓		✓					
✓	✓			✓	✓		✓	✓	✓	✓	✓	✓	✓	✓	
✓			✓	✓		✓				✓					
✓	✓					✓		✓		✓				✓	
✓					✓		✓	✓		✓	✓	✓		✓	
✓	✓				✓		✓	✓		✓	✓	✓			
✓	✓					✓		✓		✓					
			✓			✓		✓		✓					
✓	✓		✓			✓		✓		✓					
✓	✓					✓		✓		✓					
			✓			✓		✓		✓					
✓	✓					✓		✓		✓					
✓	✓			✓		✓		✓		✓			✓	✓	✓
✓	✓					✓						✓			
✓	✓				✓	✓		✓		✓	✓	✓		✓	
✓				✓			✓		✓	✓			✓	✓	✓
✓						✓		✓		✓					
✓				✓		✓		✓		✓					
				✓	✓		✓			✓	✓	✓		✓	
✓	✓	✓		✓	✓		✓			✓					✓
				✓	✓	✓		✓							✓

Name of Property	*Accessible for Disabled*	*Antiques*	*On the Water*	*Good Value*	*Car Not Necessary*	*Full Meal Service*	*Historic Building*
Eden Pines Inn			✓				
82 Chandler Street				✓	✓		
Field Farm	✓		✓	✓			✓
The Gables Inn	✓	✓					✓
Garrison Inn	✓	✓			✓	✓	✓
Gateways Inn		✓				✓	✓
Harbor Light Inn	✓	✓			✓		✓
Harborside House			✓		✓		
Honeysuckle Hill		✓					✓
Inn on Cove Hill	✓	✓		✓	✓		✓
The Inn at Fernbrook		✓					✓
Isaiah Clark House		✓		✓	✓	✓	✓
Isaiah Hall B&B Inn		✓		✓			✓
Isaiah Jones Homestead		✓		✓			✓
Ivanhoe Country House	✓	✓		✓			
Jared Coffin House		✓			✓	✓	✓
John Jeffries House	✓				✓		
Lambert's Cove Country Inn				✓		✓	
Liberty Hill		✓		✓			✓
Lord Jeffery Inn	✓	✓			✓	✓	
Martin House Inn		✓			✓		✓
Merrell Tavern Inn	✓	✓		✓			✓
Moses Nickerson House		✓					✓
Mostly Hall		✓		✓			✓
New Boston Inn	✓	✓				✓	✓

	Romantic Hideaway	Luxurious	Pets Allowed	No Smoking Indoors	Good Place for Families	Near Arts Festivals	Beach Nearby	Cross-Country Ski Trail	Golf Within 5 Miles	Fitness Facilities	Good Biking Terrain	Skiing	Horseback Riding	Tennis	Swimming on Premises	Conference Facilities
	✓						✓									
				✓	✓											
	✓	✓			✓			✓			✓	✓		✓	✓	✓
	✓	✓				✓		✓	✓		✓	✓	✓		✓	
					✓		✓						✓			✓
	✓	✓				✓		✓	✓		✓	✓	✓			
	✓	✓			✓											
	✓			✓	✓											
	✓		✓				✓		✓		✓					
				✓			✓									
	✓			✓			✓		✓		✓					
				✓	✓		✓		✓							
							✓		✓		✓					
	✓	✓		✓					✓		✓					
	✓		✓					✓	✓		✓	✓			✓	
			✓		✓		✓		✓		✓					✓
	✓				✓		✓				✓			✓		
	✓	✓			✓		✓		✓		✓					
					✓			✓			✓					
	✓						✓		✓		✓					
	✓	✓			✓	✓		✓	✓		✓	✓	✓			
	✓			✓			✓		✓		✓					
	✓	✓		✓			✓		✓		✓					
	✓			✓	✓			✓			✓		✓			

Name of Property	*Accessible for Disabled*	*Antiques*	*On the Water*	*Good Value*	*Car Not Necessary*	*Full Meal Service*	*Historic Building*
Newbury Guest House	✓				✓		
Northfield Country House		✓		✓			
Oak House		✓	✓		✓		✓
The Orchards	✓	✓				✓	
Outermost Inn			✓			✓	
The Red Lion Inn	✓	✓				✓	✓
River Bend Farm		✓		✓			✓
Rookwood Inn		✓					✓
Sally Webster Inn		✓		✓	✓		✓
Salt Marsh Farm		✓		✓			
Sea Spray Inn				✓	✓		
Seacrest Manor	✓	✓					
Seaward Inn	✓	✓	✓			✓	
Seven Sea Street					✓		
Seven South Street		✓	✓	✓	✓		✓
76 Main Street	✓	✓			✓		✓
Shiverick Inn		✓			✓		✓
Sturbridge Country Inn	✓	✓					
Summer House		✓	✓			✓	
Sunnyside Farm Bed and Breakfast		✓		✓			
Ten Lyon Street Inn		✓			✓		
Thorncroft Inn		✓			✓		
The Turning Point Inn		✓					✓
Victorian Inn		✓			✓		✓
Village Green Inn		✓		✓			✓

	Romantic Hideaway	Luxurious	Pets Allowed	No Smoking Indoors	Good Place for Families	Near Arts Festivals	Beach Nearby	Cross-Country Ski Trail	Golf Within 5 Miles	Fitness Facilities	Good Biking Terrain	Skiing	Horseback Riding	Tennis	Swimming on Premises	Conference Facilities
					✓											
	✓							✓			✓			✓	✓	
	✓	✓					✓		✓		✓				✓	
	✓	✓			✓			✓		✓	✓	✓			✓	
	✓			✓			✓				✓					
					✓	✓		✓	✓	✓	✓	✓	✓		✓	✓
	✓				✓			✓			✓	✓	✓		✓	
	✓	✓		✓	✓	✓		✓	✓		✓	✓	✓			
	✓						✓									
	✓			✓	✓	✓	✓	✓	✓		✓		✓	✓		
	✓			✓			✓		✓		✓					
	✓						✓				✓					
					✓		✓				✓					
				✓			✓		✓		✓					
					✓		✓								✓	
				✓	✓		✓		✓		✓					
	✓	✓		✓			✓		✓		✓					
	✓	✓						✓			✓					
	✓				✓		✓		✓		✓			✓	✓	
								✓			✓				✓	
	✓			✓			✓		✓		✓					
	✓	✓		✓			✓		✓		✓					✓
				✓	✓	✓		✓	✓	✓	✓	✓	✓			
	✓			✓			✓		✓		✓					
	✓	✓		✓			✓		✓		✓					

Name of Property	*Accessible for Disabled*	*Antiques*	*On the Water*	*Good Value*	*Car Not Necessary*	*Full Meal Service*	*Historic Building*
The Wauwinet	✓	✓	✓		✓	✓	✓
The Weathervane Inn						✓	
Wedgewood Inn		✓		✓			✓
Westmoor Inn		✓				✓	
Wheatleigh	✓	✓				✓	✓
Whistler's Inn	✓	✓					✓
White Elephant							
The Williamsville Inn	✓	✓				✓	✓
Windflower Inn	✓	✓				✓	✓
The Windsor House		✓				✓	✓
Yankee Clipper Inn	✓	✓	✓			✓	✓
Yankee Pedlar Inn	✓	✓		✓		✓	
NEW HAMPSHIRE							
Amos A. Parker House		✓					✓
The Bells		✓					✓
The English House	✓	✓					
Exeter Inn		✓				✓	
The Franconia Inn		✓				✓	
Governor's House Bed & Breakfast		✓			✓		✓
The Governor's Inn				✓		✓	✓
Hannah Davis House		✓					✓
Highland Farm Bed and Breakfast		✓					✓
Home Hill Country Inn & French Restaurant		✓				✓	
The Horse & Hound Inn		✓				✓	

	Romantic Hideaway	*Luxurious*	*Pets Allowed*	*No Smoking Indoors*	*Good Place for Families*	*Near Arts Festivals*	*Beach Nearby*	*Cross-Country Ski Trail*	*Golf Within 5 Miles*	*Fitness Facilities*	*Good Biking Terrain*	*Skiing*	*Horseback Riding*	*Tennis*	*Swimming on Premises*	*Conference Facilities*
	✓	✓			✓		✓				✓			✓	✓	✓
						✓		✓	✓		✓	✓	✓		✓	
	✓	✓					✓		✓		✓					
	✓						✓		✓		✓					
	✓	✓				✓		✓	✓	✓	✓	✓	✓	✓	✓	✓
	✓	✓		✓	✓	✓		✓	✓		✓	✓	✓			✓
					✓		✓		✓		✓				✓	✓
	✓							✓			✓	✓		✓	✓	
	✓				✓	✓		✓	✓		✓	✓	✓		✓	
						✓	✓		✓		✓					
	✓	✓			✓		✓				✓				✓	✓
					✓							✓				✓
	✓			✓		✓		✓			✓					
	✓								✓		✓	✓				
				✓	✓			✓			✓	✓				
			✓		✓	✓				✓	✓					✓
	✓			✓	✓			✓	✓		✓	✓	✓	✓	✓	✓
				✓		✓			✓					✓		
				✓					✓					✓		✓
	✓			✓		✓		✓			✓					
				✓		✓		✓			✓					
	✓					✓		✓			✓			✓	✓	
	✓				✓			✓	✓		✓	✓				

Name of Property	*Accessible for Disabled*	*Antiques*	*On the Water*	*Good Value*	*Car Not Necessary*	*Full Meal Service*	*Historic Building*
Inn at Christian Shore		✓			✓		✓
Inn Crystal Lake		✓	✓			✓	
The Inn at Elmwood Corners		✓					
The Inn on Golden Pond		✓	✓				
Inn at Thorn Hill		✓				✓	✓
Kona Mansion Inn		✓	✓			✓	✓
The Lavender Flower Inn		✓					
Martin Hill Inn		✓			✓		✓
Moody Parsonage Bed and Breakfast	✓	✓		✓			✓
The Mulburn Inn		✓					✓
Notchland Inn		✓				✓	✓
The Nutmeg Inn		✓					✓
The Oceanside		✓	✓				
The Pasquaney Inn on Newfound Lake		✓	✓			✓	
Red Hill Inn		✓				✓	
Rock Ledge Manor		✓	✓				✓
The 1785 Inn		✓				✓	✓
Sise Inn	✓	✓			✓		✓
Six Chimneys		✓	✓	✓			✓
Snowvillage Inn		✓				✓	✓
Sugar Hill Inn		✓				✓	
The Tamworth Inn		✓				✓	✓
The Tuc' Me Inn		✓	✓		✓		
The Victoria Inn		✓					✓
The Wakefield Inn		✓					✓

	Romantic Hideaway	*Luxurious*	*Pets Allowed*	*No Smoking Indoors*	*Good Place for Families*	*Near Arts Festivals*	*Beach Nearby*	*Cross-Country Ski Trail*	*Golf Within 5 Miles*	*Fitness Facilities*	*Good Biking Terrain*	*Skiing*	*Horseback Riding*	*Tennis*	*Swimming on Premises*	*Conference Facilities*
				✓		✓										
	✓			✓	✓		✓	✓	✓		✓	✓				
				✓	✓		✓		✓		✓					
	✓			✓	✓	✓	✓	✓			✓					
	✓	✓		✓		✓		✓			✓	✓			✓	✓
	✓		✓		✓	✓	✓	✓	✓		✓			✓	✓	✓
				✓	✓			✓	✓		✓	✓				
	✓			✓		✓										
				✓	✓	✓		✓	✓		✓					
	✓			✓	✓	✓		✓	✓		✓	✓				
	✓				✓			✓				✓			✓	
	✓			✓	✓	✓	✓	✓	✓	✓	✓				✓	✓
				✓	✓	✓	✓		✓		✓					
	✓				✓		✓	✓			✓	✓				✓
	✓				✓	✓	✓	✓			✓			✓		✓
				✓		✓	✓				✓					
	✓			✓	✓	✓		✓	✓		✓	✓		✓	✓	
	✓	✓				✓										✓
	✓				✓	✓	✓	✓	✓		✓	✓		✓		
	✓			✓	✓		✓	✓	✓			✓		✓		✓
				✓	✓	✓		✓	✓		✓	✓				✓
	✓			✓	✓						✓					✓
				✓	✓	✓	✓	✓	✓		✓					
	✓			✓		✓	✓		✓		✓					
	✓				✓						✓					

Name of Property	*Accessible for Disabled*	*Antiques*	*On the Water*	*Good Value*	*Car Not Necessary*	*Full Meal Service*	*Historic Building*
Whitneys' Inn		✓				✓	✓
The Wolfeboro Inn	✓	✓	✓		✓	✓	✓
RHODE ISLAND							
Admiral Fitzroy	✓	✓			✓		✓
Admiral Dewey Inn		✓	✓				✓
Adrian					✓		✓
Atlantic Inn		✓	✓		✓	✓	✓
Barrington Inn		✓		✓	✓		✓
Blue Dory Inn		✓	✓	✓			✓
Cliffside Inn	✓	✓					✓
Francis Malbone House		✓			✓		✓
Ilverthorpe Cottage		✓			✓		✓
The Inn of Jonathan Bowen		✓			✓		✓
The Inn at Castle Hill		✓	✓		✓	✓	✓
The Inntowne	✓	✓			✓		✓
Ivy Lodge		✓		✓		✓	✓
Manisses		✓			✓	✓	✓
Ocean House		✓	✓		✓	✓	✓
The Richards		✓		✓			✓
Rose Farm Inn		✓		✓	✓		✓
Shelter Harbor Inn	✓	✓			✓	✓	✓
1661 Inn and Guest House	✓	✓	✓		✓		✓
Stone Lea		✓	✓				✓
Surf Hotel		✓	✓	✓			✓

	Romantic Hideaway	Luxurious	Pets Allowed	No Smoking Indoors	Good Place for Families	Near Arts Festivals	Beach Nearby	Cross-Country Ski Trail	Golf Within 5 Miles	Fitness Facilities	Good Biking Terrain	Skiing	Horseback Riding	Tennis	Swimming on Premises	Conference Facilities
	✓		✓		✓	✓	✓	✓	✓		✓	✓			✓	✓
	✓	✓			✓	✓	✓	✓	✓		✓			✓	✓	✓
	✓	✓		✓	✓	✓	✓		✓			✓				✓
	✓				✓	✓	✓				✓					
							✓				✓					
	✓	✓			✓	✓	✓				✓	✓	✓			✓
				✓	✓		✓				✓					
	✓			✓			✓				✓					
	✓	✓		✓		✓	✓		✓		✓			✓		✓
	✓	✓		✓		✓	✓		✓							✓
	✓			✓	✓	✓	✓				✓					
					✓	✓	✓		✓							✓
	✓	✓				✓	✓	✓	✓		✓			✓		
					✓	✓	✓									✓
	✓	✓		✓	✓	✓	✓				✓					✓
	✓	✓		✓	✓		✓				✓					
	✓			✓	✓	✓	✓		✓		✓		✓	✓		
	✓	✓		✓		✓	✓				✓					
	✓			✓			✓				✓					
	✓	✓		✓	✓	✓	✓		✓		✓		✓	✓		✓
	✓	✓					✓				✓					
	✓	✓		✓		✓	✓				✓					
					✓	✓	✓				✓					

Name of Property	*Accessible for Disabled*	*Antiques*	*On the Water*	*Good Value*	*Car Not Necessary*	*Full Meal Service*	*Historic Building*
Victorian Ladies		✓					✓
Weekapaug Inn	✓	✓	✓			✓	✓
VERMONT							
Birch Hill Inn		✓					
Black Lantern		✓		✓			
The Darling Family Inn		✓		✓			
Eaglebrook of Grafton		✓		✓			✓
Edson Hill Manor							
1811 House		✓					✓
Fox Hall Inn		✓	✓	✓			✓
Four Columns	✓	✓					✓
The Gables	✓	✓		✓			
Governor's Inn		✓					✓
The Hermitage		✓				✓	
Hickory Ridge House		✓		✓			✓
Hill Farm Inn		✓		✓			
Inn at Long Last		✓					✓
Inn at Manchester	✓	✓					✓
Inn at Montpelier		✓					✓
The Inn at the Round Barn Farm		✓					✓
The Inn at Sawmill Farm		✓					
Inn at Weathersfield		✓					✓
Inn at Westview Farm	✓	✓		✓			
Inn on the Common		✓					

	Romantic Hideaway	Luxurious	Pets Allowed	No Smoking Indoors	Good Place for Families	Near Arts Festivals	Beach Nearby	Cross-Country Ski Trail	Golf Within 5 Miles	Fitness Facilities	Good Biking Terrain	Skiing	Horseback Riding	Tennis	Swimming on Premises	Conference Facilities
	✓	✓		✓		✓	✓	✓								
					✓		✓		✓		✓			✓		
	✓				✓	✓			✓		✓	✓		✓	✓	
	✓										✓	✓		✓		
			✓		✓	✓					✓	✓			✓	
	✓	✓						✓			✓					
					✓	✓		✓				✓	✓		✓	
	✓	✓				✓			✓		✓	✓				
	✓			✓				✓			✓	✓			✓	
	✓		✓	✓		✓		✓			✓				✓	
	✓				✓	✓		✓	✓		✓	✓			✓	
	✓	✓		✓		✓					✓	✓				
	✓				✓	✓		✓		✓	✓	✓		✓	✓	✓
	✓			✓		✓		✓			✓					
	✓				✓	✓		✓	✓		✓	✓				
				✓	✓	✓		✓			✓			✓		
					✓	✓		✓	✓		✓	✓				
		✓				✓					✓					✓
	✓	✓		✓		✓		✓	✓		✓	✓			✓	
		✓				✓		✓	✓		✓	✓		✓	✓	
	✓							✓		✓	✓					
	✓					✓		✓	✓		✓	✓				
	✓	✓			✓				✓		✓			✓	✓	

Name of Property	*Accessible for Disabled*	*Antiques*	*On the Water*	*Good Value*	*Car Not Necessary*	*Full Meal Service*	*Historic Building*
Juniper Hill Inn		✓					✓
Kedron Valley Inn		✓		✓			✓
Molly Stark Inn		✓		✓			
The Old Tavern at Grafton		✓		✓		✓	✓
Parker House		✓					✓
Queen City Inn	✓	✓		✓			
Rabbit Hill Inn	✓	✓	✓			✓	✓
Reluctant Panther	✓					✓	
South Shire Inn	✓	✓		✓			✓
Swift House Inn	✓	✓					✓
10 Acres Lodge		✓					
Vermont Marble Inn		✓					
Village Country Inn		✓		✓	✓	✓	✓
Village Inn of Woodstock		✓					✓
Waybury Inn		✓					✓
West Mountain Inn	✓	✓		✓			✓
Whetstone Inn		✓					✓
Wilburton Inn							✓
Windham Hill Inn		✓					
Ye Olde England Inn						✓	

	Romantic Hideaway	*Luxurious*	*Pets Allowed*	*No Smoking Indoors*	*Good Place for Families*	*Near Arts Festivals*	*Beach Nearby*	*Cross-Country Ski Trail*	*Golf Within 5 Miles*	*Fitness Facilities*	*Good Biking Terrain*	*Skiing*	*Horseback Riding*	*Tennis*	*Swimming on Premises*	*Conference Facilities*
	✓	✓		✓				✓			✓					✓
	✓		✓		✓	✓	✓	✓	✓		✓	✓	✓	✓	✓	
	✓			✓	✓	✓		✓	✓		✓	✓				
	✓		✓			✓		✓			✓	✓		✓	✓	✓
	✓	✓				✓		✓	✓		✓					
						✓			✓	✓						
	✓	✓		✓	✓			✓			✓	✓				
	✓	✓				✓		✓	✓		✓	✓				✓
	✓	✓		✓							✓					
	✓	✓			✓	✓		✓			✓					
	✓		✓		✓				✓			✓		✓	✓	
	✓	✓						✓			✓					
	✓	✓				✓			✓		✓	✓	✓	✓	✓	
	✓					✓		✓	✓		✓	✓	✓			
	✓					✓					✓					
	✓	✓			✓	✓		✓			✓	✓				
	✓		✓			✓		✓			✓	✓				
	✓				✓	✓		✓	✓		✓	✓		✓	✓	✓
	✓			✓		✓		✓			✓	✓				
			✓		✓	✓		✓	✓		✓	✓		✓	✓	

Connecticut

Connecticut

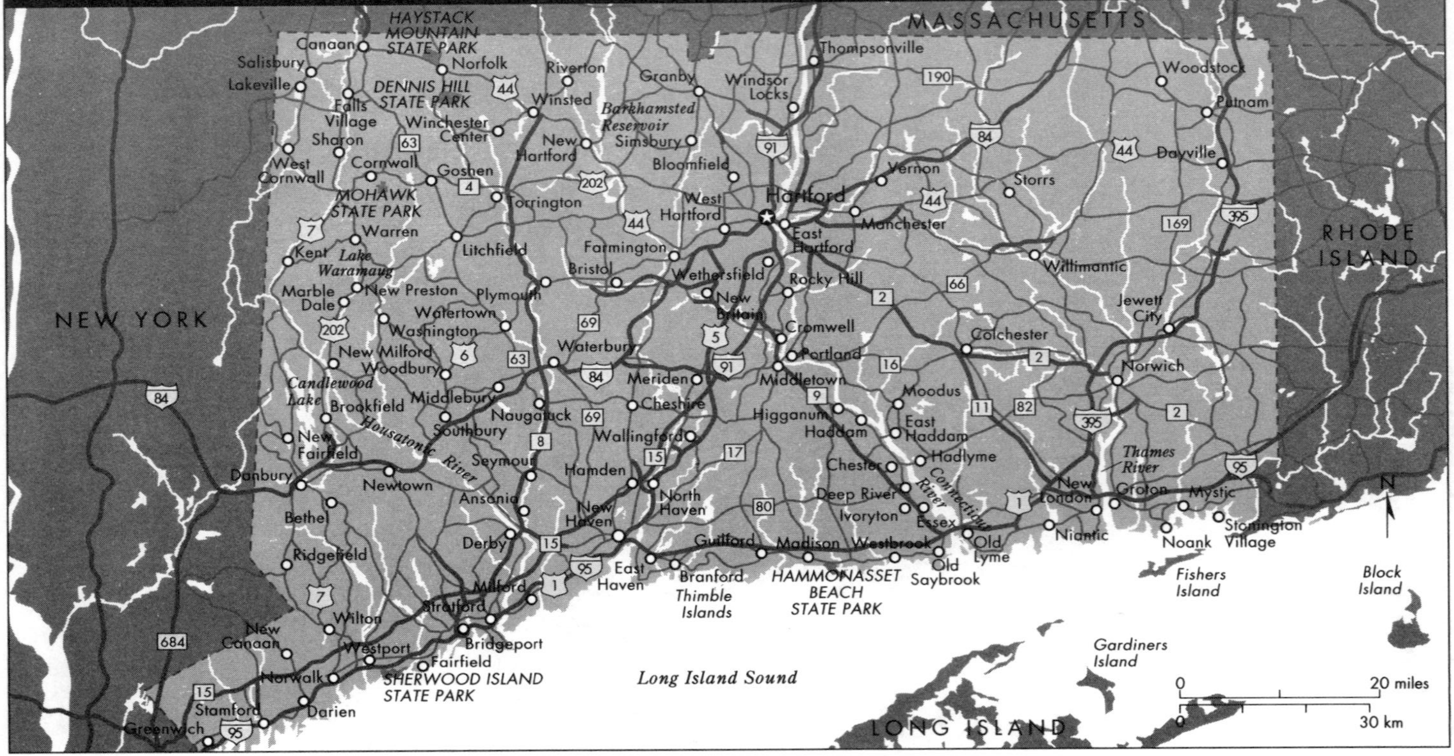

The Southwestern Coast

Much of Connecticut's shoreline between Greenwich and New Haven is an artery of the urban sprawl that radiates from New York City. Beyond the bustle of commerce, however, there are densely wooded communities of stately historic homes and winding, elm-shaded roads. Fairfield County, despite its image as "commuter country," has a pace of its own, and the odds against encountering the so-called New York attitude in southwestern Connecticut are definitely in your favor.

Long before the environmental movement took hold, people in Fairfield County saw fit to establish wilderness preserves and nature centers, principally in the upland sections, rather than directly on the coast. Today, on hundreds of safeguarded acres, these refuges from the overbuilt downtown areas offer visitors well-marked trails for hiking, bird-watching, horseback riding, and bicycling—as well as educational exhibits and hands-on activities for children.

In recent years, the most congested of the region's metropolitan areas, after suffering serious decline, have changed direction, improving in appearance and civic fortune. Stamford has gone the big-city route, with vast hotels and tall corporate towers turning its downtown into a slick steel, glass, and cement jungle. South Norwalk, fondly known now as SoNo, has taken on new life around its acclaimed Maritime Center, with trendy boutiques and restaurants cheek by jowl with expensive condominiums in renovated warehouses.

Although in the past not even the intrepid would think of swimming in this part of Long Island Sound, there's still a large, active boating and sports-fishing contingent that encourages visitors to come aboard and share the fun.

Places to Go, Sights to See

Maritime Center (10 N. Water St., Norwalk, tel. 203/852–0700). One of the state's newest attractions, this state-of-the-art aquarium/museum/IMAX theater complex in Norwalk highlights the maritime history and marine life of Long Island Sound through exhibits, educational programs, and big-screen entertainment.

Stamford Museum and Nature Center (39 Scofieldtown Rd., Stamford, tel. 203/322–1646). This 118-acre preserve has exhibits on farm tools and Native American life, as well as trails and a 19th-century working farm.

Weir Farm (735 Nod Hill Rd., Wilton, tel. 203/761–9945). Connecticut's first and only national park is dedicated to the life and art of American painter J. Alden Weir. The park's 60 rolling acres comprise studios, Weir's Federal-style house, and exhibits.

Yale University. As befits a prestigious seat of learning, the Yale campus is chockablock with history. The university offers free guided walking tours (tel. 203/432–2300), during which you can glimpse the places where Nathan Hale, William Howard Taft, and Noah Webster once studied. The *Yale Center for British Art* (1080 Chapel St., tel. 203/432–2800) has the largest collection of British paintings and sculptures outside of England.

Beaches

The numerous sandy strips along the shore may be marked "private" and "for residents only," but the only restriction generally involves access through parking, which does carry a penalty. If you can walk or bicycle to a beach, no one usually minds you settling down for some quiet sunbathing. The big public beach in the region is the **Sherwood Island State Park** (tel. 203/226–6983), 1½ miles of sand that has two large picnic groves close to the water—and there is parking here.

Restaurants

In Greenwich, **Bertrand** (tel. 203/661–4618) is the regional champion of classic and nouvelle cuisine. Westport is home to two terrific Italian eateries: **Da Pietro's** (tel. 203/454–1213) is decidedly Northern Italian and elegant, while **Bertucci's Brick Oven Pizza** (tel. 203/454–1559) serves lighter fare and caters more to families. In New Haven, you might try **Robert Henry's** (tel. 203/789–1010) for sophisticated, traditional French cuisine or **Azteca's** (tel. 203/624–2454) for exotic southwestern and Mexican dishes.

Theater and Nightlife

Bridgeport's **Downtown Cabaret** (tel. 203/576–1636) has a steady audience for its informal, spontaneous, improvisational live shows. At the **Stamford Center for the Arts** (tel. 203/323–2131) the Pilobolus Dance Theatre is frequently "at home." New Haven's **Long Wharf Theater** (tel. 203/787–4282) and **Yale Repertory Theater** (tel. 203/432–1234) offer a range of classic and new comedies and tragedies. Across town, at the nightclub-restaurant **Bopper's** (tel. 203/562–1957), the entire staff regularly lip-synchs the golden oldies to the delight of '50s and '60s buffs. A different type of spectacle as well as sport is found at **Bridgeport Jai Alai** (tel. 203/576–1976) and **Milford Jai Alai** (tel. 203/877–4242), where you can simply watch or wager on this hectic sport.

Tourist Information

Bridgeport Convention and Visitors Commission (303 State St., Bridgeport, CT 06604, tel. 203/576–8494); **Greater Stamford Convention and Visitors Bureau** (1 Landmark Sq., Stamford, CT 06901, tel. 203/359–3305); **Hill & Harbor Convention and Visitors District** (605 Broad St., Suite 208, Stratford, CT 06497, tel. 203/381–9433); **New Haven Convention and Visitors Bureau** (195 Church St., New Haven, CT 06510, tel. 203/777–8550); **Yankee Heritage District** (297 West Ave., The Gate-Lodge, Matthews Park, Norwalk, CT 06850, tel. 203/854–7825).

Reservations Services

Bed & Breakfast, Ltd. (Box 216, New Haven, CT 06513, tel. 203/469–3260); **Covered Bridge Bed & Breakfast Reservation Service** (Box 447, Norfolk, CT 06058, tel. 203/542–5944); **Nutmeg Bed & Breakfast Agency** (Box 1117, West Hartford, CT 06107, tel. 203/236–6698).

The Homestead Inn

Just south of I–95, the Connecticut Turnpike, on a tree-shaded street in Greenwich, sits a wooden frame house with an enclosed Victorian wraparound porch, Italianate cupola, and ornate bracketed eaves that set it apart as something special. And, indeed, the Homestead is very much that, since coming under the tender care of owners Lessie D. Davidson and Nancy K. Smith, and hotel manager Dorothy Jenkins. Thanks to their vision and the creativity of designers John and the late Virginia Saladino, meticulous renovation has produced a look of gentle, mellow age, the kind that usually takes centuries to achieve.

All the common rooms on the ground level get a lot of use from overnight guests and regular patrons of the celebrated restaurant, where chef Jacques Thiebeult's classic French cuisine is the daily fare. Yet the public areas still have a pristine sheen that comes only from superior maintenance. The foyer, displaying ancestral portraits set against a vivid flower-basket print wallpaper, vies with the Backgammon Room, with its green felt walls and wooden shutters, as choice spots to enjoy a cup of tea or a glass of brandy.

In the main house there are 13 guest rooms, each with its own particular decoration. One is known as the Robin Suite from the original, lovingly preserved, 18th-century stenciling on its walls. The Bridal Suite has a pale blue pencil-post bed complemented by gaily printed flowerbasket wallpaper and soft orange wing chairs. Floors are generally covered with a variety of area rugs, though one room above the dining room, with twin sleigh beds, is completely carpeted.

The 19th-century outbuilding is decorated with 20th century furnishings. The Birdcage Room is typical; it has an antique blue-and-white French birdcage whose color is echoed by a painted chest of drawers and upholstered boudoir chair. There's a fishnet canopy on the four-poster bed.

Either Lessie or Nancy is always on hand to greet the stream of dining and lodging guests, many of whom have now become familiar faces. The staff's memory for likes and dislikes and attention to details (just what you might expect in the best small hotels of Europe) make this one of the finest lodgings in America.

Address: *420 Field Point Rd., Greenwich, CT 06830, tel. and fax 203/869–7500.*
Accommodations: *14 double rooms and 3 singles with baths, 6 suites.*
Amenities: *TV, phones, electric blankets, and clock radios in rooms.*
Rates: *$87–$175; Continental breakfast. AE, DC, MC, V.*
Restrictions: *No pets. $10 surcharge for one-night stay on weekends.*

The Inn at Chapel West

Running along the New Haven Green and then into the heart of the Yale University campus, Chapel Street appears to be an infinite stretch of shops, old hotels, bookstores, and restaurants until you come to a surprise: Behind a neatly kept garden stands a freshly painted green, white, and pink Victorian mansion, complete with gingerbread trim and a carpeted stairway flanked by potted geraniums. It's amazing that this 1847 structure never fell to the wrecker's ball as its neighbors undoubtedly did; it's equally mind-boggling that someone had the vision to restore it to its present grandeur and convert it into a thriving, much-needed lodging in this vibrant college town.

Under the extremely competent management of innkeeper Melodie Pogue, the guest rooms never lack for bookings. The inn also offers complete conference facilities for groups of up to 50, with catered meals—so a whiff or the mere suggestion of something appetizing wafting through its doors at mealtimes is to be expected.

The guest rooms at the inn, though, are the stuff on which it has built its following. The owners determined to create a small hotel of uncommon luxury and it was immediately evident, at its opening in 1987, that they succeeded. Each room is decorated individually, in styles varying from Victorian to country home to contemporary. One room might have a brass bed with a checkerboard quilt, flanked by a French Provincial writing table and chair. In another, you'll come upon a golden oak four-poster bed with lace side curtains near a petit-point *fauteuil.* When you arrive, you'll find soft, fluffy robes and a bed decked with goose down pillows.

The endless debate on family-owned and -operated establishments versus those professionally run will undoubtedly, after a visit to the Inn at Chapel West, turn in favor of the latter. The staff here is delighted to guide you to the best dining in New Haven or to go the extra step and make arrangements for theater tickets, a university tour, or secretarial or baby-sitting services. It's what makes the Inn a bit of serendipity, a true urban oasis.

Address: *1201 Chapel St., New Haven, CT 06511, tel. 203/777-1201, fax 203/776-7363.*
Accommodations: *10 double rooms with baths.*
Amenities: *Air-conditioning, cable TV and phones in rooms; free parking.*
Rates: *$175; Continental buffet breakfast. AE, D, DC, MC, V.*
Restrictions: *No pets.*

The Maples Inn

The vast, sprawling, white-trimmed, yellow-clapboard Maples Inn reveals only a few of its 13 gables as it sits behind a deep lawn shaded by venerable maples on a street that's only a short drive from New Canaan's downtown shopping area. Its 12-over-12 and 9-over-9 windows that blink so invitingly at night have been welcoming guests with remarkable style since Cynthia T. Haas took over as owner nine years ago.

Ms. Haas, a longtime New Canaan resident, had always wanted to run an inn. When her chance came, she made sweeping changes, rearranging rooms, bathrooms, closets, even walls. Totally refurbishing and redecorating each of the rooms, suites, and apartments made a dramatic difference, producing a subdued but elegant, highly individual, warm, and romantic atmosphere. There's even a completely equipped four-bedroom cottage that displays the same sensitivity to beauty and comfort.

All the bedrooms have canopied four-poster, queen-size beds and contain numerous antiques and furnishings from Ms. Haas's own collection. Yet the presence of such modern equipment as phones and TVs is never intrusive. Careful maintenance produces a gleam on mahogany chests, gilt frames, and brass lamps, and the imaginative use of fabrics and paper fans is an education in design. Even the red-white-and-blue theme in one suite is in good taste.

There's a large 19th-century buffet laden with a Georgian silver coffee service on the first-floor landing, where an elegant Continental breakfast is served each morning. A setup in a hall closet provides early risers with "do-it-yourself" coffee.

The small apartments and the cottage seem to encourage long-term stays by families, and youngsters, generally respectful of the premises, are made to feel at home in the friendly, informal atmosphere. A guest might well be asked to drop off some letters at the post office or offered a treat from a box of goodies in the front desk drawer. The Maple Inn is that kind of place.

Address: *179 Oenoke Ridge, New Canaan, CT 06840, tel. 203/966–2927 or 800/959–6477, fax 203/966–5003.*
Accommodations: *6 double rooms with baths, 4 suites (1 with private screened-in porch), 6 apartments.*
Amenities: *Air-conditioning, cable TV, phones, alarm clocks, and minifridges in bedrooms; ice machine in main house; working fireplaces in 1 apartment.*
Rates: *$125–$200; Continental breakfast. MC, V.*
Restrictions: *No pets. 2-night minimum on weekends, May–Dec.*

Silvermine Tavern

Silvermine was a pre-Revolutionary town that lies within the borders of Norwalk, New Canaan, and Wilton. The tavern (part of which dates back to the early 17th century), the Country Store, the Coach House, and the Old Mill are all clustered at the intersection of Silvermine and Perry avenues in Norwalk, a short distance north of the Merritt Parkway.

If he has a moment to spare in his busy schedule of keeping this large enterprise going, innkeeper Frank Whitman, Jr., can fill you in on local history. His family has been running things here since 1955, and he grew up within the solid post-and-beam walls of the Colonial building at the heart of the present-day tavern. Frank's eyes never seem to rest because he never lets up on the high standard he sets for every detail of the food and lodging.

Though it's probably best known as a restaurant, which overlooks the Silvermine River and the millpond, the inn also has a small number of wonderful guest rooms in the main building and across the road above the Country Store. The tavern's common areas have unusual displays of primitive paintings, store signs, prints, and Early American tools and utensils, and the guest bedrooms, with their own complement of antique furnishings, have an equally pleasant atmosphere. The configuration of these rooms has evolved naturally over the ages, and the odd shapes only add to the charm. Room T-8 is entered through the bathroom, but is particularly cozy once you're inside. Some rooms have tubs but no showers because of the slanted ceilings. Wide-plank floors have hooked rugs to bridge the cracks of age, and starched white curtains grace the small, multipaned windows that glow invitingly at night, especially when there's snow on the ground.

Winter is a special season at the Silvermine, harking back to the days when the weather seemed a lot more severe. Fires crackle in the big fireplaces downstairs and a romantic smokiness seems to wrap itself around you as you settle back in a big wing chair with a good book. This scene must surely be straight out of an old-fashioned Christmas card.

Address: *194 Perry Ave., Norwalk, CT 06850, tel. 203/847–4558, fax 203/847–9171.*
Accommodations: *10 double rooms with baths.*
Amenities: *Restaurant, dining room, clock radios in rooms, air-conditioning in some rooms.*
Rates: *$80–$99; Continental breakfast. AE, DC, MC, V.*
Restrictions: *No pets. Closed Tues. year round.*

Harbor House Inn

Around the turn of the century, there was an enormous beach resort hotel called the Old Greenwich Inn. To house the servants of all the people who stayed there, a subdued Victorian beachfront cottage, with three stories and many gables, was built nearby. The Old Greenwich disappeared but the cottage endured—transformed into a comfortable guest house by the Stuttig family and managed today by the petite Dawn Stuttig under the watchful eye of her mother, Dolly. Several spacious rooms congregate around the massive lobby, and bits of stained glass filter the light here and on the second and third floors. Having grown up in the business, Dawn runs a tight ship. Unfortunately, in the interest of efficiency, the decor is rather bland. Walls are covered with modern veneer paneling and the furniture, though comfortable, is department-store standard. Simplicity is the rule, extending to the fully equipped bathrooms with Plexiglas shower stalls. Harbor House specializes in long-term stays by corporate executives.

Address: *165 Shore Rd., Old Greenwich, CT 06870, tel. 203/637–0145.*
Accommodations: *17 double rooms with baths, 6 doubles share 2 baths.*
Amenities: *Full kitchen for guest use, air-conditioning, TV in bedrooms.*
Rates: *$75; Continental breakfast. MC, V.*
Restrictions: *No pets.*

The Inn at Longshore

At the end of a long alley of stately oaks stands a late-19th-century mansion that has seen many changes over the years. Until several years ago, it was operated as a country club and public golf course by the town of Westport, which continues to run the surrounding recreational facilities. The lodgings and restaurant, which needed attention, got it through new ownership, and today the mansion is the core of a charming inn. The guest rooms have all been refurbished with excellent colonial reproductions, and all of them have a water view. The large lobby has lots of comfortable sitting areas for those guests who are not outside swimming or boating or playing golf. Moreover, a gourmet restaurant is right on the premises.

Address: *260 Compo Rd. S, Westport, CT 06880, tel. 203/226–3316, fax 203/226–5723.*
Accommodations: *9 double rooms with baths, 3 suites.*
Amenities: *Restaurant and lounge with live entertainment, air-conditioning, TV and phones in rooms, meeting room, and ballroom.*
Rates: *$125–$150; Continental breakfast. AE, DC, MC, V.*
Restrictions: *No pets. Restaurant closed Mon.*

Roger Sherman Inn

The Roger Sherman's winding porches, looking out on a broad tree-lined avenue, seem to invite relaxation. The white shingle and clapboard center-chimney Colonial dates to 1740 and has functioned as an inn since 1925. Its present owner, Henry Prieger, took over in 1988 and has done extensive refurbishing. Much of the inn's prestige has grown up around its popular restaurant and the dining rooms that are widely used for social events and business meetings. Dark paneling, hunting prints, and a blazing hearth in the bar make it a favorite indoor gathering place. The bedrooms are now furnished with colonial reproductions and an array of modern conveniences. Their antique character is felt only in such small touches as the occasional bits of woodwork, bric-a-brac, and the uneven floors. The unrelieved feeling of modernity, evidenced in the wall-to-wall carpeting, the TV sets on bureaus, and shiny plastic ice buckets, provide a glaring contrast.

Address: *195 Oenoke Ridge, New Canaan, CT 06840, tel. 203/966–4541, fax 203/966–0503.*
Accommodations: *7 double rooms with baths, 1 two-bedroom suite.*
Amenities: *Restaurant and lounge with live piano music, air-conditioning, cable TV, and phones in rooms; dry cleaning and baby-sitting available.*
Rates: *$100–$120, $175 for suite; Continental breakfast. AE, DC, MC, V.*
Restrictions: *No pets.*

The Stanton House Inn

Off busy Route 1, near the imposing Second Congregational Church, a hairpin right turn up Maple Avenue leads you to a white Federal frame house built in 1840 and enlarged in 1899 by Stanford White. Doreen Pearson, a former registered nurse, and her husband, Tog, a banking executive, have transformed this once somewhat seedy boardinghouse into a comfortable bed-and-breakfast. A number of rooms on the top floors share bathroom facilities, but the spacious bedrooms on the sprawling second floor each have their own. All have been personally decorated by Doreen who now claims expertise in dealing with upholsterers, carpenters, furniture restorers, and all manner of artisans. The results are reflected in a variety of tasteful, bright, print bedspreads and window draperies, and her light touch is apparent in the formal first-floor drawing room and dining room.

Address: *76 Maple Ave., Greenwich, CT 06830, tel. 203/869–2110, fax 203/629–2116.*
Accommodations: *23 double rooms with baths, 2 doubles share 2 baths, 1 suite.*
Amenities: *Air-conditioning, TV in rooms, phones in some rooms, copier, small conference room, working fire place in 1 room, wet bars in 7 rooms, kitchenette in 1 room.*
Rates: *$75, $135 for suite; Continental breakfast. AE, MC, V.*
Restrictions: *No smoking in bedrooms, no pets. 2-night minimum on weekends.*

Litchfield County South and Ridgefield

Southern Litchfield County contains the usual mixture of small towns and urban centers typical of the state, but it's punctuated by abundant bodies of water that provide a certain seasonal distinction. When the snow thaws, the anglers start counting the days until they can legally plunge into rivers like the Housatonic, Aspetuck, and Bantam. The shores of Lake Waramaug and Candlewood Lake are equally seductive, luring sunbathers, boating enthusiasts, and lovers of various types of water sports.

The heyday of lakeside resorts may have waned a bit, but you'll still find convivial communities of guests on the wicker settees, rattan chairs, and gliders set on the patios and porches of inns and lodgings along the water's edge.

One ongoing activity that brings many visitors to the area is the perpetual quest for treasures at the numerous antiques shops along the byways and highways. Right on the Litchfield village green there's a consignment shop that consistently stocks an amazing collection at fair prices, and Kent, New Preston, and Woodbury all have well-traveled antiques trails.

Litchfield, the county seat, and Ridgefield, in northern Fairfield County, are classic towns where prosperous Yankee merchants and landowners built monumental residences. Many of these mansions have been taken over by preservation and historical societies and are open to the public. Charity tours, announced on signposts, bulletin boards, and in the local press, open the doors to many other currently occupied dwellings.

The climate in this part of the Nutmeg State favors the growing of grapes, and consequently a wine-making industry has developed. Several vineyards welcome visitors to sample and perhaps purchase the product of their labors.

Places to Go, Sights to See

Aldrich Museum of Contemporary Art (258 Main St., Ridgefield, tel. 203/438–4519). This world-class gallery has, in addition to changing exhibits, one of the best sculpture gardens in the Northeast, as well as lectures, concerts, and films.

Lourdes in Litchfield Shrine (Rte. 118, Litchfield, tel. 203/567–1041). The grotto of Lourdes is reproduced on this 35-acre shrine maintained by the Montfort Missionaries. Its Stations of the Cross draws numerous pilgrims between May and mid-October, though the grounds are open and rites are observed year-round.

The Silo (44 Upland Rd., off Rte. 202, New Milford, tel. 203/355–0300). Band leader Skitch Henderson and his wife, Ruth, own and operate this wonderful silo and barn packed with objets de cookery, gourmet goodies and sauces, and arts and crafts.

White Flower Farm (Rte. 63, south of Litchfield Green, tel. 800/888–7756). There's bound to be a slowdown on Route 63 south of Litchfield once word gets around that the azaleas are in bloom at this world-renowned horticultural mecca. Its 10 acres of gardens and 30 acres of growing fields peak from midsummer to September, but green-thumb pros and amateurs alike flock here from early spring to late fall, drawn partially by the lure of its widely circulated catalog. It doesn't disappoint.

White Memorial Foundation (Rte. 202, west of Litchfield Green, tel. 203/567–0857). The state's largest nature center and wildlife sanctuary offers visitors 4,000 acres containing 35 miles of trails for hiking, horseback riding, and cross-country skiing. There's also a conservation center (tel. 203/567–0015) that includes special displays and programs for children. Open year-round, it's a great place to marvel at the fall foliage.

Beaches

Virtually every town that sits on one of the lakes has a public beach where all are welcome. The hitch is the need for a local parking permit. Luckily, you can walk or bicycle from most of the lodgings here to their own beach or to one nearby.

Several of the area's lakes are home to scenic state parks, including Candlewood Lake's **Squantz Pond State Park** (New Fairfield, tel. 203/797–4165) and **Lake Waramaug State Park** (New Preston/Kent, tel. 203/868–2592).

Restaurants

Charles Bistro (tel. 203/355–3266) and **Maison La Blanc** (tel. 203/354–9931) are New Milford's two finest purveyors of fine cooking. **Sacco's** (tel. 203/438–2193), in Ridgefield, effectively prepares more than 50 pasta dishes. It's much more "country casual" at the **Green General Store** (tel. 203/868–7324) in Washington, where you can take your choice of counter or table seating for breakfast or lunch. At Litchfield's **West Street Grill** (tel. 203/567–3885) you can feast on the region's most innovative new-American cuisine.

Nightlife

Bantam's Cinema IV (tel. 203/567–0006), in a small wood-frame building, is the state's oldest continually operating movie house. It thrives by showing a mixture of art films, foreign flicks, and current favorites. The **Candlewood Playhouse** (tel. 203/746–6531), close by the shores of Candlewood Lake in New Fairfield, is where summer stock once flourished and current theatrical hits are eagerly applauded today.

Tourist Information

Housatonic Valley Tourism Commission (Box 406, Danbury, CT 06813, tel. 203/743–0546 or, outside CT, 800/841–4488); **Litchfield Hills Travel Council** (Box 1776, Marbledale, CT 06777, tel. 203/868–2214).

Reservation Services

Bed & Breakfast, Ltd. (Box 216, New Haven, CT 06513, tel. 203/469–3260); **Covered Bridge Bed & Breakfast Reservation Service** (Box 447, Norfolk, CT 06058, tel. 203/542–5944); **Nutmeg Bed & Breakfast Agency** (Box 1117, West Hartford, CT 06017, tel. 203/236–6698).

Boulders Inn

Built in 1895 as a private house, the stone and shingle Boulders Inn, with its carriage house and four guest houses, sits on a gentle slope with panoramic views of Lake Waramaug. The innkeepers, Kees and Ulla Adema, came from Holland and Germany, respectively, in the '60s, and now that their children are grown and away at school, they're able to devote themselves exclusively to the running of the inn. A bit of European charm seems appropriate to this hillside retreat.

The bedrooms are a curious mixture, with picture windows, Oriental rugs, antique Victorian furniture and bric-a-brac, as well as reproduction and overstuffed pieces happily coexisting. The eight rooms in the guest houses up the hill have private decks and working fireplaces. The Carriage House was opened in 1989, with three well-furnished rooms that have their own private entrances.

In the main inn building, the large living room and adjoining TV den welcome guests for relaxed reading and conversation. A recreation room in the basement offers a pool table, darts, and an assortment of games. Across the road, the inn has a private stretch of waterfront suitable for swimming and a beach house with a hanging wicker swing for passing peaceful moments. The more adventurous may set forth in a canoe, sailboat, rowboat, or paddleboat, all provided free to guests.

At dinner, which is included in the rates, you can choose from among several outstanding dishes, including pâté with pickled vegetables, shellfish risotto, venison cassoulet with cranberry beans and smoked sausage, and herb-grilled chicken with rosemary jus and garlic-mashed potatoes. The menu changes often, so be prepared for some imaginative specials.

Running the inn is a full-time job, but Kees and Ulla manage to squeeze in time for their hobbies. He is an avid stamp collector who exhibits internationally, and Ulla's specialty can be seen in the meticulously cut lamp shades used throughout the inn.

Address: *Rte. 45, New Preston, CT 06777, tel. 203/868–0541.*
Accommodations: *10 double rooms with baths, 7 suites.*
Amenities: *Restaurant, air-conditioning in 6 rooms, minifridges and coffee makers in Carriage House and guest houses; lake swimming, boating, tennis court.*
Rates: *$225, full breakfast (Nov.–Apr.); MAP on weekends. AE, MC, V.*
Restrictions: *No pets. 2-night minimum on weekends, closed Thanksgiving weekend–mid-Dec.*

The Elms

The impressive frame house that's The Elms inn on Main Street was once the home of a Colonial cabinetmaker, who built it in 1760, near the site of the Battle of Ridgefield. After the war, in 1799, it became an inn, which now includes an adjacent building erected in 1850. Since 1951 it has been operated by the Scala family, who in 1983 did a total renovation, with the attractive results now seen throughout.

By carefully combining antiques, reproductions, and modern fixtures, they've managed to produce an atmospheric but comfortable stopping-off place for weary, and hungry, travelers. The Elms prides itself on the award-winning Continental cuisine served in its dining areas. Specialties, such as local game and wild boar (served in January), have drawn the attention of appreciative "foodies" from all over.

Although the decorating approach to the guest rooms varies from "olde days" to modern hotel, each room is furnished with such appropriate colonial-style touches as pineapple-stenciled wallpaper and hobnail spreads on lace-canopied four-poster beds. Most rooms have queen-size beds; good reading lights and comfortable Hitchcock armchairs are found throughout.

The most popular gathering spot is the lounge, where cocktails are served. Here, amid the settees, the upholstered wing chairs and cushioned Windsor chairs, beside a roaring fire, the inn's hearty Sunday brunch is also served.

The idea of lodging smack in the middle of town may not at first seem appealing, but The Elms is located on a broad avenue lined by tree-shaded mansions, close to pleasures such as band concerts in the nearby park and a short walk from antiques shops, boutiques, and historic sites. In fact, the antique map in the main dining room and the Revolutionary War relics scattered about the premises might even stir up your most patriotic sentiments.

Address: *500 Main St., Ridgefield, CT 06877, tel. 203/438–2541.*
Accommodations: *20 rooms with baths, 4 suites.*
Amenities: *Restaurant, room service 7 AM–11 PM, air-conditioning, TV and phones in guest rooms, meeting facilities for small groups (up to 15).*
Rates: $99–$130; Continental breakfast. AE, DC, MC, V.
Restrictions: No pets.

Hopkins Inn

This sprawling, Federal-style, yellow and white frame building on a hill overlooking Lake Waramaug in New Preston has grown from a 19th-century boardinghouse to a delightful 20th-century country inn. As you drive up the short street that leads to both the inn and the Hopkins Winery, it may seem like a bit of a hodgepodge, with the flag flying over the front entry, countless mullioned windows flanked by shutters, and gables, awnings, roofs, and porches. But presiding serenely over everything, the present-day innkeepers Franz and Beth Schober are the picture of efficiency.

At the inn, where dining has become celebrated, Franz is usually found in the kitchen, whence come the Austrian and Swiss dishes that form the centerpiece of the menu. His insistence on fresh ingredients extends to the maintenance of a fish tank stocked with trout, and he is also responsible for the extensive selection of wine that is carefully stored in the inn's cellar.

Beth's touch is seen just about everywhere else. She was a university librarian before taking over the inn in 1977, and her organizational skills show up in its smooth operation.

Guest rooms are all individual in shape and decor, though colonial-print wallpapers and fabrics are used extensively. Furniture runs the gamut of country style, with emphasis on crisp, ruffled bed linens; sturdy, comfortable beds; good chairs for reading; and a variety of antique decorative pieces scattered about.

Although there's a cozy, somewhat Victorian living room, there are areas set up outdoors for sitting as well as for dining, under the shade of the trees and awnings.

This is possibly the only inn in Connecticut with vineyards and a winery at its doorstep. And even when the neighboring Hopkins Winery is technically closed, the inn will often arrange private tours for guests.

The Schobers have maintained the friendly, informal atmosphere the inn exhibited in its early days. Glancing through the guest book, you'll discover many names reappearing year after year—one indication of their success.

Address: *22 Hopkins Rd., New Preston, CT 06777, tel. 203/868–7295, fax 203/868–7464.*
Accommodations: *7 double rooms with baths, 2 doubles share 1 bath, 1 double with hall bath.*
Amenities: *Restaurant; private lake beach.*
Rates: *$52–$69; breakfast extra. No credit cards.*
Restrictions: *No pets. 2-night minimum on weekends, closed Jan.–late Mar.*

West Lane Inn

Set behind a broad expanse of carefully groomed lawn, this three-story colonial-style mansion built in the late 1800s rises above a long columned sweep of porches that virtually demands relaxation. Only minutes from the center of Ridgefield and adjacent to the Inn at Ridgefield, the setting recalls a quieter time of small-town life in America.

Maureen Mayer, the owner/manager, has carefully reconstructed that atmosphere in the 12 years she has spent converting this former summer residence into a gracious country inn. As she sits on the porch sipping a cool drink, impeccably dressed and coifed, the former model and New York restaurateur is equally at ease supervising the efficient staff to maintain her high standards of comfort.

From the moment you step inside the oak-paneled lobby and (on cold days) feel the warmth of the cozy fire in the Victorian fireplace, you begin to get that "country inn" feeling. Guest rooms have well-chosen furnishings that are a slightly surprising contrast to the period style that predominates. But comfort is the byword; the queen-size and king-size beds, the upholstered barrel chairs, and the tables and lamps all seem to fit the oversize, high-ceiling rooms with their tall windows. Some of the rooms have working fireplaces that you're invited to light on chilly evenings. A few years ago, a former carriage house out back was converted to similarly furnished guest quarters, some with small kitchens.

The lobby is a gathering place for guests when the weather prohibits sitting on the porches. A brightly wallpapered breakfast room directly off the lobby is again a contrast with its modern tables and chairs.

There's a cozy intimacy at West Lane Inn that makes it easy to strike up a conversation with fellow guests on the porch or in front of the fire. You can just stretch out and listen to the sound of the birds . . . or to the carillon concert from a nearby church.

Address: *22 West La., Ridgefield, CT 06877, tel. 203/438–7323.*
Accommodations: *20 double rooms with baths.*
Amenities: *Light food available noon–10 PM, air-conditioning, TV, and phones in rooms, laundry and dry cleaning available, baby-sitting arranged.*
Rates: *$110–$160; Continental breakfast. AE, DC, MC, V; no personal checks.*
Restrictions: *No pets.*

The Curtis House

Connecticut's oldest inn (1754), located at the start of Woodbury's antiques row, may also be its cheapest: Some rooms, even with private bath, are under $50. The four-story inn, run by the Hardisty family, has seen dozens of alterations and renovations—including a complete $400 overhaul in 1900—but the TVs in some rooms look to be from the Ed Sullivan era; the phones are rotary-dial; and the floorboards, which still creak like whoopie cushions, are charmingly uneven: There's not a spot in the inn where a marble placed on the floor won't zip across the room. Decor ranges from antique to just plain old. Your quarters are likely to have a four-poster bed, a stuffed end chair in need of a new slipcover, and what you'd swear is the braided rug you last saw in your grandmother's living room. You get what you pay for, and you're not paying much. If for no other reason, stay here for the rich history and to be tended to by the friendly staff. A fireplace roars downstairs and a wonderfully cozy restaurant serves heavy but filling New England dishes, such as halibut, Yankee pot roast, pan-fried calves' liver, chicken marsala, and a rich rice-stuffed duckling in cherry-bourbon sauce.

Address: *Main St. (Rte. 6), Woodbury, CT 06798, tel. 203/263–2101.*
Accommodations: *8 rooms with baths, 6 rooms share bath.*
Amenities: *Restaurant, phones, and TVs in some rooms.*
Rates: *$40–$70; Continental breakfast extra. MC, V.*

The Homestead Inn

If you follow the blue hospital signs in downtown New Milford, you'll easily find your way to the Homestead Inn near the north end of the Village Green. Innkeepers Rolf and Peggy Hammer, formerly a marketing executive and a physical therapist, took over the rambling white clapboard Victorian house in 1985 after they retired. They now devote themselves to their guests in the main house, which dates from 1853, and the adjacent motel, where Arthur Miller and Marilyn Monroe once stayed in the '50s. The bedrooms are decorated with floral print curtains and bedspreads, and the four-poster, pencil-post, and Jenny Lind beds seem quite at home with an assortment of antiques and country-style bric-a-brac. A hearty Continental breakfast is served in the dark-beamed living room with its balloon-shaded windows and Steinway piano. It's especially cheerful in the winter, with a blazing fire on the hearth.

Address: *5 Elm St., New Milford, CT 06766, tel. 203/354–4080.*
Accommodations: *14 double rooms with baths.*
Amenities: *Air-conditioning, cable TV, and phones in rooms.*
Rates: *$65–$85; Continental breakfast. AE, D, DC, MC, V.*
Restrictions: *2-night minimum on weekends, May–Oct., and holidays.*

The Inn on Lake Waramaug

The '80s was a rocky decade for the various owners of this rambling, nearly two-century-old Colonial overlooking Lake Waramaug. Fortunately, in recent years innkeepers Chip and Meg Chapell have brought considerable charm back to this property. Still, in comparison to the nearby Hopkins and Boulders inns, a bit in the way of personality is left to be desired. The Inn at Lake Waramaug seems unable to decide whether it's a modern resort or a country inn, and therefore manages to be both adequately but neither with any great success. There are five rooms in the creaky old main house and 18 rooms in two modern out buildings closer to the lake. Most have both canopied beds and daybeds, 18 have working fireplaces, and six have lake views. Rooms in the characterful 1795 main house have wide-plank wood floors and No. 5 has a wonderful lake view, but you'll have to put up with noise from the dining room downstairs. Full breakfast and a four-course dinner are included, and the restaurant churns out some impressive New American cuisine.

Address: *North Shore Rd., Lake Waramaug, CT 06777, tel. 203/868–0563 or 800/LAKE–INN; fax 203/868–9173.*
Accommodations: *23 rooms with private bath.*
Amenities: *2 restaurants, air-conditioning, cable TV, and phone in rooms; boating equipment, tennis, game room, indoor pool.*
Rates: *$189–$229; MAP. AE, MC, V.*
Restrictions: *No smoking, no pets.*

The Mayflower Inn

The countryside is abuzz these days with talk of the completely rebuilt inn in Washington, a picture-perfect country village perched high atop a mound of old New England money. Certain suites at the Mayflower will set you back $475 a night, and one wonders how long folks will pay that sort of money out here in the sticks—even though we're talking about some awfully fancy sticks. On any given Saturday afternoon, you'll find the parking lot bumper to bumper with limos and sports cars.

The 28-acre grounds are replete with streams, trails, and a fitness center, and each of the 17 rooms and seven suites, situated among three separate buildings, is decorated individually with fine antiques and four-poster canopied beds; the walls hung with noteworthy prints and paintings, and papered in Regency stripes. If all that doesn't entice you, the mouthwatering cuisine of renowned chef, John Farnsworth, may.

Address: *Rte. 47, Washington, CT 06793, tel. 203/868–9466; fax 203/868–1497.*
Accommodations: *17 double rooms with baths, 7 suites.*
Amenities: *Restaurant; air-conditioning, cable TV, and phones in rooms; tennis; meeting facilities; heated pool; fitness center.*
Rates: *$190–$475; breakfast extra. AE, MC, V.*
Restrictions: *No smoking, no pets. 2-night minimum on weekends, 3-night minimum on holiday weekends.*

Stonehenge

Just off busy Route 7 in Ridgefield are the manicured lawns and bright white clapboard buildings of the Stonehenge restaurant and inn. Once the proud domain of celebrated chef Albert Stockli, it is operated today by Douglas Seville, a veteran of the hotel business. The original 18th-century inn was destroyed by a fire in June 1988, and, alas, the rebuilding lacks period charm. Exquisite taste has been applied to the new rooms as well as to those in the cottage and guest house, but the result has all the earmarks of the professional. None of the quirks of the true period piece has survived or been replaced. Instead, the Stonehenge is a plethora of Waverly and Schumacher prints, a 10-foot gilt-framed mirror above a king-size bed, the latest chic magazines, and wall-to-wall carpeting. The dining, however, is still magnificent, and the service is impeccable.

Address: *Box 667, Ridgefield, CT 06877, tel. 203/438–6511, fax 203/438–2478.*
Accommodations: *14 double rooms with baths, 2 suites.*
Amenities: *Restaurant, room service, air-conditioning, cable TV, and phones in rooms; outdoor pool.*
Rates: *$120–$200; Continental breakfast. AE, DC, MC, V.*
Restrictions: *No pets.*

Tucker Hill Inn

Built in 1923, this colonial-style clapboard just down the road from the village green looks like a proper contemporary New England bed-and-breakfast. In an earlier incarnation it was a tea room at a trolley stop, but when Susan Cebelenski bought it in 1985 she saw the large house as an inn, and that's what she's turned it into. After taking numerous courses on how to run a successful B&B, Susan tempered those lessons with the practical experience she'd gained dealing with the public as a retailer in New York. The result is a pleasant inn with a few spacious rooms for guests, plus cozy sitting and dining areas. Her three children and songwriter husband have their own space elsewhere in the house. The bedrooms are attractively done, with an assortment of country-style furniture, wallpapers, and fabrics that suggest the guest rooms in a modern private house. A full, homemade breakfast is served either in the big dining room or informally in the large kitchen area.

Address: *96 Tucker Hill Rd., Middlebury, CT 06762, tel. 203/758–8334.*
Accommodations: *2 double rooms with baths, 2 doubles share 1 bath.*
Amenities: *Ceiling fans in bedrooms, house phone.*
Rates: *$55–$75; full breakfast. MC, V.*
Restrictions: *Smoking only in sitting areas, no pets.*

The Southeastern Coast

As you head east from New Haven, the urban clutter of factories, apartment towers, and shopping malls dissipates gradually, and before long you encounter long stretches of road without a single man-made intrusion. Although some industry and large cities have developed where major streams flow into Long Island Sound, the area is mostly a string of small communities, proud of their individual attractions as well as their common heritage.

In a bygone era, venturesome Yankee merchants sent their ships from thriving ports in search of whale oil, rum, household goods, and spices. At one time New London was the second busiest whaling port on the Atlantic, and Mystic, long famed for shipbuilding and maritime exploits, vigorously preserves that identity today. But the seafaring adventurers have mostly disappeared, and nowadays only tiny Stonington Village can claim the distinction of a commercial fishing fleet.

Although there's substantial activity in this region year-round, it is best seen and enjoyed in the warm-weather months. All sizes and kinds of boats, from dinghies to yachts, get their barnacles scraped and suddenly dot the local waters in bright profusion. Fishing, sailing, waterskiing, and even some surfing become daily activities. Although pollution often prohibits swimming in the waters of the sound, there's still the scent of the sea, and the salt air washes over sunbathers.

Offshore exploration is a popular pastime. The Thimble Islands off the Branford coast abound with legends of pirate gold buried by the infamous Captain Kidd. And those with a scientific bent can board numerous vessels that leave Mystic and New London for oceanographic explorations under supervision. Landlubbers will find substantial marine exhibits in the region's many museums and nature centers.

Browsing in stores is probably the most inevitable activity. The coastal towns have numerous shops selling tacky nautical reproductions made elsewhere—and a few selling genuine marine artifacts. This gives you an opportunity to outsmart the shrewd Yankee and once in a while come away with a true bargain.

Places to Go, Sights to See

Milestone Energy Center (278 Main St., Niantic, tel. 203/444–4234). Fast-forward to the 20th century at this nuclear power station, where you'll find exhibits on a variety of energy sources, energy-related computer games, and multimedia programs for all ages.

Mystic Seaport. Start with a visit to the nation's oldest *maritime museum* (tel. 203/572–0711) and check out its 17 riverfront acres before moving along to *Olde Mistick Village* (tel. 203/536–4941), a commercial but picturesque recreation of an early 18th-century hamlet. You're within strolling distance of the *Mystic Marinelife Aquarium* (tel. 203/536–3323), which has more than 6,000 specimens and 49 live exhibits of sea creatures, including the 2½-acre Seal Island.

U.S. Coast Guard Academy (15 Mohegan Ave., New London, tel. 203/444–8270). A 100-acre cluster of redbrick buildings in New London is the site of this service academy. In addition to a museum and visitor's pavilion, the three-masted training bark, the *Eagle*, is open for boarding when she's in port.

U.S. Naval Submarine Base (tel. 203/449–3174). Across the Thames River in Groton, you're in submarine territory, albeit friendly waters. You can board the first nuclear-powered vessel and visit the *Nautilus* Memorial/Submarine Force Library and Museum all in one day.

Beaches

Hammonasset Beach State Park has a 2-mile strip of sand as well as facilities for swimming, camping, and picnicking. To get there, follow the crowd from Exit 62 on I–95. **Ocean Beach Park** in New London offers an Olympic-size outdoor pool with a triple water slide, a kids' pool and playground, an amusement park with miniature golf, a boardwalk with the usual concessions, and a picnic area—as well as swimming in the sound. Take I–95 and get off at Exit 82A–N/83S. **Rocky Neck State Park** in Niantic, at Exit 72 on I–95, is only a mile long, but it offers one of the nicest saltwater bathing sites in the state, including a public bathhouse, picnic grounds and shelter, campgrounds, and fishing facilities.

Restaurants

Almost any restaurant you walk into off the street will have the usual local favorites—chowder, lobster, clams, and the perennial fish fry. For superior seafood in Stonington Village, try **Harbor View** (tel. 203/535–2720) and **Skipper's Dock** (tel. 203/535–2000). The former is a bit formal and "haute cuisine," with such gourmet fare as sweetbreads. Skipper's is more rough-and-ready; its menu features such hearty dishes as Portuguese fishermen's stew.

Nightlife

In tiny Stony Creek, near Branford, you'll find year-round live theater at the **Puppet House Theatre** (tel. 203/773–8080). **Bank St. Café** (tel. 203/444–7932) in New London bills itself as the top live blues club on the East Coast and certainly tries hard for the title.

Tourist Information

Shoreline Visitors' Bureau (115 State Sq., Guilford, CT 06437, tel. 203/397–5250); **Southeastern Connecticut Tourism District** (27 Masonic St., Post Office Bldg., Box 89, New London, CT 06320, tel. 203/444–2206 or, outside CT, 800/222–6783).

Reservations Services

Bed & Breakfast, Ltd. (Box 216, New Haven, CT 06513, tel. 203/469–3260); **Covered Bridge Bed & Breakfast Reservation Service** (Box 447, Norfolk, CT 06058, tel. 203/542–5944); **Nutmeg Bed & Breakfast Agency** (Box 1117, West Hartford, CT 06107, tel. 203/236–6698).

Antiques & Accommodations

The British accent of this 1861 Victorian bed-and-breakfast in the center of North Stonington is no accident. Owner/managers Thomas and Ann Gray are avowed Anglophiles who travel regularly to England to buy things for the house. Their background as antiques appraisers and liquidators has stood them in good stead; the place is a treasure trove.

And, here's good news for guests: Everything is for sale. The Grays decided to combine their multiple interests by running an elegantly decorated small hostelry and at the same time offering the antiques for sale to their clientele. Do you like that Meissen bowl? That Welsh fireplace fender? How about the Massachusetts Sheraton four-poster in the Branscombe Room (named after an English B&B in Devon)? It could be yours... for a price.

Whether or not you buy the smallest trifle, the Grays welcome you to their home and go to great pains to provide for your comfort. The rooms are furnished, it should be noted, with *livable* antiques. In the Fireplace Room on the ground floor, though you have to walk a few steps to the bath, you have your own stereo. The bridal suite is called the Tetbury after a favorite English B&B. Honeymooners can count on being served Ann's heart-shaped Grand Marnier French toast prepared especially for them. All the rooms are filled with bright Victorian touches: fresh flowers as well as dried arrangements, and gently scented candles everywhere. A four-course candlelight breakfast of fresh local eggs, sweet cider, and crumbly buttery muffins is served every morning to guests in the main house as well as those in the adjacent 1820 farmhouse, which has been adapted to guest lodging (though it has its own huge kitchen for "do-it-yourself" cooks).

The front parlor is a pleasant place to relax or have tea, and in warm weather, so is the stone terrace out front, shaded by a flowering crabapple tree. You can sit back in the early morning sun and savor the memory of breakfast, or, as you close your eyes, you can let your thoughts drift to the turned-down bedclothes and the candle burning on your night table awaiting you at the end of the day.

Address: *32 Main St., N. Stonington, CT 06359, tel. 203/535–1736.*
Accommodations: *3 double rooms with baths, 1 single and 1 double share 1 bath, cottage with bath.*
Amenities: *Air-conditioning, box lunches available.*
Rates: *$95–$225; full breakfast. No credit cards.*
Restrictions: *Smoking only on porch, no pets.*

Bee & Thistle Inn

On a long a wide avenue in the Old Lyme historic district, behind a weathered stone wall, is a two-story 1725 Colonial house that has evolved gracefully into the Bee & Thistle Inn. Set on 5½ acres along the Lieutenant River, which joins the Connecticut to flow into Long Island Sound, the inn's broad lawns, towering trees, formal flower garden, and herbaceous borders form a perfect setting.

In the eight years since Penny and Bob Nelson left behind the corporate world and academia in New York, they have realized a family dream here. A complete turnaround in their lifestyle occurred when they decided to become innkeepers while their two children were in the last years of school. But so successful were they and such was the lure of this special place that both kids now work here: son Jeff (a former sous-chef at Boston's Ritz Carlton) in the kitchen and daughter Lori out front greeting, seating, and helping guests settle in.

Restoration has taken priority over renovation—which they have done only when comfort is at stake—and the result is the re-creation of a colonial ambience in the best sense. The scale of rooms throughout is deliberately small and inviting, with fireplaces in the downstairs parlors and dining rooms, and light and airy curtains at the multipaned bedroom windows. Almost all rooms have canopy or four-poster beds, with old quilts and afghans providing warmth when needed. Little touches change with the seasons—hanging on each door might be tiny beribboned straw hats or, at another time, sprigs of evergreen or holly. No slave to colonial New England style, Penny brings to the rooms touches of Williamsburg and even Victoriana, with such oddities as a wing chair our Puritan forebears surely wouldn't recognize.

Breakfast can be brought to your room before or after a morning soak in an herbal bath (scented soap provided). And downstairs you might encounter a harpist one evening, or take high tea late some afternoon. The romantic atmosphere is created by working fireplaces and candlelight that, coupled with high-class cuisine, can make for a memorable evening.

Address: *100 Old Lyme St., Old Lyme, CT 06371, tel. 203/434–1667 or 800/622–4946.*
Accommodations: *9 double rooms with baths, 2 doubles share 1 bath, cottage with bath.*
Amenities: *Restaurant, air-conditioning.*
Rates: *$69–$195; breakfast extra. AE, DC, MC, V.*
Restrictions: *Smoking only in some dining room areas, no children under 12, no pets. Closed first two weeks in Jan.*

Red Brook Inn

On the Gold Star Highway (Rte. 184), at the western outlet of Welles Road, you'll see one of the two buildings that make up the Red Brook Inn. The 1770 center-chimney Crary Homestead is set behind a stone wall, surrounded by a small garden on 7 acres of woodland. Innkeeper Ruth Keyes originally purchased the tavern at an auction when it was threatened at its previous site by a road-widening project. She then had it moved board by board, stone by stone, and reconstructed faithfully on its present site. She set about furnishing it with authentic Colonial-period antiques and installing the basic comforts of electricity and plumbing—judiciously modern though unobtrusive.

A transplant herself, the youthful and vigorous Ruth was a real-estate litigation appraiser in California before retirement. Today she's more at home pointing out the features of the property and cooking the hearty breakfasts served at the Red Brook. She has also mastered the intricacies of open-hearth cooking, and in November and December she prepares Saturday-night dinners for guests.

The Keeping Room, where meals are served, has a large granite fireplace and baking oven with an array of iron tools and utensils, including a rare "bottle jack" used to roast hanging game. The old stagecoach walls in the Tap Room have bare boards, which adds to the coziness of what is now a well-equipped games room, complete with Monopoly and Scrabble, dominoes and checkers. Here guests are served complimentary afternoon tea and drinks.

Bedrooms in both buildings are furnished meticulously with Colonial antiques, including canopy and four-poster beds with rare period coverings. Most rooms have working fireplaces, with fires laid in winter, waiting to be lit when you arrive. Split wood is provided to keep them going during your stay. All rooms have private baths and two rooms even have whirlpool tubs.

The New England charm of these two buildings with their fine antiques and comfortable ambience makes a stay here an unqualified pleasure. The Inn is only about twenty minutes from Mystic and the new Foxwoods Casino.

Address: *Box 327, Mystic, CT 06372, tel. 203/572–0349.*
Accommodations: *11 double rooms with baths.*
Amenities: *Cable TV, guest refrigerator, and guest phone in the Tap Room, extensive library.*
Rates: *$95–$169, $350 for 2 people for 2 nights; Colonial dinner package available on request; full breakfast and complimentary beverages. MC, V.*
Restrictions: *No smoking indoors, no pets. 2-night minimum on weekends and holidays.*

Captain Stannard House

On South Main Street in Westbrook, the two-story clapboard house with the cupola on the roof looks like a sea captain's house, and indeed it was in the 19th century. Since then it has gone through multiple changes and has been operated at various times as an inn. Today it holds sway as a bed-and-breakfast and gift shop in the hands of Verner Mattin and his wife Lee Willman, who have owned it for just over a year. They have refurbished the rooms and are in the process of landscaping the grounds. Breakfast now is served in the large bright dining room with its elegant fireplace, baby grand piano, and decorative antiques. The quaint library doubles as a lounge where drinks are served. The common area has a wood stove and pool table, and displays antiques and local crafts that are for sale.

Address: *138 S. Main St., Westbrook, CT 06498, tel. 203/399–4634, fax 203/399–0182.*
Accommodations: *6 double rooms with baths.*
Amenities: *Air-conditioning; free bikes for guest use.*
Rates: *$70–$90 year-round; Continental breakfast. No credit cards.*
Restrictions: *No smoking indoors, no children under 13, no pets.*

Harbour Inne & Cottage

On a small inlet of the Mystic River, two blocks from the train station, you'll find a 1950s-style "added on" bungalow where Charlie Lecouras, Jr., welcomes overnight guests. With its neatly clipped lawn surrounded on three sides by water, this location is ideal for spotting herons, loons, and more ccmmon waterfowl. If you want to paddle out for a better look, you can rent one of Charlie's boats or canoes and set off from his own pier. Charlie is at home most evenings, but during the day you'll probably be greeted by Dave Tuttle, a genial navy veteran and now general handyman who also makes beds and cuts the grass. Bedrooms are fairly small and have simple, modern maple furniture. The decor leans heavily on the nautical theme. Some rooms lack good bedside lamps and may be a bit cramped, but there's a cozy lounge with an open fireplace and a fully equipped kitchen for guests.

Address: *Edgemont St., Mystic, CT 06355, tel. 203/572–9253.*
Accommodations: *4 double rooms with showers, 1 double with bath, 3-room cottage for 6 with fireplace, kitchen, and bath.*
Amenities: *Cable TV and air-conditioning in rooms. Gazebo by water, picnic facilities.*
Rates: *$55–$110; no breakfast. No credit cards.*
Restrictions: *2-night minimum on weekends Memorial Day–Labor Day.*

Lasbury's Guest House

Strolling down a side street in compact Stonington Village (the preferred method of local locomotion), you'll pass by the big brick schoolhouse that has "gone condo" on your way to the Orchard Street residence of mother and daughter, Mae and Jayne Lasbury. From this small frame house built in 1860, they're proud to report that five generations of Lasburys walked to that school. But these days, they're just as pleased to show you to the little red guest house across the tiny garden, where they offer trim, quiet lodgings year-round to just a few visitors. The guest-house rooms overlook a salt marsh that drifts off to Long Island Sound. The bedrooms have no-nonsense traditional-style furniture, curtains, and bed coverings in light colors, with framed art prints announcing the annual Stonington Village Fair as part of the decor. Breakfast comes to your room in a basket and may be taken outdoors to the garden or down to the point. This is not the most comfortable of inns, but it is the only one in this delightful village.

Address: *24 Orchard St., Stonington, CT 06378, tel. 203/535–2681.*
Accommodations: *3 double rooms share 2 baths.*
Amenities: *Air-conditioning in 1 room, cable TV and minifridges in rooms.*
Rates: *$65 winter, $80 summer; Continental breakfast. No credit cards.*
Restrictions: *No pets. 2-night minimum on summer and holiday weekends.*

Old Lyme Inn

Just a short drive (less than a mile) from Exit 70 on I–95 you'll come to a bend in the road and a gray clapboard 1850s farmhouse that now forms the centerpiece of the Old Lyme Inn. Diana Field Atwood, the innkeeper of nearly 20 years, has transformed what was once a run-down Italian restaurant into a warm and attractive dining and lodging establishment in the heart of the historic district. Behind the ornate iron fence, the tree-shaded lawn, and the banistered front porch, you'll find attractive, spacious bedrooms impeccably decorated by Diana with carefully selected antiques and contemporary furnishings. When she isn't busy working for the local art academy or the Connecticut River Museum, which she serves as president, Diana will be lifting pot lids in the kitchen for whiffs of the gourmet treats served by her chef in the always-busy dining rooms. She also collects local art, some of which is displayed in the cozy common rooms on the ground floor.

Address: *Box 787B, Old Lyme, CT 06371, tel. 203/434–2600, fax 203/434–5352.*
Accommodations: *5 doubles with baths, 8 suites.*
Amenities: *Restaurant, air-conditioning, phones, and clock radios in rooms, TV and working fireplace in library.*
Rates: *$85–$140; Continental breakfast. AE, D, DC, MC, V.*
Restrictions: *Closed Jan. 1–15.*

The Palmer Inn

On a side street in the tiny village of Noank, the Palmer Inn rises majestically behind tall hedges that permit just a glimpse of its tall white Corinthian columns. This imposing southern colonial–style house was erected in 1907 by a local shipbuilder as an exact copy of a Knoxville mansion. His own artisans were responsible for the exquisite interior woodwork. Patricia White, the owner/innkeeper (who also makes the jellies and jams, muffins and breads served at breakfast), proudly points out unusual design features, such as the tile-like Lincrusta Walton wallpaper along the main stairway. Followed by Arthur and Dickens, her miniature dachshunds, she'll show you the spacious bedrooms, furnished with family heirlooms and antiques, including an ornate Eastlake bed and an original morris chair. They're complemented by Schumacher wallpapers that suit the late-Victorian period. The Balcony Room on the third floor has a fine view of Long Island Sound. Downstairs, the main parlor is almost too grand, but the library is cozy, especially with a glowing fire.

Address: *25 Church St., Noank, CT 06340, tel. 203/572–9000.*
Accommodations: *6 double rooms with baths.*
Rates: *$105–$175; Continental breakfast. MC, V.*
Restrictions: *Smoking only in library, no pets. 2-night minimum on weekends July–Oct.*

Randall's Ordinary

As you leave the Westerly-Norwich Road (Rte. 2) and continue up the short drive to this enclave of centuries-old weathered frame buildings, you could easily be a Colonial traveler seeking an inn. In the 17th century each town approved one such establishment through an ordinance, giving rise to the designation "ordinary." The original 1685 building today houses a restaurant celebrated for its open-hearth cooking and for its three primitively furnished guest rooms upstairs. Across the drive is the 1819 Jacob Terpenning barn, moved from upstate New York and converted to lodgings in 1989, with nine rooms on three floors. Innkeepers Bill and Cindy Clark have achieved period authenticity in the decor through the use of canopy and four-poster beds, simple furniture, and a smattering of antiques. However, the largely bare floors and walls also create a spartan look that could use some warming up. The tavern atmosphere of the restaurant in the main house does a lot to fill that gap. So does the dramatic Silo suite with its domed loft and skylighted living area.

Address: *Rte. 2, Box 243, N. Stonington, CT 06359, tel. 203/599–4540.*
Accommodations: *12 double rooms with baths.*
Amenities: *Air-conditioning, fireplaces in main-house bedrooms, modern baths with Jacuzzis in barn.*
Rates: *$85–$140; Continental breakfast. AE, MC, V.*
Restrictions: *No pets. 2-night minimum on holiday weekends.*

Talcott House

You can't miss the scent of salt air when you pull up to this 1890 cedar-shingled beach cottage that's now a popular shoreline bed-and-breakfast. The owner/managers Cathy and Bruce Keeton have removed all trace of clutter and have kept furnishings simple, though of the highest quality. The highly polished floor in the main salon reflects the light streaming in the front windows down its 50-foot length, from one fireplace to another at the opposite end. A ground-floor guest room has its own screened brick-floor patio looking out over the sound. The remainder of the guest rooms, upstairs, have similarly shiny floors with an assortment of attractive carpets, some brass beds, hobnail spreads, and stenciling above the pale painted walls. Three rooms facing the ocean have their own baths while another three with painted wainscoting share one bath. The Keetons, who also own and operate Viva Zapata, a Mexican restaurant in New Haven, make their breakfast special with homemade muffins, breads, and tarts.

Address: *161 Seaside Ave., Box 1016, Westbrook, CT 06498, tel. 203/399–5020.*
Accommodations: *4 double rooms with baths, 3 doubles share 1 bath.*
Amenities: *Clock radios in bedrooms.*
Rates: *$75–$95; Continental breakfast. MC, V.*
Restrictions: *No pets.*

The Whaler's Inn

Just off the Mystic River Bridge, the Whaler's Inn overlooks the passing throngs making their way along East Main Street to the heart of downtown Mystic. It's a good choice for those who want to be right in town and don't mind the summertime crowds. The Whaler's has recently been purchased from the Macbeth family by a group of local entrepreneurs who operate this former 19th-century inn more like a hotel than a country hostelry. The Whaler's complex consists of accommodations in the inn, a Victorian guest house and motor court across the parking lot, plus indoor and outdoor restaurants and a gift shop. The new owners have recently completed an extensive renovation of all the buildings and rooms. The outside has been repainted and reworked. The rooms are clean and decorated with modern Shaker furniture, and some even with canopied beds.

Address: *20 E. Main St., Mystic, CT 06355, tel. 203/536–1506 or 800/243–2588 in eastern U.S., fax 203/572–7697.*
Accommodations: *41 double rooms with baths.*
Amenities: *2 restaurants, cable TV and phones in bedrooms, courtesy car to train station and airport.*
Rates: *$65–$110; breakfast extra. Single room rates on request. AE, D, DC, MC, V.*
Restrictions: *No pets.*

Connecticut River Valley
Hartford to the Sound

As the Connecticut River flows south from the state capital to Long Island Sound, it looks beyond its banks at a broad variety of landscapes, from the high-rise urban environment of Hartford to the Colonial seaports at the mouth of the river. This kaleidoscope is really part of its great allure—if you're not happy where you are at a given moment, you don't have to go far for a change. There's the political, commercial, and cultural vibrancy of Hartford at one end of the spectrum and the relaxed charm and small-town coziness of Ivoryton at the other; the exhaust fumes of the urban end of the road contrast with the dust of ages settling on tree-shaded streets at its rural opposite.

And then, of course, there's the river itself. For many years this was a major commercial artery, with goods floating up and down its navigable waters. Industry grew up along the shorelines and poured its waste into this too-convenient source of disposal. The price of that shortsightedness is being paid today, but with the rise in ecological consciousness, the efforts to improve the quality of this beautiful waterway are seeing significant gains. Varieties of marine life that were virtually extinct are starting to reappear in abundance—much to the delight of the fishing enthusiasts, who are also finding their way back.

For a long time, the resort business that had thrived in earlier decades declined, and once-quaint tourist shops were looking dated and dilapidated. But there's been a movement toward renovation and renewal, and some are taking on new appeal with fresh coats of paint and new variations on their cutesy names. It looks as though their perseverance may get its reward from a new crop of visitors to the area.

Connecticut still has one of the highest percentages of forest and undeveloped land in the country. You don't have to go many miles inland on either side of the river to find unspoiled woodland. Many state parks and nature preserves down its entire length welcome all who respect the environment and who will leave it pretty much as it has been for centuries.

Places to Go, Sights to See

Gillette Castle State Park (tel. 203/526–2336). In 1919 the actor William Gillette, who made his fortune as the stage impersonator of Sherlock Holmes, moved into this fieldstone hillside mansion overlooking the river at East Haddam. He filled his "castle" with the ornate decor of an earlier time and lived here until his death, when the property was bequeathed to the state. The grounds are open and house tours are held from Memorial Day to the weekend before Christmas. The Victorian holiday decoration of the house is spectacular.

Goodspeed Opera House (Route 82, East Haddam, tel. 203/873–8668). A relic of the steamboat era right on the river at East Haddam, this celebrated edifice was built in 1876 by a wealthy merchant as a home for his mercantile and theatrical interests. It flourishes today as the birthplace of such Broadway hits as *Annie* and *Man of La Mancha* and the setting for acclaimed revivals of vintage musicals.

Nook Farm (Farmington Ave., Hartford, tel. 203/525–9317). You can get an idea of upper-middle-class life in the Hartford of the 1870s as well as a glimpse of our literary heritage at this intersection on the outskirts of the state capital. Here you'll find the whimsical Victorian mansion built and occupied by Mark Twain next door to the more demure cottage where Harriet Beecher Stowe lived.

Wadsworth Atheneum (600 Main St., Hartford, tel. 203/247–9111). This major art museum in downtown Hartford has more than 40,000 works, a Gallery of the Senses for the visually impaired, and changing exhibits of contemporary art.

Restaurants

Good food in Hartford ranges from French at **L'Américain** (tel. 203/522–6500) to Vietnamese at **Truc Orient Express** (tel. 203/296–2818), with excellent Italian at **Frank's** (tel. 203/527–9291) and **Carbone's** (tel. 203/296–9646). Farther south, head for haute cuisine at the justly applauded **Fine Bouche** (tel. 203/767–1277), in Centerbrook, where romance is almost inescapable in the elegant surroundings.

Theater

The performing arts have always been a mainstay all along the river and continue to draw fans year-round. In Hartford the **Bushnell Auditorium** (tel. 203/246–6807) brings in touring attractions, while the Tony Award-winning **Hartford Stage Company** (tel. 203/527–5151) generates its own hits. The Goodspeed Opera House operates on a smaller scale with new works at the **Norma Terris Theater** in Chester (tel. 203/873–8668), and the **Ivoryton Playhouse** (tel. 203/767–8348) continues its longstanding success with The River Rep during the summer season.

Boating

If you don't want to hoist your own sail or pilot your own vessel, you can still enjoy a day or evening on the river aboard a number of cruise ships that ply these waters. **Connecticut Riverboat Rides** offers hour-long voyages aboard the *Becky Thatcher* or *Silver Star*, leaving from Deep River (tel. 203/767–0103). Several **Camelot** cruises (tel. 203/345–8591) leave the dock at Haddam directly opposite the scenic Opera House. The *Lady Fenwick*, a reproduction of an 1850s steam yacht, leaving from Hartford, and the *Aunt Polly*, an excursion boat that sets off from Middletown, both offer packages that include meals and entertainment (tel. 203/526–4954).

Tourist Information

Connecticut Valley Tourism Commission (393 Main St., Middletown, CT 06457, tel. 203/347–6924); **Greater Hartford Convention & Visitors Bureau** (1 Civic Center Plaza, Hartford, CT 06103, tel. 203/728–6789).

Reservation Services

Bed & Breakfast, Ltd. (Box 216, New Haven, CT 06513, tel. 203/469–3260); **Covered Bridge Bed & Breakfast Reservation Service** (Box 447, Norfolk, CT 06058, tel. 203/542–5944); **Four Seasons International Bed & Breakfast** (11 Bridle Path Rd., West Simsbury, CT 06092, tel. 203/651–3045); **Nutmeg Bed & Breakfast Agency** (Box 1117, West Hartford, CT 06107, tel. 203/236–6698).

Copper Beech Inn

Picture a rambling Victorian country cottage, complete with carriage barn and terraced gardens set behind spreading oaks and aged beech trees on 7 wooded acres in a small town not far from a river. You've just conjured up the Copper Beech Inn. Built in the 1880s as a residence for the ivory importer A. W. Comstock, it has happily evolved into a haven for dining and lodging in the quintessential Connecticut River Valley town of Ivoryton.

The current innkeepers, Eldon and Sally Senner, took over just a few years ago but have already made their mark on the guest rooms. There are four in the main house and they have been spruced up with a fresh infusion of antique furniture and bric-a-brac, creating a warm traditional ambience.

The renovated carriage house now contains nine spacious guest rooms that were designed by the Senners. Architectural features, such as cathedral ceilings and exposed beams, give each room a distinctive character. While the rooms are essentially modern, the country theme of the main building is maintained in the furnishings and a sprinkling of appropriate antiques and graphics. All the rooms in the carriage house have French doors leading out to decks that overlook the surrounding gardens and woodland. The bathrooms here are most definitely contemporary, with large whirlpool tubs. Still, the combination of old and new, indoors and out, works to create the ambience of a country retreat, exactly what the Senners set out to do.

At one time the ground floor of the main house abounded with endless reception rooms so beloved by the Victorians. While there are still plenty of sitting areas for guests, the larger rooms have been converted to a series of thematic dining areas that are elegant and very romantic in the evening when candlelight glows on the sparkling crystal and gleaming silver. The starched linens and fresh flowers in the award-winning dining room are indicative of the high standards of the house.

You won't find anything stressful here. The beautiful grounds, comfortable guest rooms, abundant lounge space, and welcoming dining rooms may well make your quest for a quiet country inn end at the Copper Beach.

Address: *46 Main St., Ivoryton, CT 06442, tel. 203/767–0330.*
Accommodations: *13 double rooms with baths.*
Amenities: *Restaurant (closed Mon. and Tues. from Jan.–Mar.), air-conditioning, cable TV in carriage house, phones in rooms.*
Rates: *\$115–\$155; Continental breakfast. AE, DC, MC, V.*
Restrictions: *No pets. 2-night minimum on weekends.*

Riverwind

As you approach the busy downtown area of Deep River, you can't miss the dark gray clapboard building with the gingerbread trim and the sign out front that identifies Riverwind as a country inn.

Ostensibly, Miss Hickory the cat, who is usually found snoozing in front of one of the many fireplaces, is the owner of the establishment, but the innkeepers in residence, Barbara Barlow and Bob Bucknell, are always on hand to welcome guests with a cup of tea or something similarly soothing. Barbara came north from Virginia, where she'd taught school for a number of years, and fell in love with the Connecticut River Valley. When she found this 1830s Victorian, fallen sadly into disrepair, her preservationist instincts sensed a challenge. The process involved Bob, a local builder, who saw a different challenge, which he met by wooing and winning her. Maybe that's why Riverwind has so many romantic touches.

A combination of period charm and Southern hospitality is felt throughout the house in the countless carefully placed antiques and bibelots and the decanter of complimentary sherry in the parlor. In Champagne and Roses, the most spectacular guest room, a mahogany pencil-post bed under a fishnet canopy is surrounded by a vanity desk, a carved mirrored armoire, and rose-color wing chairs. You might drink the champagne that comes with this room on its private balcony at the level of the treetops.

Each room has a decorative theme, and all have antique furnishings and stenciling. The beds range from a country pine one with a painted headboard and a carved oak bed to an 18th-century bird's-eye maple four-poster bed with a canopy. The bathrooms have modern plumbing, but one has a Victorian claw-foot tub.

In the 18th century–style keeping room that was added onto the original building just a few years ago, there's a huge stone cooking fireplace. It's hard to believe it hasn't been there for centuries. This is where you'll be served Barbara's hearty country breakfast, featuring Smithfield ham, her own baked goods, and several casseroles. Freshly brewed tea and coffee are always on hand, and in the front parlor a piano is ready for those inclined to play. Touches like these lift Riverwind out of the ordinary.

Address: *209 Main St., Deep River, CT 06147, tel. 203/526–2014.*
Accommodations: *7 rooms with baths (one is a hall bath), 1 suite.*
Amenities: *Air-conditioning.*
Rates: *\$85–\$145; full breakfast, tea, coffee, and sherry. AE, MC, V.*
Restrictions: *No pets. 2-night minimum on weekends Apr. 15–Jan. 2.*

Simsbury 1820 House

Perched on a hillside above the main road through the town of Simsbury is a classic country inn—a two-story brick mansion built in 1820, with an 1890 addition on its west side. The property had ended up in the hands of the town, which didn't know what to do with it, and in 1985, it was turned over to Simsbury House Associates, to rescue it from decay, restore it to its proper status, and operate it as a country inn and restaurant.

In just a few years, the Associates have wrought a remarkable, wonderful change. The restaurant has become recognized for the excellence of its cuisine, winning praise from leading food critics. The romantic candlelight setting elicits almost as much applause as the victuals.

The bedrooms were given just as much attention as the dining room in the renovation, and the results are evident. They vary in configuration, as might be expected in a vintage building, and a judicious mix of antiques and modern furnishings works to the advantage of both. In the main house there are 19 rooms and two suites. Each has its special feature—a fireplace, a balcony, a patio, a wet bar, a dormer with a cozy window seat. If you walk under the porte cochere and cross the parking lot, you come to the old carriage house that now contains nine equally individual rooms and two suites. One, the split-level Executive Suite, has a private patio and entrance.

The room decor in the main house shows a designer's touch in the complementary use of colors—maroon, yellow, blue, green, and pink—and pattern to create a restful atmosphere. In the primarily brown and green decor of the carriage house, whimsy is added with well-chosen horse prints on bed coverings and curtains. Most rooms have imported English four-poster beds, but in one, old barn doors are used as a combination room-divider and king-size headboard. It works.

Although the common rooms in the main house are shared with restaurant patrons, there are lots of places to sit and read the paper or relax over a drink. The staff, supervised by innkeeper Kelly Hohengarten, seems to consist mostly of young people who take the time to be responsive to guests. Ms. Hohengarten should be proud.

Address: *731 Hopmeadow St., Simsbury, CT 06070, tel. 203/658–7658 or 800/879–1820, fax 203/651–0724.*
Accommodations: *28 double rooms with baths, 6 suites.*
Amenities: *Restaurant, air-conditioning, cable TV and phones in rooms.*
Rates: *$85–$135; Continental breakfast. AE, D, DC, MC, V.*
Restrictions: *Pets allowed only in carriage house.*

Barney House

Right around the corner from the busiest intersection in Farmington, you'll find a peaceful suburban street and the peach and white painted exterior of the Barney House. Built in 1832, the mansion and its 4½ acres of exquisite formal gardens have come under control of the University of Connecticut Foundation, which operates a year-round conference center on the premises. Happily for voyagers to these parts, it also accepts overnight guests by reservation. The seven large guest rooms on its upper two floors are done in a combination of antiques and modern furnishings. Some have Oriental carpets, some have area rugs, and some, wall-to-wall carpeting. All have substantial bathrooms with modern plumbing. A refrigerator and coffee setup are available for guests in the area on the second-floor landing where breakfast is served each morning. Guests are invited to enjoy the garden, pool, and tennis court, as well as the common rooms on the first floor when they're not being used for conferences.

Address: *11 Mountain Spring Rd., Farmington, CT 06032, tel. 203/677–9735.*
Accommodations: *7 double rooms with baths.*
Amenities: *Cable TV, phones, and clock-radios in rooms; 2 large and 4 small meeting rooms; outdoor pool, tennis court.*
Rates: *$79–$89; Continental breakfast. MC, V.*
Restrictions: *No pets.*

Bishopsgate Inn

To reach the Federal-style Bishopsgate Inn, just follow the Norwich Road up around the bend from the landmark Goodspeed Opera House. Here your hosts, Molly and Dan Swartz, will give you a warm welcome, including a cold drink on a hot day and vice versa. Before taking over the inn in 1986, these Midwesterners spent a number of years in Brooklyn, where Dan ran a performing-arts center and Molly was a costumer. The inn has a definite theatrical flair; pictures of guests who have appeared on the Goodspeed stage are much in evidence. Rooms in the house (built in 1818, with an addition in 1860) are not just for show, however, despite such appellations as Jenny Lind and Blue Heaven. Early American reproductions, a smattering of antiques, chenille spreads, and crisp curtains make them cozy and inviting. In addition to the downstairs sitting room, fondly called the Couch-potato Room, guests also have a small sitting area upstairs. An irresistible breakfast specialty is Molly's stuffed French toast—recipe available.

Address: *Box 290, 7 Norwich Rd., Goodspeed Landing, East Haddam, CT 06423, tel. 203/873–1677.*
Accommodations: *5 double rooms with baths, 1 suite.*
Amenities: *Air-conditioning in bedrooms, fireplaces in 4 rooms, sauna in suite.*
Rates: *$75–$100; full breakfast. MC, V.*
Restrictions: *No pets. 2-night minimum on holiday weekends.*

Griswold Inn

Stretching its 11-window length along Main Street, the Griswold Inn in Essex lays claim to being America's oldest and most famous inn. Who's going to argue? It certainly offers a great deal of testimony to its heritage everywhere you look. More than two centuries of catering to changing tastes has resulted in a kaleidoscope of decor—some Colonial, a touch of Federal, a little Victorian, and just as much modern as is necessary for present-day comfort. Guest rooms, with their candlewick spreads and muslin curtains, retain their ancient configurations complete with sloping floors, but are all air-conditioned and up-to-code in terms of safety. William Winterer, the innkeeper for two decades, has even permitted the encroachment of the communication age. Rooms now have their own telephones, although the only TV is in the lounge of the upstart 1790 Hayden House section of the "Gris." Strangely enough, there's piped-in music but no radios in the guest rooms. The dining room here draws visitors from all over and offers an enormous variety of traditional and gourmet dishes

Address: *36 Main St., Essex, CT 06426, tel. 203/767-1776, fax 203/767-0481.*
Accommodations: *18 double rooms with baths, 7 suites.*
Amenities: *Restaurant, fireplaces in 6 suites.*
Rates: *$80–$165; Continental breakfast. AE, MC, V.*
Restrictions: *No smoking in bedrooms.*

Ivoryton Inn

Once upon a time the Ivoryton Playhouse was a major venue on the star-studded "strawhat circuit." Stars such as Gloria Swanson and Rudy Vallee came to town, trod the boards, and stayed around the corner and down the road at the snappy new, welcoming Ivoryton Inn, the hostelry that was originally a boardinghouse built by a local manufacturer in the mid-19th century. Summer theater isn't what it was, and though the Playhouse still offers a season of excellent stage fare, the old gray frame building with the bright yellow awnings is no longer a celebrity hangout. Theater people still come for the convenience, the low rates, the jazz ensemble that plays in the bar every night but Monday, and for the meals in the Ivory Room restaurant. Ed Bant, who lives in nearby Essex and took over the inn in March 1990, has played the piano here for many, many years and has begun to spruce things up. The lobby, with its antique spinet piano and stenciling, offers a good preview. Meanwhile, the simply furnished, no-nonsense bedrooms are serviceable and uncluttered, if a bit charmless—the ambience here is all on the ground floor.

Address: *115 Main St., Ivoryton, CT 06442, tel. 203/767–0422, fax 203/767–0318.*
Accommodations: *26 double rooms with baths, 2 suites.*
Amenities: *Air-conditioning, restaurant, phones in rooms.*
Rates: *$85–$100; breakfast extra. AE, MC, V.*
Restrictions: *No pets.*

The Northwest Corner

The far corner, where Connecticut meets southwestern Massachusetts to abut New York State, has never been a major transportation hub. A few well-traveled state roads, Routes 7, 8, and 44, cut through the rising and falling terrain, but major interstate highways skirt the area—to the great delight of its year-round inhabitants. Even so, the corner has long been a mecca for weekend émigrés from the big cities, traditionally Boston and New York, though an increasing number are drifting in from Hartford and even Fairfield County to the south.

Its combination of large towns and small villages are spaced far enough apart to offer broad views of the commanding landscape, and the climate is generally more severe than elsewhere in the state. The foothills of the Berkshires, with Canaan Mountain dominating the western border, present just enough of a rise to challenge hikers, intermediate skiers, and campers, who flock here seasonally.

In the active summer season, the quiet hamlets of Falls Village and Norfolk come alive with famous chamber-music festivals, and Tanglewood and other cultural meccas across the border in Massachusetts draw lovers of the performing arts. Swimming, sailing, and canoeing are popular activities on mountain lakes and ponds. The Housatonic River, which wends its way from north to south, attracts avid anglers, starting with the trout season in mid-April.

Historic homes and a few small museums are scattered throughout the region, and virtually every town has a historical society that welcomes visitors and can point out some select sights—from the fountain designed by Stanford White at the southern corner of Norfolk's village green to the factory in Lakeville where the famous Holley pocketknives were made. Many of the numerous 18th- and 19th-century houses are open to the public.

Occasional special events provide a break in the general air of calm that predominates. Canaan's Railroad Days, Winsted's Laurel Festival, and the Goshen and Riverton fairs offer a glimpse of small-town America that manages not only to survive locally, but sometimes prevail.

Places to Go, Sights to See

Battell-Stoeckel Center for Music and Art (Rte. 44, Norfolk Green, tel. 203/432–1966). For the past 50 years, these splendid grounds in Norfolk have been the home of the Yale Summer School of Music and Art and the Norfolk Chamber Music Festival. In the 900-seat Shed, weekly concerts take place from late June to early August. Those on Thursday evening are free. On weekends you pay to hear performances of chamber music by the likes of the Tokyo String Quartet, clarinettist Richard Stolzman, and pianist Ruth Laredo.

Haystack Mountain, Dennis Hill, and Mount Tom. Haystack Mountain (1,716 feet) and Dennis Hill (1,626 feet), to the north and south of Route 272 as it cuts through Norfolk, offer panoramic views from Vermont to Long Island Sound. You can drive right to the top of the latter and all but the last quarter mile of the former. You have to hike a mile to the top of Mount Tom (1,325 feet), on Route 202 in Litchfield, but afterward you can swim in the lake that's part of the surrounding state park.

Northeast Audubon Center (Rte. 4, Sharon, tel. 203/364–0520). Not just for the birds, this 684-acre sanctuary has several well-marked hiking trails as well as a building housing natural-history displays, a gift shop, bookstore, and Children's Discovery Room.

Winchester Center. A bygone era is easily recalled in this tiny hamlet of 18th- and 19th-century buildings surrounding a village green and broad pasture that stretches toward the distant hills. Right next to the white fluted columns of the Congregational Church is the unique *Kerosene Lamp Museum* (Rte. 262, tel. 203/379–2612) with its impressive collection of more than 500 hanging and standing kerosene lamps dating from 1852 to 1880.

Restaurants

Just about the best home-style Italian cooking in the area takes place at **Jessie's** (tel. 203/379–0109) on Main Street in Winsted, where the spicy clam soup with homemade sausage is a must. Contemporary American cuisine, with game and fresh fish, is offered at **Freshfields** (tel. 203/672–6601), just up the road from the covered bridge that spans the Housatonic River in West Cornwall. Over in Canaan, behind the lineup of canning jars in the storefront window, the chef-owner cooks up some powerful Cajun-style delicacies at the **Cannery Cafe** (tel. 203/824–7333). Salisbury's **Chaiwalla Tea House** (tel.

203/435–9758) has achieved almost cult status as *the* place to unwind while sipping imported tea and munching on open-faced sandwiches.

Nightlife

At Torrington's **Water St. Station** (tel. 203/496–9872), you'll find live rock, R&B, or jazz groups featured Thursday through Saturday. Classical-music buffs head for not only the Norfolk Chamber Music Festival, but in summer for **Music Mountain** (tel. 203/496–2596) in Falls Village.

Canoeing

Clarke Outdoors (tel. 203/672–6365) offers canoe and kayak rentals as well as 10-mile trips from Falls Village to Housatonic Meadow State Park.

Horseback Riding

On Canaan Mountain, **Rustling Wind Stables** (tel. 203/824–7634) gives lessons and takes riders along scenic mountain trails.

Skiing

Cross-country and downhill skiers will find more than 40 miles and 23 trails (and man-made or natural snow) at **Mohawk Mountain** (tel. 203/672–6100 or 203/672–6464) in Cornwall.

Tubing

A special warm-weather local pastime is floating down the Farmington River on an inner tube rented (along with approved flotation devices) from **North American Canoe Tours** (203/739–0791) in Niantic.

Tourist Information

Litchfield Hills Travel Council (Box 1776, Marble Dale, CT 06777, tel. 203/868–2214).

Reservation Services

Bed & Breakfast, Ltd. (Box 216, New Haven, CT 06513, tel. 203/469–3260); **Covered Bridge Bed & Breakfast Reservation Service** (Box 447, Norfolk, CT 06058, tel. 203/542–5944); **Nutmeg Bed & Breakfast Agency** (Box 1117, West Hartford, CT 06107, tel. 203/236–6698).

Manor House

A pleasant stroll up a side street off the village green in Norfolk will bring you to the unique Bavarian Tudor residence that has been turned into a thriving bed-and-breakfast by its owner/managers Diane and Henry Tremblay (who own Covered Bridge Reservation Service).

After several years of working in Hartford's hectic insurance industry, they were both ready for a change in careers when they saw an advertisement for an unusual house for sale. Designed and built in 1898 by Charles Spofford, the architect of London's subway system, the house has 20 stained-glass windows designed and given by Louis Tiffany, a full Victorian complement of reception rooms, and extensive bedrooms.

The combination was irresistible. The Tremblays took over in 1985 and have gradually refurnished it and restored the Victorian atmosphere with a light touch. Henry devotes himself to the surrounding 5 acres of gardens, with beehives and a raspberry patch, whose yields find their way to the breakfast table.

The bedrooms are all furnished with antique and reproduction beds (with modern mattresses), Louis Nicole wallpapers, well-chosen bibelots, prints, mirrors, and carpets. In winter, flannel sheets and down comforters add to the warmth. The vast Spofford Room has windows on three sides, a king-size canopy bed with a cheery fireplace opposite, and a balcony. The intimate Lincoln Room still has space for an antique double sleigh bed, a white fainting couch, and a small upholstered rocking chair—along with the best view of the neighboring landscape. But the Balcony Room has the most remarkable feature—a private wood-paneled elevator (added in 1931) that works. It also has a private deck suitable for sunbathing or leisurely lolling.

In the roomy living room, with its mammoth raised fireplace, music lovers who have come to Norfolk for the annual Chamber Music Festival (within easy walking distance) may choose from the large collection of vintage recordings and compact discs. You may tickle the keys of the grand piano, which is kept in tune, or, in a quiet mood, seek the seclusion of the library and choose from its numerous volumes.

Address: *Box 447, Maple Ave., Norfolk, CT 06058, tel. 203/542–5690.*
Accommodations: *7 double rooms with baths, 1 two-bedroom suite.*
Amenities: *Cable TV and house phone in common area, working fireplaces in 2 rooms, Jacuzzi in 1 room.*
Rates: *$90–$160; full breakfast. AE, MC, V.*
Restrictions: *No smoking in bedrooms, no pets. 2-night minimum on weekends.*

Under Mountain Inn

Driving north on Route 41 from Salisbury's Main Street, you cut through sweeping fields where horses graze and silos rise in the distance. After about 4 miles, a stone's throw from the Massachusetts border, stands a white clapboard farmhouse built in the early 1700s that has become the Under Mountain Inn.

The owners, Marged and Peter Higginson, bill themselves as Innkeepers and Chef, since the inn is also a popular restaurant. Peter's British origins emerge in the decor as well as the cuisine.

Their personal stamp is found all over, from the decor of the intimate dining rooms (each with a working fireplace) to the drawing room filled with antique knickknacks and Oriental and handmade American rugs. In the back of the house is The Pub, a faithful replica of a typical English taproom, whose paneling was found, during a restoration, hidden under the attic floorboards. Since Colonial law awarded all such lumber to the king of England, Peter reclaimed it in the name of the Crown.

Upstairs, the rooms are furnished individually in a manner dubbed "English country style." Room names, such as Covent Garden and Drury Lane, recall favorite London haunts, and the decor will make anglophiles weak in the knees. The spacious Queen's Room naturally has a queen-size bed; the King's Room opposite has its counterpart. A more contemporary room has a separate entrance.

Three surrounding acres boast birch, fir, maples, and a thorned locust tree, rumored to be the state's oldest. Across the road is Fisher Pond. Guests may use its 1.8-mile footpath for a bracing stroll, that favored English form of exercise.

At dinner, which along with a full breakfast is included in the tariff, you may expect one of Peter's specialties: steak and kidney pie, roast goose, or bangers and mash—sausage and mashed potatoes to the uninitiated. Save room for the English trifle—dessert par excellence.

With the filling breakfast and dinner included in the rates, a stay here turns out to be one of the better values in the area.

Address: *482 Undermountain Rd., Salisbury, CT 06068, tel. 203/435–0242.*
Accommodations: *7 double rooms with baths.*
Amenities: *Restaurant, air-conditioning in all rooms; package deals available.*
Rates: *$160–$180; MAP. 15% service charge. MC, V.*
Restrictions: *No smoking in bedrooms, no pets. 2-night minimum on weekends.*

The White Hart

Across from the village green at the eastern end of Main Street in Salisbury, the freshly painted white colonial frame structure of the White Hart with its broad front porch clearly dominates the landscape. This venerable country inn has welcomed travelers since the early 19th century and happily continues that tradition today.

In the 1980s it fell upon hard times and passed through a succession of owners until it was sold at public auction in 1989. The new owner/managers, Terry and Juliet Moore, have operated the celebrated Old Mill Restaurant in neighboring South Egremont, Massachusetts, for the past 12 years and are well seasoned in the art of local hospitality. Today they divide their time between the two establishments, and one of them is always on hand at the White Hart during the evening and busy weekends.

Before reopening in January 1990, the Moores decided to settle for nothing less than a total renovation inside and out. The visible results of their efforts show a respect for tradition combined with the finest in contemporary materials. The green and rose printed carpeting in the lobby is also found in the upstairs hallways along with shaded beige striped wallpaper and soft-white painted woodwork. Each of the bedrooms and suites is furnished with excellent colonial reproductions. Upholstery, bedspreads, and curtains have been tailored with brightly contrasting fabrics in lively stripes, ribbons, and floral splashes. The configuration of each room is unique; instead of breaking down walls, quirks have been accommodated, giving the rooms a comfortable irregularity. Yet all have such conveniences as good lamps for reading, telephones with message lights, and modernized bathrooms. Several rooms on the eastern side have private entrances, and a few steps away, in the 1813 colonial frame building called the Gideon Smith House, similar rooms and suites are available on two levels.

Dining in either of the White Hart's two restaurants, the bright and sunny Garden Court Room/Tap Room or the elegant Julie's New American Seafood Grill, is a treat.

Address: *The Village Green, Box 385, Salisbury, CT 06068, tel. 203/435–0030, fax 203/435–0040.*
Accommodations: *21 double rooms and 2 singles with baths, 3 suites.*
Amenities: *2 restaurants, air-conditioning, cable TV and phones in bedrooms, meeting and banquet facilities.*
Rates: *\$110–\$190; breakfast extra. AE, DC, MC, V.*
Restrictions: *No smoking in main dining room; call about pets policy. 2-night minimum on weekends May–Oct., 3-night minimum holiday weekends.*

Cobble Hill Farm

About a mile from the center of New Hartford, Cobble Hill Farm is on a typical suburban street; but this farmhouse bed-and-breakfast has been here since the early 1800s, and it still comprises 40 acres of woodland and gardens, plus a spring-fed pond. Its farming days are recalled in the fresh eggs from the chicken coop and the homemade jellies and jams from the kitchen garden, orchard, and greenhouse that form the centerpiece of the ample breakfast served each morning. The owner, Jo McCurdy, has been running things here since 1986. Her special touches include a tea cart with a complete service for tea and coffee in each bedroom. The rooms vary in their eclectic country-style decor, though most have a patchwork quilt, wall-to-wall carpeting, and an antique or vintage reproduction bed. Guests are welcome throughout the house, but have their own spacious living room with a working fireplace.

Address: *Steele Rd., New Hartford, CT 06057, tel. 203/379–0057.*
Accommodations: *3 double rooms with baths (or 2 suites and 1 single with private bath).*
Amenities: *Swimming pond.*
Rates: *$95–$170; full breakfast and free tea and coffee. No credit cards.*
Restrictions: *No smoking, no pets. 2-night minimum on weekends; closed Jan.–Mar. except Presidents' Day weekend.*

The Country Goose

Three miles north of the traffic light in downtown Kent you'll find the welcoming blue sign of this cozy 1740 Colonial bed-and-breakfast. The owner, Phyllis Dietrich, can usually be found in the kitchen baking bread, muffins, and croissants for the guests' breakfast... or the cookies she keeps on a table in the upstairs hall. Or she might be washing the 20-over-20 windows upstairs and 15-over-15 downstairs, which signify that the property's builder was well-to-do. Other relics of its earlier days are the beehive oven next to the Colonial fireplace downstairs and the detailed millwork that was used near the doorways in particular. The rooms are furnished with period reproductions and antiques, including such unusual pieces as a carved white-mahogany bed and a Victorian brass bed. There's also a comfortable library set aside for guests' use.

Address: *RFD 1, Box 276, Kent–Cornwall Rd. (Rte. 7), Kent, CT 06757, tel. 203/927–4746.*
Accommodations: *3 double rooms and 1 single share 2 baths.*
Amenities: *Hiking (Appalachian Trail) nearby.*
Rates: *$75; Continental breakfast. No credit cards.*
Restrictions: *No smoking, no pets. 2-night minimum on weekends; closed Mar.–Apr. 10.*

Greenwoods Gate

This neatly preserved Federal Colonial on Route 44 in secluded Norfolk appears unassuming enough. But what one suspects, from the exterior, may be a quiet antiques shop or even a private home is in reality Connecticut's foremost romantic hideaway. Innkeeper Deanne Raymond is a cheerful host with a penchant for playing cupid. She's spared nothing to provide her guests with all the trappings of a cozy honeymooners' retreat—she's probably even gone a little over the top. Countless amenities greet guests: from chocolates and Cognac to soaps and powders to "situational" board games in every room; and champagne, fresh flowers, or a deep massage are available by advance request. The formal living room, which has wide-plank wood floors and authentic Federal windows, is decorated with period-furnishings, including a Steinway piano. But guests are just as welcome to gather in front of the TV in the casual family room or sit under the cozy kitchen's pressed-tin ceiling enjoying hot cocoa and conversation with Deanne or her daughter and co-conspirator, Marianne.

Address: *105 Greenwoods Rd. E (Rte. 44), Norfolk, CT 06058, tel. 203/542–5439.*
Accommodations: *3 suites with private bath.*
Amenities: *Spa bath in one suite, TV in common room, liquor in rooms, small gift shop.*
Rates: *$150–$175; full breakfast. MC, V.*
Restrictions: *No smoking, no pets.*

Highland Farm

At the end of a winding road and a long driveway, the porches and 14 gables of an 1879 Victorian manor house stand out, clearly identifying this once grand showcase of Litchfield County. The high ceilings and etched, beveled, and stained glass on doors and windows, along with some period antiques and reproductions, help preserve the crisp edge of that era. Though the rooms contain some modern furniture, the Victorian spirit is predominant.

New Hartford natives Jim and Marion Kavanaugh have turned their retirement years into running a simplified bed-and-breakfast operation on these premises with the instincts of seasoned innkeepers. Fresh flowers and the local newspaper are found in each room; there's a cozy small sitting room on the upstairs landing, and the typically formal downstairs front parlor is also reserved for guests.

Address: *107 Highland Ave., New Hartford, CT 06057, tel. 203/379–6029.*
Accommodations: *2 double rooms share 1 bath, 1 suite.*
Rates: *$70–$95; Continental breakfast. No credit cards.*
Restrictions: *Smoking in downstairs public area only.*

Old Riverton Inn

You can't miss the blue-and-white Colonial frame building in Riverton, directly across the bridge over the Farmington River from the Hitchcock Chair Factory. This tiny and serene village's original name was Hitchcockville, and the inn predates even the factory, having been a popular stagecoach stop on the Hartford-Albany route in 1796. Its present owners, Mark and Pauline Telford, continue the tradition of hospitality, particularly in the popular dining room, which is open to the public for lunch and dinner Wednesday through Sunday. The bedrooms have the appealing architectural irregularity of age, but the decor, with its mixture of old and new, is less successful. The huge suite with its wall-to-wall carpeting and minifridge distinctly lacks charm. The rooms on the third floor are generally smaller.

Address: *Rte. 20, Riverton, CT 06065, tel. 203/379–8678; fax 203/379–1006.*
Accommodations: *11 double rooms with baths, 1 suite.*
Amenities: *Restaurant, air-conditioning, cable TV in bedrooms; tubing, fishing, and swimming nearby. Pets allowed with prior approval.*
Rates: *$65–$150; full breakfast. AE, D, DC, MC, V.*
Restrictions: *2-night minimum on holiday weekends.*

Toll Gate Hill Inn & Restaurant

On the north side of the road from Litchfield to Torrington, watch for the white sign that marks the entrance to the secluded Toll Gate Inn. Since 1745 the main house (which was moved to its present site in 1923) has been a popular way station for travelers. The current proprietor, Fritz Zivic, is justifiably proud of the restoration, which went into high gear in 1983. Guest rooms, decorated with vibrant colonial prints, checks, and stripes, are provided with comfortable period-style furniture. The rooms and suites in the converted schoolhouse and Captain William Bull House that complete the complex have similar decor. The tavern and the more formal dining room, celebrated for New American gourmet cuisine, hark back to the 18th century. Private parties take place in the ballroom, a hidden treasure of a second-story room with a high ceiling and a tiny fiddler's loft, where live music is often played for the diners below.

Address: *Box 1339, Litchfield, CT 06759, tel. 203/567–4545 or 800/445–3903.*
Accommodations: *15 double rooms with baths, 5 suites.*
Amenities: *Restaurant, air-conditioning, cable TV and phones in rooms, working fireplaces in 3 rooms and all suites.*
Rates: *$110–$175; Continental breakfast. AE, D, MC, V.*

Wake Robin Inn

A long curving driveway through carefully landscaped "wilderness" on 15 acres takes you to the pillars and porches of the 1896 frame building that forms the hub of the Wake Robin Inn. Annexes, extensions, and outbuildings have been added, some more successfully than others, to this colonial-style former girls' school, to take care of the people who flock to Connecticut's Lake Wononscopomuc. The bedrooms are individually furnished with brightly printed fabrics; spool, four-poster, and sleigh beds; and have assorted oddities—such as the staircase in No. 25 that leads nowhere. The rooms in the aptly designated motel have standard hotel-chain furnishings and are merely functional. Rooms in the main house, recently refurbished, are the most desirable. A professional staff oversees the lodging part of things, while the celebrated dining room is supervised by a master chef.

Address: *Rte. 41, Lakeville, CT 06039, tel. 203/435–2515, fax 203/435–2000.*
Accommodations: *23 double rooms with baths in main house, 16 doubles with baths in motel, 2 suites.*
Amenities: *Restaurant, cable TV and phones in rooms in main house; outdoor pool.*
Rates: *$95–$225; breakfast extra. AE, MC, V.*
Restrictions: *No pets in main house.*

Yesterday's Yankee B&B

It's surprising to find a 1744 Cape Cod house in this part of the state, but it suggests that visitors from afar began coming here even then. Right on Main Street as you come into Salisbury from the east, it is today surrounded by aged maple trees that seem to shelter it from traffic. Doris and Dick Alexander, a high school English teacher and architect/builder, have converted their family home with an eye to preserving the best historical features, such as the wide-board floors, while modernizing where appropriate, for example, the bathroom. Bedrooms are furnished with simple, traditional furniture, braided rugs, and down comforters. Gourmet breakfast from the up-to-date kitchen always includes some of Doris's home-baked bread, rolls, or muffins and is served at a long trestle table in the original keeping room.

Address: *Box 442, Rte. 44, Salisbury, CT 06068, tel. 203/435–9539.*
Accommodations: *3 double rooms share 1 bath.*
Amenities: *Air-conditioning in bedrooms; box lunches available.*
Rates: *$65–$80; full breakfast. MC, V.*
Restrictions: *No smoking on 2nd floor, no pets. 2-night minimum on weekends Memorial Day–Oct.*

Rhode Island

Rhode Island

MASSACHUSETTS
Slatersville
Woonsocket
Diamond Hill
Cumberland Hill
Manville
Harrisville
Pascoag
Chepachet
GEORGE WASHINGTON MANAGEMENT AREA
Harmony
Greenville
Central Falls
Pawtucket
North Providence
Providence
East Providence
MASSACHUSETTS
South Foster
North Scituate
Clayville
Scituate Reservoir
Cranston
Barrington
Warren
Warwick
Apponaug
Washington
CONNECTICUT
Bristol
Prudence Island
Homestead
East Grenwich
Tiverton
ARCADIA MANAGEMENT AREA
Narragansett Bay
Portsmouth
Exeter
Wickford
Conanicut Island
Hope Valley
Middletown
Little Compton
Jamestown
Newport
Sakonnet
Kingston
GREAT SWAMP MANAGEMENT AREA
Peace Dale
Wakefield
Worden Pond
Narragansett
Ashaway
Galilee
Westerly
Watchaug Pond
Charlestown
Matunuck
Point Judith
TO WATCH HILL
Misquamicut
TO NEW LONDON
Rhode Island Sound
Sandy Point
Block Island Sound
New Harbor
Old Harbor
TO MONTAUK
Block Island
N
0
20 miles
0
30 km

Newport

Perched gloriously on the southern tip of Aquidneck Island and bounded on three sides by water, Newport has three substantial claims to fame: It's one of the great sailing cities of the world, for many years site of the America's Cup yachting race; it boasts a peerless collection of 19th-century mansions, monuments to the glories of the Gilded Age; and it hosts world-class jazz, folk, and classical music festivals every summer.

Newport's first age of prosperity was in the late 1700s, when it was a port city almost as important as Boston or New York. Many homes, shops, churches, and government buildings from the Colonial era still stand, now restored to their original condition and open to visitors.

In the mid- to late 19th century, Newport became the fashionable summer playground of America's wealthiest families. Having taken the grand tour of Europe and seen its magnificent castles, the well-to-do displayed their newfound sophistication by building their own extravagant mansion-size "cottages" along Newport's Bellevue Avenue. Each cottage was more elaborate than the one built just before it, culminating in the grandiose excess of Cornelius Vanderbilt II's The Breakers, whose luxurious appointments rival world-famous museums.

Newport on a summer afternoon can be exasperating, its streets jammed with day-trippers, its traffic slowed to a crawl by a succession of air-conditioned, exhaust-spewing sightseeing buses. Yet it's worth braving the crowds to attend the city's summer music festivals—the Newport Music Festival for two weeks in mid-July (tel. 401/846–1133), the Newport Folk Festival in late July (tel. 401/847–3709), and the JVC Jazz Festival in mid-August (tel. 401/847-3700). In the fall, winter, and spring, visitors can enjoy a visit to Newport without having to contend with throngs, although from mid-November to March, many of the mansions are closed or are open only on weekends. The weather stays fairly warm well into November, and there are many special events in December as the city celebrates "Christmas in Newport."

Places to Go, Sights to See

The Breakers (Ochre Point Ave., tel. 401/847–6543). Beginning in 1893, it took 2,500 workmen two years to complete this 70-room summer home for the small family of Cornelius Vanderbilt II; 40 servants were required to keep the establishment running. The four-story limestone villa is loaded with marvels: there's a music room with a gold ceiling, a fireplace built of rare blue marble, rose alabaster pillars in the dining room, and a porch with a mosaic ceiling that took Italian craftsmen six months lying on their backs to install.

Cliff Walk. This 3-mile-long trail, which begins at Easton's Beach and runs along Newport's cliffs, offers a waterside view of many of the town's mansions. It is a challenging walk, not recommended for the elderly or infirm or for children under age 6, but it rewards the energetic with breathtaking vistas.

Hammersmith Farm (Ocean Dr. near Ft. Adams, tel. 401/846–7346). The childhood summer home of Jacqueline Bouvier Kennedy Onassis, and the site of her wedding to John F. Kennedy, this is the only working farm in Newport. The house is decorated in such a casual, comfortable style, and is filled with so much Bouvier and Kennedy memorabilia, that it feels as though its owners have just stepped out of the room. The elaborate landscape was designed by Frederick Law Olmsted.

International Tennis Hall of Fame and **The Tennis Museum** (Newport Casino, 194 Bellevue Ave., tel. 401/849–3990). A magnificent building of the Newport Casino, designed by Stanford White, now exhibits photographs and other artifacts celebrating a century of tennis history. The first National Tennis Championships were held here in 1881.

Museum of Yachting (Ft. Adams and Ocean Dr., tel. 401/847–1018). Browse through galleries of pictures of the incredible yachts of the Vanderbilts, the Astors, and the Belmonts.

The Newport Historical Society (82 Touro St., tel. 401/846–0813). A large collection of Newport memorabilia, furniture, and maritime items are on display. Here you can pick up a brochure that outlines a walking tour through the historic downtown; guided walking tours also leave from the Historical Society building on Friday and Saturday in summer.

Redwood Library (50 Bellevue Ave., tel. 401/847–0292). Built in 1748, this library is a superb example of the work of noted Colonial architect Peter Harrison. This wooden building, designed to look like a Roman temple, has its exterior painted to resemble marble. Inside you'll find a wonderful collection of paintings by Early American artists.

Trinity Church (Queen Anne Sq., tel. 401/846–0660). Built in 1724, this Colonial treasure is especially notable for its three-tier wineglass pulpit, the only one of its kind in America.

Beaches

Easton's Beach (Memorial Blvd.), known locally as First Beach, is popular for its carousel and for miniature golf. **Sachuest Beach** (Sachuest Point area), also called Second Beach, is adjacent to the Norman Bird Sanctuary; dunes, high waves, and a campground make it popular with singles and surfers. **Third Beach** (Sachuest Point area), on the Sakonnet River, has a boat ramp and is a favorite of windsurfers.

Restaurants

At **The Black Pearl** (Bannister's Wharf, tel. 401/849–2900), a popular waterfront restaurant with nautical decor, diners may choose between the tavern and the more formal Commodore's Room. Recommended is swordfish with Dutch pepper butter. **The Wave Café** (580 Thames St., tel. 401/846–6060) is open for breakfast, lunch, and dinner; the principal attractions are a large selection of cheeses and smoked meats; a salad and fruit bar; and such Italian specialties as stromboli, lasagna, and pizza.

Tourist Information

Newport County Convention and Visitors Bureau (23 America's Cup Ave., tel. 401/849–8048 or 800/326–6030) has telephones linked to motels for placing reservations, an orientation film, and cassette tours.

Reservations Services

Bed and Breakfast of Rhode Island, Inc. (Box 3291, Newport, RI 02840, tel. 401/849–1298); **Pineapple Hospitality, Inc.** (47 N. 2nd St., New Bedford, MA 02747, tel. 508/990–1696); **Bed and Breakfast Newport Reservation Service** (33 Russell Ave., Newport, RI 02840, tel. 401/846–5408); **Aquidneck Island Reservation Service** (88 William St., Newport, RI 02840, tel. 401/846–4331).

Cliffside Inn

In January 1993, Norbert and Annette Mede celebrated their first anniversary as the new innkeepers of the Cliffside Inn. They had much to celebrate: In that year their renovations included turning an unused attic room into a luxurious guest room with skylights, a king-size bed, and a Jacuzzi.

The Cliffside Inn, located on a quiet side street, overlooks the ocean and is close to Newport's Cliff Walk. Originally a summer cottage called Villa du Côte, the house was built in 1880 for Governor Thomas Swann of Maryland. In another incarnation, it housed the prestigious St. George's prep school. Now restored to mint Victorian condition, the inn has come into its own as a special hideaway filled with cozy nooks and crannies and flooded with daytime sunlight from its many bay windows.

A screened porch arrayed with comfortable wicker furniture makes a good lounging spot in summer. The large center hallway, with its original gleaming hardwood floor, leads to a spacious parlor, which has a Victorian fireplace bedecked with an ornate antique mirror. The parlor is furnished with several Victorian sofas and easy chairs, as well as a small piano and even an antique telephone booth.

Each guest room is unique; all are decorated with Victorian furniture and Laura Ashley fabrics. The rooms have names, recalling past residents or referring to the various decors—it's a touch some may find coy, but it comes in handy when you're recommending a special room to a friend. Miss Beatrice's Room, for example, is a large room with a window seat and an antique "Lincoln-style" queen-size bed, with its massive carved headboard and footboard in cherry wood. The bathroom, with marble and raised wood paneling, has a whirlpool bath. The Veranda Room is a light, airy room with a huge bay window, a double bed, and a private entrance. Miss Adele's Room has a rose-colored mantelpiece that has been refashioned as the headboard of the double bed.

Address: *2 Seaview Ave., Newport, RI 02840, tel. 401/847–1811 or 800/845–1811.*
Accommodations: *12 double rooms with baths.*
Amenities: *TV in common room, 4 rooms with fireplaces.*
Rates: *$125–$205; full breakfast and afternoon appetizers. MC, V.*
Restrictions: *No pets; no smoking.*

Francis Malbone House

Colonel Francis Malbone made a sizable fortune as a shipping merchant, succeeding well enough at his trade to build, in 1760, a most impressive yellow-brick mansion and countinghouse just across Thames Street from the harbor where he kept his boats at anchor. His home, restored over the past 15 years, opened to guests in 1990, becoming Newport's only Colonial mansion operating as an inn. It's only a 10-minute walk from downtown, too, a plus for visitors interested in historic Newport.

The design of the house is attributed to the great architect Peter Harrison, who also designed Newport's Touro Synagogue, Brick Market, and Redwood Library. A pair of formal parlors occupy the front of the house; the present dining room, once the kitchen, features an authentic Colonial brick fireplace with a beehive oven. All the public rooms are tastefully furnished with Colonial reproduction pieces, which the innkeeper, Jim Maher, says will be replaced with antiques piece by piece over time. That change will be significant, because right now the reproductions are characterless, making the house seem so "perfect" that it looks a little like a stage set. Jim, an actor by training, has lived in Newport for many years and is part of a new generation of innkeepers: they are more professionally trained than most bed-and-breakfast operators, yet they offer a personal welcome you only rarely find in a hotel.

A grand staircase with hand-carved balusters leads to the guest rooms, which are spacious and full of natural light, and have views of either the garden or the harbor; furnishings are elegant, although the reproduction pieces here are also slated for eventual replacement with authentic antiques. Guests may rent the Counting House next door, a small building with distinctive, tall windows and dark wood paneling. Connected to the main house through the library (but also accessible through private entrances from the street and the garden), it can function either as a single room or as part of a suite.

Though the house stands on busy Thames Street, it is set well back from the sidewalk behind its white picket fence. The large, lushly landscaped garden in the back, with a gurgling ornamental fountain and wrought-iron furniture, makes a green retreat where breakfast is served in the summertime.

Address: *392 Thames St., Newport, RI 02840, tel. 401/846–0392.*
Accommodations: *9 double rooms with baths.*
Amenities: *Off-street parking; most rooms with fireplaces.*
Rates: *$125–$200 Apr. 15–Nov. 1, $80–$95 Nov. 2–Apr. 14; Continental breakfast. AE, MC, V.*
Restrictions: *No smoking.*

The Inn at Castle Hill

The Inn at Castle Hill is perched in jaunty isolation, far from the madding crowd of downtown Newport, on a 40-acre peninsula with three private beaches. Built as a summer home for scientist and explorer Alexander Agassiz, the inn is a rambling shingled structure of curves, gingerbread woodwork, turrets, and jutting porches, imitating the chalets of Dr. Agassiz's native Switzerland. Outbuildings dot the grounds, including Agassiz's former laboratory, a series of waterside cottages (rented by the week), and Harbor House, where Grace Kelly lived while filming *High Society.*

Inside the inn, many original furnishings reflect Agassiz's fondness for Chinese and Japanese art, particularly bronzes and porcelain. The lounge, with Oriental rugs and richly patterned period wallpaper, has two small Victorian sofas nestled next to an unusual hand-carved fireplace, its design similar to a stained-glass rose window in a Gothic cathedral. Three water-view dining rooms include the professor's original study; the Sunset Room; and the original dining room, whose carved sideboard conceals two safes designed for silver and other valuables. The dining rooms attract a certain number of nonguests, particularly for Sunday brunch, and on summer Sunday afternoons, a top-notch outdoor barbecue with music features such favorites as rack of lamb, veal Française, Dover sole, and shrimp stuffed with clams. (Try to avoid arriving during this popular weekly event.)

The six spacious oceanside rooms in the main house, which must be booked at least four months in advance, are furnished with Victorian antiques and comfortable chairs, decorated with bright floral fabrics, and have enormous bathrooms. Room 6, with a large bay window, was built for Mrs. Agassiz; Room 7, Dr. Agassiz's bedroom, has walls and a ceiling of inlaid oak and pine; Room 8, decorated with white wicker furniture, features an old claw-foot bathtub in which you can relax while watching traffic crawl across the Jamestown Bridge. In Room 9, novelist Thornton Wilder wrote *Theophilus North* while listening to the distant ringing of the bell at the Castle Hill Lighthouse. An upstairs suite combines a large living room and a bedroom. The six modest guest rooms in Harbor House need refurbishing.

Address: *Ocean Dr., Newport, RI 02840, tel. 401/849–3800.*
Accommodations: *12 double rooms with baths, 3 doubles share 1 bath, 1 suite.*
Amenities: *Restaurant.*
Rates: *$80–$225 June–Oct., $50–$180 other times of year; Continental breakfast. AE, MC, V.*
Restrictions: *No pets. Closed Dec. 24–25, restaurant closed early Nov.–mid-Apr.*

Ivy Lodge

Behind the front door of this elegant Queen Anne Victorian, designed by Stanford White, waits an amazing sight: a 33-foot-high Gothic-style oak-paneled entry, with a three-story turned-baluster staircase. Tucked in at an angle at the foot of the staircase is a brick fireplace, built in the shape of a moorish arch, where a welcoming fire burns on fall, winter, and spring afternoons.

Veteran innkeepers Maggie and Terry Moy live at Ivy Lodge. Their manner is low-key and gracious; they know how to make guests very comfortable. The sumptuous breakfast served here might include such delicacies as smoked fish, bananas flambé, bread pudding, or fresh strawberries and popovers with whipped cream.

Ivy Lodge, which was built in 1886 for a prominent Newport physician, has eight guest rooms, all of which have been newly carpeted, painted, and wallpapered and are tastefully decorated with a combination of Victorian antiques and good-quality reproductions; rooms are spacious and give a sense of privacy. Here and there, a few of the older furnishings look a little shabby; the Moys, aware of this, are on a continual campaign of improvement. Over the past year, much refurbishing has been accomplished: The inn's exterior has been repainted, and two large bedrooms—the Turret Room and the Ivy Room—have been added. The Turret Room, decorated in peach and green, has a king-size bed and a private bath with a Victorian claw-foot tub. The Ivy Room has a queen-size four poster bed with French cut white linens, Waverly ivy wallpaper, and a private bath.

A 20-foot-long mahogany table that seats 18 dominates the long dining room, with floor-to-ceiling bay windows at one end. Also on the main floor, a bright sitting room with floral wallpaper and wicker furniture is invitingly filled with books and magazines. The airy living room features pink-and-white-striped Art Deco sofas, thick carpeting, and a huge fireplace. A wraparound porch gives onto a lovely garden filled with many specimen plants.

While Ivy Lodge is neither as large nor as opulent as the fabled mansions on nearby Bellevue Avenue, it is every bit as gracious. Fantasies of living in Newport in its 19th-century heyday may well be realized here.

Address: *12 Clay St., Newport, RI 02840, tel. 401/849–6865.*
Accommodations: *8 double rooms with baths.*
Rates: *$100–$165 May–Nov. 1. $100 off-season rate for any room; full breakfast and afternoon tea. AE, MC, V.*

Victorian Ladies

At first glance, the location of the Victorian Ladies may give pause, for this bed-and-breakfast is situated on a busy thoroughfare, Memorial Boulevard. But once you're inside, double-pane windows and air-conditioning muffle the street noise, and the sumptuous furnishings and the friendly attention of hosts Don and Helene O'Neill fully compensate.

Don and Helene bought their home in 1985 after a B&B trip to California convinced them that they would enjoy being hosts at their own establishment. They found a fairly run-down property built about 1840 consisting of a private home and an accompanying carriage house. Don was able to restore the place himself, thanks to his years of experience as a carpenter for the Newport Restoration Foundation.

The mansard exterior of the Victorian Ladies is now painted slate gray and burgundy; the two buildings are connected by a flower-filled latticed courtyard that serves as an outdoor breakfast area in the summer. Inside, the inn is splendidly decorated, each room reflecting Helene's creativity and eye for design.

The living room, mauve and light blue, has a crystal chandelier, cozy fireplace, floral wallpaper, several plump-pillowed couches, and many ornamental objects from the Far East. The adjoining dining room reflects the color scheme of the living room but has more of a country feeling, with a large, simple pine table and sideboard where ample traditional breakfasts of eggs and bacon or ham are served.

Each guest room is different, though the general look is frilly: Flounces and lace are brightened by house plants and fresh flowers. A favorite of many guests is the honeymoon suite: Its romantic canopy bed is festooned with chintz, echoed at the windows by matching balloon shades. As in so many other rooms in the inn, the bed here is heaped with ruffled pillows handmade by Helene. Another guest room features children's lace dresses on the walls, set off by a black background with a rosebud print; all the furnishings and accessories are carefully coordinated to this color scheme. The rooms are furnished with an eclectic collection of antiques, reproductions, and modern pieces, which coexist in harmony.

Address: *63 Memorial Blvd., Newport, RI 02840, tel. 401/849–9960.*
Accommodations: *9 double rooms with baths.*
Amenities: *Air-conditioning, TV in bedrooms, off-street parking.*
Rates: *\$135–\$165 May 15–Nov. 1, \$85–\$105 Nov. 2–May 14; full breakfast. MC, V.*

Admiral Fitzroy

"What's that unbelievable smell?" people ask innkeeper Brenda Johnston. "That's oatmeal bread," she answers, adding, "I couldn't bake in the middle of the day when I worked at TWA!"

The Admiral Fitzroy, built as a convent in 1854, has been fancifully redecorated: An inventive artist was given the challenge of handpainting each of the inn's rooms and a lot of the furniture, and she made the most of her opportunity. One room sports shiny green walls with a ceiling border of intricately interlocking scalloped leaves; another features a blue sponge-painted surface with a cheerful ceiling border of wildflowers. There are sleigh beds and brass bedsteads, mostly reproduction Victorian pieces, all covered with down duvets and lacy linens. In each room a handmade Swedish cupboard contains a TV, refrigerator, and an electric teakettle.

Address: *398 Thames St., Newport, RI 02840, tel. 401/847–4459 or 800/343–2863, fax 401/846–4289.*
Accommodations: *18 double rooms with baths.*
Amenities: *Air-conditioning, phones in bedrooms, hair dryers, elevator, 2 rooms with private decks; off-street parking.*
Rates: *$75–$145 May–Sept.; Continental breakfast and afternoon tea. AE, DC, MC, V.*
Restrictions: *2-night minimum on summer weekends, 3-night minimum on holiday weekends and during the Newport festivals.*

The Inn of Jonathan Bowen

Down the street from bustling Bowen's Wharf, in the heart of Newport's Gaslight district, you'll find the Inn of Jonathan Bowen. It's actually two buildings: the Jonathan Bowen House, built in 1804, and an adjacent main building, built in 1915. Both were extensively renovated in the late 1980s, resulting in a facility that is in excellent condition, yet retains much of the original colonial and Victorian charm.

Paul Brandeis, manager and part owner of the inn, is a gregarious, self-described "exile from the Garment District" in New York City. Turn-of-the-century vintage furniture abounds, and each guest room is outfitted with an antique armoire. Many rooms also feature Victorian writing tables, cedar chests, and chaise longues, and some have working fireplaces.

The clientele at this inn is generally young and urban. On some late summer nights, he warns, it's possible to hear passersby on the streets; to avoid that, book an off-street room.

Address: *29 Pelham St., Newport, RI 02840, tel. 401/846–3324, fax 401/847–7450.*
Accommodations: *8 double rooms with baths, 2 doubles share a bath, 2 apartments.*
Amenities: *Ceiling fans.*
Rates: *$85–$195; Continental breakfast. MC, V.*
Restrictions: *2-night minimum on weekends, 3-night minimum on holiday weekends.*

The Inntowne

Innkeepers Paul and Betty McEnroe provide a warm, welcoming atmosphere for their guests, including serving afternoon tea in the lounge. The Inntowne is located just off Thames Street in a bustling part of Newport. In spite of the busy location, once you step inside this pleasant gray clapboard building, you are welcomed with warmth and a very professional level of comfort.

The rooms at the Inntowne are big, clean, and bright, decorated with floral wallpaper, low-hung pictures, and colonial reproduction pieces, creating an ambience somewhere between "rustic tavern" and "motel modern." Light sleepers may prefer a room on one of the upper floors, which get less street traffic noise. A fourth-floor sun deck is open to guests.

Address: *6 Mary St., Newport, RI 02840, tel. 401/846–9200 or 800/457–7803, fax 401/846–1534.*
Accommodations: *26 double rooms with baths.*
Amenities: *Phones in bedrooms, kitchen facilities in some rooms, small patios off some rooms, 24-hour front desk; access to health club facilities at the nearby Marriott, parking.*
Rates: *$110–$250 May 16–Oct. 31, lower rates midweek and Nov. 1–May 15; Continental breakfast. AE, MC, V.*
Restrictions: *Closed Dec. 24–25.*

Coastal Rhode Island

When the old Route 1 was superseded by I–95 some 20 years ago, something wonderful happened—or rather didn't happen. Coastal Rhode Island (the South County, as it's known locally, though no such county exists on any official map) was left behind in time. The 19th-century resorts of Watch Hill and Narragansett, with their Victorian "cottages" perched over clean broad beaches, maintained an air of genteel refuge. The quiet town of Westerly, right over the border from Connecticut, preserved several fine older homes that have recently been meticulously restored, either as private residences or as historic sites open to the public. South Kingstown, which contains the shady green campus of the University of Rhode Island, kept all the charm of a college town without surrendering to tacky development. In fact, the region as a whole is surprisingly unblighted by the march of malls and tract housing that overtook other, more accessible, areas.

A good deal of the rolling landscape of slow-paced South County is still farmland—in fact, around Wickford in North Kingstown, in Rhode Island's so-called plantation country, many farms that date back to the Colonial era are intact; some of them can be visited today. With 19 preserves, state parks, beaches, and forest areas, including three in Charlestown alone—Burlingame State Park, Ningret Park, and the Trustom Pond Wildlife Refuge—South County is a region that respects the concept of wilderness. For summertime tourists, of course, the most important attraction of the area may be its mile after mile of vast, sandy beaches.

Places to Go, Sights to See

Galilee. Several miles south of Narragansett off Route 108 is one of the busiest fishing ports on the East Coast. It also has two excellent seafood restaurants: *Champlin's* (tel. 401/783–3152) and *George's of Galilee* (tel.

401/783–2306). Galilee is the point of departure for several excursion boats, as well as a ferry (tel. 401/789–3502) to Block Island.

Narragansett. At the end of the 19th century, wealthy vacationers from New York and Boston arrived by train at this posh resort, or took the steamboat over from Newport for lunch at the *Narragansett Casino.* Though the railroad link and the steamboat no longer operate, a section of the casino survived a disastrous 1900 fire: *The Towers,* a Victorian turret rising above Ocean Road now houses the Narragansett Chamber of Commerce. At the end of Ocean Road, there's a beautiful ocean vista at the *Point Judith Lighthouse.*

South County Museum (tel. 401/783–5400). Located on the grounds of Canonchet farm in Narragansett, this museum features reconstructions of many typical New England buildings.

Watch Hill. This Victorian beach village is a good place to shop for jewelry, summer clothes, and antiques. Stop by to watch the hand-carved horses whirling around on the Flying Horses Carousel, the oldest merry-go-round in America (built in 1867), then stroll out on Napatree Point, a long sandy spit with a protected wildlife area.

Westerly. Two spots worth visiting in Westerly are Wilcox Park, an 18-acre plot at the intersection of High and Broad streets designed by Frederick Law Olmsted and Calvert Vaux, featuring a garden for the visually impaired and handicapped; and the late-18th-century Babcock-Smith House (124 Granite St., tel. 401/596–4424), nearby, where Benjamin Franklin was a frequent visitor.

Beaches

The turquoise waters of busy **Misquamicut State Beach** (at Rte. 1A in Westerly) are popular with young people. **East Beach** (off Rte. 1, access from East Beach Rd., Charlestown) offers 2 miles of dunes, backed by the clear waters of Ninigret Pond; to get here, you'll have to hike a distance from the car. **East Matunuck State Beach** (south of Rte. 1 in Matunuck, off Succotash Rd.) features high surf, picnic areas, and a bathhouse.

Restaurants

Shelter Harbor Inn (10 Wagner Rd., Rte. 1, Westerly, tel. 401/322–8883) offers gourmet Continental dining in a tranquil country setting. The **South Shore Grill** (210 Salt Pond Rd., South Kingstown, tel. 401/782–4780) has great waterfront views and a wood-fired grill. On a summer evening, you can enjoy a traditional Rhode Island shore dinner (steamed clams, lobster, corn on the cob, coleslaw, and clam chowder) at **Aunt Carrie's** (Rte. 108 and Ocean Rd., Point Judith, tel. 401/783–7930), on the ocean.

Nightlife

At the **Windjammer** (tel. 401/322–0271), on Atlantic Avenue in Westerly, there's dancing to rock bands in a room that holds 1,800. Groups of national renown who've played there in recent years include Huey Lewis and the News, Cyndi Lauper, and Joan Jett.

Tourist Information

South County Tourism Council (Box 651, Narragansett, RI 02882, tel. 401/789–4422 or 800/548–4662).

Reservations Services

Bed and Breakfast of Rhode Island, Inc. (Box 3291, Newport, RI 02840, tel. 401/849–1298); **Pineapple Hospitality, Inc.** (47 N. 2nd St., New Bedford, MA 02747, tel. 508/990–1696).

The Richards

Imposing and magnificent, this English manor-style mansion, built of granite quarried on the site, was the brainchild of Joseph Peace Hazard, scion of one of the founding families of Rhode Island. There's a mysterious story of how Hazard came to build his summer home; ask the current owner, Nancy Richards, and she'll be delighted to share it with you. Nancy and Steven Richards and their two teenage daughters, who bought the house in 1987, are only the third family to own it since its construction more than a century ago, so the legends have been passed along intact.

Meticulously restored and listed on the National Register of Historic Places, the Richards' home has a broodingly Gothic mystique that is almost the antithesis of a summer home. From the wood-paneled common rooms downstairs, French windows look out onto a lush landscape, with a grand swamp oak the centerpiece of a handsome garden. The library, its shelves lined with interesting books, often has a fire crackling in the fireplace on chilly late afternoons. Each morning, in the baronial dining room, equipped with an early 19th-century English sideboard, Nancy serves a breakfast consisting of fresh fruit, strudel, cereal, coffee, and muffins as well as such main courses as eggs Florentine and oven pancakes.

Although only four of the 12 bedrooms are open to guests (an additional suite is in the planning stages), they are in a separate wing, so you never have the sense of intruding upon the family. Each guest room is furnished with 19th-century English antiques; the brass bed, two 19th-century sleigh beds, and a canopy bed are particularly interesting. Two of the rooms have private baths, in one of which is a linen press original to the house. Each room has a working fireplace (which visitors are welcome to use), down comforters, and tasteful furniture upholstered in floral fabrics, as well as cut-glass decanters of sherry for a later-afternoon sip.

Nancy and Steven know their stuff, having operated bed-and-breakfasts in the Narragansett area for the past two decades, and their manner is welcoming yet unobtrusive. They've found a property worthy of their talents with this superbly restored house, offering visitors luxurious accommodations in a quiet rural setting.

Address: *144 Gibson Ave., Narragansett, RI 02880, tel. 401/789–7746.*
Accommodations: *2 double rooms with baths, 2 doubles share 1 bath.*
Rates: *$55–$85; full breakfast. No credit cards.*
Restrictions: *No smoking, no pets. 2-day minimum on summer weekends, 3-day minimum on holidays.*

Shelter Harbor Inn

Though it's set beside busy Route 1 (with neither sea nor harbor in sight), the Shelter Harbor Inn is surprisingly peaceful, buffered from the highway by a rolling lawn. On the grounds you'll find the main building, a two-story farmhouse built from 1800 to 1810, and the original coach house and barn, where more guest rooms have been quietly tucked away.

The lobby, library, sun porch, and restaurant are decorated with a quirky choice of antiques. For instance, there's an enormous Hoosier hutch and a Simplex wall clock, which many guests cite as their favorite antique in the place. Each guest room is furnished differently, with a combination of Victorian antiques and reproduction pieces; bedspreads and curtains are in muted floral patterns. Purists may be disappointed that the working fireplaces featured in some rooms are modern and somewhat tacky in design—not in the style of the inn's original construction—but this is one of the few inns in the area that allows visitors to light fires in their rooms. Several of the rooms with fireplaces also have decks (the corner room, #9, is a particular favorite), and if you climb to the roof there's another deck, with a hot tub and barbecue, open to guests. Some of the furnishings in the guest rooms show signs of wear and could be replaced.

The inn's restaurant serves three meals a day and receives rave reviews from locals despite prices that range a little on the high side; lighter fare is served in the veranda bar. A breakfast worth getting up for is included in the room rate. One breakfast specialty is ginger blueberry pancakes; fresh seafood is frequently featured on the dinner menu.

This efficiently run inn is a good choice for a romantic getaway. The management is friendly, unobtrusive, and professional. Owner Jim Dey, a self-described "Wall Street exile," bought the inn in 1976, and has masterminded many of its renovations himself. Though he and his wife, Debbye, no longer live on the property, they are here most of the time. If you arrive on a summer or fall afternoon, you are likely to see Jim rolling around the inn's front lawn on his ride-on mower, a job he reserves for himself, he says, because it gives him time to think.

Address: *10 Wagner Rd. (Rte. 1), Westerly, RI 02892, tel. 401/322–8883.*
Accommodations: *24 double rooms with baths.*
Amenities: *Restaurant, bar, air-conditioning, TV and phones in bedrooms; paddle tennis, croquet.*
Rates: *$82–$106; full breakfast. AE, D, MC, V.*
Restrictions: *No pets. 2-day minimum on weekends Memorial Day–Thanksgiving, 3-day minimum on holidays.*

Stone Lea

Situated a mile south of the town of Narragansett, just off winding Ocean Drive, Stone Lea is a large shingle-covered house that offers panoramic ocean views. Built in 1883, it was designed by the famous architectural firm of McKim, Mead and White, who were also responsible for Narragansett's most classic buildings, the Coast Guard House, Towers, and Casino. Rotundas and bay windows sprout all over this handsome summer house, and inside you'll find big windows, lots of light, and elaborate detail, such as the carved wood paneling in the main entrance hall and stairway. A favorite perch for many guests is the window seat on the stair landing.

Converted to a bed-and-breakfast in the early 1980s, Stone Lea has been operated since 1987 by Carol and Ernie Cormier, a friendly couple who try to make guests feel at home (although you may feel that you should fluff the pillows when you rise from the sofa). The rooms are quiet and spacious, although the most memorable feature of the place is the glorious ocean view. Every guest room offers a glimpse of the water, and some face directly onto the sea. The furnishings are "getting more Victorian all the time," according to the Cormiers, who hope eventually to equip the house entirely with period furniture. Before this is accomplished, however, you may find some pieces that look a little shabby, such as the chaise longue in Room 7. The chaise is nevertheless well situated for an afternoon of staring at the ocean, and Ernie defends its threadbare condition by saying, "It's a little worn out—but sit in it. Have you ever felt anything more comfortable?" He's right.

The living room is a friendly spot, furnished with a player piano and a reproduction of an antique pool table. It also displays Ernie's collection of antique car models: He is a real buff. In the dining room, lined with shelves bearing antique china, Carol serves breakfasts of homemade muffins, coffee cake, coffee breads, and fresh fruits. The air of tranquillity here is a real plus, and this is, overall, one of the nicest places to stay in Narrangansett.

Address: *40 Newton Ave., Narragansett, RI 02882, tel. 401/783–9546.*
Accommodations: *7 double rooms with baths.*
Amenities: *Cable TV in common area.*
Rates: *$60–$125; Continental breakfast. No credit cards.*
Restrictions: *No smoking, no pets. 2-day minimum on weekends in summer, 3-day minimum on holidays; closed Thanksgiving, Christmas, New Year's Eve.*

Weekapaug Inn

At the end of curving Dunn's Corners Road, past a line of gracious, well-maintained vintage beachfront homes, waits an enchanting inn where time seems to have stood still since 1939. The Weekapaug Inn has been operated by the Buffum family every summer since 1899, with only one interruption—when it was destroyed by the hurricane of 1938. Even in the face of that catastrophe, the family acted quickly, rebuilding the inn from scratch several hundred yards away from its former waterside site and reopening just one week late in the summer of 1939.

The building seems more a mansion than an inn, with a peaked roof, stone foundation, and huge wraparound porch. It's perched on a peninsula surrounded on three sides by salty Quonochontaug Pond; just beyond a barrier beach is Block Island Sound (the inn rents boats to interested guests). Like a set from the old TV series *Father Knows Best*, there's a comfy tidiness about the furnishings in the common rooms and bedrooms, where every surface looks freshly painted, waxed, or varnished. The decor of the bedrooms is cheerful, if not particularly remarkable, and each room is big and bright, with wide windows offering impressive views.

Many guests have been regulars here for several summers—some as many as 45 or 50 years—although newcomers are more than welcome ("We like to see fresh faces here," comments caretaker Horst Taut). Standards in the restaurant are very high; a new menu every day features four to six entrées, emphasizing seafood, and a full-time baker makes all the desserts, breads, and rolls. Thursday-night cookouts feature swordfish, steak, and chicken, as well as seasonal vegetables.

The Weekapaug Inn is a complete summer vacation spot, offering a full range of diversions: access to a nearby private golf course, tennis, lawn bowling, sailing, windsurfing, rowing, fishing, access to a private beach, shuffleboard, croquet, ping-pong, billiards, and weekly movies. Though many of its guests are middle-aged and older, the inn's children's program has made it a favorite of families, too. A full-time children's program director runs two daily sessions, with special excursions and projects that make even the youngest feel welcome.

Address: *15 Spring Ave., Weekapaug, RI 02892, tel. 401/322–0301.*
Accommodations: *33 double rooms with baths, 21 singles with baths.*
Amenities: *Restaurant.*
Rates: *$140–$155 per person; three meals. No credit cards.*
Restrictions: *No pets, BYOB. 2-day minimum on weekends, 3-day minimum on holidays, closed Labor Day–June 13.*

Admiral Dewey Inn

Constructed in 1898 as a seaside hotel and now listed on the National Register of Historic Places, this shingled, blue-shuttered inn stood unused for many years until Joan and Hardy LeBel bought it and restored it to its original condition. Today, its 10 guest rooms—some offer views of the ocean, others are cozy and tucked in the eaves—have been furnished with matching sets of Victorian furniture, each of a different style. One room has a grain-paneled suite, another has sponge-painted furniture, another is Gothic. Ask Joan, an inveterate antiques collector and dealer, to tell you about the style of whichever room you're staying in.

Joan, a former teacher, and Hardy, a retired Air Force lieutenant colonel who served with NATO, are outgoing and helpful, and enjoy their new lifestyle as innkeepers. They offer a Continental breakfast of fresh fruits, juices, muffins, breads, and beverages served either outdoors on the terrace, or at an 1840 harvest table that expands to seat 40. Beachgoing is about the only activity in this summer community of Matunuck Beach, but you're never far away from anywhere else in Rhode Island.

Address: *668 Matunuck Beach Rd., South Kingstown, RI 02879, tel. 401/783–2090.*
Accommodations: *10 double rooms, 8 with baths.*
Rates: *$80–$125 May–Sept., $60–$100 Oct.–Apr.; Continental breakfast. MC, V.*
Restrictions: *No smoking in house.*

Ilverthorpe Cottage

The Watts family, who had owned Ilverthorpe Cottage since it was built in 1896 (look for the date carved in the mantel of the rough-stone fireplace in the front hall), moved out every summer to rent it to a small, loyal succession of "summer people." Chris and John Webb now operate it as a bed-and-breakfast, continuing the long tradition of hospitality for which the cottage is renowned. Listed on the National Register of Historic Places, Ilverthorpe is resplendent with Victorian gingerbread, bric-a-brac, and a wraparound porch, and the decoration inside runs toward plump lace cushions and potpourri, with many pieces of authentic Victorian furniture.

Though it's a small property, with a definite aura of home, Chris and John work constantly to provide new amenities for their many repeat visitors (last summer they screened in the porch). Breakfast is a highlight at Ilverthorpe, with specialties including Belgian waffles and "breakfast pizza" (quiche with fresh fruit on top). The bread served here is baked daily.

Address: *41 Robinson St., Narragansett, RI 02882, tel. 401/789–2392.*
Accommodations: *2 double rooms with baths, 2 doubles share a bath.*
Rates: *$65–$70; full breakfast. No credit cards.*
Restrictions: *Smoking only in common rooms, no pets. Closed Labor Day–Memorial Day.*

Ocean House

If you don't mind a ramshackle setting as long as it's full of ocean views and charm, consider a visit to the Ocean House, perched atop Watch Hill. In operation since just after the Civil War, it has been run by the Brankert family since 1938 (Grandpa Brankert bought it just before the 1938 hurricane, says his grandson Michael, the current assistant manager). A long porch running the length of the hotel offers magnificent views of the sunset. Its restaurant, housed in a cheerful setting of ballroom proportions, serves three hearty meals a day, two of which are included in the price of the room. A set of rickety stairs leads down to a spectacular private beach on tranquil Block Island Sound. Furnishings in the rooms are not distinguished—they might be described as "maple eclectic"—but almost every room sports an ocean view. With such panoramas, creaky beds and splintery floors tend to seem trivial.

Address: *2 Bluff Ave., Watch Hill, RI 02891, tel. 401/348-8161.*
Accommodations: *56 double rooms with baths, 3 single rooms with baths.*
Amenities: *Restaurant, cocktail lounge.*
Rates: *$115–$190; breakfast and one other meal. MC, V.*
Restrictions: *No pets. 2-night minimum on weekends, 3-night minimum on holidays, closed Labor Day–late June.*

Block Island

Situated 13 miles off the Rhode Island coast, Block Island has been a popular tourist destination since the 19th century. Despite the large number of visitors who come here each year, the 11-square-mile island's beauty and privacy have been preserved; its 365 freshwater ponds make it a haven for more than 150 species of migrating birds. History, natural wonders, and tranquillity combine to make Block Island a special refuge from the rigors of modern living.

While it is possible to get to Block Island by small plane (New England Airlines, tel. 800/243–2460, or Action Air, tel. 800/243–8623), most visitors arrive on the ferries, which cross Long Island Sound year-round from Galilee, Rhode Island, and in the summers also from Providence and Newport; New London, Connecticut; and Montauk (Long Island), New York. It isn't necessary to bring your car, because most distances are easily covered on foot or by rented bicycle, and taxis are readily available. The island's year-round population of some 700 people swells to nearly 5,000 from mid-June to Labor Day, when regular summer residents move into their island homes and overnight guests fill the hotels. Spring and fall are also beautiful here, with an extra-quiet atmosphere and refreshingly cool evenings.

Block Island's original inhabitants were Native Americans, who called it Manisses, or Isle of the Little God. In 1524, the Italian explorer Giovanni da Verrazano renamed it Claudia, after the mother of the French king. Revisited in 1614 by the Dutch explorer Adraen Block, the site was given the name Adrian's Eyelant, which later became Block Island. In 1661 the island was settled by colonists seeking religious freedom; the farming and fishing community they established still exists today. The Old Harbor, where the ferries dock, is the island's only village, its streets lined with a friendly, eclectic clutter of shops, restaurants, inns, and hotels.

Places to Go, Things to See

Block Island Historical Cemetery. Prowl around this graveyard on the top of Job's Hill to read the island's history on tombstones dating from the 1700s.

Block Island Historical Society (Old Town Rd., tel. 401/466–2481). Permanent and special exhibits of the society celebrate the island's farming and maritime past.

Clay Head Nature Trail. Pick up this walk at its well-marked entrance on Corn Neck Road, to explore along ocean cliffs and through scrub woodlands; meander down side trails for the most spectacular views. In summer, guided tours run a few times a week; look for announcements in the *Block Island Times,* or call the Chamber of Commerce for information.

Mohegan Bluffs. Take Spring Street south out of the village to the Mohegan Trail, where at the southern tip of the island you'll find dramatic ocean views from a height of 150 feet. Stop inside the *Southeast Light* (tel. 401/466–5009), an 1873 brick building with gingerbread detailing.

The North Light at Sandy Point. At the northernmost tip of Block Island, a 7-mile hike or bike ride from town, this lighthouse was built in 1867 of Connecticut granite hauled to the site by oxen. It's currently being restored to house a maritime museum, although the project is not slated for completion until 1995. Watch out for the thousands of seagulls nesting in the rocks leading up to the lighthouse.

Rodman's Hollow. Along Champlins Road, this is one of Block Island's five wildlife refuges. It is also a natural wonder—a ravine formed by a glacier. Many winding paths trace the deep, dramatic cleft in the hills all the way down to the sea.

Beaches

Block Island is ringed with beaches, but the only one patrolled by lifeguards is **State Beach,** part of Crescent Beach, off Corn Neck Road.

Restaurants

Ballard's Inn (Old Harbor, tel. 401/466–2231) is a noisy, lively spot that caters to the boating crowd. At **Finn's Seafood Bar** (Water St., tel. 401/466–2473) you can eat inside or go out on the deck, which offers a panoramic view of the harbor. The smoked-bluefish pâté is wonderful. The cheerful **Harborside Inn** (Ferry Landing, tel. 401/466–5504) features native seafood and an extensive salad bar. **The BeacHead** (Corn Neck Rd., tel. 401/466–2249) is a favorite local spot where you can catch up on island gossip or stare out at the sea. Have a burger, or try the spicy chili.

Tourist Information

Block Island Chamber of Commerce (Drawer D, Block Island, RI 02807, tel. 401/466–2982).

Reservations Services

Bed and Breakfast of Rhode Island, Inc. (Box 3291, Newport, RI 02840, tel. 401/849–1298); **Pineapple Hospitality, Inc.** (47 N. 2nd St., New Bedford, MA 02747, tel. 508/990–1696).

Atlantic Inn

When rocking in a comfortable chair on the wide, shady porch of this classic summer hotel, you may feel a sense of déjà vu, for planted at the bottom of the rise is a small building that looks disconcertingly similar to the Atlantic Inn. "It's a miniature of the hotel that the owners built for the children who visit here," explains innkeeper Nicole Tricomi-Moore. "There's even some miniature furniture to go in there." Talk about catering to guests down to the smallest detail!

Built in 1879, the Atlantic Inn is a long, white clapboard hotel with a red roof, bravely fronting the elements on a hill above the ocean. Big windows, high ceilings, and a sweeping staircase contribute to the breezy atmosphere. Guest rooms, which are capacious though not huge, are lined up on long, straight hallways. The inn is furnished with turn-of-the-century furniture, much of it golden oak. The generally austere feel of the place is softened by predominantly pastel colors, and homey touches abound: There are handmade boat models in the dining room. The overall effect is refreshingly unfrilly, creating a restful ambience that accords well with the bracing effect of the clean ocean air.

Continental breakfast is served, and on holiday weekends a full buffet breakfast awaits. The restaurant is open for dinner mid-June–mid-September. The 2½-acre grounds are carefully maintained, and boast large wildflower, herb, and vegetable gardens (the produce of which is used in the kitchen); two all-weather tennis courts; and a smooth green croquet lawn, allowing for a game of mallets and wickets at a moment's notice.

And then there are the views. Isolated from the hubbub of the Old Harbor area, at the Atlantic Inn it's possible to perch on a hillside and muse on the patterns the wind makes in the long grasses, on the rippling of waves across the many small ponds within sight, or on the sparkle of the not-too-distant ocean.

The proprietors also own the Captain Willis House, which faces New Harbor. This house has 10 bedrooms with shared baths.

Address: *High St., Box 188, Block Island, RI 02807, tel. 401/466–5883.*
Accommodations: *21 double rooms with baths.*
Amenities: *Restaurant; phones in bedrooms; electric fans; common area with large-screen TV, games, and books.*
Rates: *$100–$165 June 15–Sept. 15, $55–$105 fall and spring; Continental breakfast (full buffet breakfast on holiday weekends). AE, MC, V.*
Restrictions: *No pets. 2-night minimum and 3-night minimum on weekends June–Aug., closed Nov.–Mar.*

Hotel Manisses

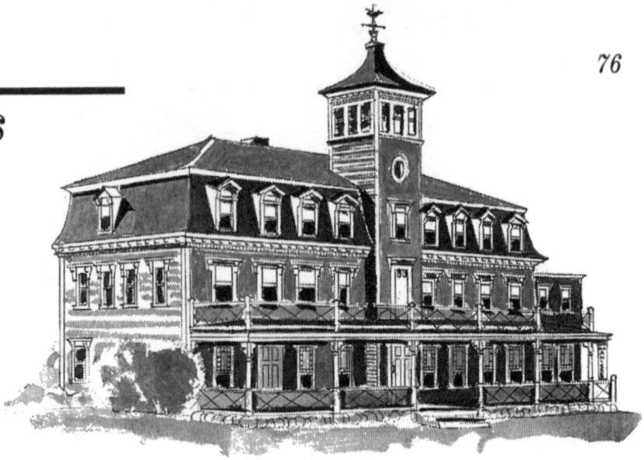

As you stroll along Spring Street on a foggy night, your eye might be caught by a translucent glow in the sky. Continue down the street and you'll discover the source: the magnificent brass chandelier suspended inside the cupola of the Manisses, like a beacon of welcome from a bygone era.

The Manisses is an 1870 Victorian gem, restored with loving care and constant diligence by its owners and operators—Joan and Justin Abrams, their daughter Rita Draper, and her husband, Steve. (The family also owns and operates the nearby 1661 Inn and Guest House; *see* below.) No expense has been spared in the inn's renovation and decoration, but what's perhaps more important, the Drapers and Abrams families work hard to make their guests feel comfortable, relaxed, and pampered. While not intruding on guests' privacy, the hosts have refined to a high art the successful innkeeper's usual attention to detail. As Rita Draper escorts guests to their rooms, her eye constantly sweeps over the territory, checking to make sure that every plant has been watered and that every lace doily and antimacassar is neatly in place.

Furnishings were clearly chosen with care. Many of the guest rooms, named after famous shipwrecks, are filled with unusual Victorian pieces painstakingly restored, such as the many-leveled bureau in the Princess Augusta Room. Even more intriguing are the knickknacks occupying every available bit of space, such as the ivory toilet-set on the bureau in one room. Afternoon tea and bedside decanters of brandy show an extra level of thoughtfulness. The restaurant, too, is a standout, with inventive cuisine drawing upon local seafood, homemade bread, and fresh vegetables grown in the Manisses garden. Breakfast for guests at the Manisses, which is served at the 1661 Inn, a one-minute walk up the road, is copious: eggs, sausage, cornbread, smoked bluefish, muffins, and much more.

Address: *Spring St., Box 1, Block Island, RI 02807, tel. 401/466-2063, fax 401/466-2858.*
Accommodations: *17 double rooms with baths.*
Amenities: *Restaurant, ceiling fans, whirlpool baths in some rooms; petting farm next door featuring llamas, goats, and black swans.*
Rates: *$130–$250 May 15–mid-Oct., $75–$175 mid-Oct.–May 14; buffet breakfast served at nearby inn. AE, MC, V.*

The 1661 Inn & Guest House

If your island vacation fantasy includes lounging in bed while gazing at swans on the marshes and a roiling sea, consider booking an oceanside room at The 1661 Inn and Guest House. For that matter, any room here is comfortable and relaxing. Owners Joan and Justin Abrams and operators Rita and Steve Draper (*see* the Hotel Manisses, *above*) are noted for their attention to detail. Even if your room doesn't face the water, you can loll on the inn's expansive deck or in a lounge chair on the gentle oceanside slope and enjoy the panorama of the water below.

In the front hallway, there's a wall full of pictures of the inn contributed by former guests, suggesting what a special experience staying here has been for many people. Recently refurbished from top to bottom, the inn has fewer rooms than it once did, which gives guests larger bedrooms with more luxurious appointments. Many rooms offer whirlpool baths, often accompanied by Victorian "fainting couches" that allow the whirlpool-induced glow to linger. Each room is different, each decorated with an eye to detail. For example, the floral wallpaper in one room matches the colors of the handpainted tiles at the top of that room's antique bureau. Another room features a collection of handmade wooden ship models. Yet another, a duplex looking out to sea, has an antique canopy bed.

No matter how lost you may get in the comfort of your surroundings, be sure to get up in time for breakfast, a splendid experience in any season but especially so in summer, when guests can sit outdoors on the canopied deck. The ample buffet may consist of fresh bluefish, corned-beef hash, Boston baked beans, sausage, Belgian waffles, roast potatoes, French toast, scrambled eggs, hot and cold cereal, fruit juices, and fresh muffins. Afternoon cocktails are also served, with such hors d'oeuvres as bluefish pâté and super-spicy nachos.

Adjacent to the inn is the Guest House, with smaller rooms and some shared baths. Though the atmosphere here is slightly more spartan, the prices are quite reasonable, and all the inn's amenities remain available.

Address: *Spring St., Block Island, RI 02807, tel. 401/466–2421 or 401/466–2063, fax 401/466–2858.*
Accommodations: *9 double rooms with baths in inn; in guest house, 5 doubles with baths, 4 doubles share 2 baths.*
Amenities: *Phones in bedrooms, 4 rooms accessible to wheelchairs.*
Rates: *$75–$300 Memorial Day–Aug. and weekends through Columbus Day, $55–$150 other times; full buffet breakfast. AE, MC, V.*
Restrictions: *No pets.*

Barrington Inn

When a former Welcome Wagon hostess decides to open a bed-and-breakfast, you can bet she'll do things right. Joan Ballard, who, with her husband, Howard, owns and operates the Barrington Inn, has an innate sense of hospitality. Though it clearly takes plenty of work to run the inn without a large staff, Joan in repose is gracious, frank, and witty—great qualities in an innkeeper.

The inn, originally an island farmhouse built in 1886, was restored by Joan and Howard when they bought it in 1982. It is furnished with a friendly assortment of antiques, some dating from the mid-19th century. A number of delightfully eccentric decorations are also displayed throughout the inn, such as a "tin plate" painting and a French hand-painted mirror that is Joan's particular pride and joy.

Because the inn is located on a rise, there are good views from every window. Three rooms feature decks that overlook Trim's Pond, the Great Salt Pond, and the ocean. The decks afford beautiful sunset views.

Address: *Box 397, Beach & Ocean Aves., Block Island, RI 02807, tel. 401/466–5510.*
Accommodations: *6 double rooms with baths, 2 apartments.*
Amenities: *TV and VCR in common room.*
Rates: *$90–$140 mid-June–Labor Day; Continental breakfast. MC, V.*
Restrictions: *No pets. Closed Nov. 20–Mar.*

Blue Dory Inn

Located at the edge of the busy Old Harbor area, the Blue Dory Inn has been a guest house since its construction in 1898 by Brunell Dodge, a Block Island fisherman. Dodge was also an artist; an example of his wood-burning skills hangs over the doorway of the inn's Victorian-style parlor, which is furnished with floral wallpaper and a curved sofa.

Ann Loedy, owner and manager, runs a most tidy and efficient inn here, consisting of one main building and three smaller outbuildings. Several rooms overlook Crescent Beach. Couples looking for a romantic hideaway often enjoy the Tea House, with its porch looking out on the beach. An expanded Continental breakfast is served in summertime on a pretty flagstone patio. Because parking is a problem here, it's recommended that you keep your car on the mainland—everything on Block Island is within walking or biking distance, anyway.

Address: *Dodge St., Box 488, Block Island, RI 02807, tel. 401/466–2254.*
Accommodations: *13 double rooms with baths.*
Amenities: *Cable TV in lobby.*
Rates: *$100–$170 Memorial Day weekend and June 15–Labor Day, $55–$130 other times; Continental breakfast. AE, MC, V.*
Restrictions: *Smoking barely tolerated, no pets.*

Rose Farm Inn

Judy and Robert Rose are two of the few innkeepers on Block Island who were born and bred here. In 1988, they restored the house built by Robert's grandfather at the turn of the century. The sense of belonging and rootedness they bring to their operation makes their welcome all the heartier.

Each of the pleasantly uncluttered rooms at the Rose Farm Inn offers bucolic views—some of the ocean, some of nearby ponds. The furnishings are a combination of original antiques and high-quality reproductions. Of the turn-of-the-century walnut bed in one room, Judy says proudly, "Golden oak was common at that time. Walnut was very *unusual.* Look at the beautiful grain in that piece!" Another intriguing item is a Victorian ladies' hotel bureau, with a special compartment for hats and gloves. The breakfast room is furnished in wicker and decorated with hanging plants, and a spacious front porch makes a perfect setting for reflective moments.

Address: *Roslyn Rd., Box E, Block Island, RI 02807, tel. 401/466–2021.*
Accommodations: *8 double rooms with baths, 2 doubles share 1 bath.*
Amenities: *Cable TV in common room, refrigerator and ice machine available for guests.*
Rates: *$85–$140; Continental breakfast. MC, V.*
Restrictions: *Closed Columbus Day–Memorial Day.*

Surf Hotel

The Cyrs—Beatrice, Ulric, and Lorraine—have operated the Surf Hotel since 1956. Located a stone's throw from the ferry dock, in the heart of the Old Harbor area, *and* with Crescent Beach just outside its back door, the hotel seems to have changed very little over the years; in fact, in many ways, it's not hard to imagine what the hotel was like when it first opened in 1876. Dark winding hallways give onto smallish, tidy guest rooms decorated with a jumble of antiques and "simply old" pieces. The dining room's ceiling is the original tin; Victorian curios abound, such as the perambulator stuffed with 1890s baby dolls, each wearing a startled expression. The front porch, offering a spectacular ocean view, is furnished with comfortable high-backed rockers, inviting contemplation of the blue waters below.

The guest rooms have their own sinks but share toilets and baths—as Lorraine Cyr points out, when the building was built, bathrooms were a pretty unusual commodity—but return guests (and there are *many* of them) seem not to mind sharing.

Address: *Dodge St., Block Island, RI 02807, tel. 401/466–2241.*
Accommodations: *20 double rooms and 20 singles; all share 9 baths.*
Amenities: *Barbecue grill in backyard for guests.*
Rates: *$45–$80; Continental breakfast. No credit cards.*
Restrictions: *No pets. Closed Columbus Day–Memorial Day.*

Massachusetts

Massachusetts

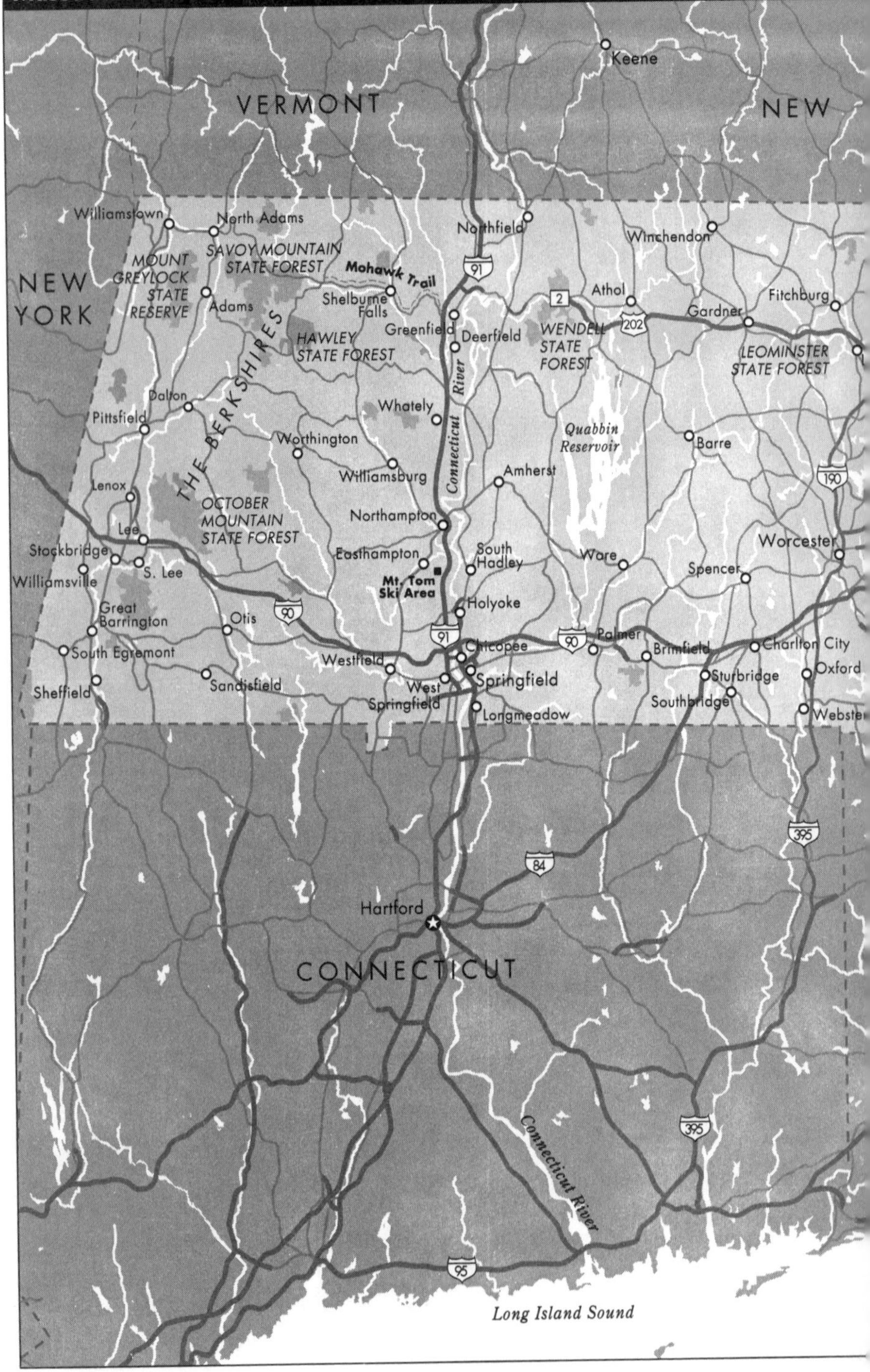
VERMONT
NEW
NEW YORK
Keene
Williamstown
North Adams
Northfield
Winchendon
MOUNT GREYLOCK STATE RESERVE
SAVOY MOUNTAIN STATE FOREST
Mohawk Trail
91
Adams
Shelburne Falls
2
Athol
Fitchburg
Gardner
202
Greenfield
Deerfield
WENDELL STATE FOREST
LEOMINSTER STATE FOREST
HAWLEY STATE FOREST
THE BERKSHIRES
Dalton
Pittsfield
Whately
Connecticut River
Quabbin Reservoir
Barre
Worthington
Williamsburg
Amherst
190
Lenox
OCTOBER MOUNTAIN STATE FOREST
Northampton
Lee
Worcester
Stockbridge
Easthampton
South Hadley
Ware
Spencer
S. Lee
Williamsville
Mt. Tom Ski Area
Holyoke
Great Barrington
Otis
90
91
Chicopee
90
Palmer
Brimfield
Charlton City
South Egremont
Westfield
Springfield
Sturbridge
Oxford
Sheffield
Sandisfield
West Springfield
Longmeadow
Southbridge
Webster
395
84
Hartford
CONNECTICUT
395
Connecticut River
95
Long Island Sound

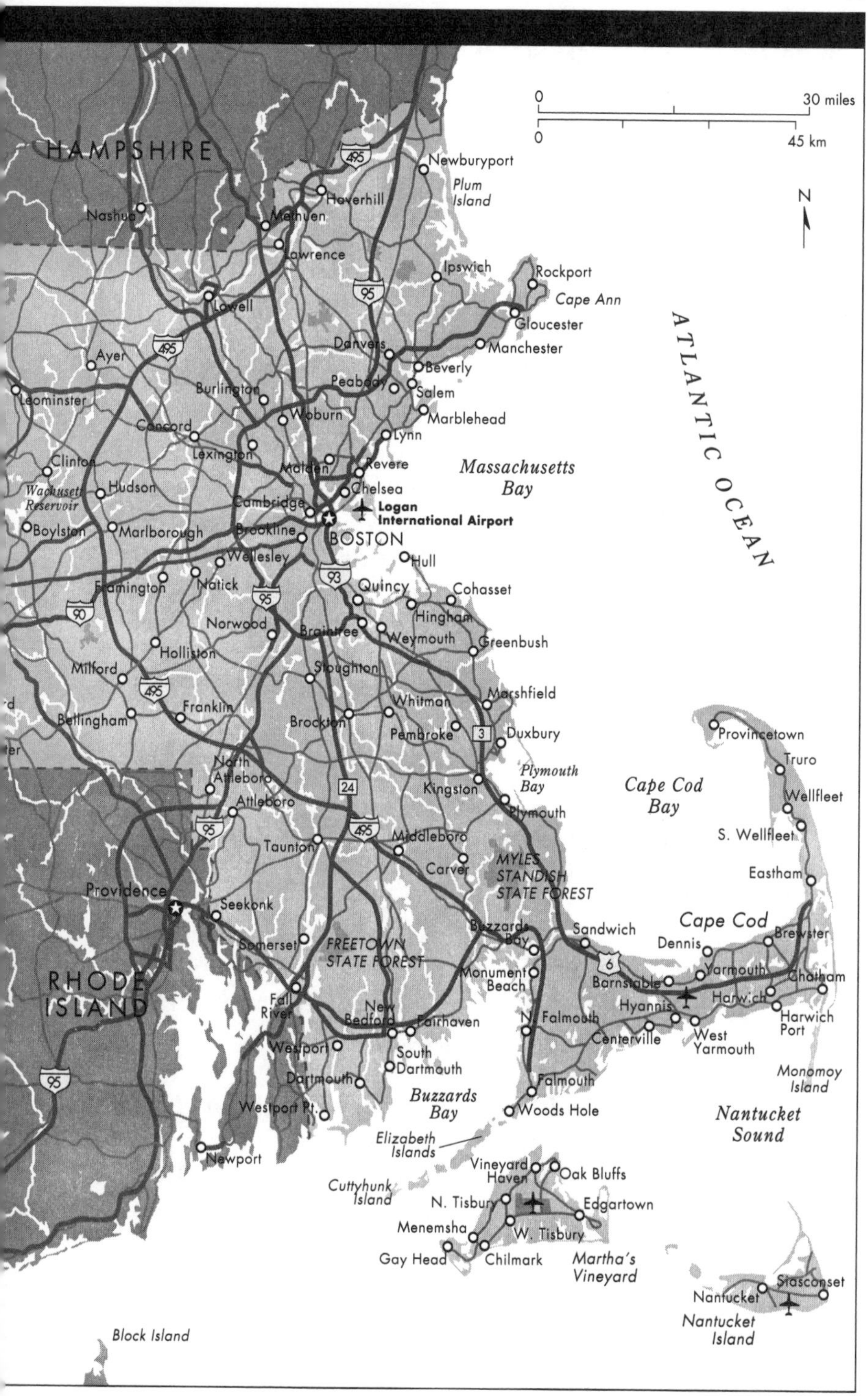
HAMPSHIRE
RHODE ISLAND
ATLANTIC OCEAN
Massachusetts Bay
Cape Cod Bay
Cape Cod
Plymouth Bay
Buzzards Bay
Nantucket Sound
0
30 miles
0
45 km
N
BOSTON
Logan International Airport
Providence
Newburyport
Plum Island
Haverhill
Nashua
Methuen
Lawrence
Ipswich
Rockport
Cape Ann
Gloucester
Lowell
Manchester
Ayer
Danvers
Beverly
Peabody
Salem
Leominster
Burlington
Woburn
Marblehead
Concord
Lynn
Lexington
Malden
Revere
Clinton
Chelsea
Hudson
Wachusett Reservoir
Cambridge
Boylston
Marlborough
Brookline
Hull
Wellesley
Framingham
Natick
Quincy
Cohasset
Hingham
Norwood
Braintree
Weymouth
Greenbush
Holliston
Milford
Stoughton
Marshfield
Whitman
Franklin
Bellingham
Brockton
Pembroke
Duxbury
Provincetown
North Attleboro
Truro
Kingston
Wellfleet
Attleboro
Plymouth
S. Wellfleet
Taunton
Middleboro
Carver
MYLES STANDISH STATE FOREST
Eastham
Seekonk
Sandwich
Brewster
Buzzards Bay
Dennis
Somerset
FREETOWN STATE FOREST
Yarmouth
Monument Beach
Barnstable
Chatham
Fall River
New Bedford
Harwich
Hyannis
N. Falmouth
Harwich Port
Fairhaven
Centerville
West Yarmouth
Westport
South Dartmouth
Monomoy Island
Dartmouth
Falmouth
Westport Pt.
Woods Hole
Elizabeth Islands
Newport
Vineyard Haven
Oak Bluffs
Cuttyhunk Island
N. Tisbury
Edgartown
Menemsha
W. Tisbury
Gay Head
Chilmark
Martha's Vineyard
Siasconset
Nantucket
Nantucket Island
Block Island
495
95
93
90
24
3
6

Southeastern Massachusetts

Travelers often zip through the large southeastern section of the state on their way somewhere else—usually, Cape Cod. Yet those who take the time to explore this region will be rewarded with many surprises—and far fewer Winnebagos and tour buses (except perhaps around Plymouth Rock) than in other parts of the state. One place of interest is Quincy, the birthplace of presidents John Adams and John Quincy Adams, which is reached by Route 3, south of Boston, and by following the meandering roads closer to the coast. Continuing farther south and heading over to Route 3A, you'll pass through the seaside towns of Hingham, Cohasset, Greenbush, and Marshfield. Several public beaches are also accessible down side roads. A little farther south, visitors can enjoy the storybook town of Duxbury, first settled in the 17th century by the Pilgrims soon after they arrived in Plymouth. From here, you can rejoin Route 3 just outside Duxbury, but a more interesting drive south on Route 3A leads to Kingston, another Pilgrim settlement, and 4 miles farther, to Plymouth.

If you choose instead to head south of Boston on Route 24, you'll arrive at the seaports of Fall River and New Bedford in about an hour's time. Each city reached its peak of prosperity in the 19th century, and, in both places, travelers can visit restored buildings of that era as well as more than 50 outlet stores. Boats from New Bedford Harbor depart each day for Martha's Vineyard and Cuttyhunk Island.

Perhaps because of the lemminglike rush of most tourists to Cape Cod, southeastern Massachusetts unfortunately offers few places to stay outside the standard chain motels. Most of the bed-and-breakfast operations are quite small, often providing no more than two rooms. In this section, only one B&B of this size is included, because it is exceptional.

Places to Go, Sights to See

Dartmouth. The *Children's Museum* (Gulf Rd., tel. 508/993–3361), housed in a former dairy barn on 60 acres of open land, features a hand-carved saltwater aquarium, a rain forest exhibit, a teddy bear collection, hiking trails, and more.

Fall River. Industrial docks and enormous factories hark back to the city's past as a major textile center. The city also served as a port, however, and its most interesting site is *Battleship Cove* (access from I–95, Exit 5, beside the Taunton River, tel. 508/678–1100), which harbors several museums, the 35,000-ton World War II battleship USS *Massachusetts,* and the attack sub USS *Lionfish.* The *Marine Museum at Fall River* (70 Water St., tel. 508/674–3533) displays ship models, steam engines, and memorabilia from the *Titanic* and the Old Fall River Line.

New Bedford. Home of the largest fishing fleet on the East Coast, this former whaling capital has a delightful historic district with cobblestone streets near the waterfront, where antiques and boating supplies are for sale. At the *New Bedford Whaling Museum* (18 Johnny Cake Hill, tel. 508/997–0046), exhibits include a model of the square-rigger *Lagoda,* a superb collection of scrimshaw, whaling journals, and a huge selection of whaling gear. *Seamen's Bethel* (Johnny Cake Hill) is a 19th-century chapel that was immortalized at the beginning of Melville's *Moby Dick.* New Bedford also has a *Glass Museum* (50 N. 2nd St., tel. 508/994–0015), with 2,000 pieces in its collection, and one of the finest upscale designer outlets (651 Orchard St., tel. 508/999–4100) in the country.

Plymouth. This pleasant residential and industrial community with steep streets leading down to the harbor cherishes its history as the site of Plymouth Colony, the first permanent New England settlement, established by the English Pilgrims in the 17th century. Visitors can begin at *Plymouth Rock,* the boulder right next to the harbor, which is traditionally accepted as the initial landing spot of the Pilgrims who disembarked from the *Mayflower* in 1620. Travelers can also visit the *Mayflower II* (State Pier, tel. 508/746–1622), a replica of the original Pilgrim ship, and *Plimouth Plantation* (Warren Ave., Rte. 3A, 3 mi south of Plymouth, tel. 508/746–1622), a reconstruction of a Pilgrim village of 1627, with furnished homes, gardens, and actors in period dress demonstrating household skills.

Beaches

Several of the beaches along the South Shore and on Buzzards Bay are under the jurisdictions of the towns in which they are located; watch out for local parking regulations. State beaches in the area include **Demarest Lloyd State Park** in Dartmouth, **Fort Phoenix State Beach** in Fairhaven, **Horseneck Beach** in Westport, and **Nantasket Beach** in Hull.

Restaurants

In Plymouth, seafood is the specialty at the **Inn For All Seasons** (tel. 508/746–8823), with pleasant gardens in the back and the charm of a faded country mansion. **Crane Brook Tea Room** (tel. 508/866–3235), in Carver, offers fine French-influenced fare in an antiques-filled dining spot set at the edge of a pond. Dartmouth's **The Bridge Street Café** (tel. 508/994–7200) features tasty seafood dishes as well as a casual bistro menu in a quaint harborside setting. In Fall River, **Leone's** (tel. 508/679–8158), conveniently close to Battleship Cove, has three decks of tables overlooking the river; specialties include lobster, prime ribs, and pasta. **Candleworks Café** (tel. 508/992–1635) serves well-prepared seafood on the ground floor of a beautifully restored Federal-style candle factory.

Tourist Information

Coastal South Shore information is handled by the **Plymouth County Development Council** (Box 1620, Pembroke, MA 02359, tel. 617/826–3136). For New Bedford and Fall River information, try the **Bristol County Development Council** (70 N. 2nd St., New Bedford, MA 02740, tel. 508/997–1250).

Reservations Services

Pineapple Hospitality (Box F821, 47 2nd St., Suite 3A, New Bedford, MA 02742, tel. 508/990–1696).

Allen House

Getting here is a bit of an adventure. The Allen House is the sole inn on tiny Cuttyhunk Island, 6 miles out to sea from New Bedford harbor. Part of the Elizabeth Islands, Cuttyhunk is the only island in the group that still offers public accommodations. If you don't own a boat, you'll have to take *Alert II,* the small ferry that travels here year-round. Or you can scoot over on a seaplane. But persevere, for the trip is worth it.

You can walk every inch of the unspoiled island—2 miles long by 1 mile wide—in three hours. The winter population of 40 swells to 500 in the summertime, but the island never seems crowded. Guests can see deer, rabbits, and wildflowers along the quiet roads, and they can watch the sunset from World War II bunkers. Bird-watching is at its best during the spring and fall.

The Allen House has been run since 1984 by two sisters, Margo Solod and Nina Solod Brodeur, who took over the inn from their father, the original innkeeper. The 100-year-old building has been used as a rooming house since the 1920s; it sits with its annex on a hill overlooking Vineyard Sound and Buzzards Bay. The tasteful furnishings are old but in good condition—the owners refuse to call them antiques, though others probably would. Rooms have been individually decorated and are kept in tiptop shape; all feature wonderful views of the idyllic surroundings. Two newer cottages are also rented in June and September; one has one room, one bath, and the other has three rooms and one bath.

The inn offers a bright, amiable, high-quality restaurant with a glassed-in porch that overlooks the water. It seats 75 and specializes in fresh seafood caught just off the island. Wine and liquor are not for sale on the island, but visitors can bring their own bottles.

Guests can enjoy the blissful ambience at Allen House, even at the height of the season, when nerves at a busier resort might fray. The place caters to an eclectic clientele; guests may include parents with children, couples, anglers, retirees, and single men and women; they are all welcome here. But Cuttyhunk isn't a place for a lively vacation, and those who swear by the inn would just as soon keep it that way.

Address: *Cuttyhunk, MA 02713, tel. 508/996–9292.*
Accommodations: *11 double rooms and 1 single share 4 baths, 2 cottages.*
Amenities: *Restaurant, TV in guest lounge, pay phone in restaurant.*
Rates: *$60–$85 June 29–Sept. 1; Continental breakfast. MC, V.*
Restrictions: *No pets, BYOB. 2-night minimum on weekends, closed mid-Oct.–late May.*

Durant Sail Loft Inn

Since his arrival in New Bedford in 1988, Michael Delacey has put his background in historic preservation to use; he's been a tireless volunteer in many community activities, including the restoration of the New Bedford lightship and the city's waterfront park. Michael is proud of his adopted home; his "let's pitch in and do it right" approach is evident at the Durant Sail Loft Inn as well. The only full-service accommodation for many miles around, the inn prides itself, justifiably, on its high level of service. This is most definitely the only lodging in the New Bedford area that is prepared to shine your shoes and send up a midnight snack.

In the heart of the fishing-pier area, the inn is located in the old Bourne Counting House, a huge granite industrial structure built in 1847 by Captain Edward Merrill, a whaling master. From its guest rooms, visitors have a bird's-eye view of the activities at the country's busiest fishing port. The building was completely renovated in 1979 under the auspices of the City of New Bedford and the Massachusetts Historic Commission and is one of many 19th-century jewels that have been restored in the waterfront area.

Although the modern furnishings in the bedrooms are undistinguished, the rooms are spotless and comfortable, with thick towels and an array of toiletries in the bathrooms; sitting areas; plush, blue-and-beige rugs; and cheerful bedspreads and upholstery. Each room bears the name of a whaling captain from New Bedford's past, and pictures of old sailing vessels decorate the walls.

Guests can choose between the more formal dining area of the Lisboa Antiga restaurant or the casual area which the locals patronize. The fare is authentic Portuguese; baked fish in a wine sauce and steak grilled in an earthenware frying pan are the two most popular specialities. For those who want the most traditional of Portuguese dishes, there is also *bacalhau assado* (baked cod fish). The restaurant opens at 5:30 AM for the local fishermen, so you can enjoy a full breakfast here if you wish for more than the complimentary Continental breakfast served in the inn.

Address: *1 Merrill's Wharf, New Bedford, MA 02740, tel. 508/999–2700, fax 508/990–7863.*
Accommodations: *16 double rooms with baths.*
Amenities: *Restaurant and café, air-conditioning, TV and phones in rooms, 24-hour room service, laundry service, newspaper delivery, secretarial services, translator; theater-ticket, restaurant, and rental-car reservations made. A function room for up to 200 people has been added.*
Rates: *$68–$88 year-round; Continental breakfast. AE, DC, MC, V.*
Restrictions: *No pets.*

Salt Marsh Farm

Located on the historic Isaac Howland homestead farm at the quiet end of a harborside road in South Dartmouth, this two-story, mint-condition Georgian farmhouse (circa 1727) is run by Sally and Larry Brownell and has been in Sally's family since World War II. In the back of the house lie 90 acres of grounds, where nature trails lead to huge maples and oaks, a 40-acre salt marsh, and the sparkling waters of Little River.

The Brownells have turned over the front of their home to their bed-and-breakfast guests, who may lounge by the fireplace in the living room filled with books on local nature lore and history. A large gallery-type family room, where you'll probably see jigsaw puzzles laid out, runs the length of the house. The building is full of pewter, silver, and choice antiques, virtually all of which were passed down through Sally's or Larry's families. Some of the pieces date back hundreds of years, such as the massive mahogany sideboard in the intimate dining room, where portraits of four of Sally's Colonial ancestors gaze down on the scene.

Though three rooms are actually available to guests, only two may be rented at a time, under local law. Two of the small chambers offer twin four-poster beds, and the third has a double bed. Sally's handmade quilts often cover the beds, and freshly picked flowers decorate the rooms. One bathroom features an oversize, claw-foot tub and a tub-height window with a view of the grounds.

Sally is an accomplished cook who makes good use of her vegetable garden. Her breakfast repertoire includes five-grain pancakes (she buys the grain at a nearby gristmill); fresh eggs from the Brownells' henhouse, prepared in any number of ways; prizewinning blueberry muffins; and double-dipped French toast with a special orange sauce and what Sally calls "mystery" syrup. "I never tell the guests what it's made of until they've tried it," she says. "But they always ask for more."

The town beach is within biking distance, and New Bedford is about 6 miles away. Padanaram is the local name of South Dartmouth and is used on many signposts.

Address: *322 Smith Neck Rd., South Dartmouth, MA 02748, tel. 508/992–0980.*
Accommodations: *3 double rooms with baths.*
Amenities: *TV and phone in common areas; bicycles and a bicycle built for two may be borrowed; private nature trails.*
Rates: *$75 summer, $65 winter; full breakfast. MC, V.*
Restrictions: *No smoking indoors, no pets, no children under 5. 2-night minimum on summer weekends and holidays.*

The Windsor House

The large white building that houses this inn was built in 1803 by Nathaniel Windsor, a merchant sea captain. Three upstairs rooms, recently refurbished, feature fireplaces and Colonial-style reproduction furniture. The brown Gurnet Room has a queen-size canopy bed; the Snug Harbor Room with green decor has twin canopy beds. The larger Powder Point Suite with blue decor has a double bed, a pull-out couch, and a small adjoining room.

Downstairs, guests can relax in an English-style pub built in the 1930s with wood from a Pilgrim-period church next door. The pub benches were church pews. The carriage house restaurant opens onto a patio at lunchtime, and the more formal main dining room has post-and-beam construction. Fresh seafood is served along with such entrées as chicken Neptune, stuffed with lobster and broccoli.

Managers and part owners Myles and Kathy McGuire are hoteliers who know how to make you feel at home. Guests can walk to a beach, and golf, tennis, swimming, and cross-country skiing are nearby.

Address: *390 Washington St., Duxbury, MA 02332, tel. 617/934–0991.*
Accommodations: *3 double rooms with baths.*
Amenities: *2 restaurants, pub.*
Rates: *$80–$90 Apr.–Oct.; full breakfast. AE, MC, V.*
Restrictions: *No pets.*

Cape Cod

Traditionally associated with quaint little villages, weathered-shingle cottages, long dune-backed beaches, fog-enshrouded lighthouses, and clam chowder, the Cape has become so popular that it risks losing the charm that brought everyone here in the first place. More and more open land has been lost to new housing developments and strip malls, built to serve a burgeoning population. During the summer, visitors must seek out the tranquillity that once met them at every turn. Yet peace can still be found, for much of the Cape remains compellingly beautiful and unspoiled, and always there is the sea, offering the chance to reconnect with elemental things.

Sixty miles southeast of Boston, and separated from the rest of Massachusetts by the 17.4-mile Cape Cod Canal, this craggy peninsula jutting out 70 miles into the Atlantic Ocean is always likened in shape to an outstretched arm bent at the elbow, its fist turned back toward the mainland at Provincetown. The moderate coastal climate fosters an abundance of plant and animal life. Barrier beaches attract a stunning variety of shore and sea birds, and the marshes and ponds are rich in waterfowl. Stellwagen Bank, just north of Provincetown, is a prime feeding ground for whales and dolphins; sandbars are playgrounds for harbor seals. Nature preserves laced with walking and bicycling trails encompass pine forests, marshes, swamps, cranberry bogs, and other terrains. Across dunes anchored by sturdy poverty grass sprawl beach plums, pink salt-spray roses, and purple beach peas.

A less happy result of the Cape's coastal location is that, on the Atlantic side especially, the tides regularly eat away at the land, sometimes at an alarming rate: Many lighthouses, some built hundreds of feet from the water's edge, have fallen into the sea, and others are now in danger of being lost. In the mid-19th century, Henry David Thoreau described, in his book Cape Cod, *walking the length of the coast, which he called "the edge of a continent wasting before the assaults of the ocean." Thanks to the establishment of the Cape Cod National Seashore in 1961, one can still walk almost 30 miles of Atlantic beach virtually without seeing a trace of human habitation.*

Through the creation of national historic districts, similar protection has been extended to the Cape's loveliest man-made landscapes. The largest and most pleasing is along the Old King's Highway (Route 6A), where the Cape's first towns—Sandwich, Barnstable, and Yarmouth—were settled by 1639. Lining this tree-shaded country road, which traverses the entire north shore, are early saltboxes, fancier houses built later by prosperous sea captains, and traditional cottages, shingles weathered to a silvery gray, with soft pink roses spilling across them. Here, too, are the white steepled churches, taverns, and village greens that preserve the spirit of old New England, along with some of the Cape's many surviving windmills.

Most villages have their own small museums, often set in houses that are themselves historic. Borning and keeping rooms, summer and winter kitchens, beehive ovens, a spinning wheel, a stereopticon, a hand-stitched sampler, and other remnants of the past add up to a visual history of the lives of the English settlers and their descendants. The travels of whaling and packet-schooner seamen and captains in the area are recalled through such items as antique nautical equipment, harpoons, charts, maps, journals, scrimshaw created during the years-long whaling voyages, and gifts brought back from exotic ports.

The economy of the Cape today is mainly dependent on tourism, so a plethora of services and entertainment exists to promote it. The area also provides a variety of amusements for children. In addition to traditional New England clambakes—where you can sample fiery red lobsters, briny steamers, corn on the cob, baked potatoes, and maybe linguiça *for a touch of the Cape's Portuguese flavor—eating places range from fried-clam shacks and rustic fish houses to elegant restaurants. Shoppers find no end of crafts and antiques stores and art galleries; theater buffs choose from many good community groups and college and professional summer stock. Of course, there's plenty of fishing and water sports, and everywhere bay and sound beaches—calm or wild, dune- or forest-backed, blanket-paved or secluded—offer just about every option for seekers of summer sun and sea.*

"The season" used to be strictly from Memorial Day to Labor Day, but the boundaries have blurred; many places now open in April or earlier and close as late as November, and a core remain open year-round. Unfortunately, most of the historic sites and museums, largely manned by volunteers, still adhere to the traditional dates and are inaccessible in the off-season.

Each of the seasons invites a different kind of visit. During the summer, you have your choice of relaxing at a beach or filling your schedule with museum visits and other activities—or whatever mix of the two suits you. In the fall, crowds are gone, prices are lower, and the water sometimes remains warm enough for swimming. Gently turning foliage reaches its peak around the end of October, with areas around the freshwater marshes, ponds, and swamps offering the brightest displays. Fall and winter are oyster and scallop season, and all the restaurants still open feature the freshly caught delicacies. In the winter, many tourist-oriented activities and facilities shut down, but accommodations (including fireplace-warmed inns) go for as little as half the summer rates, and you can walk the beaches in often total solitude. Spring does get a bit wet; still, the daffodils come bursting up from roadsides, and everything begins to turn green. By April, shops and restaurants start to open, and locals begin to prepare for another summer.

Places to Go, Sights to See

Band Concerts. Every town has these fun slices of Americana. Chatham has particularly lively and popular concerts, held on Friday evenings during the summer at *Kate Gould Park* (tel. 508/945–2160) on Main Street; as many as 500 people fox-trot on the dance floor, and there are special dances for children and sing-alongs for all.

Cape Cod National Seashore. The 27,700-acre national park includes and protects 30 miles of beaches on the Cape's Atlantic coast, as well as woods, swamps, marshland, vast dunes, and several historic structures (including the United States' first transatlantic wireless station and an old life-saving station). Lacing through the areas are self-guided nature trails and biking and horse trails. For more information on what the park has to offer, including an extensive program of guided walks, boat trips, and lectures, visit one of the visitor centers off Route 6 (Salt Pond, Eastham, tel. 508/255–3421, closed Jan.–Feb.; Province Lands, Provincetown, tel. 508/487–1256, closed Jan.–Mar.), which also have nature displays, films, and gift shops. In January and February, information is available at Seashore headquarters, at the Marconi Station (off Route 6, South Wellfleet, tel. 508/349–3785).

Chatham Fish Pier. The unloading of the boats as the fishing fleet returns to the pier on Shore Road in the early afternoon is a big event, drawing crowds who watch from an observation deck.

Cranberry Harvests. Cranberries are big business on the Cape. If you drive along Route 6A in Sandwich in early fall, while the surrounding foliage starts taking on the rich colors of autumn, you can watch the cranberries being harvested—a sight not to be missed. First, a bog is flooded with 12 to 18 inches of water, then men in great waders walk a machine with wooden paddles around in it to loosen the berries. Bright red cranberries float on the surface of the water, and more men in waders corral the berries within floating wooden booms, directing the flow into a gathering machine. A conveyor belt deposits them snugly in huge dump trucks to be carted away.

Heritage Plantation (Grove and Pine Sts., Sandwich, tel. 508/888–3300; closed Nov.–mid-May). At this extraordinary 76-acre complex, you'll find extensive and beautifully maintained gardens—daylily, fruit tree, rhododendron—crisscrossed by walking paths. Also here are museums showcasing classic and historic cars; antique firearms, hand-painted miniature soldiers, and military uniforms; Colonial tools, Currier and Ives prints, Americana (such as antique toys and mechanical banks), and a working 1912 carousel. During the summer, evening concerts are held on the grounds.

John F. Kennedy Hyannis Museum. While fundraising continues on a complete museum dedicated to JFK's Cape Cod years, a photographic exhibit is on view at 397 Main Street, Hyannis. The photographs, which span the years 1934 to 1963, have been culled largely from the collection of the

John Fitzgerald Kennedy Library in Boston.

John F. Kennedy Memorial. The Kennedys have had homes in Hyannis Port, an area of quietly posh estates, since 1929; during John F. Kennedy's presidency, the family compound became the summer White House. This memorial—a quiet esplanade with a plaque and fountain pool overlooking Lewis Bay, on which the late president often sailed—was erected in 1966 by the townspeople. To reach it from Hyannis, take Main Street to Ocean Street.

Lighthouses. Go to *Chatham Light* (Shore Rd.) for a great view of the harbor, the offshore bars, and the ocean beyond. Coin-operated telescopes offer a close look at the famous "Chatham break," where a 1987 storm blasted a channel through a barrier beach. *Highland Light* in Truro (off Rte. 6), the Cape's oldest lighthouse, is where Thoreau boarded for a spell in his travels. *Nobska Light* in Woods Hole (Church St.) gives spectacular views of the nearby Elizabeth Islands and of Martha's Vineyard, across the sound.

Monomoy National Wildlife Refuge. This two-island sanctuary off Chatham is an important stop along the North Atlantic Flyway for migratory waterfowl (peak times: May and late July), providing resting and nesting grounds for 285 species. White-tailed deer live here, and harbor seals frequent the shores in winter. A very peaceful place of sand and beach grass, tidal flats and dunes, and an old lighthouse, Monomoy can be visited on tours offered by the *Audubon Society* (tel. 508/349–2615); you can also get a boat at Chatham Harbor (tel. 508/945–9378) to taxi you over in season.

Nickerson State Park. This park (Rte. 6A, Brewster, tel. 508/896–3491), encompassing more than 1,700 acres of white pine, hemlock, and spruce forest and eight freshwater kettle ponds, offers the Cape's best tent camping; it is also open for fishing (ponds are stocked with trout and bass), biking (8 miles of paved trails), bird-watching, canoeing and sailing, picnicking, and, in winter, ice fishing, skating, and cross-country skiing.

Pilgrim Monument. Dominating the skyline of Provincetown is this 252-foot-high stone tower, erected between 1907 and 1910 to commemorate the landing of the Pilgrims in Provincetown Harbor and the signing of the Mayflower Compact before they moved on to Plymouth. Climb the 116 steps for a panoramic view of the dunes, the harbor, the town, and the entire bay side of Cape Cod. At the base is a museum (tel. 508/487–1310) with exhibits on whaling, shipwrecks, and scrimshaw; a diorama of the *Mayflower;* and more. Through 1993, an exhibit on the *Whydah*—the only pirate ship ever recovered, sunk in a 1717 storm and found off Wellfleet in 1984—includes a laboratory doing conservation work on retrieved artifacts.

Provincetown. A destination in itself, Provincetown (Chamber of Commerce, tel. 508/487–3424) is a quiet fishing village in the winter. During the summer it becomes a lively place with important art galleries and museums, wonderful crafts shops, whale-watch excursion boats, good restaurants and people-watching, and lots of nightlife (including drag shows). Recently it was designated a historic district, preserving for posterity its cheerful mix of tiny waterfront shops (former fish shacks) and everything from a 1746 Cape house to a mansarded French Second Empire building. See the town via the *P-town Trolley* (tel. 508/487–9483); see the dunes by Jeep with *Art's Dune Tours* (tel. 508/487–1950).

Sandwich. A picture-perfect New England town, Sandwich is centered by an idyllic pond with shade trees, ducks, fishing children, and a waterwheel-operated gristmill reached by a wooden bridge. You can spend a day wandering in and out of several museums, such as the *Yesteryears Doll Museum* (143 Main St., tel. 508/888–1711; closed Nov.–mid-May), whose collection includes such exotica as lacquer-and-gold miniatures of a Japanese emperor and empress and their court; the *Hoxie House* (Water St., tel. 508/888–1173; closed mid-Sept.–mid-June), a furnished and exhibit-filled 1675 saltbox that was never modernized with electricity or plumbing; the *Thornton W. Burgess Museum* (4 Water St., tel. 508/888–4668), dedicated to the native son who created an American Peter Rabbit and featuring nature- and Burgess-related exhibits; and the *Sandwich Glass Museum* (129 Main St., tel. 508/888–0251; closed Jan.), displaying the pressed and blown glass that made the town famous.

Train Tour. *Cape Cod Scenic Railroad* (Main and Center Sts., Hyannis, tel. 508/771–3788; tours mid-June–Oct.) runs 1¾-hour excursions—past ponds, cranberry bogs, and marshes—between Sagamore and Hyannis, with stops at Sandwich and the canal.

Whale-watching. Provincetown is the center for whale-watch excursions, which run spring–fall. On boats of the *Dolphin Fleet* (tel. 508/349–1900 or 800/826–9300), scientists conducting marine research tell you the histories and habits of the mammals. The office (and those of other outfitters) is at MacMillan Wharf, the departure point for the boats. Tours are also available out of Barnstable Harbor (tel. 508/362–6088 or 800/287–0374 in MA).

Beaches

All the Atlantic Ocean beaches, though cold, are otherwise superior—wide, long, sandy, dune-backed, with great views, usually lifeguards and rest rooms, but no food. **Coast Guard Beach,** backed by low grass and heathland, and **Nauset Light Beach** are both off Route 6 in Eastham (for Coast Guard, park at the Salt Pond Visitor Center—*see* Cape Cod National Seashore, above). In Dennis, off Route 6A, **Corporation Beach** (full services) is a long, broad crescent of white sand; **Chapin Beach** (no services), backed by low dunes, has long tidal flats that allow walking far out at low tide; and sandy-bottomed **Scargo Lake** (rest rooms) is a freshwater lake with a picnic area. **Old Silver Beach** (full services) in North Falmouth, off Route 28, is especially good for small children because a sandbar keeps it shallow at one end and makes tidal pools with crabs and minnows. **Sandy Neck Beach** in West Barnstable is a 6-mile barrier beach between bay and marsh, excellent for walking. **West Dennis Beach** (full services) runs 1½ miles along the warm south shore and includes a playground and Windsurfer rentals.

Shopping

Throughout the Cape you'll find shops selling the fine wares of weavers, glassblowers, potters, and other craftsmen, especially along Route 6A (the Old King's Highway), which also has many antiques shops and antiquarian booksellers. Provincetown was an art colony in the early 1900s and remains an important art center, with many galleries and frequent exhibitions of Cape and non-Cape artists; its crafts offerings are also among the area's most original and sophisticated. Wellfleet has a number of arts and crafts galleries as well, in a quietly artsy setting. Hyannis's Main Street is the Cape's busiest, fun for strolling and people-watching. For buying, head to Provincetown or to Chatham, which has generally traditional antiques and clothing shops and a subdued but charming old-Cape atmosphere. Seven **Christmas Tree Shops** are perennial Cape favorites for fun discounted paper goods, candles, home furnishings, whatever. The largest is in Hyannis (Route 132, tel. 508/778–5521), another at Exit 1 off Route 6 in Sagamore (tel. 508/888–7010).

Theater

In 1915, a group of successful writers and unknowns, including Eugene O'Neill, began a playhouse in Provincetown. Since then, theater has thrived on Cape Cod, in its early days featuring such fledgling actors as Bette Davis and Henry Fonda. The **Barnstable Comedy Club** (Village Hall, Rte. 6A, Barnstable, tel. 508/362–6333) is the most notable of the amateur groups, many of which perform in the off-season. For summer stock, there's the Equity **Cape Playhouse** (off Rte. 6A, Dennis, tel. 508/385–3911) and the non-Equity **Falmouth Playhouse** (off Rte. 151, North Falmouth, tel. 508/563–5922). The **Wellfleet Harbor Actors Theatre** (W.H.A.T.; by town pier, tel. 508/349–6835) presents less traditional summer fare, including satires and farces. The **College Light Opera Company** (Highfield Theatre, end of Depot Ave., Falmouth, tel. 508/548–0668) presents operettas in the summer starring music majors from Oberlin College and elsewhere.

Tourist Information

Cape Cod Chamber of Commerce (Junction of Rtes. 6 and 132, Hyannis, MA 02601, tel. 508/362–3225); **Provincetown Business Guild** (115 Bradford St., Box 421–89, Provincetown, MA 02657, tel. 508/487–2313; focuses on gay tourism).

Reservations Services

House Guests Cape Cod and the Islands (Box 1881, Orleans, MA 02653, tel. 800/666–4678); **Bed and Breakfast Cape Cod** (Box 341, West Hyannis Port, MA 02672–0341, tel. 508/775–2772); **Orleans Bed & Breakfast Associates** (Box 1312, Orleans, MA 02653, tel. 508/255–3824 or 800/541–6226; covers Lower Cape, Harwich to Truro); **Provincetown Reservations System** (tel. 508/487–2400 or 800/648–0364; also shows, restaurants, and more).

Captain Freeman Inn

This impressive Victorian facing Brewster's little town square was built in 1866 by a packet-schooner captain and fleet owner. Converted to an inn in the 1940s, it was bought in December 1991 by Carol Covitz, a former marketing director for a Boston computer company.

Carol has done a splendid job renovating the house. She restored the exterior's original Victorian greens, with contrast colors for the brackets and columns of the wrap-around veranda. The veranda itself got a new floor of oiled mahogany, and has rockers and a screened section facing the pool. Inside, Carol had a jewel to work with. The ground floor is spacious and bright, with 12-foot ceilings and windows. Fine architectural details include the ornate Italian plaster ceiling medallions and marble fireplace brought back from the captain's travels.

Like the common areas, first-floor guest rooms feature 12-foot ceilings, grand windows, and ceiling medallions. Second- and third-floor front rooms offer 8½-foot ceilings and large windows with views of a white church and the square. In a 1989 addition are three "Luxury Suites"—spacious bedrooms with queen canopy beds, sofas, fireplaces, cable TV and VCRs, minifridges, and French doors leading to small enclosed porches with private whirlpool spas. Guest rooms have hardwood floors, local art, and individual heat controls; they are done in antiques and Victorian reproductions, with nice touches like crystal or brass lamps, eyelet spreads and all-cotton sheets, and some beds have lace or fishnet canopies.

Carol's breakfasts showcase skills honed in professional cooking classes. (In winter she sometimes offers her own weekend cooking school.) Such dishes as potato-cheddar pie, Italian *stradas*, and compotes are served on the screened porch or by the fire in the dining room.

Out back, the 1½-acre lawn is bordered in wild grapes, blackberries, and highbush blueberries. Hurricane fencing surrounds the pool and its deck, which is edged in garden and set with lounge chairs. A bay beach is a five-minute walk away.

Address: *15 Breakwater Rd., Brewster, MA 02631, tel. 508/896–7481 or 800/843–4664.*
Accommodations: *9 double rooms with baths, 3 doubles share 1 bath.*
Amenities: *Common minifridge, ice machine, sink, movie library; outdoor heated pool, croquet, badminton, bikes.*
Rates: *$75–$115, $185 suites; full breakfast and afternoon tea. AE, MC, V.*
Restrictions: *No smoking, no pets. 2-night minimum in season, other weekends.*

Captain's House Inn

Finely preserved architectural details, superb taste in decorating, opulent baked goods, and an overall feeling of warmth and quiet comfort make this perhaps the finest of the Cape's small inns. Behind a high hedge about half a mile from the town center is a 2-acre estate comprising the main inn, a white Greek Revival built in 1839 by packet-boat captain Hiram Harding; the attached Carriage House, a three-quarter Cape; and the Captain's Cottage, a full Cape with a 200-year-old bow roof, set in its own yard.

Though the general style of the inn is Williamsburg—with historic-reproduction wallpapers, mostly king- or queen-size canopy or other antique beds, and upholstered wing chairs, as well as fluffy comforters and modern tile baths—each guest room has its own personality. Carriage House III is spacious and serene, with an antique canopied four-poster, tapestry-upholstered wing chairs, and nubby white and wheat wall-to-wall carpeting under a high cathedral ceiling. In the Captain's Cottage, the spectacular Hiram Harding Room has 200-year-old hand-hewn beams and a wall of Early American raised walnut paneling centered by a large fireplace, a seating area with a sofa, an antique spinning wheel, and a rich red Oriental carpet.

In the main inn, the variable-width pumpkin pine floors of the entry hall softly shine with age. Here and in the parlor, where a hearth fire sets a welcoming tone, impeccably chosen antiques are accompanied by luxurious Oriental carpets and oil paintings of sea captains. French doors lead to the white and bright glassed-in sun room, where breakfast and a lavish English tea (with homemade scones, jams, and cream) are served on Wedgwood and crystal at individual tables.

Dave and Cathy Eakins bought the inn in 1983 after leaving jobs in New York City as an investment manager and an office manager, respectively. Cathy, who does all the decorating and cooking, is a quietly gracious host. Dave—a more gregarious "type A," as he puts it—tends to much of the business. A well-trained staff ensures that their high standards are maintained while allowing the innkeepers time to provide the level of personal service one expects from a fine country inn.

Address: *371 Old Harbor Rd., Chatham, MA 02633, tel. 508/945–0127, fax 508/945–9406.*
Accommodations: *14 double rooms with baths, 2 suites.*
Amenities: *Individual heat and air-conditioning in rooms, triple sheeting.*
Rates: *$129–$199; Continental breakfast and afternoon tea. AE, MC, V.*
Restrictions: *No smoking, no pets. Closed mid-Nov.–mid-Feb.*

Chatham Bars Inn

Perched majestically atop a rise overlooking Pleasant Bay, just a stroll from the shops of Chatham, is this ultimate oceanfront resort in the old style. Once a kind of private club for the wealthy, Chatham Bars remains a traditionally classy inn. Built as a hunting lodge in 1914, the inn consists of the crescent-shape main building and 26 one- to eight-bedroom cottages (either in wooded groupings near the main inn or across the street on the bluff above the beach) on 20 landscaped acres. It has been completely overhauled by owners Alan Green and William Langelier to create a casual Cape Cod elegance—though you'll feel free to dress in your best in season (no jeans or T-shirts in common areas after 6 PM).

Off the grand entry hall is the airy and bright South Lounge, with groupings of white wicker and chintz, large potted palms, and an enormous fireplace; the brick terrace, with views out to the bay and the famous sandbars; and a year-round casual restaurant and bar. Simple elegance is the theme in the main dining room, with an expansive view of the sea from the window wall. The decor is bright and crisp, with a deep green rug setting off the white accents. A lavish breakfast buffet is served here each morning, with fresh fruits, sliced meats and smoked fish, finger pastries, and more; hot dishes are also available. The dinner menu centers on creative New England fare. A beachfront grill has lighter meals and clambakes in summer.

Most rooms have decks. All the cottages have common rooms, some with fireplaces. Throughout, rooms are carpeted in shades of sand and sea and are attractively decorated with furnishings including traditional pine, more modern upholstered pieces, Queen Anne reproductions, gilt-framed art, and Laura Ashley touches.

An excellent time to sample the inn's offerings is from October through May, through inexpensive midweek bed-and-breakfast packages or well-organized mystery, swing dancing, or other theme weekends.

Address: *Shore Rd., Chatham, MA 02633, tel. 508/945–0096 or 800/527–4884, fax 508/945–5491.*
Accommodations: *130 double rooms with baths, 20 suites.*
Amenities: *3 restaurants, all rooms with phones and cable TV, lending library, cottages with common minifridges; private beach, 4 tennis courts, lessons, putting green, heated outdoor pool, fitness room, volleyball, harbor cruises, movies, cocktail parties, shuffleboard, children's program (July–Aug.), newspaper, babysitting, launch service; golf course adjacent.*
Rates: *$150–$325, 1- or 2-bedroom suites $325–$650; breakfast extra. MAP available. AE, DC, MC, V.*
Restrictions: *No pets.*

The Inn at Fernbrook

When Boston restaurateur Howard Marstons built his mansion in this quiet village of Centerville, just outside Hyannis, he hired the best—Frederick Law Olmsted, designer of New York's Central Park—to landscape it. Complete with man-made ponds, formal gardens, a vineyard, and hundreds of trees brought from all over the world by Marstons's sea captain father, the park they created made an elegant setting for the Queen Anne Victorian gem that is today The Inn at Fernbrook.

Though the original 17-acre estate has dwindled to 2, the eponymous fern-rimmed brook remains, as does part of Olmsted's design. Pebbled paths wind past a sunken, heart-shape sweetheart garden of red and pink roses, set in a heart-shape lawn; exotic trees (a Japanese cork, a weeping beech); a windmill; a vine-covered arbor; and two fish ponds where Japanese koi swim amid water hyacinths and lilies.

The 1881 house itself, now on the National Register of Historic Places, is a beauty, from the turreted white exterior to the fine woodwork and furnishings within. All rooms have antique or reproduction beds, 1930s-style wood table radios, and decanters of sherry with antique glasses. Some have sitting areas with bay windows, fireplaces, canopy beds, Victorian sofas, and pastel Oriental carpets on floors of cherry, maple, or oak. The spacious third-floor Olmsted Suite has two bedrooms and a living room with a fireplace under cathedral ceilings, as well as a sun deck; there's also a cottage by itself across the lawns.

Breakfast is friendly and delicious, served in the formal dining room. Brian Gallo—who left the hotel business in 1986 to join his friend Sal Di Florio in converting the house into an inn—cooks the meals, and Sal serves. On Sunday Brian regales guests with tales of the house's past: Here, onetime owner Herbert Kalmus, inventor of the Technicolor process, hosted such Hollywood friends as Gloria Swanson and Cecil B. deMille, and in the 1960s, Cardinal Spellman (who was using the house as a summer retreat) entertained John F. Kennedy and Richard Nixon. In the afternoon, minted iced tea or hot tea can be taken (on request) in the living room or on the veranda, with its wicker furniture and hanging baskets of pink geraniums.

Address: *481 Main St., Centerville, MA 02632, tel. 508/775–4334, fax 508/778–4455.*
Accommodations: *4 double rooms with baths, 1 double suite, 1 cottage (no kitchen).*
Rates: *$115–$135, cottage $105, suite $185; full breakfast. AE, MC, V.*
Restrictions: *No smoking in bedrooms, no pets. 2-night minimum summer weekends.*

Moses Nickerson House

After raising four children, Elsie Piccola opened a room or two in her New Jersey home to overnight guests—and found she liked it. So when husband Carl retired from his liquor business in 1989, they decided to look around for a house they could operate together as a B&B. "Divine intervention" led them to this just-converted 1839 home, a white Greek Revival with gray-blue shutters and large fan ornament (incidentally, just across the street from the Captain's House Inn).

Named for the whaling captain who built the house, their B&B today expresses their love of fine antiques, attention to detail, and warm, thoughtful hospitality. The formal dining room gleams with crystal used at breakfast in the glassed-in sun room, which looks out onto a garden and fountain. In the afternoon, Elsie and Carl join guests for tea or wine in the parlor, which features a fireplace, an Aubusson rug, a lyre-base Duncan Phyfe table, Cape Cod cranberry glass, and a hand-carved Mexican horse inlaid with agates.

All the rooms have wide-board pine floors, pedestal sinks, and firm queen-size beds with comforters, color-coordinated linens, and lots of pillows; several have gas-log fireplaces. Special touches include stenciling in closets, scented drawer liners, padded clothes hangers, and dimmer switches on reading lamps.

Room 7 is clubby and masculine, with Ralph Lauren fabrics, dark leathers and woods, and a fireplace; on the walls hang hunting hats and horns. In lovely Room 4, a feather bed sits aloft a high canopy bed mounted by stepstool; a wood rack displays antique laces and linens, and the blue of a hand-hooked Nantucket rug is echoed in the pale blue walls. Off the parlor is Room 1, with a romantic antique four-poster and armoire hand-painted with roses, and a blue velvet Belgian settee invitingly placed before a fireplace.

Address: *364 Old Harbor Rd., Chatham, MA 02633, tel. 508/945–5859 or 800/628–6972.*
Accommodations: *7 double rooms with baths.*
Amenities: *Individual heat in rooms, complimentary fruit and sherry, turndown service.*
Rates: *\$99–\$149; full breakfast and afternoon wine or tea. AE, MC, V.*
Restrictions: *No smoking, no pets. 2-night minimum summer weekends, 3 nights on major holidays, closed Jan.–Valentine's Day.*

Ashley Manor

Set off from the Old King's Highway by a high privet hedge is this gabled Colonial, built in 1699 with additions. The brick patio out back overlooks the inn's 2 quiet acres, complete with tree-shaded tennis court and a new little rose-trellised fountain garden.

Inside, the public rooms are large and bright; the living room has a fireplace, Oriental rugs, and a grand piano. Guest rooms combine antiques with such modern comforts as coffeemakers and large baths with hair dryers; all but one has a fireplace. One has a private terrace under the trees; a separate cottage room has a kitchenette for light cooking and sliders out to a deck.

Innkeepers Donald and Fay Bain—formerly a New York lawyer and an advertising executive, respectively—preside over a gourmet breakfast, served by fire- and candlelight on Lowestoft and Spode china in the formal dining room or on the terrace.

Address: *3660 Main St. (Rte. 6A), Box 856, Barnstable, MA 02630, tel. 508/362–8044.*
Accommodations: *2 double rooms with baths, 4 suites.*
Amenities: *All-weather tennis court, bicycles, croquet.*
Rates: *$100–$165; full breakfast, and afternoon wine and refreshments. AE, MC, V.*
Restrictions: *Smoking restricted, no pets. 2-night minimum on weekends June–Sept., sometimes longer on holiday weekends.*

Augustus Snow House

From baths with whirlpools to Gucci toiletries, luxury is the operative word at this inn, a turn-of-the-century Princess Anne Victorian with gabled dormers and a wraparound veranda. Thoroughly restored by owner Anne Geuss, it has been decorated in painstaking period detail, including reproduction and antique furnishings, dark Victorian-print wallpapers, and antique brass bathroom and lighting fixtures. Room 5 is an exception, done in a light, airy country style in cornflower blue and pale yellow.

In the afternoon, the two oak-paneled Victorian front rooms are opened to the public for an English tea. The pretty restaurant downstairs, offering creative American cuisine, features old brick and raised-wood paneling over a carpet of roses. At breakfast, order whatever you like.

In season, guests can relax in a wicker-filled screened porch. In the off-season there is no common room.

Address: *528 Main St., Harwich Port, MA 02646, tel. 508/430–0528 or 800/339–0528 in MA.*
Accommodations: *5 double rooms with baths.*
Amenities: *Restaurant, tea room, phones, and cable TV in rooms, 3 rooms with whirlpool tubs, turndown service.*
Rates: *$135–$150; full breakfast. AE, MC, V.*
Restrictions: *No smoking in common areas, no pets. 2-night minimum weekends in season.*

Bacon Barn Inn

All the great, hand-hewn beams and open space of an 1830 dairy barn have been combined with the rosy loveliness of the English country style to create a warm and expansive bed-and-breakfast, surrounded by a lawn and gardens, just off Route 6A and a short walk to the village.

Innkeeper Mary Giuffreda and her husband, Robert, a Boston contractor, bought this converted gray clapboard barn with cupola in 1989. She put her love of decorating to work, creating romantic rooms where white walls and beam-crossed ceilings (some cathedral) form a bright background for flowered chintzes, hand-hooked rugs, dried roses, and painted boxes, all in shades of rose and blue.

The guest rooms are on the second floor. The feeling of the loft it once was is retained in the spacious, high-ceilinged common room (also done in rose florals). Gourmet breakfasts are served on the sun porch or at the dining table by the common room's fireplace.

Address: *3400 Main St., (Rte. 6A), Box 621, Barnstable, MA 02630, tel. 508/362–5518 or (for area codes 617 and 508) 800/696–5518.*
Accommodations: *3 double rooms with baths.*
Amenities: *Common cable TV, croquet.*
Rates: *$85; full breakfast. No credit cards.*
Restrictions: *No smoking, no pets. 2-night minimum mid-May–Oct.*

Bay Beach

If you're looking for a place where you can step out your sliding glass doors and in a minute be plunging into the sea, this B&B is calling your name. A mile's walk from Sandwich center via a boardwalk, this modern bayfront house is surrounded on three sides by beach grass.

The decor is contemporary, with lots of light wood, skylights, sand-color carpeting, rattan, pastel fabrics, and brass. The spacious guest rooms have air conditioning, minifridges, cable TV, phones, and bright new baths with hair dryers and heat lamps; some have CD/cassette players and radios.

The Sandcaper, a popular honeymoon suite, has a two-person Jacuzzi. Behind the bed is a mirrored wall.

Emily and Reale Lemieux, innkeepers since 1988, believe in remaining unobtrusive yet always within reach. Breakfast is set out buffet style so you can enjoy it in your room, on your private deck, in the living room, or on the waterfront common deck.

Address: *1–3 Bay Beach La., Box 151, Sandwich, MA 02563, tel. 508/888–8813.*
Accommodations: *4 double rooms with baths.*
Amenities: *Lifestep and Lifecycle machines, newspaper; private beach, beach chairs, bikes.*
Rates: *$125–$175; Continental breakfast, wine and cheese on arrival.*
Restrictions: *No smoking, no pets. 2-night minimum weekends, 3 nights on holidays; closed Veteran's Day–Apr.*

Beechwood

This 1853 Queen Anne Victorian, painted yellow and pale green and trimmed with gingerbread is on the tree-lined Old King's Highway. Wrapping it on three sides is a porch where wicker chairs and rockers sit beneath wind chimes in the shade of an ancient weeping beech.

Hosts Anne and Bob Livermore—a former teacher and engineer, respectively, who moved here from St. Louis in 1986—have kept up the theme inside. In the parlor, mahogany and red velvet furnishings blend with Victorian-patterned wallpaper. In a cozy adjacent room with wainscoting, a pressed-tin ceiling, and a fireplace, breakfast is served at tables covered in lace and set with hurricane lamps, flowers, china, and crystal. Pedestal sinks, antique plumbing and lighting fixtures, wicker pieces, Oriental rugs, and lacy curtains pick up the theme in the guest rooms, done in a lighter, early Victorian style. An exception is Rose, featuring a high, queen-size mahogany four-poster bed, a crocheted canopy and spread, and a red velvet fainting couch.

Address: *2839 Main St. (Rte. 6A), Barnstable, MA 02630, tel. 508/362–6618.*
Accommodations: *6 double rooms with baths.*
Amenities: *Air-conditioning in 1 room, fireplaces in 2 rooms, minifridges.*
Rates: *$100–$135; full breakfast, afternoon tea on request. AE, MC, V.*
Restrictions: *No smoking in common rooms, no pets. 2-night minimum weekends in season.*

Brewster Farmhouse

This 1845 farmhouse blends gently with its surroundings, across from a 19th-century windmill on historic Route 6A. Through its portals, however, some lovely 20th-century surprises await you. Sliding glass doors lead from the small, fireplaced common area to a patio with café tables. Beyond is a 2-acre backyard rimmed with apple trees and grapevines and centered by a pool and spa.

Joe Zelich and Robert Messina, former teachers from New York, moved to the Cape in 1984 to run a hotel and bought this place in July 1992. They have created sophisticated guest rooms with large modern baths, Lane reproduction furnishings, wood shutters, quilts, goose-down pillows, thick white towels, terry robes, hair dryers, and sherry and chocolates by the bed.

The large downstairs rooms include one with a fireplace, one with a king-size rice bed and sliders out to a private patio, and a third with a mammoth acorn-carved queen four-poster bed.
Address: *716 Main St., Brewster, MA 02631, tel. 508/896–3910 or 800/892–3910, fax 508/896–4232.*
Accommodations: *3 double rooms with baths, 2 doubles share 1 bath.*
Amenities: *Cable TV in rooms, air-conditioning, turndown service, fax; heated pool, spa, beach towels and blankets.*
Rates: *$85–$140; full breakfast and afternoon tea. AE, DC, MC, V.*
Restrictions: *No smoking in bedrooms, no pets. Closed Jan.–Mar.*

Honeysuckle Hill

Along a particularly rural stretch of Route 6A sits this homey B&B run since 1986 by former St. Louisan Barbara Rosenthal. Listed in the National Register of Historic Places, the 1810 farmhouse is furnished in a cozy Cape version of English country, including chintz, Claire Murray hooked rugs, and unintimidating antiques. The Victorian-and-chintz Rose Room has a wood-burning fireplace. Though supplemented by upscale amenities like English toiletries and feather beds with Laura Ashley linens, down comforters, and handmade quilts, more characteristic of the tone of the place are such touches as ice water and homebaked cookies by the bedside.

Barbara and her two small dogs may join you in the spacious Great Room, with a wood-burning potbellied stove, TV, games table and dart board, and two great clocks: a carved Black Forest cuckoo that plays "Edelweiss" and a charming Bristol-made grandfather clock. Double French doors look onto the backyard's flowering trees, honeysuckle and wisteria vines, fish pond, and rock garden.

Address: *591 Rte. 6A, West Barnstable, MA 02668, tel. 508/362–8418 or 800/441–8418.*
Accommodations: *3 double rooms with baths.*
Amenities: *Air-conditioning, common cable TV with VCR; bicycles, beach towels, chairs, umbrellas, croquet.*
Rates: *$90–$110; full breakfast and afternoon tea. AE, D, MC, V.*
Restrictions: *No smoking in dining room.*

Isaiah Clark House

The main house—a three-quarter Cape with colonial-style decor—retains the flavor of its 1780 origins, in painted variable-width floorboards, old fireplace mantels and moldings, narrow staircases, and the original keeping room. Some rooms have queen canopy beds, wood-burning fireplaces, or Oriental rugs, and one has a bed under a skylight that lets you view the stars. The Rose Cottage is good for families, with a kitchen, a dining room, a sitting room with fireplace, and a backyard barbecue.

Innkeeper Charles DiCesare offers such delights as cranberry pancakes with three-berry butter at breakfast. It is served either in the keeping room or on the sunny deck overlooking the backyard, where you'll find 5 acres of woods, gardens, and a pond, adjacent to a nature preserve.

Address: *1187 Rte. 6A, Box 169, Brewster, MA 02631, tel. 508/896–2223 or 800/822–4001, fax 508/896–7054.*
Accommodations: *8 double rooms with baths, 4 doubles share 2 baths.*
Amenities: *Air-conditioning, phones, and cable TVs in main house rooms; common TV with VCR and movies, stereo, CD, piano; turndown service; bikes, games, beach chairs and towels, airport or train-station pickup.*
Rates: *$80–$108 double rooms with baths, $68 doubles with shared bath; full breakfast, afternoon tea, evening cookies and milk on request. AE, D, MC, V.*
Restrictions: *No smoking in bedrooms, no pets. 2-night minimum weekends in season.*

Isaiah Hall B&B Inn

Lilacs and pink roses trail along the white picket fence outside this 1857 Greek Revival farmhouse. Inside, the cheerful, unfussy decor features country antiques, some canopy beds, floral-print wallpapers, and such homey touches as quilts and priscilla curtains.

In the main house's Early American common room, a coal-burning stove is set inside the fireplace of the original kitchen, complete with beehive oven and proofing cabinet. In the attached carriage house, rooms have a Cape Cod, cabin-like look, with three stenciled white walls, one knotty pine; several have small balconies overlooking a wooded lawn with grape arbors, berry bushes, and a net for games. A camp like TV room features a potbellied stove.

Innkeeper Marie Brophy has provided such thoughtful extras as radio alarm clocks, ironing boards, full-length mirrors, and robes in every room. Make-it-yourself popcorn, tea and coffee, and soft drinks are always available.

Address: *152 Whig St., Dennis, MA 02638, tel. 508/385–9928 or 800/736–0160, fax 508/385–5879.*
Accommodations: *10 double rooms with baths, 1 double shares bath with housekeepers in season.*
Amenities: *Common TV and fridge, no-smoking rooms; croquet, badminton, picnic tables, grills.*
Rates: *$55–$98; Continental breakfast. AE, MC, V.*
Restrictions: *No pets. 2-night minimum in season and holidays, closed mid-Oct.–Mar.*

Isaiah Jones Homestead

The third of our Isaiahs was built in 1849, and everything in it reflects the early Victorian era—from fine antiques, Oriental carpets, and elegant window treatments to such period accents as fringed lamp shades, leather-bound books, and a beaded bag on a dresser. Innkeeper Shirley Jones Sutton, who acquired the inn in 1992, serves breakfast by candlelight, and the sitting room offers a fireplace.

The two first-floor rooms have 11-foot ceilings and knockout antique-reproduction beds, including a massive Empire four-poster with fish-net canopy and a high mahogany bed with pineapple finials on posts encrusted with leaf carvings. Up the curving staircase is the sweet Lombard Jones Room, with white eyelet bedding, white wicker, mosquito-net tenting over the bed. The Deming Jarves Room, the pièce de résistance, has seafoam-green wallpaper, a pile rug, and a stunning suite of burled birch, including a tester bed (with burgundy damask spread and half-canopy), an armoire, and a cheval mirror. The mauve-tile bath has a whirlpool tub.

Address: *165 Main St., Sandwich, MA 02563, tel. 508/888–9115 or 800/526–1625.*
Accommodations: *5 double rooms with baths.*
Amenities: *1 room with fireplace.*
Rates: *$85–$119; full breakfast, afternoon tea. AE, D, MC, V.*
Restrictions: *Smoking only on front porch, no pets.*

Liberty Hill

Beth and Jack Flanagan's 1825 Greek Revival mansion with a portico of white fluted columns stands on a rise in an attractive setting of flower-edged lawn. Guest rooms are large and bright, with high ceilings, tall windows, interesting moldings, painted floorboards, and individual heat controls. The decor is uncluttered but warm, with soft colors (peach, light colonial blue, cream), fine antiques, upholstered chairs, thick carpets or Oriental rugs on wide-board floors, Laura Ashley fabrics, Roman shades, and pretty wallpapers. The third-floor Waterford Room, up a private staircase, features a king-size bed and a large bath.

Gourmet breakfasts, such as baked eggs with shrimp sauce, or soufflés, are served at individual tables. In the afternoon, cookies and tea or iced tea can be taken on the veranda or in the common room, formally furnished in the Queen Anne and Chippendale styles.

Address: *77 Main St. (Rte. 6A), Yarmouth Port, MA 02675, tel. 508/362–3976 or 800/821–3977.*
Accommodations: *5 double rooms with baths.*
Amenities: *2 rooms with air-conditioning, common TV, minifridge with mixers; train or airport pickup.*
Rates: *$90–$125; full breakfast and afternoon tea. Dinner on request. AE, MC, V.*
Restrictions: *No smoking in dining room, no pets. 2-night minimum on major holiday weekends.*

Mostly Hall

This inn, behind a high wrought-iron fence, looks very much like a private estate. Built in 1849 by a sea captain for his New Orleans bride, the gray clapboard structure has a porch that wraps the entire first floor, and a dramatic cupola. Named for its large central hallways, the inn offers corner rooms with leafy views, shuttered casement windows, reproduction queen-size canopy beds, floral wallpapers, and wall-to-wall carpeting. Ground-floor rooms have 13-foot ceilings. Most baths are small.

Jim and Caroline Lloyd, innkeepers since 1986, are warm and helpful hosts. Jim's love of clocks is reflected in the fireplaced Victorian-eclectic sitting room, where an 1890 Paris mantel clock and four others chime the hour. Caroline shines at breakfast, with such treats as French toast stuffed with cream cheese and walnuts. The inn is just steps from the shops of Falmouth and a few miles away from Woods Hole and the Vineyard ferry.

Address: *27 Main St., Falmouth, MA 02540, tel. 508/548–3786 or 800/682–0565.*
Accommodations: *6 double rooms with baths.*
Amenities: *Air-conditioning in rooms, common TV/VCR, piano, lending library; bicycles.*
Rates: *$105; full breakfast and afternoon tea. MC, V.*
Restrictions: *No smoking, no pets. 2-night minimum usually in season, weekends year-round; closed Jan.–mid-Feb.*

Village Green Inn

In 1986, two former schoolteachers, Linda and Don Long, turned this turreted white Victorian (actually built in 1804 and Victorianized in 1894) across from the Falmouth green into a bed-and-breakfast. In doing so, they preserved the fine old woodwork and hardwood floors (one with inlay from 1890, in a front room with a view of the green from a picture window topped by stained glass) and such atmospheric details as an elaborately designed forced-hot-water radiator and the embossed-tin ceiling and half-wall (the other half is raised oak paneling) in one bath. To this promising start they added tasteful furnishings and modern comforts. The spacious guest rooms have antique and reproduction queen-size beds, comforters, dust ruffles, floral-print wallpapers in soft Victorian colors, and some working fireplaces.

Breakfast includes such hot entrées as apple-filled German pancakes or chili-cheese egg puffs. Seasonal beverages, such as sherry, hot cider, or lemonade, are served on the veranda, set with wicker and hanging geraniums, or in the elegant guest parlor, with a Victorian fireplace.

Address: *40 W. Main St., Falmouth, MA 02540, tel. 508/548–5621.*
Accommodations: *4 double rooms with baths, 1 suite.*
Amenities: *Cable TV in suite, common TV, piano; bikes.*
Rates: *$90–$110; full breakfast. AE, MC, V.*
Restrictions: *Smoking on porch only, no pets. 2-night minimum on holiday weekends.*

Wedgewood Inn

Next door to Liberty Hill is another handsome Greek Revival building on the National Register of Historic Places, this one from 1812. White with black shutters, the facade has a front door with sidelights and fanlight and a large fan ornament over a third-floor window. Inside, the decor is sophisticated country, a mix of fine Colonial antiques, handcrafted cherry pencil-post beds, upholstered wing chairs, Oriental rugs on wide-board floors, English sporting prints and maritime paintings, brass accents, antique quilts, Claire Murray hooked rugs, period wallpapers, and wood-burning fireplaces. Two spacious suites have canopy beds, fireplaces, and porches; one has a separate den with a sofa bed and a bay window.

Innkeeper Gerrie Graham cooks elegant breakfasts such as Belgian waffles with whipped cream and strawberries, or egg dishes with hollandaise. Milt, her husband, a former Boston Patriot and FBI agent, serves breakfast and helps guests make plans for the day. In the afternoon, a tray of tea and cookies is brought to rooms.

Address: *83 Main St., Yarmouth Port, MA 02675, tel. 508/362–5157 or 508/362–9178.*
Accommodations: *4 double rooms with baths, 2 suites.*
Amenities: *Air-conditioning in rooms, common TV; bicycles.*
Rates: *$105–$130, $130–$150 suites; full breakfast and afternoon tea. AE, DC, MC, V.*
Restrictions: *No smoking in common areas, no pets.*

Martha's Vineyard

Much less developed than mainland Cape Cod, yet more diverse and cosmopolitan than neighboring Nantucket, Martha's Vineyard is an island with a split personality. From Memorial Day through Labor Day the island is a vibrant, star-studded event. Edgartown is flooded with day-trippers who've come to wander its tidy streets lined with chic boutiques and stately Federal and Greek Revival homes built by whaling captains. Oak Bluffs has a boardwalk-town atmosphere, with pizza and ice-cream shops, a popular dance club, and several bars, all teeming with the high-spirited, tanned young people.

Multicolor towels blanket the spectacular, miles-long beaches, while the harbors fill with snapping sails and gleaming luxury yachts. Summer residents, including such celebrity regulars as Walter Cronkite, Jacqueline Onassis, and Carly Simon, fill the cottages and homes. Island concerts, theater, dance, and lectures feature first-rate performers and speakers, while the many nature preserves, a county fair, farmers' markets, and fireworks viewed from the Oak Bluffs green provide earthier pleasures.

The Vineyard's summer persona is the one most people come for, but to some, its other self is even more appealing, for in the off-season the island becomes a place of peace and simple but breathtaking beauty. On drives or bike rides through the agricultural heart of the island, there's time to linger over views of grazing sheep, horses, even llamas, in fields bounded by dry stone walls, ponds, and sea. The beaches, always lovely, can then be appreciated in solitude, and the water seems to sparkle more under the crisp blue skies.

The locals, too, are at their best in the off-season. After struggling to make the most of the short money-making season, they reestablish contact with friends and take up pastimes previously crowded out by work. Cultural, educational, and recreational events are offered year-round, and a number of inns, restaurants, and shops remain open to serve visitors wise enough to seek out the island's quieter charms.

Places to Go, Sights to See

Felix Neck Wildlife Sanctuary. Felix Neck (tel. 508/627–4850), off the Edgartown-Vineyard Haven Road, is laced with 6 miles of self-guided trails traversing marshland, fields, woods, and seashore. Activities such as guided nature and birding walks are held regularly.

Flying Horses. In Oak Bluffs, the many lures for children (an arcade, a slush shop . . .) include an 1876 carousel that still offers the brass ring.

Gay Head Cliffs. These dramatically striated red-clay cliffs at the island's western tip are its major tourist site, as a parking lot perpetually full of buses will attest. The approach to the overlook—from which the Elizabeth Islands are visible across the sound—is lined with shops selling Native American crafts and fast food (Gay Head is a Native American township). A casual restaurant, the *Aquinnah* (tel. 508/645–3326), commands a great view, especially at sunset.

Menemsha. This little fishing village on the west coast is one of New England's most charming. The jumble of fishing and pleasure boats and of drying lobster pots and nets along the dock may seem familiar—location shots for the movie *Jaws* were filmed here. Besides fish markets and summer boutiques, the village offers a beach (good for sunset picnics), fishing from the jetty, and a seasonal restaurant, *Home Port* (tel. 508/645–2679), with fresh seafood and wonderful vistas of sunset. Save room for an ice-cream sundae across the way.

Oak Bluffs Camp Ground. In a little enclave of town, dozens of Carpenter Gothic Victorian cottages, gaily painted and trimmed in lacy filigree, are gathered tightly together, just as the tests they replaced once were. The cottages were built in the late 1800s by Methodists who in 1835 began to come to the area for a retreat; Oak Bluffs then turned into a popular Victorian summer playground. The spirit of the Camp Meeting is revived in a community sing, held Wednesday nights in season.

Beaches

Joseph Sylvia State Beach, between Oak Bluffs and Edgartown, is a mile-long sandy beach on Nantucket Sound. The calm, warm water makes it popular with families. **Menemsha Beach,** adjacent to the fishing village, is a sandy beach on Vineyard Sound, backed by dunes. Located on the western side of the island, it is a great place to catch the sunset. **South Beach** is a popular 3-mile ribbon of sand on the Atlantic, with strong surf and sometimes riptides. From Edgartown, take the 2-mile bike path to Katama or catch the half-hourly shuttle at the corner of Main and Church streets. **Wasque Beach,** on Chappaquiddick Island, is reached via a ferry from Edgartown (it runs from about 7 AM to midnight in season) and then a drive or bike ride east. Part of a wildlife refuge, it offers heavy surf, good bird-watching, and relative isolation.

Restaurants

Lambert's Cove Country Inn (tel. 508/693–2298) in West Tisbury and the **Beach Plum Inn** (tel. 508/645–9454) in Menemsha offer fine Continental dining in attractive wooded settings. The sophisticated **Oyster Bar** (tel. 508/693–3300), in the center of Oak Bluffs, has a raw bar and an extensive daily selection of fresh seafood cooked virtually any way. Also in Oak Bluffs is **Zapotec** (tel. 508/693–6800), with inexpensive, creative Mexican food and an intimate, fun atmosphere.

Dance Clubs

Hot Tin Roof (tel. 508/693–0320), at the airport, is larger and has a bit more live rock and reggae music than the year-round **Atlantic Connection** (tel. 508/693–7129) in Oak Bluffs, which has a fancy light system.

Tourist Information

Martha's Vineyard Chamber of Commerce (Box 1698, Beach Rd., Vineyard Haven, MA 02568, tel. 508/693–0085).

Reservations Services

Martha's Vineyard and Nantucket Reservations (Box 1322, Vineyard Haven, MA 02568, tel. 508/693–7200); **Accommodations Plus** (RFD 273, Edgartown, MA 02539, tel. 508/627–7374); **House Guests Cape Cod and the Islands** (Box 1881, Orleans, MA 02653, tel. 508/896–7053 or 800/666–4678).

Charlotte Inn

On a quiet street in the center of well-groomed Edgartown is an inn that stands out like a polished gem. Gery Conover, owner for over 20 years, and his wife, Paula, oversee every detail with meticulous care and obvious pride to make sure their guests find everything fresh, pretty, welcoming—and perfect. From the original structure, an 1860 white clapboard home that belonged to a whaling-company owner, the Charlotte has grown into a five-building complex connected by lawns and a private courtyard. Ivy-bordered brick walkways lead past pockets of garden to flower-filled nooks perfect for reading or reflection. Across the street is the early 18th-century Garden House; one gorgeous room has French doors out to a private terrace looking onto a large English garden.

True Anglophiles, the Conovers have furnished the inn through antiquing trips to England—and continue to do so, since each room is redone completely every five years. Guest rooms feature mahogany furniture, brass lamps, original art, richly colored wallpapers, lush fabrics, and down-filled pillows, comforters, and chair cushions. One room in the veranda-wrapped 1850 Summer House has a fireplace and a baby grand piano.

The most exquisite accommodations on the island are here, in the Coach House. Set above a re-created estate garage lined with gleaming wainscoting, the suite features cathedral ceilings, a Palladian window, French doors, a green marble fireplace, and sumptuous furnishings. Everywhere you look, there's something wonderful: sterling silver lamps, Minton bone china, white cutwork-lace bed linens.

The main inn's ground floor is spacious and elegant, with the gallery's sporting and marine art and contemporary works displayed throughout. A shop selling small antiques will move across the street in 1993. Its space in the inn will become a mahogany-paneled common room.

The fine restaurant, L'étoile, set in a glassed-in summerhouse with patio, serves dinner and Sunday brunch. It mixes luxuriant greenery, spotlighted oil paintings, and surprising antique accents, such as leather-bound books perched on the rafters. The contemporary French menu highlights native seafood and game.

Address: *S. Summer St., Edgartown, MA 02539, tel. 508/627–4751.*
Accommodations: *21 double rooms with baths, 3 suites.*
Amenities: *Restaurant, gallery, shop; air-conditioning, TV, and phones in some rooms, fireplaces in 5 rooms; common TV.*
Rates: *$195–$350, suites $350–$450; Continental breakfast (Mon.–Sat.) and afternoon tea. AE, MC, V.*
Restrictions: *No pets. Restaurant closed Jan.–mid-Feb.*

Lambert's Cove Country Inn

Approached via a narrow, winding road through pine woods, this secluded retreat is everything a country inn should be. The 1790 farmhouse is set amid an apple orchard, a large English garden bordered by lilac bushes, and woods that hide a tennis court. In spring, an ancient tree is draped in blossoms from 20-foot wisteria vines (photo spot for many weddings held here); in fall, a Concord grape arbor scents the air.

The inn's common areas are elegant, with rich woodwork and large flower arrangements, yet also make you feel at home. Most impressive is the gentleman's library, part of the additions made in the 1920s. This large, airy room features booklined white walls, a fireside grouping of upholstered wing chairs, rich red Oriental carpets on a polished wood floor, and French doors leading out to the orchard. A cozier reading area on the second-floor landing offers a sofa and shelves of books and magazines.

The guest rooms are in the main house and in two adjacent buildings. Most main-house rooms have a soft, soothing country look, framed by Laura Ashley wallpapers; two at the back can convert to a suite with a connecting sitting room with sleep sofa and sliders opening onto a backyard deck. Rooms in the other houses have a bit more rustic feel. Two rooms upstairs in The Barn have exposed beams; downstairs, one large room with a sofa bed has sliders out to a deck. The Carriage House has camp-style decks and screened porches. Comfort is the focus, meaning unfussy furnishings, firm beds with electric blankets, and bright, cheerful baths with extra-thick towels.

Fine dining is part of the experience, and the romantic restaurant serves unpretentious, excellent Continental cuisine in an intimate atmosphere of soft lighting and music. The popular Sunday brunch is served on a deck overlooking the orchard, weather permitting.

Innkeepers since summer 1992 are Russ Wilson and Marchele Kowalski, whose previous experience includes stints with Marriott, Hilton, and the Los Angeles Biltmore.

Address: *Lambert's Cove Rd., West Tisbury, RR1, Box 422, West Tisbury, MA 02575, tel. 508/693–2298, fax 508/693–7890.*
Accommodations: *15 double rooms with baths.*
Amenities: *Restaurant (dinner and Sun. brunch; off-season, weekends only); some rooms with air-conditioning, 1 room with fireplace, common TV; tennis court, beach passes.*
Rates: *$120–$145; Continental breakfast. AE, MC, V.*
Restrictions: *No smoking in common areas, no pets. 3-night minimum most weekends July–Aug.*

Oak House

Among the summer homes along the coast road just outside Oak Bluffs center stands the Oak House bed-and-breakfast. Built in 1872 and enlarged and lavishly refurbished in the early 1900s, this wonderful Victorian beach house features a playful gingerbread-trimmed pastel facade and a wrap-around veranda with much-used rockers and even a swing or two.

Inside, the reason for the inn's name becomes clear: Everywhere you look, you see richly patinated oak, in ceilings, wall paneling, wainscoting, and furnishings. The two bedrooms that constitute the Captain's Room are fitted out like cabins in a ship, with oak wainscoting covering walls and ceilings. The best of the rooms with balconies (some just large enough for a chair) is the Governor Claflin Room, with French doors that open wide to let in a broad expanse of sea and sky. Unfortunately, cars whiz past on the road below, which some people may find distracting (a room at the back is one solution).

When the Convery family bought the Oak House in 1988, they created several tiny bathrooms out of existing closets. One spacious hall bath, with peach-painted pressed-tin walls and ceiling, a dressing table, and the inn's only tub, was turned into a private bath for the very feminine Tivoli Room. (Each room has a distinct personality.)

Alison Convery's island antiques shops provided much of the inn's superb furniture, brass lamps, sea chests, and such. The entrance hall evokes an elegant Victorian private home, with high ceilings, a baby grand piano, a hand-cranked organ, potted palms, and an impressive central staircase lined with sumptuous red Oriental carpeting. The glassed-in sun porch has lots of white wicker, plants, floral print pillows, and original stained-glass window accents.

In the afternoon, guests wander back from the beach (across the street) to meet and chat over tea. Homemade lemonade and iced tea, along with elegant tea cakes and cookies, are provided by Alison's daughter Betsi Convery-Luce, the warm and open innkeeper and a Cordon Bleu-trained pastry chef.

Address: *Sea View Ave., Box 299, Oak Bluffs, MA 02557, tel. 508/693–4187.*
Accommodations: *8 double rooms with baths, 2 suites.*
Amenities: *4 rooms with air-conditioning, TV in 1 room and in suites, common TV.*
Rates: *$110–$160, $220 suites; Continental breakfast and afternoon tea. D, MC, V.*
Restrictions: *No pets. 3-night minimum most summer weekends, closed mid-Oct.–mid-May.*

Outermost Inn

In 1990, Hugh and Jeanne Taylor finished converting the sprawling, gray-shingle home they built 20 years ago—and are raising their two children in—into a bed-and-breakfast. Hugh's redesign takes full advantage of the superb location, at the sparsely populated outermost western end of the island. Standing alone on acres of wide-open moorland, the two-story house is wrapped with picture windows that reveal breathtaking views of sea and sky in three directions; to the north are the Elizabeth Islands and, beyond, mainland Cape Cod. The sweeping red and white beams of the Gay Head Lighthouse, just over the moors on the Gay Head Cliffs, add an extra touch of romance at night.

White walls and polished light-wood floors of ash, cherry, beech, oak, and hickory create a bright, clean setting for simple contemporary-style furnishings and local art. Fabrics used throughout the inn are all natural—in the dhurrie rugs, the down-filled cotton comforters, and the all-cotton sheets. Several corner rooms offer window walls on two sides. The Lighthouse Suite has a private entrance, a skylit bath, and a separate living room with a butcher-block dining table. The Oak Room has French doors that open onto a private deck with a great view of the lighthouse.

The wraparound porch, set with hammocks and rocking chairs, is ideal for relaxing and watching birds and deer. Breakfast is served there or in the dining room, with fireplace and window wall. In the afternoon complimentary hors d'oeuvres and setups for drinks are provided on request. In season, the inn operates a restaurant (by reservation only), offering a mix of gourmet and home cooking prepared by a Culinary Institute–trained chef—another excuse for guests not to wander far from the nest.

When you are ready to venture out, the owners are happy to help with arrangements for all kinds of activities. Hugh (of the musical Taylor clan) has sailed the local waters since childhood, and he will charter out his 50-foot catamaran to guests for excursions to Cuttyhunk Island. There's a privately accessed beach just a five-minute walk away.

Address: *Lighthouse Rd., RR 1, Box 171, Gay Head, MA 02535, tel. 508/645–3511, fax 508/645–3514.*
Accommodations: *6 double rooms with baths, 1 suite with bath.*
Amenities: *Phones in rooms, 1 room with whirlpool bath, TVs on request; beach passes.*
Rates: *$195–$220; full breakfast. AE, MC, V.*
Restrictions: *Smoking only on porch, no pets.*

Thorncroft Inn

Set amid 3½ wooded acres about a mile from town and the Vineyard Haven ferry, the Thorncroft is like a little piece of English countryside. Beyond a manicured lawn bordered in neat boxwood hedges and flowering shrubs is the tidy Craftsman bungalow, gray-green with white shutters and a dormered second story, built in 1918 as the guest house of a large estate.

Since they bought the place in 1981, Karl and Lynn Buder have renovated it from top to bottom, furnishing it beautifully with a mix of antiques and reproductions to create an environment that is elegant yet soothing, somewhat formal but not fussy. In addition, they built a Carriage House out back featuring two rooms geared for romance, with large whirlpool baths (one backed by mirrored walls) and fireplaces. Two other irresistible inn rooms have attached private hot tub rooms with screens just under the roof that let in fresh air for an Alpine effect.

Considering Lynn's master's degree in business administration and Karl's in public administration, it is not surprising that the Thorncroft—now their only business—is run as efficiently as it is.

The fine Colonial and richly carved Renaissance Revival antiques—including matched sets—are meticulously maintained. Beds are firm, floors thickly carpeted, tiled bathrooms modern and well lighted. Room fireplaces (used only in the off-season) are piled with wood and kindling each day, ready for the touch of a match. Ice buckets, wineglasses, and corkscrews are provided in each guest room, as is a notebook of information on the area. The bedrooms are wired for computer modems—for those who just *can't* leave work behind. And for those who can, there's a bookcase full of magazines on an amazing range of subjects—and a wicker sun porch in which to read them, if you like.

Breakfast is an organized affair. You sign up for one of two seatings the night before. A bell calls you to the table, where guests meet and exchange touring tips over such tasty entrées as almond French toast and sausage-cheese pie.

Address: *278 Main St., Box 1022, Vineyard Haven, MA 02568, tel. 508/693–3333 or 800/332–1236, fax 508/693–5419.*
Accommodations: *12 double rooms with baths, 1 suite.*
Amenities: *Air-conditioning, phones, and fireplaces in 9 rooms; whirlpools, hot tubs, cable TV, and minifridges in some rooms; turndown service, newspaper, common TV, and minifridge.*
Rates: *$129–$299; full breakfast and afternoon tea. AE, D, MC, V.*
Restrictions: *No smoking, no pets.*

Admiral Benbow Inn

Separated from the busy road between Vineyard Haven and Oak Bluffs by a white picket fence and a tree-shaded lawn, this small, homey bed-and-breakfast, converted in 1985, remains much as it was when it was built for a minister at the turn of the century. Throughout the house, the elaborate woodwork has been preserved. The Victorian parlor boasts a stunning nonworking fireplace, with a frame of carved wood and ceramic bas-relief.

The guest rooms (try to avoid a room on the side facing the gas station) are furnished in a pleasant hodgepodge of antiques, including brass beds and some Victorian pieces. Victorian-inspired wallpapers add to the period feel. In the country-formal dining room, innkeeper Lynn Brew—a young mother who lives upstairs with her husband and two small children—serves a cold breakfast buffet of pastries, fruits, granola, cereals, and juices, as well as hot entrées.

Address: *520 New York Ave., Box 2488, Oak Bluffs, MA 02557, tel. 508/693–6825.*
Accommodations: *7 double rooms with baths.*
Amenities: *TV in common area.*
Rates: *$85–$130; full breakfast and afternoon tea. AE, MC, V.*
Restrictions: *No smoking, no pets. 2-night minimum weekends, 3 nights on holidays; closed Jan.*

Aldworth Manor

A 10-minute walk from Main Street brings you to a secluded inn that offers graciously appointed rooms and lots of space. The two-story house, built in 1902 with a 1920s addition, was converted to an inn and completely renovated in 1989 by Lynne Nippes, who made the move from New York with husband Ernest on his retirement, after summering here for years.

Bedrooms feature thick carpeting in soft pastels, floral wallpapers and borders, pedestal sinks, and carved antique and reproduction beds piled with pillows and quilts or crocheted coverlets. Two rooms have fireplaces, including the suite, which also has a high queen-size canopy bed and *lots* of floral chintz.

The welcoming common areas include a large living room with a fireplace, a game table, and a grand piano. In the dining room, a brass chandelier and silver tea services bring a formal note to breakfast—or you can escape to the patio's tables overlooking 2 acres of gardens and trees.

Address: *26 Mt. Aldworth Rd., Box 4058, Vineyard Haven, MA 02568, tel. 508/693–3203.*
Accommodations: *6 double rooms with baths, 1 suite.*
Amenities: *Common cable TV and minifridge, turndown service; beach chairs, towels, and coolers.*
Rates: *$119–$145, suite $189; Continental breakfast and afternoon tea. No credit cards.*
Restrictions: *No smoking, no pets.*

The Bayberry

A stay at The Bayberry—a Cape-style house with peaked roof and weathered gray shingles, about 5 miles outside Vineyard Haven—is like a visit to Grandma's. Innkeeper Rosalie Powell displays her many antiques collections—majolica, Devonshireware, pewter—in her comfortable living room, where guests can enjoy the fireplace or piano or read before a bay window looking onto 4 acres surrounded by meadows and woods.

Guest rooms have an old-fashioned look, with some antique pieces—a marble-top dresser, a rolltop desk, a four-poster pineapple bed—and such homey touches as handmade quilts and rugs hooked by Rosalie. But the only thing fancy about this bed-and-breakfast is the breakfast, served in the fireplace-warmed country kitchen on antique pine tables set with linens, candles, and blue-and-white Staffordshire china, or on the backyard patio, with birdsong as background music. Such entrées as french toast with grilled bananas and Grand Marnier sauce are accompanied by warm popovers and breads.

Address: *Old Courthouse Rd., North Tisbury; Box 654, West Tisbury, MA 02575, tel. 508/693–1984.*
Accommodations: *3 double rooms with baths, 2 doubles share 1 bath.*
Amenities: *Guest refrigerator; croquet, beach passes and towels.*
Rates: *$100–$140; full breakfast and afternoon tea. MC, V.*
Restrictions: *No smoking indoors, no pets.*

Beach Plum Inn and Cottages

This 10-acre retreat's main attractions are a secluded woodland setting, a panoramic view of the ocean and Menemsha Harbor, and a romantic upscale restaurant with window walls that take advantage of it (be sure to reserve a table for a time when you'll catch one of the spectacular sunsets). Owners Paul and Janey Darrow preside at an afternoon cocktail hour on the lawn, where guests meet while enjoying the view and the gardens.

The inn rooms—some with private decks affording great views—have modern furnishings (brass and glass), small new baths, and wall-to-wall carpeting. The cottages (one with a whirlpool bath), scattered among the trees, are decorated in casual beach style, with wicker or other simple furnishings.

Address: *North Rd., Menemsha, MA 02552, tel. 508/645–9454 or 800/528–6616.*
Accommodations: *5 double rooms, 4 1- or 2-bedroom cottages, all with baths.*
Amenities: *Restaurant, some rooms with air-conditioning, turndown service, fax; tennis court, beach passes.*
Rates: *$175–$250; full breakfast. MAP available. AE, D, MC, V.*
Restrictions: *Closed mid-Oct.–mid-May.*

Breakfast at Tiasquam

Set on acres of farmland and forest is this bed-and-breakfast, built in 1987 in a contemporary design with 20 skylights, sliding glass doors, and private decks that connect the interior with the natural setting. The location invites bike rides on country roads, walks in the woods, or just relaxing in a hammock.

The decor is spare and soothing, emphasizing fine craftsmanship, as in the woodwork and the baths' hand-thrown ceramic sinks. A few pieces of art adorn the white walls; except for seafoam green carpeting, earth tones dominate. Some rooms offer decks; one has a cathedral ceiling, a wood-burning stove, and a large bath with whirlpool.

Owner Ron Crowe's background is in food service, so it's not surprising that breakfast gets special emphasis. The hearty spread of fruits, breads, and more may feature such unusual entrées as fresh albacore tuna or corn-blueberry pancakes, served at a hand-crafted dining room table.

Address: *off Middle Rd., RR 1, Box 296, Chilmark, MA 02535, tel. 508/645–3685.*
Accommodations: *2 double rooms with baths, 6 doubles share 3½ baths (2 outdoor showers).*
Amenities: *TV and stereo in common area; rental car and bikes, ferry or airport pickup, beach passes.*
Rates: *$105–$185; full breakfast. No credit cards.*
Restrictions: *No smoking, no pets.*

Captain Dexter House

This bed-and-breakfast, set in an 1843 sea captain's house at the quiet edge of the shopping district and three blocks from the ferry, has an intimate, historic feeling about it. The guest rooms are small but beautifully appointed, with period-style wallpapers, velvet wing chairs, and 18th-century antiques and reproductions, including several four-poster beds with lace or fishnet canopies and hand-sewn quilts.

The Captain Harding Room is more spacious, with the original wood floor covered by an Oriental carpet, a wood-burning fireplace, bay windows, a canopy bed, a sofa, a desk, and a large, bright bath. Other baths are tiny; the Captain West Room has a charming one, done up in pink and green with a pink claw-foot tub under a peaked roof. All the third-floor rooms have interesting architectural features, such as dormer windows and oddly shaped roofs and walls. Breakfast is served in the formal dining room, encouraging guests to socialize. There's also a fireplaced living room and a garden patio.

Address: *100 Main St., Box 2457, Vineyard Haven, MA 02568, tel. 508/693–6564.*
Accommodations: *7 double rooms with baths, 1 suite.*
Amenities: *Fireplaces in 2 rooms, guest refrigerator.*
Rates: *$110–$165; Continental breakfast and afternoon tea. AE, MC, V.*
Restrictions: *Smoking restricted, no pets. closed Jan.–Mar.*

Daggett House

The flower-bordered lawn that separates the main house from the harbor makes a great retreat after a day of exploring the town, a minute away. The 1750 Colonial house, with weathered gray shingles, a white picket fence, and a lavish garden incorporates an old tavern and breakfast room, open to the public in summer. Much of its 1660 ambience has been preserved, including a secret stairway that's now a private entrance to an upstairs guest room.

All three inn buildings—including the Captain Warren house across the street and a three-room cottage between the main house and the water—are decorated with fine wallpapers, antiques, and reproductions (some canopy beds). The Widow's Walk Suite has a rooftop hot tub with a great view of Edgartown Harbor, as well as a formal dining room and a kitchen; another suite has a hot tub on a private water-view balcony. Plans call for adding room phones and working fireplaces.

Address: *59 N. Water St., Box 1333, Edgartown, MA 02539, tel. and fax 508/627–4600 or 800/HOTEL–14.*
Accommodations: *20 double rooms with baths (1 with kitchenette), 3 housekeeping suites.*
Amenities: *Restaurant, air-conditioning in 3 rooms, common TV, beach towels; laundry service and box lunches available.*
Rates: *$120–$175; Continental breakfast. AE, MC, V.*
Restrictions: *No pets.*

Sea Spray Inn

In 1989, artist and art restorer Rayeanne King converted her Victorian summer house into a year-round bed-and-breakfast that still feels like a summer house. It is in a quiet spot in Oak Bluffs, on a drive circling an open, grassy park by the bike path and road that lead to Edgartown. Beyond the park, and just a few minutes' walk from the inn, is a sandy ocean beach. Public tennis and golf are within walking distance.

The decor is simple—no expensive antiques—and restful, highlighted by cheerful splashes of color, including furniture and floors painted in lavender, baby blue, and pink. In the Honeymoon Room, an iron-and-brass bed is positioned for watching the sunrise through bay windows draped in lacy curtains; the cedar-lined bath has an extra-large shower. The Garden Room has a king-size bed with gauze canopy and a private enclosed porch.

The inn has plenty of room for lounging, either on the wide wrap-around porch, set with rockers and wicker and looking onto the park, or in the lovely, airy living room.

Address: *2 Nashawena Park, Box 2125, Oak Bluffs, MA 02557, tel. 508/693–9388.*
Accommodations: *5 double rooms with baths, 2 doubles with shared bath.*
Amenities: *Common TV, refrigerator; barbecue grill.*
Rates: *$75–$125; Continental breakfast. MC, V.*
Restrictions: *No smoking, no pets.*

Shiverick Inn

Staying at this grand 1840 house with mansard roof and cupola is a bit like staying at an elegant private residence. The American and English 18th- and 19th-century furnishings throughout are exceptional. Rich fabrics and wallpapers and such accents as Oriental rugs, gilt-edged mirrors, cut-glass lamps, and antique art are impeccably chosen.

Thoroughly remodeled in 1987, with no expense spared, the inn was bought in April 1992 by Denny and Marty Turmelle, who left corporate careers in Manchester, New Hampshire, to become innkeepers. One or the other presides over breakfast, which is served on china and crystal in a lovely summerhouse-style room with a wood-burning fireplace.

Off the second-floor library is a terrace with a pretty view of a white steepled church; a flagstone patio has a small garden.

Address: *Corner of Pease's Point Way and Pent La., Box 640, Edgartown, MA 02539, tel. 508/627–3797 or 800/723–4292.*
Accommodations: *10 double rooms with baths, 1 sitting room connects to 1 or 2 adjacent rooms to form a suite with sleep sofa.*
Amenities: *Most rooms with air-conditioning and fireplace; library with cable TV, stereo, and minifridge; bike rentals.*
Rates: *$160–$170, $225 suites; Continental breakfast. AE, MC, V.*
Restrictions: *No smoking, no pets.*

Victorian Inn

An 1857 whaling captain's home listed on the National Register of Historic Places, this gingerbread-trimmed Victorian building has some antiques, including canopy and four-poster beds, but is generally furnished simply. Kathy Appert—a onetime occupational therapist—took over the inn in 1990 and is continually upgrading the furnishings and decor.

While spacious rooms on the high-ceilinged third floor are lovely, with French doors leading to balconies (some with a view of the harbor in the distance), other rooms have rough edges, such as old metal stall showers or linoleum floors in bathrooms, some of which are quite small. One whimsical touch: a teddy bear in every room. All rooms also have decanters of sherry.

In season, breakfast is served in the flower-brightened courtyard, a quiet, pretty place shaded by trees. Lemonade and cookies are set out in the afternoon.

Address: *24 S. Water St., Edgartown, MA 02539, tel. 508/627–4784.*
Accommodations: *14 double rooms with baths.*
Rates: *$110–$198; full breakfast in season, Continental Columbus Day–Memorial Day. AE, MC, V.*
Restrictions: *No smoking, no pets. 2-night minimum in season.*

Nantucket

At the height of its prosperity, in the early to mid-19th century, the little island of Nantucket became the foremost whaling port in the world. Before the boom years ended, some of the hard-won profits went into the building of grand homes that still survive as an eloquent testimony to Nantucket's glory days. Indeed, Nantucket town hardly seems changed since its whaling days; its cobblestone streets remain lit by old-fashioned street lamps, and its hundreds of 17th- to 19th-century houses—with weathered gray shingles or clapboard painted white or gray—have been beautifully preserved.

Hard times must take their share of the credit for this preservation—after the boom came the bust, when there was no money to tear down and rebuild and, in fact, few residents left to do it. Still, Nantucket's past has also been kept alive as the result of conscious effort. A very strict code now regulates any changes that can be made to structures within the town, part of a national historic district that encompasses most of the island. The code's success is obvious in a restful harmony of architectural styles; virtually nothing jars. In spring and summer, when the neat gardens are in bloom and the houses are blanketed with cascading pink roses, it all seems perfect.

In addition, through a land bank and other conservation organizations, more than a third of the 12- by 3-mile island's acreage is protected from development, and more parcels are continually acquired for preservation as open lands. Most of these areas, marked with signs on the roadside, are open to the public for nature walks, hiking, bird-watching, or swimming, and some are accessible via one of several paved, scenic bike paths.

In town (there is, by the way, only one) you'll find many first-class art galleries, crafts shops, and boutiques, along with a number of historical museums and fine restaurants.

Beyond are the moors—swept with fresh salt breezes scented with bayberry, wild roses, and cranberries—and miles of clean, white-sand beaches. The breezy openness of the island, along with its location 30 miles out to sea, gives Nantucket a feeling of isolation and allows visitors a respite from the rush and regimentation of life elsewhere. The style of the place—though long a bastion of the very wealthy—is decidedly casual and low-key.

Summer, of course, is the main season: All the shops, restaurants, museums, and entertainment options the island has to offer are accessible, and plenty of beach time can be expected. In spring and fall, crowds are much thinner and prices lower, yet many tourist facilities remain open. Spring (which can be wet and foggy) brings daffodils in profusion; its arrival is welcomed with the Daffodil Weekend festival, featuring, among other events, an antique-car parade down a route lined with millions of the blooms. In fall, the weather is still lovely, and the moors are covered with a mantle of purple, brown, and rust. Winter will appeal mainly to hearty lovers of solitude, stark landscapes, romantic inns with fireplaces, and freshly caught scallops; tourists will find little else to attract them to the island at this time.

Places to Go, Sights to See

Coatue–Coskata–Great Point. An unpopulated spit of sand comprising three wildlife refuges, Coatue is open for picnicking, surfcasting, or just enjoying the surroundings. Its beaches, dunes, salt marshes, and stands of oak and cedar provide a habitat for birds. Because of dangerous currents, swimming is strongly discouraged, especially within 200 yards of Great Point Light. The refuge is reached via the gatehouse at the end of Wauwinet Road, by foot or four-wheel-drive vehicle, for which you need a permit (tel. 508/228–2884). *Beach Excursions Ltd.* (tel. 508/228–5800) runs Jeep tours.

Cranberry Bogs. Between Siasconset and town are two working bogs surrounded by conservation land—especially pleasing in October, when the bright red berries are harvested by flooding the bogs. The Milestone Bog is off Milestone Road (with a parallel bike path); off the Polpis Road is the Windswept Cranberry Bog, with a parking area.

Eel Point (tel. 508/228–2884). Accessible only by foot (take a right off the Madaket bike path onto Eel Point Rd.), this unspoiled conservation area 6 miles from town has arguably the most beautiful beach on the island. A small stretch of land with harbor on one side, shoal-protected ocean on the other, and low grasses with wild grapes, roses, bayberries, and other scrub in between, the area attracts vast numbers of birds. The extensive sandbar makes the water clear, calm, and shallow; the surf fishing is good.

First Congregational Church (62 Centre St.; closed mid-Oct.–mid-June). Climb the 92 steps of the 120-foot tower for a view of moors, ponds, beaches, offshore islands, and the winding streets and rooftops of town.

Hadwen House (96 Main St., tel. 508/228–1894; closed Columbus Day–Memorial Day). A guided tour of this all-white, porticoed Greek Revival mansion—one of a side-by-side, nearly matching pair known as the Two Greeks—points out the grand circular staircase, fine plasterwork, marble fireplace mantels, and other architectural details. Regency, Empire, and Victorian furnishings are accented with 19th-century portraits and decorative objects. Across the street are the famous **"Three Bricks"**—identical, elegant brick mansions set off by white-columned Greek Revival porches, built between 1836 and 1838 by whaling merchant Joseph Starbuck for his three sons; his daughter married William Hadwen, builder of the Two Greeks.

Museum of Nantucket History (Straight Wharf, tel. 508/228–3889). This museum gives an overview of the geology and history of the island from its beginnings. Displays include an early fire-fighting vehicle, ship models, audiotapes, and photographs. A 13-foot diorama shows the bustling waterfront before the Great Fire of 1846, which destroyed the wharves and 400 buildings—about a third of all those in the town.

Nantucket Whalewatch (Hy-Line dock, Straight Wharf, tel. 508/283–0313, 800/942–5464, or 800/322–0013 in MA) runs naturalist-led whale-watching excursions in season.

Oldest House (Sunset Hill, tel. 508/228–1894; closed Columbus Day–Memorial Day). The most striking feature of this 1686 saltbox, the island's oldest structure, is the massive central brick chimney with brick horseshoe adornment. Other highlights are the diamond-pane leaded-glass windows, enormous hearths, and cutaway panels that show 17th-century construction techniques.

Old Mill (tel. 508/228–1894; closed Columbus Day–Memorial Day). At the top of South Mill Street is this 1746 Dutch-style octagonal windmill, built with lumber from shipwrecks. When the wind is right, the wood gears of the mill still grind cornmeal, which is for sale. The white sails flying on this hilltop site are a joy to behold.

Siasconset. This village of pretty lanes with tiny rose-covered cottages and driveways of crushed white shells is reached by a road or a level 7-mile bike path. An actors' colony around the turn of the century, 'Sconset (as it's known) today offers summer visitors a sandy, uncrowded beach, three fine restaurants, a box-lunch place, and a few services, such as a liquor store and a market (everything shuts down come autumn).

Whaling Museum (Broad St., tel. 508/228–1736; closed Christmas–mid-Apr.). Set in an 1846 spermaceti-oil refinery, this excellent museum gives a real feel for Nantucket's whaling past. Exhibits include a fully rigged whaleboat, harpoons, scrimshaw, a whale skeleton, replicas of cooper and blacksmith shops, and a 16-foot-high lighthouse prism.

Beaches

Children's Beach is a calm harborside beach, an easy walk from town, with a park and playground. A short, easy bike ride from town (or accessible by shuttle bus), lively **Jetties Beach** is popular with families for its calm surf, snack bar, Windsurfer rentals, and adjacent tennis courts. **'Sconset Beach** (or **Codfish Park**), reached via the 'Sconset bike path or a shuttle, is a golden-sand beach with moderate to heavy surf. Three miles from town by bike path or shuttle bus, **Surfside** is the premier surf beach, with a wide strand of sand.

Restaurants

Chanticleer (9 New St., 'Sconset, tel. 508/257–6231; closed Columbus Day–Mother's Day), serving classic French fare, is generally considered the island's top restaurant. Lunch in the rose garden, with a flower-bedecked carousel horse in the center, is a delight. The in-town top spot is the **Club Car** (1 Main St., tel. 508/228–1101), with flawless Continental cuisine, and a piano bar in an attached railway car. **The Brotherhood of Thieves** (23 Broad St., no phone), a very old-English pub restaurant, attracts long queues for its convivial atmosphere—thanks partly to the live folk music at night and to the hundreds of beers, ales, and exotic alcoholic concoctions available from the bar.

Tourist Information

Nantucket Chamber of Commerce (Pacific Club Bldg., Main St., Nantucket, MA 02554, tel. 508/228–1700); **Nantucket Information Bureau** (25 Federal St., tel. 508/228–0925).

Reservations Services

Nantucket Accommodations (Box 217, Nantucket, MA 02554, tel. 508/228–9559); **Martha's Vineyard and Nantucket Reservations** (Box 1322, Lagoon Pond Rd., Vineyard Haven, MA 02568, tel. 508/693–7200 or 800/649–5671 in MA); **House Guests Cape Cod and the Islands** (Box 1881, Orleans, MA 02653, tel. 508/896–7053 or 800/666–4678).

Centerboard Guest House

The look of this inn, a few blocks from the center of town, is unique on the island. In the high-ceilinged guest rooms, white walls (some with murals of moors and sky in soft pastels), blond-wood floors, white or natural wood furniture, white slatted shutters, and natural woodwork with a light wash of mauve tint create a cool, spare, dreamy atmosphere. There's more white still, in the lacy linens and puffy comforters on the featherbeds, each mounded with four pillows. Restrained touches of color are added by small stained-glass lamps, antique quilts, dishes of pink crystals, and fresh flowers.

No. 4 is the largest regular room, with a queen-size bed, a sofa, and an oversize shower; No. 2 has two antique brass and white-painted iron double beds. The small but pleasant studio apartment has a kitchen, two double beds in cabinetry-like berths on a ship, a separate twin bed in its own cubbyhole (fun for a child), a dining area, and a private entrance.

The first-floor suite is a stunner. Its large living room evokes the house's Victorian origins, with an 11-foot ceiling, the original parquet floor, a working fireplace topped by an elaborately carved oak mantel, and antique accents (a carved duck, a tapestry firescreen, lighting fixtures, and books). A nice modern touch is the wet bar. A lush hunter-green and rose Oriental carpet, sleep sofa, and upholstered chairs nicely complement the eggplant-color walls and the richness of the wood. Off the small separate bedroom, with a custom-built cherry four-poster bed topped by a high fishnet canopy, is the also-small bath, whose highly polished darkwood cabinetry is set off by a rich green marble floor, double shower, and whirlpool tub.

Manager of the inn since it opened in 1987 after a complete renovation is Reggie Reid, a New Jersey native and an island habitué for over 20 years. She sets out cold cereals, fruit, muffins, Portuguese bread, teas, and coffees in the sunny dining room amid such artistic touches as a sand-and-shell assemblage under glass and an 18th-century corner cupboard spilling antique-blue and purple dried hydrangeas.

Address: *8 Chester St., Box 456, Nantucket, MA 02554, tel. 508/228–9696.*
Accommodations: *4 double rooms with baths, 1 studio apartment, 1 suite.*
Amenities: *TV, phone, and minifridge in rooms; common TV with VCR accessible on room TVs (rent tapes in town); beach towels.*
Rates: *$145, $245 suite; Continental breakfast. AE, MC, V.*
Restrictions: *No pets. 2-night minimum most weekends.*

Jared Coffin House

Amid the shops, restaurants, and activity of downtown stands this complex that is a perennial favorite because of its location, dependability, conveniences, and class. It consists of six structures dating from the 18th century to the 20th, and all are well maintained and landscaped. The landmark main inn is the most impressive.

In 1845, Jared Coffin, a wealthy shipowner, built this glorious three-story redbrick Greek Revival with Ionic portico, parapet, hip roof, and cupola (ask for a key to go up in it and check out the panoramic view). In 1847 it became a stopover for travelers, in 1961 the Nantucket Historical Trust restored it, and today it is watched over by Phil and Margaret Read—owners since 1976.

The first-floor public rooms are elegant, yet welcoming—with Oriental rugs and antique Sheraton and Chippendale furniture, portraits, and clocks. In cool weather, you can sit by the fire sipping drinks brought to you from the basement bar and restaurant, the Tap Room. Breakfast and dinner are served in the formal restaurant, Jared's, a lovely, high-ceilinged room with salmon walls, pale green swag draperies, Federal antiques, and chandeliers with frosted-glass globes. The front desk is also in the main house, as is "Mrs. K" (alias Winifred Kittila), the concierge for more than a decade, who always knows what's going on.

The house's nine guest rooms (and those in the Eben Allen Wing and the Swain House) are beautifully furnished with 19th-century antiques (giltwood mirrors, a carved pineapple four-poster bed, upholstered chairs), Oriental carpets, and lace curtains. Second-floor corner rooms are the largest and nicest, with a sitting area and more windows. The inexpensive single rooms—a rare commodity on the island—are small but tastefully done.

The Harrison Gray House, an 1842 Greek Revival across Centre Street, offers bigger rooms with large baths, as well as a common living room and a sun porch with TV; both it and the 1821 Henry Coffin House have queen canopy beds. The Daniel Webster House, built in 1964, with uninspired decor by Ethan Allen, is adjacent to the outdoor café and has a conference room.

Address: *29 Broad St., Nantucket, MA 02554, tel. 508/228–2400 or 800/248–2405, fax 508/228–8549.*
Accommodations: *52 double rooms with baths, 8 singles with baths.*
Amenities: *2 restaurants, color TV (except in the main house) and phones in rooms, some minifridges; concierge late May–mid-Oct. and holidays.*
Rates: *$135–$170, singles $75–$100; full breakfast. AE, D, DC, MC, V.*

76 Main Street

Built by a sea captain in 1883 as a private residence, 76 Main—now a gracious bed-and-breakfast inn—sits just above the bustle of the shops on quiet, mansion-lined upper Main Street. The original mansard roof has been obscured by an unfortunate Federal-style facade, with a fretted parapet and platinum gray shutters on the white wood siding; the mansard, however, is still visible at the sides.

A long, serpentine granite staircase leads to a beautifully restored Victorian entry hall, shining with rich woods—from the elegant patterned floor to the elaborately carved cherry staircase. Massive, dark-stained redwood pocket doors with bull's-eye moldings close the hall off from the very Victorian sitting room and the former dining room and parlor, now the two best guest rooms.

These two rooms share the hall's emphasis on fine wood, as well as its high ceilings. No. 3 has not only wonderful woodwork but also a two-tone wood floor, a carved armoire, and twin four-poster beds set off by Oriental-style blue-and-white wallpaper. The spacious No. 1 has three large windows, upholstered chairs, brass lamps, and a bed with eyelet spread and canopy.

The second- and third-floor hallways, with maple and oak flooring topped with Oriental rugs and runners, lead to rooms furnished less grandly but well, with Ethan Allen reproductions, braided rugs, handmade quilts over all-cotton sheets, country curtains, and light patterned wallpapers. Everything is sparkling clean. Some rooms on the dormer-punctuated third floor have skylighted baths, casement windows, or window seats.

In a single-story, motel-like annex out back (built in 1955, when the facade was added), you'll find six rooms with private entrances. Although they have low ceilings and are a bit dark, the rooms are large enough for families of up to five. Furnished in a more colonial style, with industrial carpeting, pretty wallpapers, and velour-upholstered armchairs, they are available in season only.

The inn's breakfast buffet is set out either in the breakfast room, on a long wood table over which guests get to know one another easily, or out back on the flagstone patio. Usually officiating is innkeeper Mitch Blake or the owner, Shirley Peters.

Address: *76 Main St., Nantucket, MA 02554, tel. 508/228–2533.*
Accommodations: *18 double rooms with baths.*
Amenities: *Cable TV and minifridges in annex rooms.*
Rates: *$115–$130; Continental breakfast. AE, MC, V.*
Restrictions: *No smoking, no pets.*

Ten Lyon Street Inn

In 1986, Ann Marie and Barry Foster opened this bed-and-breakfast on a quiet street about a five-minute walk from the town center. Barry's work—completely rebuilding the three-story Colonial-style house from its foundations—was pretty much done, but Ann Marie's had just begun. Since then, she has used her decorating skills, from upholstering to antiques restoration, to make this a most individual and eye-pleasing inn. Her touch is evident from the moment you pass through the gate into the small, flower-filled yard. Exotic bulbs, lilacs, and other perennials curve around the lawn, while during spring and summer pink and peach roses climb the trellises against the house's weathered gray shingles.

Barry, an electrical contractor, wanted to give the house something of a historic feel, so to the smooth, white plaster walls and ceilings and light-wood moldings he added such touches as new golden-pine floors in planks of variable widths, salvaged Colonial-era mantels, and hefty antiqued red oak ceiling beams.

Guest rooms have a spare, uncluttered look, yet are warmed by details. The white walls make a clean stage for exquisite antique Oriental rugs in deep, rich colors and some choice antiques, such as English pine sleigh beds and a tobacco-leaf four-poster bed; chairs upholstered in English florals; and such romantic fabrics as white lace curtains and a Battenberg lace canopy. The beds have hand-stitched quilts, down comforters, and all-cotton sheets (which Ann Marie actually irons). Bathrooms are bright white, with maize- and white-striped runners on the shiny floors and delicate wall hangings—white with a touch of color—brought from Ann Marie's native Austria. Several baths have separate showers; all have antique porcelain pedestal sinks and brass fixtures.

Room 1, the showpiece, has a 19th-century French country tester bed romantically draped in gauzy white mosquito netting. The large room is made lush with stunning red Turkish carpets, potted palms, gilt mirrors, and little antique gilt-wood cupids on either side of the bed.

Ann Marie serves a healthy Continental breakfast; the muffins are low in sugar and fat, the jellies low in sugar, yet all is delicious. Unfortunately, there's not much in the way of a common room.

Address: *10 Lyon St., Nantucket, MA 02554, tel. 508/228–5040.*
Accommodations: *7 double rooms with baths.*
Rates: *$120–$160; Continental breakfast. AE, MC, V.*
Restrictions: *No smoking indoors, no pets. Closed mid-Dec.–mid-Apr.*

Westmoor Inn

The tradition of gracious entertaining established when the Vanderbilts built their Nantucket summer house in 1917 continues today in its incarnation as a bed-and-breakfast.

After a day of exploring the island, guests gather for a predinner wine and cheese reception. Mornings, they meet again in the sunny, all-glass breakfast room over a buffet of yogurt, fruit salad, granola, croissants, home-baked scones or nut breads, juices, and more. Tables are set with white damask, flowers, and white china. Nice touches like ramekins of jams and butter, a bowl of ice around the milk pitcher on the buffet, a selection of daily newspapers, and soft classical music help make the experience especially enjoyable.

The entry, with sweeping staircase, has the air of the manor house. Off the entry is the living room, with a grand piano and a game table, as well as a glassed-in sun porch with white wicker chairs and a TV (for those inevitable rainy days). Outside the yellow Federal-style mansion with widow's walk and portico, a wide lawn set with Adirondack chairs and a garden patio secluded behind 11-foot hedges invite summer lounging.

Guest rooms are bright and white, with eyelet comforters and pillows, framed botanicals and old prints, and some very nice antiques; all have phones (only for outgoing calls). Third-floor rooms have lots of dormers and angles, with stenciling on the white eaves. The second floor features highly polished wide-board pine floors. Most baths are very nice and modern; a few need updating (old metal shower units and tile floors)—specify if it matters to you. One first-floor "suite" has a giant bath with extra-large Jacuzzi and French doors opening onto the lawn. The third-floor master bedroom, with a king bed and a queen sofa-bed, has a broad view of moors and the ocean beyond to the north; to the east, it looks onto a neighbor's private baseball diamond.

A mile from the shops and restaurants, and just a short walk from an uncrowded ocean beach and the Madaket bike path, the inn is a good choice for those who prefer spaciousness and seclusion to the bustle and closeness of Nantucket town.

Address: *Cliff Rd., Nantucket, MA 02554, tel. 508/228–0877.*
Accommodations: *14 double rooms, 3 separate apartments with new kitchens.*
Amenities: *Bicycles, beach towels.*
Rates: *$100–$225; Continental breakfast, wine and cheese. AE, MC, V.*
Restrictions: *No smoking, no pets. 3-night minimum mid-June–mid-Sept., closed early Dec.–Apr.*

Century House

When you arrive at the Century House, innkeeper Jean Heron greets you with all her considerable warmth and energy. She and her husband and fellow innkeeper, Gerry Connick, bought the inn in 1984 to get away from corporate life.

The sprawling, late Federal–style inn, built in 1833 by a sea captain (it is the oldest continuously operated guest house on the island), is just a few minutes' walk from town. A wide veranda with rocking chairs wraps the front and sides of the house.

Guest rooms are very casual, homey, and bright, with wallpapers and fabrics in the Laura Ashley light-floral style, such country furnishings as wicker and painted wood, and spatter-painted wide-board floors. Down comforters and some canopy beds add touches of luxury.

A breakfast buffet—highlighted by homemade granola, fruits, juice, bagels, muffins, fresh-baked breads, and cinnamon-flavored coffee—is served in a pine-paneled country kitchen or on the veranda.

Address: *10 Cliff Rd., Box 603, Nantucket, MA 02554, tel. 508/228–0530.*
Accommodations: *8 double rooms with baths, 4 doubles with sinks share 2 baths.*
Amenities: *Common TV.*
Rates: *$75–$165; Continental breakfast and afternoon happy hour. MC, V.*
Restrictions: *No smoking indoors, no pets. May close in winter.*

Cliff Lodge

When the innkeeper is an interior designer, you can expect a certain flair from your room, and at Cliff Lodge you certainly find it. Gerrie Miller, who moved here from Rhode Island in 1989, has made guest rooms big, bright, and airy, with lots of sky blue and crisp white, pastel hooked rugs on spatter-painted floors, country curtains and furnishings, light floral wallpapers, and white eyelet linens. Built in 1771, the lodge preserves lots of old-house flavor, in moldings, wainscoting, and wide-board floors. Modern touches are room phones and small TVs tucked in cupboards. Some baths are very small. The very pleasant apartment has a fireplace in the living room, a private deck and entrance, and a large eat-in kitchen.

In addition to the attractive common rooms, both with wood-burning fireplaces, guests may take afternoon tea or cocktails in the wicker sun porch, on the garden terrace, or on the roofwalk patio, with a great view of the harbor. And there's parking available—a rarity in town.

Address: *9 Cliff Rd., Nantucket, MA 02554, tel. 508/228–9480.*
Accommodations: *11 double rooms with baths, 1 apartment.*
Amenities: *Common refrigerator and coffeemaker; beach towels, croquet, barbecue grill.*
Rates: *$100–$150, $190 apartment ($1,275 weekly); Continental breakfast. AE, MC, V.*
Restrictions: *No smoking in bedrooms, no pets. Closed Jan., weekdays in Feb.*

Corner House

Poufy down comforters and plenty of down pillows, pretty linens, and firm mattresses on interesting beds (antique, reproduction, canopy, brass, tall-post) practically guarantee a sweet night's sleep at this B&B a block or two from town center. The 1790 main inn has much old-house flavor. Its wide-board floors carry the patina of age, as well as the cracks and tilts. The living room and original keeping room each have walls of detailed Colonial woodwork centered by a fireplace. Here Sandy Knox-Johnston and her British husband and fellow innkeeper, John, join guests for a convivial afternoon tea, which can also be taken on the wicker-filled screened porch or the garden terrace.

Inn accommodations vary widely. In the main house, some tiny third-floor rooms have rough plaster walls and exposed beams; others have separate sitting areas or daybeds in alcoves, perfect for reading. In a nearby post-and-beam house designed by Sandy, a still-practicing architectural restorer, skylighted pine-beam cathedral ceilings rise over upstairs rooms with sleeping lofts.

Address: *49 Centre St., Box 1828, Nantucket, MA 02554, tel. 508/228–1530.*
Accommodations: *14 double rooms with baths, 1 suite.*
Amenities: *Some rooms with TVs and minifridges, common TV, fax available.*
Rates: *$85–$145; Continental breakfast and afternoon tea. MC, V.*
Restrictions: *No smoking in bedrooms, no pets. Closed mid-Jan.–mid-Feb.*

Martin House Inn

A nicely refurbished bed-and-breakfast in an 1803 house with dormers and a widow's walk, Martin House, just off the main thoroughfare, offers mostly spacious rooms with white lacy curtains, four-poster or canopy beds, and Oriental and dhurrie rugs. A large first-floor room, just off the entrance hall, has an exceptional tobacco-leaf pattern, four-poster bed with cloth canopy and backing, and a tiny bathroom. The country-look third-floor rooms are under the eaves, and could be bumpy business for tall folks.

New Yorkers Ceci and Channing Moore bought the inn in 1991 after Channing left a career in banking; souvenirs of a Hong Kong stint are their Siamese cat, Sam, and alley cat Calli.

A breakfast of home-baked breads and muffins (including raspberries from the backyard patch), granola, and fruits can be enjoyed in the formal dining room, on the veranda, or in the living room, with fireplace, piano, sofa, and cozy window seats.

Address: *61 Centre St., Box 743, Nantucket, MA 02554, tel. 508/228–0678.*
Accommodations: *9 double rooms with baths, 2 doubles and 2 singles share 1 bath.*
Amenities: *Common TV and piano, 2 rooms with fireplaces.*
Rates: *$75–$140, $45 single; Continental breakfast. AE, MC, V.*
Restrictions: *No smoking in bedrooms, no pets. 2-night minimum usually in season.*

Seven Sea Street

This inn on a quiet side street in the center of town was built in 1987 in the colonial style, with a widow's walk (take a seat up there for a great harbor view, or relax in the leafy backyard). Though the all-new furnishings are also in that style and in antique colors (federal blue, colonial red), the place has a bit of a Scandinavian look. A post-and-beam construction in light pine and red oak, it features exposed-beam ceilings, pine-trimmed white walls, and highly polished wide-board floors. Each room has a desk area, a braided rug, a queen-size pencil-post field bed with fishnet canopy and quilt, a rocking chair, and a bathroom with a two-seat fiberglass stall shower and brass fittings. A suite with an adjoining sitting room with sofa bed is available for families.

One of the two small common rooms has a Franklin stove; the breakfast room has a fireplace, as well as a microwave and a coffeemaker for guests' use. Innkeepers Matthew and Mary Parker produce *Nantucket Journal*, a magazine on island living.

Address: *7 Sea St., Nantucket, MA 02554, tel. 508/228–3577.*
Accommodations: *8 double rooms with baths.*
Amenities: *All rooms with phone, cable TV, minifridge; whirlpool room.*
Rates: *$165, suite $210; Continental breakfast. AE, MC, V.*
Restrictions: *No smoking; no pets. 2-night minimum most weekends, 3 nights on holidays.*

Summer House

Those hoping to get away from it all might look to this bastion of easy classiness in the village of Siasconset, 7 miles from town. Here, across from 'Sconset Beach, around a flower-filled lawn, stand the rose-covered gray-shingle cottages we associate with Nantucket summers. Each is furnished in a blend of unfussy, breezy beach style and romantic English country motifs—white walls, white lace and eyelet curtains and spreads, Laura Ashley floral accents, and English stripped-pine antiques. Some cottages have one bedroom, some have two; some offer fireplaces or kitchenettes; most have marble baths with whirlpools.

The inn's restaurant, with white painted and wicker furniture, lots of flowers, hanging plants, and paintings of Nantucket scenes, serves creative American cuisine emphasizing seafood and attracts a stylish clientele. Piano music can be heard nightly in season in the bar/lounge. Breakfast is laid out on a shaded porch overlooking the gardens and the sea. Overlooking the ocean is a pool, with a café serving light lunches and frozen drinks.

Address: *Ocean Ave., Box 313, Siasconset, MA 02564, tel. 508/257–9976.*
Accommodations: *8 cottages with baths.*
Amenities: *Restaurant; pool, poolside restaurant and bar, private beach.*
Rates: *$275–$325 1-bedroom, $375 2-bedroom; Continental breakfast. AE, MC, V.*
Restrictions: *No pets. Closed Nov.–late Apr.*

The Wauwinet

An exquisite setting, impeccable furnishings, and extensive amenities characterize this most luxurious hotel. A minute's walk through the dunes leads to miles of Atlantic Ocean beach; you'll find little else here, at the gateway to the Coatue–Coskata–Great Point wildlife preserve. Jitney service to and from town, 8 miles away, and airport and ferry pickup are provided.

This historic 19th-century hotel was given a $3-million renovation in 1988. Each guest room is decorated in country/beach style, with stripped pine or other antiques. The restaurant, Topper's, is one of the island's best, serving New American cuisine in a summerhouse setting. The patio is especially nice at sunset. An elegant breakfast is brought to your room or served in the restaurant.

Address: *Wauwinet Rd., Box 2580, Nantucket, MA 02584, tel. 508/228–0145 or 800/426–8718, fax 508/228–6712.*
Accommodations: *29 double rooms with baths, 5 cottages.*
Amenities: *Restaurant, bar, air-conditioning, cable TV with VCR in rooms, turndown service, room service, business services, concierge, videocassette library; 2 Har-Tru tennis courts, sailboard and Sunfish rentals and lessons, croquet, 18-speed mountain bikes, boat trips, Coatue jeep tours.*
Rates: *$290–$450; full breakfast. AE, DC, MC, V.*
Restrictions: *No pets. 3-night minimum summer and holiday weekends, closed Dec.–Mar.*

White Elephant

For years a hallmark of service and style, the Elephant offers above all a choice location, right on Nantucket harbor. All that separates it from the bobbing boats is a wide lawn, boasting a large new pool and whirlpool spa and a waterside outdoor café.

Rooms in the deck-wrapped main hotel have stenciled pine armoires, sponge-painted walls, and floral fabrics. The Breakers offers more luxurious accommodations with harbor-view window walls, as well as minibars and minifridges. Some rooms have French doors that open onto the lawn or a private deck—*very* romantic.

Groups of cottages done in the English country style, some with full kitchens, range from handsome to some in a pine grove. The entire property has been renovated since 1989, and everything is fresh and new. All rooms have phones and cable TV; some have VCRs and air-conditioning.

Address: *Easton St., Box 359, Nantucket, MA 02554, tel. 508/228–2500 or 800/475–2637, fax 508/228–7197.*
Accommodations: *48 double rooms, 32 1- to 3-bedroom cottages.*
Amenities: *Restaurant, lounge with entertainment, room service, concierge, minifridges, fax; heated pool, croquet court, putting green, boat slips.*
Rates: *$235–$425, cottages $275–$650; breakfast extra. AE, D, DC, MC, V.*
Restrictions: *No pets. Closed mid-Sept.–Memorial Day.*

Boston

New England's largest city and the cradle of American independence, Boston is 360 years old, far older than the republic it helped to create. Its most famous buildings are not merely civic landmarks but national icons; its great citizens are not the political and financial leaders of today but the Adamses, Reveres, and Hancocks who live at the crossroads of history and myth.

At the same time, Boston is a contemporary center of high finance and higher technology, a place of granite and glass towers rising along what once were rutted village lanes. Its enormous population of students, artists, academics, and young professionals has made the town a haven for foreign movies, late-night bookstores, racquetball, sushi restaurants, New Wave music, and unconventional politics.

Best of all, Boston is meant for walking. Most of its historical and architectural attractions can be found in compact areas, and its varied and distinctive neighborhoods reveal their character and design to visitors who take the time to stroll through them.

Places to Go, Sights to See

Boston Common is the oldest park in the United States and was once used for grazing cows. Across Charles Street from the Common is the **Public Garden,** where the famous swan boat rides are given on the 4–acre pond.

The **Charlestown Navy Yard** (tel. 617/426–1812) is the home of the **USS *Constitution,*** nicknamed Old Ironsides, and is a designated national historic site. In addition to the *Constitution,* visitors may tour the USS *Cassin Young,* a World War II destroyer; the museum; the commandant's house; and the collections of the Boston Marine Society.

The **Esplanade,** a strip of park that runs along the Charles River for the entire length of the Back Bay, is home to the **Hatch Memorial Shell,** where the Boston Pops plays each summer. More than a pleasant place for a stroll, a run, or a picnic, the Esplanade is home port for the fleet of small sailboats that dot the Charles River Basin, and the **Union Club Boathouse,** private headquarters for the country's oldest rowing club.

Faneuil Hall and **Quincy Market** face each other across a small square thronged with people at all but the smallest hours. In this indoor and outdoor mall, you'll find a plethora of shops, souvenir vendors, restaurants, bars, and dance clubs.

The 70–acre **Franklin Park Zoo** (Dorchester, tel. 617/442–2002) features an excellent walk-through aviary, and the new Tropical Forest Pavilion, home to gorillas and 32 other species of mammals, reptiles, birds, and fish.

The mile-and-a-half **Freedom Trail** is marked on the sidewalk by a red line that winds its way past 16 of Boston's most important historic sites. The walk begins at the Freedom Trail Information Center on the Tremont Street side of Boston Common. Sites include the State House, Old Granary Burial Ground, King's Chapel, Globe Corner Bookstore, Old State House, Boston Massacre site, Faneuil Hall, Paul Revere House, Old North Church, Copp's Hill Burying Ground and the USS *Constitution.*

Two blocks west of the MFA is the **Isabella Stewart Gardner Museum** (tel. 617/566–1401), a trove of spectacular paintings, sculpture, furniture, and textiles. At the center of the building is a magnificent courtyard, fully enclosed beneath a glass roof, in which there are always fresh flowers.

The **Museum of Fine Arts** (tel. 617/267–9300) features an extensive American artist collection, including John Singer Sargent, Winslow Homer, Edward Hopper, and John Singleton Copley. It boasts the most extensive collection of Asiatic art gathered under one roof, and its collection of antique musical instruments is world-renowned. This museum also hosts major traveling exhibitions.

The **Museum of Science** (tel. 617/723–2500) features more than 400 exhibits covering astronomy, astrophysics, anthropology, medicine, computers, earth science, and more. Also on the premises is the **Mugar Omni Theater** (tel. 617/523–6664), a state-of-the-art film projection and sound system with a 76–foot, four-story domed screen.

Central Wharf is the home of the **New England Aquarium** (tel. 617/973–5200) where you'll find seals, penguins, a variety of sharks, and other sea creatures—more than 2,000 species in all, some of which make their homes in the aquarium's four-story, 187,000-gallon observation tank, the largest of its kind in the world.

Beaches

While Boston is on the water, the nicest beaches are outside the city. However, there are local public beaches such as **Malibu Beach** in Dorchester, and **Pleasure Bay** in South Boston. Call for information on these Metropolitan District Commission-run beaches (tel. 617/727–5215). Several excellent beaches a short distance from the city make lovely day trips. Among the nicest are **Nantasket Beach** in Hull, **Crane's Beach** in

Ipswich, **Plum Island** in Newburyport, and **Wingaersheek Beach** in Gloucester.

Restaurants

Boston offers something for every taste and wallet size. **Julien** (tel. 617/451–1900) serves some of the finest classic French cuisine in town. **Durgin-Park** (tel. 617/227–2038) serves homey New England fare in a casual, if noisy, atmosphere. **Biba** (tel. 617/426–7878) is an inventive, and enormously popular restaurant featuring new American fare. **Ristorante Lucia** (tel. 617/523–9148) is considered by some aficionados the best Italian restaurant in the North End. **Legal Sea Foods** (tel. 617/426–4444) and the **Union Oyster House** (tel. 617/227–2750) serve the seafood Boston is famous for. **Casa Romero** (tel. 617/536–4341) features authentic Mexican cuisine. **Figs** (Charlestown, tel. 617/242–2229) specializes in gourmet pizza.

Nightlife

The **House of Blues** (Cambridge, tel. 617/491–2583), owned by Dan Akroyd, among others, is the latest nightspot, featuring live blues music. **Axis** (Boston, tel. 617/262–2424) features urban, underground dance music, and **Avalon** (Boston, tel. 617/262–2424), next door, offers top 40 dance tunes. **Quest** (Boston, tel. 617/424–7747) is a primarily gay (but mixed gender) dance club. For jazz, try the **Regattabar** (Boston, tel. 617/937–4020) or **Scullers** (Boston, tel. 617/783–0811). **John Harvard's Brew House** (Cambridge, tel. 617/868–3585) is a well-stocked alehouse. The **Comedy Connection** (Boston, tel. 617/248–9700) books national and local talent.

Reservations Services

Bed & Breakfast Agency of Boston (47 Commercial Wharf, Boston 02110, tel. 617/720–3540 or 800/248–9262); **Bed & Breakfast Associates Bay Colony Ltd.** (Box 57166, Babson Park Branch, Boston 02157, tel. 617/449–5302 or 800/347–5088); **New England Bed and Breakfast, Inc.** (1753 Massachusetts Ave., Cambridge 02138, tel. 617/498–9819); **Bed and Breakfast Cambridge and Greater Boston** (Box 665, Cambridge 02140, tel. 617/576–1492 or 800/888–0178).

Tourist Information

Greater Boston Convention and Visitors Bureau (Box 490, Prudential Tower, Boston, MA 02199, tel. 617/536–4100); **Massachusetts Office of Travel and Tourism** (100 Cambridge St., 13th floor, Boston, MA 02202, tel. 617/727–3201 or 800/447–MASS).

A Cambridge House Bed-and-Breakfast

Massachusetts Avenue is a busy, two-lane highway, but this 1892 yellow clapboard house, listed on the National Register of Historic Places, is set well back from the street. As you cross the wide front porch and enter the gorgeously decorated hallway, the outside noise and bustle vanish into a calm, well-ordered, Victorian glow.

In fact, the ground floor public rooms are the house's best features: they're dominated by gloriously carved cherry paneling and floor-to-ceiling fireplaces (the fireplace in the lobby is made of intricately carved African mahogany). The parlor and library show off hand-worked fire screens, elegant Victorian couches, bureaus, piano, and hard-wood floors with Oriental rugs. A full breakfast is served in the handsome dining room, with its glass chandelier, Oriental rug, and corner china cabinet with silver coffee service.

A paneled staircase featuring portraits and a grandfather clock on the landing leads to the second floor and the best room in the house—the "suite" (actually, it's only one room). The room has thick carpets, a canopy bed, a working fireplace, a chaise longue, an alcove with a desk, and padded walls covered in fabric that complements the gray and pink of the bedskirts and drapes. Third floor guest rooms are furnished with canopy or sleigh beds, fireplaces, and Victorian antiques. Most rooms in the carriage house, while tastefully furnished, are extremely small; despite wall-size mirrors installed in some to create a sense of space, you can only just walk around the bed.

Ellen Riley bought the house in 1985 and intended to use it as a private residence. She converted a couple of rooms into guest accommodations "just for fun," and got carried away by the bed-and-breakfast spirit. When she's not around, the inn is managed by polite and helpful innkeepers.

The house is just four blocks from the nearest subway station, and Harvard University is one stop away. There are plenty of shops and restaurants in the immediate vicinity, and 10 minutes on the subway will take you into the heart of Boston. And you can park your car for free!

Address: *2218 Massachusetts Ave., Cambridge, MA 02140, tel. 617/491–6300 or 800/232–9989, fax 617/868–2848.*
Accommodations: *5 rooms with baths, 11 rooms share 8 baths.*
Amenities: *Air-conditioning, cable TV, and phones in rooms, some rooms have fireplaces; parking.*
Rates: *$79–$169 (singles $20 less); full breakfast and afternoon tea. AE, MC, V.*
Restrictions: *No pets, no smoking. 2-night minimum on weekends May–Oct.*

82 Chandler Street

Located in Boston's recently revitalized South End, on a quiet, tree-lined street of tall, redbrick row houses, this bed-and-breakfast is just a five-minute walk from the city center, a 10-minute taxi ride from the airport, and around the corner from Amtrak's Back Bay station. Constructed in 1863, the building sits on former tidal marshlands which were filled in to provide housing space for the city's growing middle class. Its mansard roof and redbrick, brownstone trim are trademarks of 19th-century Boston homes.

Owners Denis Coté and Dominic Beraldi bought the house in 1978, and after major renovation, turned it into apartments. In 1983, however, when one tenant moved out, they decided to try their hand at innkeeping. According to Denis, a social worker for 25 years, innkeeping is a positive kind of social work, "but more enjoyable, since you're helping people to have a good time, rather than to survive!"

A full breakfast, including pancakes, French toast, or crepes is served family style in the big, sunny penthouse kitchen with exposed brick walls, plants, skylights, and a row of windows overlooking the city's rooftops. The bedroom across the stairwell is the "Room with a View": Its wide bay window looks out on downtown Boston and several landmark skyscrapers. The walls are exposed brick, the floors are polished pine with Oriental rugs, there's a working marble fireplace, and a skylight in the bathroom. Ask for this room first when making reservations (especially since all rooms cost the same).

82 Chandler Street is very much an "up and down" house: all other guest rooms open off the staircase and are "color coded" with green, red, blue, or yellow schemes. Front rooms have large bay windows and two have working fireplaces; all are spacious and sunny, with white enamel and brass headboards, pedestal sinks, Oriental rugs, plus a kitchen area with refrigerator and microwave oven.

Ever devoted to his guests' well-being, Denis provides a wealth of tourist information, directions, and advice on the best sights to see. Although guests can use two nearby parking lots (costing from $8 to $16 per day), parking is problematic throughout Boston and you're better off without a car.

Address: *82 Chandler St., Boston, MA 02116, tel. 617/482–0408.*
Accommodations: *5 double rooms with baths.*
Amenities: *Air-conditioning, phones, and kitchen-areas in rooms; some rooms have fireplaces; breakfast room; TV available.*
Rates: *$75–$110; full breakfast. No credit cards.*
Restrictions: *No pets, no smoking. 2-night minimum Apr.–Nov.*

Newbury Guest House

This elegant, redbrick and brownstone row house was built in 1882 as a private home in Boston's fashionable Back Bay, still *the* place to live in Boston. A father and son team, Nubar and Mark Hagopian, bought the four-story house in 1990, and after extensive restoration and renovation, opened it as a bed-and-breakfast in January 1991. Guests enter below street level through a combination lobby, sitting, and breakfast room with polished floors, and reproduction Victorian furnishings. In summer, the Continental breakfast of breads and pastries is served outside on a brick patio.

The location of this inn is perfect: Newbury Street—famous for its gas street lamps, broad sidewalks, leaded windows, and neat front gardens—is the city's smartest shopping street, home to a wide selection of clothing stores, antiques shops, art galleries, hair salons, and dozens of sidewalk cafés, restaurants, and trendy bars. It's also a short walk to the Public Garden, Boston Common, Copley Square, and many other attractions.

Guest rooms open off the beautifully carved oak staircase of this tall, narrow house. The spacious two-room suite on the first floor features an arched stained-glass window, hand painted in the 1880s by an artist from Tiffany's. The suite has a cherry sleigh bed, nonworking fireplace, and intricately cut plaster moldings. A guest room on the same floor has a cherry bedroom set, carved wainscot paneling, and stained glass in the doors.

Throughout the rest of the house, "bay" guest rooms have couches and oriel windows overlooking Newbury Street; less expensive "traditional" rooms have wing chairs and are smaller—however, as Mark points out, they're not as small as the "small" rooms at Boston's famous Ritz-Carlton Hotel, just a few blocks away! Several rooms have cherry four-poster beds and nonworking fireplaces; all feature reproduction Victorian furnishings, dark-stained pine floors and rugs, queen-size beds, and a wide variety of original artwork on consignment from local galleries.

There's metered street parking just outside, and the inn offers a limited number of spaces to guests for $10 per night. You don't need a car here, but if you will have one, consider reserving a space in advance.

Address: *261 Newbury St., Boston, MA 02116, tel. 617/437–7666.*
Accommodations: *15 double rooms with baths.*
Amenities: *Living room, air-conditioning, cable TV, phones in rooms; limited parking (extra).*
Rates: *$75–$145; Continental breakfast. AE, D, DC, MC, V.*
Restrictions: *No pets.*

Beacon Hill Bed and Breakfast

Susan Butterworth had owned this six-story, brick Victorian row house with huge bay windows in Beacon Hill for more than 20 years, when five years ago, after her sons left for college, she decided to turn it into a bed-and-breakfast. The historic neighborhood is characterized by narrow, twisting streets lit by gas lamps and lined with trees.

Guest rooms are enormous, with great oriel windows, built-in bookshelves, and fireplaces (alas, nonworking). Rooms contain some Victorian antiques—one has a metal four-poster bed—but upstairs there's a more contemporary theme, with loud black-and-white check wallpaper in the hallways and light-blue modern couches in the bedrooms. Breakfast is served downstairs in a large room with red decor, Victorian antiques, and a bay window overlooking the river.

The bed-and-breakfast has no parking available, and since you can walk to everything from this central location, don't bring the car! If you do, the nearby Boston Common Garage is your best bet.

Address: *27 Brimmer St., Boston, MA 02108, tel. 617/523–7376.*
Accommodations: *3 double rooms with baths.*
Amenities: *Air-conditioning, TV in rooms, public phone, breakfast room.*
Rates: *$95–$120; full breakfast. No credit cards.*
Restrictions: *No pets, no smoking. 2-night minimum on weekends Apr.–Nov.*

Beacon Inns

These two Beacon Street inns, owned by the Gloth family and located in Brookline, manage to combine clean, spacious, and stylish rooms with easy access to the city for a very reasonable rate.

1087 is a four-story brick Victorian town house with a beautiful oak staircase and a floor-to-ceiling lobby fireplace surrounded by carved wood and columns. Guest rooms are large, with detailed wainscot paneling, period wallpapers, and desks and chairs.

Rates are slightly lower at 1750. Although big, rooms are on the dark side, with painted-wood paneling, brick nonworking fireplaces, and faded wallpaper; rooms on the top floor have sloping ceilings. Both inns are run by friendly live-in managers.

Both inns have streetcar stops almost right outside the door—it's a 15-minute ride to the city center from 1750, a 10-minute hop from 1087.

Address: *1087 and 1750 Beacon St., Brookline, MA 02146, tel. 617/566–0088.*
Accommodations: *1087: 6 rooms with baths, 5 rooms share 3 baths. 1750: 3 rooms with baths, 10 rooms share 3 baths.*
Amenities: *Air-conditioning in some rooms, TV in rooms, public phone; limited parking.*
Rates: *1087: $39–$59; 1750: $29–$48; Continental breakfast. AE, MC, V.*
Restrictions: *No pets at 1087; pets by arrangement at 1750.*

The Bertram Inn

Built in 1903 as a private home, the Bertram Inn is an elegant Victorian mansion located on a quiet suburban street in Brookline, a few minutes' walk from the subway and a ten-minute ride into the center of Boston. The impressive entrance hall features a grand staircase and heavy, carved rocking chairs; to the left, a sitting and breakfast room is warmed by an elaborate fireplace topped by a heavy Chinese wood carving. A stunning bedroom on this floor has a big, marble, working fireplace, lead-paned windows, heavy curtains, and cherry paneling. Other bedrooms have Victorian antiques, bookshelves, Oriental rugs, working brick fireplaces, pedestal sinks, and claw-foot tubs.

In 1993, owner Bryan Austin began work to put more private baths into the second floor rooms, and renovated the porch, where breakfast is served in summer. This is a quiet, calm place to stay within easy reach of the city—and you can park your car for free!

Address: *92 Sewall Ave., Brookline, MA 02146, tel. 617/566–2234.*
Accommodation: *12 double rooms, 9 with private baths, 3 share 1 bath.*
Amenities: *Air-conditioning in some rooms, TV in rooms, living room, public phone; porch, parking.*
Rates: *$45–$94; Continental breakfast. MC, V.*
Restrictions: *No smoking in public rooms, no pets. 2-night minimum on weekends.*

The John Jeffries House

Named for the father of modern opthamology, the John Jeffries House was built a hundred years ago as part of the neighboring Massachusetts Eye and Ear Infirmary; in 1987, the square, four-story brick building was converted into a large inn. New managers are striving to create a friendly and stylish ambience, typified by the downstairs parlor, with wingback chairs, a fireplace, polished pine floors, and thick Oriental rugs. In 1993, renovation began on the guest rooms: The idea is to add brass and more distinctive features to the rather generic accommodations. Presently, rooms are decorated in pastel shades, with reproduction Colonial furnishings, and most are small, two-room suites with a sitting area and kitchen facilities; some are rather dark.

The inn sits at a major intersection, but triple-glazed windows keep out all the noise. One side of the John Jeffries faces characterful Charles Street at the bottom of Beacon Hill.

Address: *14 Embankment Rd., Boston, MA 02114, tel. 617/367–1866, fax 617/573–4181.*
Accommodations: *22 rooms, 24 suites, all with baths.*
Amenities: *Air-conditioning, parlor, TV and phones in rooms, kitchen facilities; reduced rates at local parking garage.*
Rates: *$70–$115 (some seasonal discounts); Continental breakfast. D, MC, V.*
Restrictions: *No smoking in some rooms, no pets.*

North Shore

The sliver of Atlantic seacoast known as the North Shore stretches from the grimy docklands of Boston's northern suburbs, past Rockport's precariously perched rows of wooden fishing shacks, to the fine Federal mansions of proud Newburyport, just south of the New Hampshire border. These North Shore towns present a world of contrasts: Salem claims a history of witches, millionaires, and maritime trade; Rockport is home to many artists' studios; and its neighbor, Gloucester, serves as a workaday port with a substantial fishing fleet. In Newburyport, redbrick storefronts give way to clapboard fishing cottages along a sandy road leading to dunes, beaches, extensive salt marshes, and numerous nature reserves.

During the short summer season, and in early fall, you'll experience the region at its brightest—and busiest. Most past visitors will probably remember the towns as bustling, sunglasses-and-sandwich-shop meccas, where finding a room is almost—but not quite—as difficult as finding a parking space. In the long, peaceful off-season months, travelers will find it nearly as hard to locate a room—not because the inns are full, but because some businesses in the region close down after October. Winter and early spring have much to offer nature lovers, hikers, and those in search of scenic seaside tranquillity. Locals enjoy the summer on the North Shore as much as visitors. The offerings at this time of year are what vacations are about: beaches, ice cream, crafts shops, seafood, boats, museums, nature trails, and top-quality country inns.

Places to Go, Sights to See

Crane's Beach. Near Ipswich, this white stretch of sand, over 5 miles long, is part of a 735-acre nature reserve that incorporates a salt marsh. Here, as at other North Coast beaches, biting flies invade on intermittent "bug days" throughout the summer.

Gloucester. The town's most famous landmark is the statue of a man at a ship's wheel, facing the ocean, and dedicated to those "who go down to the sea in ships." The monument is fitting, for Gloucester, the oldest seaport in the nation, is still a major fishing port. The town is also home to Rocky Neck, the oldest working artists' colony in America.

Marblehead. The small seaside town was founded by fishermen from Cornwall, England, in 1629, and the twisting, narrow streets of the historic district resemble those in typical Cornish fishing villages. Today, the town is one of the major yachting centers on the East Coast. The redbrick *town hall* (Washington St., tel. 617/631–0528) contains the well-known patriotic painting, *The Spirit of '76.*

Newburyport. Some of the finest Federal mansions in New England line the streets of this small historic town. They were built by prosperous 19th-century sea captains when Newburyport was a thriving port, famous for its clipper ships. The town's redbrick center has been completely revitalized and is now a shopping area. In the restored Customs House on the waterfront, the *Maritime Museum* (25 Water St., tel. 508/462–8681) has shipbuilding exhibits. A causeway connects Newburyport with *Plum Island* (tel. 508/465–5753), which has a long sandy beach and a wildlife refuge.

Rockport. At the tip of Cape Ann, Rockport was originally a fishing village but it developed as an artists' colony in the 1920s. Today, it's an arty, touristy New England town, with an incredible concentration of galleries and fine crafts stores, attracting large crowds in the summer.

Salem. Salem may not be the prettiest town on the North Shore, but it's rich in history. The infamous witchcraft trials took place here in 1692, and the *Salem Witch Museum* (Washington Sq. N, tel. 508/744–1692) accurately portrays the hysteria that engulfed this Puritan community. Later on, Salem became a prime U.S. port, with trade links to China and India. Salem's merchants were America's first millionaires, and their mansions still flank the streets. *Salem Maritime* (175 Derby Rd., tel. 508/744–4323), operated by the National Trust, is situated beside Derby Wharf. Tours take in the Customs House, the Government Warehouse, and historic shipowners' homes. The *Peabody and Essex Museum* (East India Sq., tel. 508/745–1876), the country's oldest continuously operating museum, houses a fine collection of exotic items brought back by merchant ships. Visitors should also stop off at the *House of Seven Gables* (54 Turner St., tel. 508/744–0991), immortalized by Salem-born author Nathaniel Hawthorne in his novel of the same name.

Whale-watching. For the best tours on the North Shore, try the whale-watch excursions. The whales are so numerous between May and October that you're practically guaranteed to see at least half a dozen, and on "good" days you may well see 40 or more.

Restaurants

Seafood is the North Shore specialty, from deep-fried clams "in the rough" to haute cuisine lobster dinners. Rockport is a dry town, with no liquor stores and no alcohol available in the restaurants, but you can usually bring your own. Recommended seafood restaurants include **White Rainbow** (tel. 508/281–0017) in Gloucester; **The Landing** (tel. 617/631–6268), beside Marblehead Harbor (outdoor dining in summer); **Scandia** (tel. 508/462–6271), and **David's** at the Garrison Inn (tel. 508/462–8077), both in Newburyport.

Dance Clubs

Popular local spots include **The Grog** (Newburyport, tel. 508/465–8008), with live blues and rock bands Thursday through Sunday nights, and downstairs at **Roosevelt's** restaurant (Salem, tel. 508/745–9608), where local bands play rock and roll Wed.–Sat. evenings.

Tourist Information

The umbrella organization for the whole region is the **North of Boston Visitors and Convention Bureau** (Box 3031, Peabody, MA 01961, tel. 508/532–1449). The following cover more specific areas: **Cape Ann Chamber of Commerce** (33 Commercial St., Gloucester, MA 01930, tel. 508/283–1601); **Essex North Chamber of Commerce** (29 State St., Newburyport, MA 09150, tel. 508/462–6680); **Rockport Chamber of Commerce** (Upper Main St., Rockport, MA 09166, tel. 508/546–6575); **Salem Chamber of Commerce** (32 Derby Sq., Salem, MA 01970, tel. 508/744–0004).

Reservations Services

Bed and Breakfast Marblehead and North Shore (Box 35, Newtonville, MA 02160, tel. 617/964–1606 or 800/832–2632, fax 617/332–8572); **Greater Boston Hospitality** (Box 1142, Brookline, MA 02146, tel. 617/277–5430); **Bed and Breakfast Associates Bay Colony Ltd.** (Box 57166, Babson Park Branch, Boston, MA 02157, tel. 617/449–5302 or 800/347–5088, fax 617/449–5958).

Addison Choate Inn

Rockport offers an excellent selection of inns, and the Addison Choate is one of the best. Shirley Johnson, an interior designer, bought the inn in 1992 with her husband, Knox, a landscape architect, and together they set about enhancing the historical character of an already attractive property.

Made of white clapboard, the long, narrow, two-story house, built in 1851, was the famed site of Rockport's first bathtub. The inn is a minute's walk from the town center and two blocks away from the Rockport-Boston railway station. Beyond the main building, the carriage house contains two one-bedroom apartments, and still farther is a large, fenced-in outdoor swimming pool. Spacious rooms in the main inn have big, tiled bathrooms and are individually decorated. The navy and white Captain's Room boasts a dark wood four-poster bed with a net canopy, polished pine floors, handmade quilts, Oriental rugs, and paintings of ships. The Chimney Room has a white brick chimney passing through it, wide-board floors, a Victorian oak bureau with mirror, and rocking chair with a hand-woven seat. Other rooms contain Hitchcock rockers and headboards, spool beds, filligree brass beds, quilts, local paintings, and wooden antiques. The "Room with a View" was converted from a loft, and its two huge windows have sea views over the rooftops, while the bathroom features a stained-glass skylight. The bedroom has wide pine floorboards, patterned fabrics, and white wicker furniture.

The large carriage house apartments offer first-floor living space and kitchens; one contains an iron spiral staircase leading to a bedroom with cathedral ceilings, wooden beams, and a skylight; the other has stained glass windows and a deck.

The living room has a Greek revival mantelpiece, cozy reading nooks, and Classical antique and modern furnishings. An extended Continental breakfast with home-baked goods is served in the dining room; in summer, guests can sit on the porch overlooking the inn's perennial garden. Knox's hobby since childhood has been bird-watching, and he offers guided bird-watching tours around the greater Rockport area.

Address: *49 Broadway, Rockport, MA 01966, tel. 508/546–7543.*
Accommodations: *7 double rooms with baths, 2 one-bedroom apartments.*
Amenities: *Air-conditioning; gardens, parking, outdoor pool.*
Rates: *$65–$100; Continental breakfast. MC, V.*
Restrictions: *No smoking, no pets. 2-night minimum on weekends; in season, 2-night minimum on holidays.*

Clark Currier Inn

This three-story clapboard mansion is the newest inn in Newburyport—and the best. Built by shipping merchant Thomas March Clark in 1803, the lodging is a typical example of the Federal architecture for which Newburyport is famous. The interior has been completely renovated to reveal many period splendors, such as wide-board polished wood floors, window seats, original colonial-style shutters, wood stoves, and a Federal "good morning" staircase—so-called because two small staircases join at the head of a large one, permitting family members to greet one another on their way down to breakfast.

Guest rooms, named after former owners or residents of the house, are all spacious and carefully decorated in period style, with Federal antiques. Some feature pencil-post beds; one has a reproduction sea captain's bed complete with drawers below, and another contains a sleigh bed dating from the late-19th century. Many of the rooms have fireplaces with carved wood surrounds, but these are not in use. Typical of the Federal home, ceilings become lower as you reach the upper stories, so in first-floor rooms the ceilings are 11 feet high, but only 7 feet on the third floor, where guest bedrooms are converted from former servants' quarters; upstairs, the ambience is less formal, but still authentic.

Bob Nolan, an international banker and currency trader in New York City, and his wife, Mary, a political science teacher at Rutger's University in New Jersey, stepped out of their high-stress jobs back in 1990 to take on the Clark Currier. They wanted a more family-oriented lifestyle for themselves and their daughter Melissa, now 8, and believe they've found the perfect situation in Newburyport. Since taking over, they opened up the ground floor to create a large living room with working fireplace, antique desks, couches, and bookcases. A second floor library has books and writing desks, and a display of antique toys on the landing outside. The inn offers afternoon tea, and a buffet-style breakfast of breads and muffins in a recently converted kitchen, besides in-room extras like candy dishes, restocked daily by Melissa! In summer, guests can eat outside in the garden with its rocking chairs and gazebo.

Address: *45 Green St., Newburyport, MA 01950, tel. 508/465–8363.*
Accommodations: *8 double rooms with baths.*
Amenities: *Air-conditioning, TV in lounge.*
Rates: *$65–$95; Continental breakfast. AE, MC, V.*
Restrictions: *No pets.*

Eden Pines Inn

Built in 1900 as a private summer cottage, Eden Pines stands so close to the ocean that the whole place seems about ready to sail off to sea—in fact, two of the wood decks already did, which prompted owner-managers Inge and John Sullivan to build a storm-proof brick deck that has survived for 15 years. The house looks out to the twin lights of Thatcher's Island; below the deck lie rocks and the raging (or lapping) waves. The Sullivans bought the inn 21 years ago, and they utilize its location to the utmost. The large bedrooms have great ocean views, and five out of six have secluded private balconies. Rooms are eclectically furnished, with a mixture of modern rattan or wicker and a few older pieces picked up at antiques shops. A "fresh" look predominates, however, with green and pale blue painted walls, modern floral fabrics, bright white moldings, and pastel-toned carpets; one room has a nonworking white painted-brick fireplace. The large bathrooms offer marble units and brass fixtures.

Downstairs, the living room features a fireplace with stone surround and dark-stained, pine-paneled walls. The breakfast room, with its white trellises, wood-plank walls, and straw matting, opens onto the oceanside deck; the room's huge windows provide excellent sea views.

For even better ocean vistas, take a look at the Sullivans' other property just down the street, the four-bedroom Eden Point House, which they rent by the week. It stands on a rock, surrounded by the sea on three sides, and is of a contemporary, open-plan design, with a semicircular living room; a stone, floor-to-ceiling fireplace surround; a high cathedral ceiling; and a large modern kitchen.

Eden Pines Inn and Eden Point House are a five-minute drive from Rockport center, and two minutes by car from the nearest beach.

Address: *Eden Rd., Rockport, MA 01966, tel. 508/546-2505.*
Accommodations: *6 double rooms with baths.*
Amenities: *Air-conditioning, cable TV in rooms; dip pool, croquet lawn.*
Rates: *$80–$120, Continental breakfast. MC, V.*
Restrictions: *No pets. 3-night minimum on holiday weekends, closed mid-Nov.–mid-May.*

Harbor Light Inn

On a bustling narrow street at the heart of Marblehead's historic district, this Federal-style inn is the best place to stay in town; it competes with the Clark Currier Inn in Newburyport as one of the classiest, most relaxing, and most authentic inns on the whole of the North Shore. If you take the Harbor Light Room and stand on tiptoe, you can see the lighthouse in the harbor; otherwise you'll only have an occasional glimpse of the sea. Nevertheless, you're bound to be impressed with the building's interior—wide-board hardwood floors, chintz chairs, silver ice buckets and candy bowls, original shutters that fold into the wall, and Chinese rugs. As for the beds, you can choose between a pencil-post bed and a hand-carved mahogany four-poster bed with a floral canopy. Newly added bathrooms have huge mirrors and skylights, and some contain whirlpool baths as well.

The old building dates from the early 1700s, with one wing constructed in the 19th century. When innkeepers Paul and Suzanne Conway bought the place in a state of disrepair in 1986, they opened up the third floor and added a completely new section to the back of the house. They're veteran, energetic innkeepers, whose hard work and attention to detail have resulted in a luxurious inn with excellent amenities but undisturbed original features. The character of individual rooms varies tremendously—those in the earlier structure have more original features, such as unusual arched doorways, working fireplaces, and wideboard floors. On the third floor, however, rooms have skylights, exposed brick, cathedral ceilings, and wooden beams. In the new addition, rooms are modern in concept and in decor, and some offer private decks.

In 1992, the innkeepers bought the building next door and over the next year expanded the inn, adding seven more big, beautiful bedrooms with working fireplaces, four-poster beds, and painted wood paneling. One room has an old-fashioned bathroom with claw-foot tub, the top floor room has exposed beams and a large, modern bathroom. The inn has two parlors with Chippendale furniture, wing chairs and open fireplaces; Continental breakfast is served in the recently added dining room.

Address: *58 Washington St., Marblehead, MA 01945, tel. 617/631–2186.*
Accommodations: *19 double rooms with baths, 1 suite.*
Amenities: *Air-conditioning, cable TV in rooms, 2 parlors, dining room, conference room; outdoor pool.*
Rates: *$90–$185; Continental breakfast. AE, MC, V.*
Restrictions: *No pets. 2-night minimum on weekends July–Oct.*

Inn on Cove Hill

This immaculate, well-maintained inn has an excellent location on a pretty hillside street, just two minutes' walk from the center of Rockport. The square, Federal-style house was built in 1791, reportedly with money from a cache of pirate gold discovered at nearby Gully Point. Although some guest rooms are small (a few are really tiny), they're so carefully decorated in the Federal style, with white draperies and spreads, white wicker chairs, bright flowery print papers, and white painted brass headboards, that they can be called "cozy" with a clear conscience. Other rooms feature such details as Laura Ashley floral-print wallpapers, patchwork quilts, unfinished wooden antiques, canopy and half-canopy beds, spool beds, iron door latches, wooden bathroom fixtures, wide-board floors, and pastel-toned Oriental rugs. Two rooms in an 1850s addition have been furnished in the Victorian style, with brass and wicker, and one bathroom contains an original claw-foot bathtub and bathroom set. The overall "country" style is executed with taste: You won't be ambushed by duck pillows or rag dolls at every turn.

The second and third floors are reached via two narrow spiral staircases (first-floor bedrooms are available), the front staircase has 13 steps, representing the original 13 Colonies. Both upper stories have decks, and the third floor affords a good view over the rooftops to Rockport Harbor and Bearskin Neck.

The guest lounge retains its original wide-board pine floors and dentil cornice moldings; furnishings include a mixture of Federal-style antiques, velvet wing chairs, rockers, and more modern, matching couches. There's no public breakfast room, so a rather scanty Continental breakfast (fresh muffin, juice, and coffee) is served on Wedgwood or Royal Doulton English bone china in the bedroom or outside in the garden at tables around an old pump.

Innkeepers John and Marjorie Pratt spent their honeymoon here, and returned years later to buy the place. They've been running the inn since 1978, and in that time have done a good deal of restoration, removing 1950 cover-up features to expose original wood paneling and floors. The Pratts are excellent hosts with a great sense of humor.

Address: *37 Mt. Pleasant St., Rockport, MA 01966, tel. 508/546-2701.*
Accommodations: *9 double rooms with baths, 2 doubles share 1 bath.*
Amenities: *Fans, TV in rooms.*
Rates: *$45–$94; Continental breakfast. No credit cards.*
Restrictions: *No smoking, no pets. 2-night minimum Jul.–Aug. and on weekends May–Jun. and Sept., closed late Oct.–Apr.*

Yankee Clipper Inn

The white Georgian mansion that forms the main part of this imposing, perfectly located Cape Ann establishment stands surrounded by gardens, challenging the waves from a rocky headland that juts out into the ocean. Constructed as a private home in the 1930s, this three-story oblong building with big square windows has been managed as an inn by one family for more than 40 years. Guest rooms in the mansion vary in size, but they're generally large; with the sea on three sides, all rooms (except one) have fabulous views. Many of them also offer weatherized porches, such as the one that wraps around the enormous suite where John and Jacqueline Kennedy stayed when the late president was still a Massachusetts senator. Furnished with Queen Anne– and Victorian-style reproductions, the rooms contain four-poster or canopy beds, chaise longues, and wicker porch furniture.

Across the lawns in a newer structure called the Quarterdeck, picture windows in all the rooms provide impressive ocean views. Modern and stylish, the spacious (some are huge) well-designed rooms have wood-paneled or blue/green painted walls, seascape paintings, wing chairs, and modern couches. The top-floor rooms are particularly attractive with their sloped ceilings, large bathrooms, and sitting areas.

On the other side of the street from the main inn is the Bullfinch House, an 1840 Greek Revival home, appointed with dark wood antiques, floral print papers, lacy curtains, and pineapple four-poster beds.

Guests dine at the main inn, on a sunny porch with wrought-iron chairs, again overlooking the sea. Just behind the porch, the lounge has a huge fireplace with a mahogany surround and large floral stencils at either side. Dusky pink tones, pink velvet couches, and heavy-framed painted portraits recreate a Victorian atmosphere. Below the lounge, a conference center caters to business clientele. The well-managed inn has a friendly staff, and careful touches abound—the outdoor swimming pool, for example, is attractively landscaped and virtually invisible from the road. The Yankee Clipper is located more than a mile north of Rockport, so guests will need transport in and out of town.

Address: *96 Granite St., Box 2399, Rockport, MA 01966, tel. 508/546–3407.*
Accommodations: *27 double rooms with baths, 6 suites.*
Amenities: *Restaurant, lounge, air-conditioning; outdoor pool.*
Rates: *\$69–\$196; full breakfast. AE, MC, V.*
Restrictions: *No pets. Closed Dec. 20–26.*

Garrison Inn

This square, four-story Georgian redbrick building was first constructed as a private home in 1809 and became an inn around the turn of the century. Set conveniently on a small square, a few blocks from Newburyport's downtown and the waterfront, the Garrison is a high quality inn with excellent dining. On the formal side, the inn will appeal to travelers who enjoy business-style conveniences: cable TV, telephones, and room service. Spacious rooms contain Colonial reproductions, and exposed walls show off Newburyport's famous red brick. The best guest rooms are the unusual top-floor suites; furnished with 19th-century reproduction couches and wing chairs, they have fireplaces and are on two levels, with either a contemporary spiral staircase or a Colonial staircase leading from the sitting room to the sleeping area above.

The two restaurants, David's and Downstairs at David's, are top of the line both for food and service, and offer a childcare facility where kids can play and eat while parents enjoy their own meal in peace!

Address: *11 Brown Sq., Newburyport, MA 01950, tel. 508/465–0910.*
Accommodations: *24 rooms with baths, 6 suites.*
Amenities: *2 restaurants, air-conditioning, cable TV in rooms and lounge, room service, live entertainment.*
Rates: *$75–$85, $120–$130 suites; breakfast extra. AE, DC, MC, V.*
Restrictions: *No pets.*

Sally Webster Inn

Sally Webster was a member of Hannah Jumper's so-called hatchet gang, which smashed its way through the town's liquor joints one evening in 1856 and succeeded in turning Rockport into the dry town it remains today. Sally lived in this house for much of her life, and guest rooms are named after members of her family. The inn, run by the Webster family (no relation to Sally), is classy, small, and relaxing. Bedrooms contain pineapple four-poster, brass, canopy, or spool beds; pine wide-board floors with Indian and Belgian rugs; rocking chairs; and nonworking brick fireplaces, which shelter old curiosities, such as a cranberry rake or a bread bin. Other furnishings include Chippendale, Sheridan, and Queen Anne antiques. Breakfast is served on mismatched china in the long, narrow dining room with its glass-fronted cabinets and display of pewter. The guest lounge is known as Sally's share, because she inherited it after her father's death. It houses Webster family artifacts, a piano, a brick fireplace, and paintings by Rockport artists. The inn lies close to the beach.

Address: *34 Mt. Pleasant St., Rockport, MA 01966, tel. 508/546–9251.*
Accommodations: *6 double rooms with baths.*
Amenities: *Dining room, lounge.*
Rates: *$68–$78; Continental breakfast. MC, V.*
Restrictions: *No pets. 2-night minimum weekends June–Oct.; open weekends only Feb., Mar., Apr., Nov., closed Dec. and Jan.*

Seacrest Manor

The motto here is "decidedly small, intentionally quiet," and Seacrest Manor certainly lives up to these expectations. The 1911 clapboard mansion sits on a hill overlooking the sea, surrounded by carefully tended gardens. Inside, you'll find two long sitting rooms with leather chairs and bookshelves; they were redecorated in 1992 with dark green silk fabrics, and the huge wall mirror from the old Philadelphia Opera House was regilded. The hall and staircase are festooned with paintings by local artists—some of which depict the inn. The simply furnished bedrooms feature white bedspreads, brick (nonworking) fireplaces, floral print papers, and wood paneling. Some rooms provide sea views, while others have large private decks.

By the working fireplace in the dining room, a kingly breakfast is served on Wedgwood crockery. Innkeepers Dwight MacCormack and Leighton Saville are justly proud of their culinary delights (especially the spiced oatmeal). Many special touches enhance your stay: complimentary newspapers, a shoe-shine service, custom toiletries, a nightly turndown service.

Address: *131 Marmion Way, Rockport, MA 01966, tel. 508/546–2211.*
Accommodations: *6 rooms with baths, 2 rooms share 1 bath.*
Amenities: *TV in some rooms.*
Rates: *$70–$110; full breakfast. No credit cards.*
Restrictions: *No pets. 2-night minimum weekends, 3-night minimum holidays, closed Dec. 1–Mar. 30.*

Seaward Inn

At the end of a quiet promontory a mile south of Rockport, this cedar-shingled inn built at the turn of the century lies just across a narrow lane from the sea. In the main building the medium-size rooms have Colonial furnishings; the best of these at the front provide an ocean view. Third-floor bedrooms offer sloping ceilings and old-fashioned beige-toned floral-print wallpapers. Common rooms include a large winterized porch with a flagstone floor, a lounge with an open fireplace, and three dining rooms, one of which has a brick floor and bay windows. Clothespins serve as napkin holders, and guests write their name on the peg—when they return to the inn, their peg hangs waiting for them on a string, along with thousands of others that adorn the dining-room wall. Breakers, across the street, is a shingled house on the ocean. Its nine rooms are particularly spacious: One suite features a working fireplace, another has a private deck, and a third opens onto the lawn facing the sea. Another nine-room building and eight cottages are also for rent, some with pine paneling and working fireplaces.

Address: *62 Marmion Way, Rockport, MA 01966, tel. 508/546–3471.*
Accommodations: *38 double rooms with baths.*
Amenities: *Restaurant; pool, putting green, bicycles, playground.*
Rates: *$98–$138, full breakfast (MAP available). MC, V.*
Restrictions: *No pets. Closed mid Oct.–mid May.*

Seven South Street

This white clapboard house on the hill, dating back to 1750, operates as a cozy, colorful, country-style bed-and-breakfast inn. Each curiously shaped, prettily decorated guest room has a distinct character. Open fireplaces in the rooms are not for use; the bricks have been painted white, and most contain dry flower arrangements. All rooms are cheerful, if on the small side.

A 17th-century sampler hangs on the wall, some rooms have brass or four-poster beds, and a few beds are covered with handmade quilts; one room has its own entrance and a deck. Breakfast is served in the dining room, which has heavy beams an open fireplace, pewter chandeliers, and wood paneling. A small lounge contains a piano; its walls are covered with the work of local artists. The inn is situated on South Street, beyond The Inn on Cove Hill and the Sally Webster Inn; it's only a few minutes' walk to downtown, and less than five minutes' walk to the beach.

Address: *7 South St., Rockport, MA 01966, tel. 508/546–6708.*
Accommodations: *3 double rooms with baths, 2 doubles and 1 single share 1 bath, 2 housekeeping apartments, 1 studio cottage that sleeps four.*
Amenities: *Dining room, lounge; pool.*
Rates: *$55–$78, apartments $450 and $550 per week; cottage $600 per week, Continental breakfast. No credit cards.*
Restrictions: *No pets. Closed Dec. 1–Feb.*

Harborside House

Located in Marblehead's historic district and overlooking the water, Harborside House was built in 1850 by a ship's carpenter. Susan Livingston has lived here 28 years, and operated the house as a successful bed-and-breakfast since 1985. This is what the British mean by "B&B": a family home with three upstairs bedrooms turned over to guests. Visitors share a downstairs living room, which has a working brick fireplace and wood paneling, and eat a breakfast of home-baked goods and homemade cereal in a pleasant dining room or on the deck outside. Bedrooms have polished wide-board floors and Oriental rugs; two have perfect views over Marblehead harbor with its hundreds of sailboats, the third overlooks a lovely garden. Susan, who works as a dressmaker from home, is a considerate and interesting host, providing information folders about the area, as well as in-room journals where guests can write about the highlights of their stay for future arrivals. The house is a short walk from all of Marblehead's attractions, and offers parking space, a much sought-after commodity in the historic district.

Address: *23 Gregory St., Marblehead, MA 01945, tel. 617/631–1032.*
Accommodations: *1 room with bath, 2 rooms share 1 bath.*
Amenities: *TV in rooms, shared phone; parking.*
Rates: *$60–$85; Continental breakfast. No credit cards.*
Restrictions: *No smoking, no pets.*

Amelia Payson Guest House

One of the best places to stay in Salem, the Amelia Payson Guest House is within walking distance of all the town's attractions, only a block or so away from the many museums in the historic district, and a brief stroll across the common from the town center and the sea. Built in 1845 for Amelia and Edward Payson, the Greek Revival house has bright, airy rooms with floral-print wallpaper, brass and four-poster canopy beds, nonworking marble fireplaces, and white wicker. The parlor downstairs contains a grand piano, while upstairs a reading room is full of visitor information. A Continental breakfast of fresh fruit and home-baked breads is served family-style in the elegant dining room. Ada and Don Roberts bought the building in 1984, restored the dilapidated vacant house to its present condition, and have been operating successfully as an inn since 1985.

Address: *16 Winter St., Salem, MA 01970, tel. 508/744–8304.*
Accommodations: *3 double rooms with bath, 1 studio.*
Amenities: *Breakfast room, TV in rooms, 2 parlors; parking.*
Rates: *$75–$95; Continental breakfast. AE, MC, V.*
Restrictions: *No smoking, no pets.*

The Pioneer Valley

The Pioneer Valley, a string of historic settlements along the Connecticut River from Springfield in the south up to the Vermont border, formed the western frontier of New England from the early 1600s until the late 18th century. The fertile banks of the Connecticut River first attracted farmers and traders. Today, the northern regions around Amherst, Deerfield, and Greenfield remain rural and tranquil, supporting fruit farms, agricultural businesses, small towns, and villages with typical New England architecture. Farther south, power mills, factories, and the earliest industrial cities in North America developed along the river; here the landscape is less scenic, though it is still of great historic interest. Pioneers in education came to this region, too, to found America's first college for women. Today five major colleges, as well as numerous smaller institutions and well-known preparatory schools, are located in the region, which has a thriving cultural and artistic community life.

Places to Go, Sights to See

Amherst. Three of the valley's five major colleges—the University of Massachusetts, Amherst College, and Hampshire College—are located here, and not surprisingly, Amherst caters to youthful tastes, reflected in its numerous bookstores, bars, and cafés. The town was also the home of poet Emily Dickinson; the poet's *Homestead* (280 Main St., tel. 413/542–8161) can be visited by appointment.

Historic Deerfield. A peaceful village with a violent past, Deerfield lies near the northern end of the Pioneer Valley, a short drive east on Route 5 from 1–91. In 1675, Pocumtuck Indians attacked the community of newly settled farmers in the Bloody Brook Massacre, killing or driving out every white inhabitant. Returning pioneers were set upon again in 1704, by the Indians and the French together, and only one house—the Indian House—survived that raid intact. Ironically, it was torn down in 1848 because there were no funds for its restoration; a replica was constructed in 1929, and can now be visited, as can 12 other 17th- and early 18th-century house museums (The Street, tel. 413/774–5581) along the main throughfare. As period homes, some contain antique furnishings and decorative arts; others exhibit collections of textiles, silver, pewter, and ceramics.

Mount Tom State Reservation. One of several reservations in the Pioneer Valley, *Mount Tom* (tel. 413/527–4805), off Route 5, has 20 miles of hiking trails, and facilities for orienteering, fishing, cross-country skiing, and ice skating. Nearby, the *Mount Tom Ski Area* (tel. 413/536–0516) offers downhill skiing in winter and a summer resort with a wave pool, water slide, and alpine slide.

Northampton. This small town is the site of Smith College, which opened in 1875 with 14 students: Today it accommodates almost 3,000 women undergraduates. Northampton was also the longtime home of the 103th U.S. President, Calvin Collidge. He practiced law here, served as mayor from 1910 to 1911, and returned to the town after his presidential term. A leaflet of walking tours around the historic city is available at the tourist information booth (tel. 413/584–1900) opposite the Hotel Northampton.

Old Sturbridge Village. About 20 miles east of Springfield, Sturbridge Vilalge is the star attraction of central Massachusetts. A model New England village of the early 1800s with 40 buildings, Old Sturbridge (tel. 508/347–3362) covers a 200-acre site, and as one of the best period restorations in the country, it shouldn't be missed. Working exhibits include a 200-year-old newspaper printing press, a blacksmith and forge, a water-powered woolcarding mill, and a sawmill. In the elaborately furnished individual houses, "interpreters" in period costume demonstrate skills, such as spinning and cooking, and talk about 18th-century life. You can ride the streets in a horse-drawn carriage and visit a farm and a village store.

South Hadley. Mount Holyoke College, the first women's college in the United States, was founded here in 1837. Surrounded by spacious grounds and mellow brick buildings, the *College Art Museum* (tel. 413/538–2245) contains exhibits of Asian, Egyptian, and classical art. Poet Emily Dickinson, born in nearby Amherst, studied here.

Springfield. The largest city in the Pioneer Valley, Springfield is a sprawling industrial town where modern skyscrapers rise between grand historic buildings. Its main claim to fame, however, is that Dr. James Naismith invented basketball here in 1891. The *Naismith Memorial Basketball Hall of Fame* (W. Columbus Ave., tel. 413/781–6500) honors the game's greatest celebrities and features a cinema, a basketball fountain, and a moving walkway from which visitors can shoot baskets. At the musuem quadrangle near downtown are four others: the *Connecticut Valley Historical Museum* (tel. 413/732–3080); the *George Walter Smith Art Museum* (tel. 413/733–4214), with a private collection of Japanese armor, ceramics, and textiles; the *Museum of Fine Arts* (tel. 413/732–6092), with French Impressionist paintings; and the *Springfield Science Museum* (tel. 413/733–1194).

Restaurants

A number of inns in the Pioneer Valley offer traditional dining, featuring such New England specialties as seafood, pot roast, rack of lamb, and Indian pudding. Recommended inns are the **Deerfield Inn** (Deerfield, tel. 413/774–5587), **The Whately Inn** (Whately, tel. 413/665–3044), **Wiggins Tavern** (Northampton, tel. 413/584–3100), and the **Publick House** (Sturbridge, tel. 508/347–3313).

Dance Clubs

The Collegiate population ensures a lively club and nightlife scene in the Pioneer Valley. Popular spots include **Iron Horse** (Northampton, tel. 413/584–0610), with a variety of folk, blues, jazz, Celtic, and new-wave music seven nights a week; **The Vertex** (Rte. 9, Hadley, tel. 413/586–4463), specializing in rock and blues; and **Sheehan's Café** (Northampton, tel. 413/586–4258), featuring rock and roll and blues six nights a week.

Tourist Information

Pioneer Valley Convention and Visitors Bureau (1500 Main St., Springfield, MA 01115, tel. 413/787–1548); **Worcester County Convention and Visitors Bureau** (33 Waldo St., Worcester, MA 01608, tel. 508/753–2920).

Reservations Services

American Country Collection of B&B (4 Greenwood Lane, Delmar, NY 12054, tel. 518/439–7001, fax 518/439–4301); **The Greater Springfield/Berkshire Bed and Breakfast Homes** (Main St., Box 211, Williamsburg, MA 01096, tel. 413/268–7244).

The Allen House

Dozens of bed-and-breakfast inns fall under the general term of "country-style"—a few have good antiques and interesting decor. But inns that are restored with historic precision and attention to every last detail are rare indeed: The Allen House, honored with a Historic Preservation Award from the Amherst Historical Commission in 1991, is one of them.

Alan Zieminski, a biochemist at the University of Massachussetts, has lived in the 1886 Queen Anne, stick-style house since the late '60s. He bought it in 1988, and once he and his wife, Ann, began putting their vague ideas of restoration into practice, the project took on a life of its own. Along with Alan's brother Jonas, the family soon became experts in Aesthetic period—a Victorian movement heavily influenced by trade with Japan.

Guest rooms are museum-like representations of the Aesthetic era. Impressive period wallpapers decorate the walls. Sunflowers, the Aesthetics' emblem, are everywhere. Furnishings include some original Charles Eastlake pieces, such as the matching burled walnut bedhead and dresser in the upstairs Eastlake room; other rooms have Eastlake reproductions, wicker "steamship" chairs, pedestal sinks, screens, carved golden oak or brass beds, goose-down comforters, painted wooden floors, and claw-foot tubs. Public rooms are just as impressive as bedrooms: The breakfast room has Anglo-Japanese reproduction wallpapers, an intricately carved fireplace, and its original grass reed matting, imported from Japan, on the floor. The sitting room floor also has its original covering—Victorian oilcloth, the forerunner of linoleum, and an 1880s Oriental hand-stiched rug.

When the Zieminskis bought the house, it was a kind of time capsule full of original, if faded, relics. The upstairs hallway is lined with pictures found stashed away in a locked room. Modern advantages are cable TV in the living room, tourist information, poetry books, afternoon tea, a hearty cooked breakfast, and free pick-up service to guests from the nearby train and bus stations. It's a short walk from the center of Amherst, rates are reasonable, and the hosts—who seem a little overwhelmed by what they've achieved—are extremely pleasant company.

Address: *599 Main St., Amherst, MA 01002, tel. 413/253-5000.*
Accommodations: *5 double rooms with baths.*
Amenities: *Living room with cable TV, breakfast room, ceiling fans; parking, pay-phone, afternoon tea.*
Rates: *$45–$95; full breakfast. No credit cards.*
Restrictions: *Smoking on veranda only, no pets. 2 night minimum weekends in season.*

Deerfield Inn

Perfectly situated on the street that's realy a string of museums, the peaceful Deerfield Inn, with its columned facade and white clapboard exterior, harks back to a gentler era. Built in 1884, it was substantially modernized after a fire in 1981, which explains the square, spacious guest rooms, reminiscent of more modern hotels. The style and grace of the light, airy interior owes much to the flair and imagination of the young, enthusiastic innnkeepers, Karl Sabo and his English wife, Jane, who bought the place in 1987, leaving their fast-track lives in New York's Greenwich Village for "something different."

The couple has worked hard on redecoration, for example, having reproduction period wallpapers custom designed for the reception room, tavern, and many of the bedrooms. Guest rooms, with light floral themes, are furnished with sofas, bureaus, eclectic Federal-style antiques, and replicas of Queen Anne beds and Chippendale chairs. Some rooms have four-poster or canopy beds.

The large, sunny dining room on the first floor is elegantly decorated with silverware, Federal-style chairs, and antique side tables, are graced with candlelight in the evening. The cuisine is first rate, and the inn has a well-deserved reputation for dining. Specialties on the menu include saddle of vension sautéed with chestnuts in black-currant sauce, rack of lamb with Dijon mustard and garlic, and salmon with scallops; several dishes are based on recipes from old cookbooks in the village museum. Jackets and ties are suggested, though not required, an approach that sums up the inn's nature—it is formal enough to make your stay a special event, but friendly enough to create a relaxed and welcoming atmosphere. From May to October, a cheerful café serves inexpensive sandwiches and salads during the day.

Just down the road are the dozen 17th- and early 18th-century house museums of Historic Deerfield (*see* Places to Go, Sights to See, above), which provide year-round lectures and tours. The Barnard Tavern has a ballroom with a fiddlers' gallery, and several hands-on displays: you can climb into the rope bed and write on the slates. The Memorial Hall Museum displays tributes to the Native American Pocumtuck, as well as relics from the village's history.

Address: *The Street, Deerfield, MA 01342, tel. 413/774–5587.*
Accommodations: *23 double rooms with baths (2 rooms wheelchair-accessible).*
Amenities: *Restaurant, coffee shop, lounge, air-conditioning, TV, and phones in 4 rooms.*
Rates: *$122; full breakfast. AE, DC, MC, V.*
Restrictions: *Closed Dec. 24–26.*

Sturbridge Country Inn

Originally a farmhouse, this white 1840s building on Sturbridge's busy Main Road has become one of the best places to stay for visitors to Old Sturbridge Village, just a short walk away. An imposing Greek Revival facade brings to mind a grand municipal edifice rather than a farmhouse, and sets a high level of expectation, which the interiors more than match. Guest rooms, all of which have working fireplaces, are furnished with colonial reproductions that blend with the modern design. And every room has a whirlpool bath.

Although all the rooms have impressive colonial-style decor, those on the first floor are smaller and simpler. Upstairs, Rooms 7 and 8 are "theme rooms"—one features wicker furnishings, the other brass, and each offers a glass-enclosed sun porch. Both these rooms are grand, with exposed hand-hewn beams and steps that lead down from the whirlpool bath to the large bedroom. The best room of all, however, is the vast suite that occupies the whole of the third floor; it features cathedral ceilings, a large whirlpool bath in the living room, a wet bar, and big windows.

Guests are served a light Continental breakfast in the first-floor lounge, where innkeeper Kevin MacConnell, whose brother runs the inn, has succeeded in mixing old styles with modern comforts. The lounge has an open fireplace and colonial-style furnishings and decor, but the open-plan architecture and cathedral ceilings lift the area into the 20th century and create a light and gracious ambience. In the summer, an adjoining garden area and gazebo are opened to guests. Only one caveat here: The plumbing gurgles, and ground floor rooms can be noisy as a result.

Address: *530 Main St., Box 60, Sturbridge, MA 01566, tel. 508/347–5503.*
Accommodations: *9 double rooms with baths, 1 suite.*
Amenities: *Air-conditioning, cable TV, fireplaces, whirlpool baths in bedrooms.*
Rates: *\$69–\$149; Continental breakfast. AE, D, MC, V.*
Restrictions: *No smoking in some bedrooms, no pets.*

Yankee Pedlar Inn

The Yankee Pedlar has grown outward from a central yellow clapboard building, and now comprises several annexes of superbly decorated guest rooms, as well as an "opera house" for dances and banquets. Each annex has a different theme; rooms have four-poster beds, Currier and Ives prints, nightstands, desks, and other antiques. The spaciousness of the suites—some with fireplaces—make them worth the minimal extra cost. Although every room at this inn is unique, one of the best places to stay is the all-pink Victorian-style bridal suite. It's a wonderful extravaganza of deep carpets, dripping lace, draperies, mirrors, and bird cages, complete with Victorian valentines on the mantelpiece. If you prefer something simpler, the inn offers an alternative: the neighboring carriage house, with classic canopy beds, rustic antiques, cathedral ceilings, and exposed beams.

Antiques in the public rooms include a pre-Prohibition bar, decorative wood panels from the local (now demolished) Kenilworth Castle, a collection of copper pots, and dozens of old photographs of the region. Thursday through Saturday evenings a banjo and piano player entertain in the Oyster Bar, which is equipped with a popcorn machine in the shape of a street vendor's cart. The place feels like a popular London pub from the Victorian era, but with an added touch of class. The restaurant (J.J. Hilderth's, after the judge who first owned the house) serves good American fare with an emphasis on seafood and steak. The owners, Larry Audette, Rod Cameron, and John Samosko, bought the inn in 1990. Holyoke residents, they have a background in the restaurant business. They employ a large staff for the frequent private parties in the inn's many function and dining rooms, and have begun an ongoing refurbishing program.

The inn has only one disadvantage for vacationers—the location. Although it's convenient—only a short distance off I-91—it stands at a major intersection. Rooms near the road have triple-glazed windows, which keep out the noise. Holyoke has several museums, but it is not a tourist mecca. On the plus side, the inn is near several colleges, including Mount Holyoke, Smith, Amherst, and the University of Massachusetts.

Address: *1866 Northampton St., Holyoke, MA 01040, tel. 413/532–9494.*
Accommodations: *45 double rooms with baths, 2 single rooms with baths, 16 suites.*
Amenities: *Restaurant, 2 bars, outdoor café, air-conditioning, cable TV in rooms, 4 banquet rooms.*
Rates: *$69–$95; Continental breakfast. AE, D, DC, MC, V.*
Restrictions: *No pets.*

The Publick House and Colonel Ebenezer Crafts Inn

These two inns operate under the same management, and offer a wide variety of services with very distinct styles. The Publick House was founded, (confusingly enough, by Ebenezer Crafts) in 1771, and recently underwent a major renovation. It's a big, sprawling old inn with extensive dining rooms lit by pewter chandeliers, and a menu emphasizing the same traditional Yankee meals that were served 200 years ago, from individual lobster pies to double-thick loin lamb chops. Four meals are served daily, all year round, and breakfasts are sometimes cooked on the open hearth. Accommodations at the Publick House consist of fairly small, "olde-worlde" bedrooms with uneven wide-board floors, some canopy beds, and plain wooden antiques. The Chamberlain house next door features suites in the same style, while contemporary accommodations are available at the new Country Lodge with its modern motel-style rooms.

Just over a mile away, the Crafts Inn is a quiet alternative to the hustle and bustle of the Publick House. A restored Colonial Farmhouse built in 1786, it features eight spacious guest rooms with canopy or four-poster beds, antique desks, painted wood panels, and polished hardwood floors. Third floor rooms have sloping gable roofs. Downstairs, guests share a library, sun porch, and a large lounge with Colonial furniture and an enormous brick fireplace; there's also an outdoor pool. Breakfast consists of baked goods, and afternoon tea is also served.

Address: *Rte. 131, On-the-Common, Sturbridge, MA 01566, tel. 508/347–3313 or 800/782–5425, fax 508/347–5073.*
Accommodations: *17 rooms with bath (Publick House); 3 suites and one room with bath (Chamberlain House); 100 modern rooms with bath (Country Lodge); 8 rooms with bath (Crafts Inn).*
Amenities: *3 restaurants, conference rooms, bar; tennis court, pool, shuffleboard, playground, bike rentals (Publick House). Air-conditioning, library, living room; pool (Crafts Inn).*
Rates: *$69–$120, suites $99–$175; breakfast extra (Publick House), Continental breakfast (Crafts Inn). AE, DC, MC, V.*
Restrictions: *No pets, no smoking (Publick House guest rooms).*

Lord Jeffery Inn

The gabled Victorian-style brick inn with green shutters is ideally located on the green between the town center and Amherst College Campus; although it's at the heart of Amherst, the lodging remains quiet and calm. Colonial furnishings and the lounge's open fireplace make for an inn-like atmosphere in the public rooms, and new owners are gradually replacing the standardized floral decor in the bedrooms with simpler, cream-painted plaster walls and pastel-painted woodwork. In fact, the business-style atmosphere which used to predominate is being toned down, with a friendlier, less formal style of management. Some rooms have working fireplaces, and all contain Colonial reproductions as well as modern conveniences like cable TV and phones. When making reservations, it's a good idea to try and book either a room with a balcony overlooking the garden courtyard or a first-floor room that opens onto the garden. Also keep in mind that the inn can get fully booked during key college weekend events. The inn's large restaurant, with its white painted beams, chandeliers, and open fireplace, is first rate.

Address: *30 Boltwood Ave., Amherst, MA 01002, tel. 413/253–2576.*
Accommodations: *44 double rooms with baths, 6 suites.*
Amenities: *Restaurant, tavern, air-conditioning, phones, cable TV in rooms.*
Rates: *$80–$120; breakfast extra. AE, DC, MC, V.*
Restrictions: *No pets.*

Northfield Country House

Andrea Dale, once an executive at Saks Fifth Avenue, gave up her job in favor of the quiet life. She certainly found what she was looking for in Northfield House, and so should you, if the main purpose of your vacation is to get away from it all. This big English manor house sits on 16 acres of ground atop a small rise, overlooking the countryside and Northfield village in the distance. Thick woods border the long curving driveway, and landscaped gardens filled with daffodils, tulips, and summer flowers surround the house. Andrea, a welcoming but discreet host, has renovated the place extensively, rebuilt porches, and added an outdoor pool. Northfield was constructed about 100 years ago by a shipbuilder, which accounts for the abundance of such handcrafted woodwork as the heavy paneling and thick chestnut beams in the open-plan living room. Guest rooms vary in size—avoid the smallest ones, which are former servants' quarters. Rooms contain Victorian antiques, brass beds, chairs, and mirrors, and the best have working fireplaces with stone surrounds.

Address: *School St., RR 1A, Box 617, Northfield, MA 01360, tel. 413/498–2692.*
Accommodations: *7 double rooms share 4 baths.*
Amenities: *Lounge; pool, gardens.*
Rates: *$50–$80; full breakfast. MC, V.*
Restrictions: *No smoking in bedrooms, no pets.*

Sunnyside Farm Bed and Breakfast

Guests have the whole of the second floor to themselves in this 1864 farmhouse, but you're made to feel very much part of the family by hosts Dick and Marylou Green. The yellow house with black shutters and a red barn attached has been in Marylou's family for generations, and formerly operated as a tobacco farm. Now the fields are let out to the Nourse Strawberry Farms, where you can pick your own berries in season.

Country-style guest rooms vary in size from tiny to large—the best and the biggest is the room at the front, furnished with twin beds and country maple antiques that were either handed down by the family or bought at auctions. Framed fine-art prints hang on the walls, and all rooms have views across the fields. Guests are invited to sit with the Greens in their first-floor livingroom where there's a TV; the only other public space for visitors is a small small library on the first floor. Breakfast, served family-style in the dining room with its wood-burning stove, often includes homemade jams and muffins, berries, eggs and bacon, or pancakes.

Address: *11 River Rd., Whately (Box 486, South Deerfield, MA 01373), tel. 413/665–3113.*
Accommodations: *5 double rooms share 2 baths.*
Amenities: *Pool.*
Rates: *$40–$75; full breakfast. No credit cards.*
Restrictions: *No smoking in bedrooms, no pets.*

The Berkshires

The Berkshires—about 2½ hours by car from both Boston and New York—embrace some of the most attractive countryside in Massachusetts: rolling hills, extensive woodlands, and characteristic New England villages. The county has been a popular vacation destination since the mid-1800s, when wealthy New Yorkers and Bostonians were building their "summer cottages" here, and it continues to attract its fair share of wealthy weekenders from the big cities. Though many of the older mansions have now been converted into schools or hotels, much of their elegance and interesting architecture has been preserved.

One of the best (if busiest) times to visit the area is in fall, when the gentle, tree-covered slopes are ablaze with autumn foliage. Summer is another peak period, with the Berkshires' vibrant and varied cultural life in full swing. The annual series of concerts at Tanglewood has turned into New England's best-known music festival, but this event is accompanied by a host of other regional musical and theatrical performances in a variety of settings. Even in winter, the region is popular for its family-oriented downhill ski areas and for cross-country skiing.

With all these advantages, the region is hardly undeveloped. You'll find dozens of country inns, ranging from deluxe palazzi and baronial castles requiring evening dress at dinner to relaxed country farmhouses with homemade jam for breakfast. Despite the abundance of accommodations, rooms are scarce during the Tanglewood Festival, rates are high, and the narrow roads are frequently jammed. The influx of affluent travelers keeps prices up, whether you're shopping for antiques or reserving a motel room.

Places to Go, Sights to See

Great Barrington. The biggest town in the southern Berkshires is a mecca for antiques hunters, as are the villages of South Egremont, just south on Route 23, and Sheffield, south on Route 7.

Hancock Shaker Village (on Rte. 20, 5 mi west of Pittsfield, tel. 413/443–0188). Founded in the 1790s, the village of Hancock thrived in the 1840s, when 300 Shakers made their living farming, selling seeds, making medicines, and producing household objects. The best buildings to visit here are the Round Stone Barn with its labor-saving devices and the Laundry and Machine Shop, with its water-powered instruments.

Lenox. At the heart of the "summer cottage" region, Lenox fairly bursts with old inns and majestic buildings: Particularly worth visiting are *The Mount* (tel. 413/637–1899), former summer home of novelist Edith Wharton, the first woman to win the Pulitzer Prize; *Chesterwood* (tel. 413/298–3579), where sculptor Daniel Chester French spent his summers for 33 years; and *Arrowhead* (tel. 413/442–1793), the house where Herman Melville wrote Moby Dick. *Tanglewood* (tel. 413/637–1940), summer venue of the Boston Symphony Orchestra, is New England's best-known music festival, featuring world-famous performers. Ideally located in a hillside forest clearing with marvelous views, this 200-acre site attracts thousands of fans in July and August.

Mt. Greylock. The highest peak in Massachusetts, at 3,491 feet, is surrounded by the Mount Greylock State Reservation (Rockwell Rd., Lanesborough, tel. 413/499–4262/3), which encompasses 10,327 acres and provides facilities for bicycling, fishing, hiking, horseback riding, and snowmobiling.

Stockbridge is an archetypal New England small town, with a history of literary and artistic inhabitants—one of the most famous was painter Norman Rockwell. A new museum with the largest collection of Rockwell originals in the world opened in 1993, just outside Stockbridge on Rte. 183.

Williamstown. This north Berkshire town is dominated by the grand, weathered stone buildings of Williams College. The *College Art Museum* (Main St., tel. 413/597–2429), emphasizing American and contemporary art, and the *Sterling and Francine Clark Institute* (225 South St., tel. 413/458–9545), with paintings by Renoir, Monet, Pisarro, and Degas, are worth visiting. Williamstown is at the westernmost point of the *Mohawk Trail,* a 67-mile scenic stretch of Route 2 that takes in several interesting sites, including the Western Gateway Heritage State Park and Hail to the Sunrise, a monument to the Native American. The route follows a section of a former Native American path that ran from the villages of western Massachusetts to New York's Finger Lakes.

Restaurants

Many of the best Berkshire restaurants are at country inns that focus primarily on traditional and New England cuisine. Lobster, regional game, and such favorites as rack of lamb are the most common fare. Some inns require formal dress at dinner. Good inn restaurants can be found at **Gateways Inn** (tel. 413/637–2532), **The Candlelight Inn** (tel. 413/637–1555), and **Wheatleigh** (tel. 413/637–0610) in Lenox; **The Williamsville Inn** (tel. 413/274–6118) in West Stockbridge; and **The Orchards** (tel. 413/458–9611) in Williamstown.

Dance Clubs

The emphasis in the Berkshires is definitely on classical entertainment; however, **The Lion's Den** (tel. 413/298–5545) downstairs at the Red Lion Inn in Stockbridge has folk music and contemporary bands every evening, and **The Night Spot** (tel. 413/637–0060) at Seven Hills Inn in Lenox stages jazz and blues music on summer weekends.

Tourist Information

Berkshire Visitors Bureau (Berkshire Common, Pittsfield, MA 01201, tel. 413/443–9186 or 800/237–5747); **Lenox Chamber of Commerce** (Lenox Academy Bldg., 75 Main St., Lenox MA 01240, tel. 413/637–3646); **Mohawk Trail Association** (Box 722, Charlemont, MA 01339).

Reservations Services

Nutmeg B&B Agency (Box 1117, West Hartford, CT 06127, tel. 203/236–6698 or 800/727–7592, fax 203/232–2989); **American Country Collection of B&B** (4 Greenwood Lane, Delmar, NY 12054, tel. 518/439–7001, fax 518/439–4301); **Berkshire B&B Homes** (Main St., Box 211, Williamsburg, MA 01096, tel. 413/268–7244, fax 413/268–7243); **Pineapple Hospitality Inc.** (Box 7821, New Bedford, MA 02742, tel. 508/990–1696).

Apple Tree Inn

This country inn has much to recommend it, particularly its setting on a gently sloping hillside with marvelous views over the Stockbridge Bowl and Laurel Lake, and literally across the street from Tanglewood's main gates. You're so close to the music festival that on a summer evening, you won't even need a ticket—you can listen to concerts from the inn's own gardens; because the inn is surrounded by 22 acres of land, planted with apple orchards and 450 varieties of roses, you may well decide to do just that.

Originally constructed in 1885, the main building features public areas furnished with Victorian antiques and the unexpected yet effective piece of modern art. Guests enter via the parlor, with its arches, Persian rugs, open fireplace, velvet couches, grand piano, hanging plants, and German nutcrackers on the mantelpiece. In the tavern room, oak-paneled walls support a collection of antique sleds, old tools, and a water buffalo head that stares out over the fireplace. The main restaurant, a circular 1960s addition, has a marquee-like ceiling with spokes of light bulbs. Picture windows afford excellent views over the lawns and orchards.

Upstairs, guest rooms are furnished with a variety of antiques, including four-poster and brass beds, Victorian washstands, and wicker pieces. Four rooms have working fireplaces, and several have window seats with fabulous views over the hills and the lake. The generally spacious rooms come in unusual shapes with individual characters, especially the ones on the top floor, with eaves, gables, and skylights. However, there are some smaller rooms to avoid, especially #5 (The Blue Skylight Room), which is over the kitchen and can become hot and noisy, particularly in the busy summer season. The nearby lodge has 21 motel-like rooms.

The Apple Tree Inn has an interesting past, and belonged at one point to Alice of "Alice's Restaurant"—though she catered primarily to dinners, not guests. Greg and Aurora Smith, who've run the establishment for the past 10 years are proud of the inn's current popularity.

Address: *224 West St., Lenox, MA 01240, tel. 413/637–1477.*
Accommodations: *Inn: 29 double rooms with baths, 2 doubles share 1 bath, 2 suites; lodge: 21 doubles with baths.*
Amenities: *Restaurant and tavern, air-conditioning in bedrooms, cable TV in suites and lodge rooms; pool, tennis court.*
Rates: *Inn: $80–$290, lodge: $60–$145; Continental breakfast. AE, D, DC, MC, V.*
Restrictions: *No pets. 2-night minimum on weekends (3 nights on weekends July–Aug. and Oct.), closed mid Jan.–end Apr.*

Blantyre

Lenox has many fine country inns, but the palatial Blantyre, on 85 magnificent acres, is outstanding. The service is superb. In 1989, Blantyre was voted best of the Relais et Châteaux group. Built in 1901, Blantyre's design is based on an ancestral Scottish home, and its castle-like Tudor architecture is unique to the region. Senator John Fitzpatrick and his family, who also own the Red Lion Inn in Stockbridge, acquired the estate in 1980, and with it the mammoth task of restoring a dilapidated giant to its proper stature. Some of the furnishings in the great hall are original, as are the plaster relief ceilings, the intricately carved oak paneling, and the leather-backed wallpaper.

While the hall, with its heavy carved wooden furnishings (and wooden rocking horse in full heraldic gear), appears imposingly solemn, the long, cream-toned music room next door evokes a lighter mood, with inlaid chess tables, an antique Steinway grand piano, a harp, antique Dutch and Italian cabinets, and exquisite chairs and couches. Doors open onto a terrace set with tables overlooking two large, perfectly manicured croquet lawns.

Staying at Blantyre is an expensive occasion, so make the most of it by reserving one of the five best rooms, all in the main house. Although the entire property is stylishly finished, the rooms in the carriage house and cottages can't compare with these spacious accommodations, which have hand-carved four-poster beds, bay windows, high ceilings, working fireplaces, chintz chairs, overstuffed chaise longues, boudoirs, walk-in closets, and Victorian bathrooms. The huge Paterson Suite has two bathrooms, a sitting room with fireplace, a pineapple four-poster bed, and matching wallpapers, linens, and draperies in pale green. If these rooms are booked, the smaller Ashley Suite or the carriage house's split-level suites beside the pool are next best.

The first-rate service rests in the hands of Scottish manager Roderick Anderson. The many extras include bathrobes, toiletries, newspapers, turn-down service, and wine, cheese, and fruit.

Address: *Rte. 20, Lenox, MA 01240, tel. 413/637–3556 or 413/298–3806, fax 413/637–4282.*
Accommodations: *13 double rooms with baths, 10 suites.*
Amenities: *Restaurant; air-conditioning, cable TV and phones in rooms, 5 rooms have fireplaces, room service; heated pool, whirlpool bath, sauna, 4 tennis courts, 2 croquet lawns.*
Rates: *$210–$525; Continental breakfast. AE, DC, MC, V.*
Restrictions: *No pets. 2-night minimum on weekends, closed early Nov.–mid-May.*

Field Farm

Neither your average bed-and-breakfast, nor your typical Berkshire cottage estate, this former home of art collector Lawrence H. Boedel has been owned by the Trustees of Reservations since 1984. The Trustees weren't too sure what to do with it until experienced innkeepers David and Judy Loomis came along a couple of years ago and suggested they turn it into a B&B. The starkly geometric exterior of this 1948 American modern-style structure, its cedar walls painted in sickly brown, contrasts unromantically with the profusion of attractive period homes in the region. But consider its advantages: The 254 acres of private, wooded grounds contain a pond, a pool, a tennis court, and cross-country ski trails—and all this comes at a reasonable price. The place is not yet well-known, and because it has only five guest rooms, staying here is like living on your own country estate.

The interior is unashamedly square, and the house, designed as a sort of display case for Boedel's art collection (which went to the Williams College museum after his death), feels a bit like a modern museum. Most of the 1950s oak, cherry, and walnut furniture in use was handmade by Boedel, while other pieces were designed especially for the house—even the plastic doorknobs were custom made, quite a coup in the 1940s. Modern sculptures decorate the gardens. Guest rooms on the first floor are square and large (some are huge), with modern furnishings, painted brick walls, spotlighting, big picture windows, and expansive views over the grounds toward distant hills. Three bedrooms have private decks, and two have working fireplaces surrounded by custom-made tiles depicting animals, birds, and butterflies. Downstairs in the large public sitting room, you'll discover another working fireplace and more modern art. Incidentally, Boedel, his wife, and their dog are buried in a private graveyard by the parking lot.

Dave and Judy Loomis, who are responsible for the successful operation of this unique B&B, also run River Bend Farm (*see* below), another authentic restoration dating from a much earlier period.

Address: *554 Sloan Rd. (off Rte. 43), Williamstown, MA, 01267 tel. 413/458-3135.*
Accommodations: *5 double rooms with baths.*
Amenities: *Breakfast room, lounge; outdoor pool, pond, tennis, cross-country skiing.*
Rates: *$90; Continental breakfast. No credit cards.*
Restrictions: *No pets.*

Gateways Inn

A formal, elegant, and expensive Lenox inn with a superb restaurant, Gateways was built in 1912 by Harley Proctor of Proctor and Gamble as a summer home he named Orleton. The oblong, white clapboard mansion, fittingly enough, resembles a bar of Ivory soap. When Proctor owned the house, it was surrounded by 7 acres of lawns, formal gardens, and boasted a carriage house and a tennis court. The inn is situated on Walker Street, only steps away from the center of Lenox, which could be named "inn row" considering the number of establishments that line the road.

Upon entering Gateways, you step into an impressive entrance hall with oval windows; from here, a grand mahogany open staircase lighted by a skylight leads to the second-floor guest rooms. The best of these, in the east corner, is the huge Fiedler Suite, named after Tanglewood conductor Arthur Fiedler, who stayed here regularly. The suite has two working fireplaces, one each in the bedroom and the sitting room, and a pleasantly large dressing room off the bathroom. Several other rooms have fireplaces, and one suite features a quirky square pillar between the couch and the bed. All rooms have been individually decorated with light period reproduction wallpapers, and furnished with Colonial and Victorian antiques, four-poster or canopy beds, and rich Oriental rugs. The west corner room boasts an eight-piece maple and black-walnut Victorian bedroom set.

Public rooms downstairs include a small parlor with Colonial furnishings and a series of four dining rooms: The Rockwell Room is named after painter Norman Rockwell, who dined in a sunny corner here every week. These tastefully designed areas have chandeliers and tapestries on the walls. Entrées on the extensive (and fairly expensive) menu include rack of lamb, breast of chicken with crawfish, truffles, crepes in a honey liqueur sauce, and pheasant in a light game sauce; the chef's award-winning cuisine is one of the inn's major assets. In both the restaurant and guest services, the staff is suitably distant but very polite.

Address: *71 Walker St., Lenox, MA 01240, tel. 413/637–2532.*
Accommodations: *6 double rooms with baths, 1 suite.*
Amenities: *Restaurant, air-conditioning, TV in lounge.*
Rates: *\$85–\$185, \$185–\$295; Fiedler Suite; Continental breakfast. AE, D, DC, MC, V.*
Restrictions: *No pets.*

Merrell Tavern Inn

This Federal-style red clapboard building with a columned facade, listed on the National Register of Historic Places, remained uninhabited for almost 100 years, until the present owners bought it in 1981. They installed heat, running water, and electricity, and reopened the Merrell Tavern as one of the most beautifully authentic inns in the Berkshires. Innkeepers Charles and Faith Reynolds are retired schoolteachers who were honored with a Preservation Award from the Massachusetts Historical Commission in 1982. They are friendly, interesting, but unobtrusive hosts; Faith weaves and Charles likes working on the grounds.

Built about 1794 and turned into a stagecoach inn in 1817, the lodging is blessed with some good-size bedrooms that offer polished wide-board floors and area rugs, painted plaster walls, iron door latches, and mellow wood antiques. Most beds are pencil four-posters, some have simple white canopies, and four rooms contain working, Count Rumford-style wood-burning fireplaces. The necessity of abiding by a 500-year covenant that protects the building's historic aspect means small (but beautifully decorated) bathrooms—on the third floor, where rooms were built in the shell of the old ballroom, some bathrooms are housed in the former drovers' sleeping quarters.

The original keeping room, now the guest parlor, features a grand piano, beehive oven, and large cooking fireplace with a Franklin stove. A breakfast of pancakes, French toast, or omelets is served in the original tavern room, which contains an open fireplace and the only complete "birdcage" Colonial bar in America. Look for the 19th-century detail: the wood grain on the bar and the doors is handpainted, not natural; the pulley wheels on the ceiling were used to raise and lower the original candle chandelier (now in a Boston museum). The inn is about a mile east of Stockbridge, beside busy Route 102, but it's well back from the road. Behind the building, 2 acres of landscaped gardens with a gazebo descend gently to the Housatonic River.

Address: *Main St., Rte. 102, South Lee/Stockbridge, MA 01260, tel. 413/243–1794 or 800/243–1794.*
Accommodations: *10 double rooms with baths.*
Amenities: *Air-conditioning, breakfast room, parlor, phones in rooms.*
Rates: *$75–$135; full breakfast. AE, MC, V.*
Restrictions: *No smoking on first floor, no pets. 2-night minimum on summer weekends, 3-night minimum on holiday weekends, closed Dec. 24 and 25.*

River Bend Farm

One of the oldest buildings in the Berkshires, this property was constructed in 1770 by Colonel Benjamin Simonds, a founder of Williamstown and a commissioned officer of the Berkshire militia during the American Revolution. The restoration of River Bend Farm is totally authentic and it is listed in the National Register of Historic Places: to stay here takes you back to another era. The Loomises share a lifelong love of restoration and used to spend their days sailing and restoring "big old wooden schooners." Then they turned their talents to "a big old wooden house."

Guests enter through the kitchen and are greeted by an open range stove and an oven hung with dried herbs. Chairs hang on pegs on the walls, Shaker style, and the room is filled with 18th- and 19th-century country antiques, from wood washtubs and spoon racks to flatirons and dozens of cooking implements. Also downstairs is a small formal sitting room with a fireplace, but "formal" only means the walls are plastered—upstairs it's another story. Bedroom walls consist of wide wood panels, some of them painted in their original colors (the Loomises scraped their way through layers of paper and paint to discover them); others are whitewashed, or made of simple scrubbed wide planks as are the floors and doors. Window draperies are "tab curtains" (no hooks, just cloth loops) of unbleached muslin. Accurate colonial-style reproductions of candle chandeliers hang from the ceilings, and sconces with candles are fixed to the walls. Some rooms feature brick (nonworking) fireplaces. Beds are either four-posters with canopies or rope beds with feather mattresses, and antique pieces decorate the rooms—a spinning wheel here, a wing chair there, or a chamber pot in the corner.

Speaking of chamber pots . . . the farm's only disadvantage is that five guest rooms share two bathrooms, one of which is located on the ground floor. It's an absolute Aladdin's cave of utilitarian antiques including washbowls, jugs, lamps, butter tubs, and hanging herbs.

The Loomises serve a healthy Continental breakfast that includes homemade bread and honey. Outdoors, guests have access to the river for canoeing, and can visit a warm spring pool, ¼ mile up the river. Williamstown is about an eight-minute drive away.

Address: *643 Simonds Rd., Williamstown, MA 01267, tel. 413/458-5504 or 413/458-3121.*
Accommodations: *5 double rooms share 2 baths.*
Rates: *$70 ($60 singles), Continental breakfast. No credit cards.*
Restrictions: *No smoking in guest rooms, no pets. Closed after Thanksgiving–late Apr.*

Wheatleigh

Wheatleigh was built in 1893, a wedding present for an American heiress who brought nobility into her family by marrying a Spanish count. Set among 22 wooded acres, the mellow brick building, based on a 16th-century Florentine palazzo, is nothing short of baronial. Step into the great hall: the sheer style of the open staircase, the balustraded gallery, and the large Tiffany windows is breathtaking. Everything here is vast, including most guest rooms—and the beds! Rooms have high ceilings, intricate plaster moldings (more than 150 artisans were brought from Italy to complete the detailed decoration), and English antiques; eight have working fireplaces with big, elegant marble surrounds. Prices are vast as well, at over $400 per night in high season, but for the clientele—most of whom look like they're escaping high pressure, big-city executive posts—it's no doubt worth the money.

Though it has much to recommend it, Wheatleigh has suffered from a mixed reputation over the years, with rumblings about the service and the unconventional—some said tasteless—mixture of antique and modern styles. The furnishings have been toned down to mostly classical pieces, the place has been repainted, and the rooms were refurbished in 1993 to give the inn an elegant new front. The service too seems up to scratch, and virtually anything is available to guests, from in-room massage to breakfast in bed.

The main restaurant, another huge room with elegant marble fireplaces and cut glass chandeliers, has an excellent reputation for its "contemporary classical" cuisine; the $65 prix fixe menu (with 18% service charge) includes roast antelope, pheasant, rabbit, and lobster; the Grill Room also serves full meals in a more casual setting.

Address: *Hawthorne Rd., Lenox, MA 01240, tel. 413/637–0610.*
Accommodations: *17 double rooms with bath.*
Amenities: *2 restaurants, air-conditioning, sauna, room service; tennis, pool.*
Rates: *$110–$425; breakfast extra. AE, D, DC, MC, V.*
Restrictions: *No pets. 3-night minimum stay during Tanglewood and holiday weekends.*

Whistler's Inn

Elegant, ornate, and somehow exotic, Whistler's Inn stands apart from its nearby competitors, with lavish Louis XVI antiques in the parlor; heavy, dark wood furniture in the baronial dining hall; and African artifacts in the office. Innkeepers Joan and Richard Mears, with their easy, well-traveled style, maintain an extraordinary ambience at this English Tudor mansion, built in 1820 by railroad tycoon Ross Wynans Whistler.

The Mearses, who have owned Whistler's since 1978, are widely traveled hosts, making for some interesting conversation. Richard, a published novelist, is currently working on a new book, and Joan, formerly a teacher of art and English, is also writing a novel.

Public rooms are impressive, with Chippendale furniture, ornate antiques (including Louis XVI palace mirrors, candelabra, clocks, and love seats), chandeliers, original artwork, Persian rugs, and marble fireplaces. A Steinway grand piano graces the music room/parlor, and next door is a well-stocked library, where complimentary sherry, port, or afternoon tea is offered to guests. The dining room or the sun porch provides a restful setting for breakfast. You may wish to take a look at the Mearses' first-floor office—it features many souvenirs brought back from their travels, including African pieces and a large wooden elephant puppet from a maharaja's palace.

Guest rooms are attractively decorated with designer draperies and bedspreads. They vary in size from the large master bedroom to two small chambers beneath the eaves, and all are furnished with antiques. One room features a Chippendale armoire, some rooms have working fireplaces, and most of them offer superb views across the small valley that includes 7 acres of private gardens, as well as a croquet lawn and a badminton court for guests. This peaceful place is only a short walk from the center of Lenox.

Address: *5 Greenwood St., Lenox, MA 01240, tel. 413/637–0975.*
Accommodations: *12 double rooms with baths.*
Amenities: *Dining room, air-conditioning (70% of rooms), library; gardens, croquet, badminton.*
Rates: *$65–$180, full breakfast and afternoon tea. AE, MC, V.*
Restrictions: *No smoking in public rooms, no pets. 3-night minimum on weekends July, Aug., Oct., and Dec.*

Brook Farm Inn

This big brown clapboard Victorian house is named after a literary community that emerged near Boston in 1841, and like the old Brook Farm, this inn has become a focal point for poets, who hold readings and classes here. The library, with its dark wood antiques, Oriental rugs, and open fireplace, contains 750 volumes of poetry and about 75 poets on tape.

Joseph Miller, who bought the inn in 1992 with his wife, Ann, inherited the literary tradition with reservations. "I was afraid of it," he admits. "My background is in construction—what did I know about poetry! But it really has a life of its own, and now I thoroughly enjoy it. The inn's guest rooms contain four-poster and canopy beds, wing chairs, and old bureaus; five rooms have fireplaces. The special room lies in the garret, converted from an old loft, consisting mainly of ceiling and skylights, with exposed beams, floral print fabrics and stencils on the walls. Every room has a collection of excellent reading materials.

Address: *15 Hawthorne St., Lenox, MA 01240, tel. 413/637-3013.*
Accommodations: *12 double rooms with baths.*
Amenities: *Air-conditioning (3rd floor), ceiling fans, library; pool.*
Rates: *$60–$165; Continental breakfast and afternoon tea. AE, MC, V.*
Restrictions: *No pets. 3-night minimum weekends July–Sept., 2-night minimum weekends Oct. and holidays.*

The Candlelight Inn

Next door to Gateways Inn on "inn row" in Lenox, this bed-and-breakfast exudes style without stuffiness. Dining is particularly important here—you can choose among four dining rooms set with sterling silver. These areas range from an airy room with arched windows and a sun terrace to a darker, Old World space with a large open fireplace, paneled walls, and exposed beams. In summer, tables are set up in the pleasant courtyard outside. John Hedgecock, who always wanted to own an inn, left his job as a New York banker to study at the French Culinary Institute, also in New York, in preparation for his new career. The menu features such specialties as grilled snails, Italian fisherman's stew, rack of lamb, and grilled breast of duckling. John bought the inn in 1987 and runs it with the help of his wife, Rebecca, and their two daughters. The large bedrooms have been renovated with floral print wallpapers and Colonial and Victorian antiques, including wing chairs and writing desks. Rooms on the top floor feature sloping ceilings and skylights. The inn is a short stroll from the middle of Lenox.

Address: *53 Walker St., Lenox, MA 01240, tel. 413/637-1555.*
Accommodations: *8 double rooms with baths.*
Amenities: *Restaurant, air-conditioning, bar.*
Rates: *$95–$160; Continental breakfast. AE, MC, V.*
Restrictions: *No pets.*

Cliffwood Inn

This exquisite, classic colonial-style building is located unobtrusively on a residential Lenox side street. Built in the 1890s for an ambassador to France, Cliffwood incorporates many European touches, such as the oval dining room with its similarly shaped windows and Belgian, French, and Italian 15th- and 16th-century antiques brought back from the Continent by owners Joy and Scottie Farrelly. The living room features inlaid wood floors, huge wall mirrors, a white marble fireplace, Oriental rugs, and a 15th-century Italian desk. In summer, breakfast is served on the outside terrace overlooking the pool.

On the second-floor landing, the custom-made bookcase matches the room's arched windows and dentil moldings. Six of the seven guest rooms have working fireplaces (one is in the bathroom), and most contain canopy beds. One room offers a simple, Amish-made net canopy bed in golden oak. Persian and Chinese rugs cover the oak and pine floors, and top-floor rooms are graced with sloping roofs and windows in the eaves.

Address: *25 Cliffwood St., Lenox, MA 01240, tel. 413/637–3330.*
Accommodations: *7 double rooms with baths.*
Amenities: *Air-conditioning; pool.*
Rates: *$78–$190; Continental breakfast (no breakfast winter weekdays). No credit cards.*
Restrictions: *No pets. 4-night minimum July and Aug. weekends, 2-night minimum holidays.*

Dalton House

Although the original house is 170 years old, this reasonably priced establishment has been modernized, and offers a simple alternative to more traditional local inns. Dalton is not Lenox, for a start—it's a busy village whose character has been dominated by Crane's paper mills for over 150 years. Inside the pink clapboard house with rose shutters, guests share a split-level sitting room, with cathedral ceiling and skylight, exposed beams, pine floors, and a wood-burning stove. They dine outside on the deck or in a sunny new breakfast room with pine chairs and tables. Most bedrooms are situated in the 1967 wing of the main house. They're cheerful, if smallish, with orange and brown floral print drapes and wallpapers. Suites and rooms in the recently converted carriage house are larger, with exposed beams, period furnishings, rocking chairs, and quilts. Gary and Bernice Turetsky opened this bed-and-breakfast in 1975, and eventually sold their florist business to go into innkeeping full time.

Address: *955 Main St., Dalton, MA 01226, tel. 413/684–3854.*
Accommodations: *9 double rooms with baths, 2 suites.*
Amenities: *Air-conditioning, TV in rooms, breakfast room; outdoor pool, picnic area, deck.*
Rates: *$58–$100; Continental breakfast. AE, MC, V.*
Restrictions: *No smoking in public rooms, no pets. 2-night minimum on summer and fall weekends.*

The Gables Inn

Another venerable Walker Street inn, this accommodation is famous because it was home to novelist Edith Wharton for two years before she moved into the Mount, her new "cottage" down the road. Built in 1885, the Queen Anne–style mansion has undergone extensive renovations. Experienced innkeepers Frank and Mary Newton refurbished the eight-sided library where Wharton wrote short stories, and refurnished the bedrooms with authentic, 19th-century antiques.

The room where Wharton once slept offers a big four-poster bed with a pink and white canopy, a mauve sofa, and a rich Oriental rug. Several rooms feature particular decorative themes, such as the Show Biz Room with its old posters of Hollywood movies and signed photos of film stars and the Edith Wharton suite, which has a canopy four-poster, carved wood fireplace, sitting area, and two pedestal sinks in the large bathroom. More modern touches are the indoor pool with a whirlpool, and a tennis court.

Address: *103 Walker St., Lenox, MA 01240, tel. 413/637–3416.*
Accommodations: *3 suites, 15 double rooms with bath, 2 doubles share 1 bath.*
Amenities: *Air-conditioning, cable TV (2 rooms), VCR (suites).*
Rates: *$60–$195; Continental breakfast. D, MC, V.*
Restrictions: *No pets. 3-night minimum during Tanglewood, 2 nights on fall and holiday weekends.*

Ivanhoe Country House

The Appalachian Trail runs right by this rural bed-and-breakfast, and, according to host Carole Maghery, who has been taking in guests here since 1969, deer graze on the lawn in winter. The house was built in 1780, and various wings were added at later dates, with the result that the home is on various levels, with curious staircases and passageways throughout. The ample guest sitting room contains antique desks, a piano, and comfortable couches; it's also well stocked with reading material. Most of the guest rooms are large, all have pleasant country views, and several offer private balconies or porches—one comes complete with its own ping-pong set. Rooms are furnished with antiques, and some contain brass beds. There is no dining room, so guests have breakfast delivered to their rooms. Dick Maghery raises golden retrievers on the house's 20 acres of grounds, which contain a scenically landscaped outdoor pool.

Address: *Undermountain Rd., Rte. 41, Box 158, Sheffield, MA 01257, tel. 413/229–2143.*
Accommodation: *9 double rooms with baths, 1 2-bedroom suite with kitchen.*
Amenities: *Air-conditioning in some rooms, individual refrigerators; outdoor pool.*
Rates: *$55–$99, dogs $10 extra; Continental breakfast. No credit cards.*
Restrictions: *2-night minimum on weekends July–Labor Day, 3-night minimum on holiday weekends.*

New Boston Inn

This distinctive gray clapboard building with bright red trim is the oldest inn in the Berkshires. It was built as an inn in 1737 (a large extension was added in 1796) and has remained one ever since. The present owners, from Cape Cod, bought the place in 1985 and have carried out extensive restoration and renovation work. Original interior features include the 24-inch "kings boards" that make up the floor of the tavern room and bar, and the unfinished pine and maple panels and corner cupboard on the wall. The sloping door frames, floors, and ceilings are a constant reminder of the age of the building, as is the large, blue-and-white second-floor ballroom, part of the 1796 extension. Guest bedrooms feature colonial-style furniture, wide-board floors, painted wood beams, cedar-lined closets, floral print drapes, and beautifully executed stencils on the walls (a favorite design is the Shaker tree of life). The inn is situated in the tiny village of Sandisfield, in a quiet corner of the southern Berkshires. Dinner is available in the 1737 House Restaurant on the premises.

Address: *Intersection Hwys. 8 and 57, Box 120, Sandisfield, MA 02155, tel. 413/258–4477.*
Accommodations: *8 double rooms with baths.*
Amenities: *Restaurant, tavern, bar.*
Rates: *$55–$135; full breakfast. AE, D, MC, V.*
Restrictions: *No smoking, no pets. 2-night minimum weekends, 3-night minimum holidays.*

The Orchards

The first impression is not too auspicious—pale orange stucco exterior, no orchards, and a location amid motels, gas stations, and supermarkets on a commercial strip of Route 2, a mile from the center of Williamstown. But try to reserve judgment until you're inside this small, fancy hotel, built in 1985. Church pews and a heavy wood pulpit adorn the corridors, and the lounge offers thick carpets, fresh flowers, cases of silverware, and an open fireplace surrounded by an 18th-century carved oak mantel.

Some guest rooms have four-poster beds, all have English antiques, and uniform beige wallpapers with floral patterns. Business travelers will appreciate the in-room desks, bathroom phones, and discreetly hidden TVs. Vacationers should note that there's little difference between the least expensive rooms and those in the middle price range; try to avoid a room with a parking-lot view.

Address: *222 Adams Rd. (Rte. 2), Williamstown, MA 01267, tel. 413/458–9611, outside MA 800/225–1517, fax 413/458–3273.*
Accommodations: *49 rooms with baths.*
Amenities: *Restaurant, air-conditioning, cable TV, room service, tavern; outdoor pool, sauna, whirlpool.*
Rates: *$125–$195; full breakfast. AE, DC, MC, V.*
Restrictions: *No pets.*

The Red Lion Inn

Nobody can write about the Berkshires without including this grande dame of New England inns, built in 1773. Numerous famous people have stayed here, and the place was frequented by artist Norman Rockwell, who lived just around the corner. The wood-beamed restaurant, its tables set with pewter, provides a stylish place to dine; it's conveniently located in the heart of Stockbridge. That said, it seems that much of the Red Lion's fame stems from its status. Many guest rooms are small, and those in the main building open off a long, dark corridor. In general, accommodations in the numerous houses that have been annexed to the inn are more appealing. Rooms are traditionally decorated, with floral print wallpapers and curtains from the mail-order store that is owned by the innkeepers and operates out of the inn. Other furnishings include Early American and Victorian antiques, rocking chairs, couches, Oriental rugs, and Rockwell prints. A polite and pleasant staff operates the Red Lion, which has been owned by the Fitzpatricks for more than 25 years.

Address: *Main St., Stockbridge, MA 02162, tel. 413/298–5545, fax 413/298–5130.*
Accommodations: *108 rooms, 75 with baths, 10 suites.*
Amenities: *Restaurant, air-conditioning, exercise room, bar, meeting rooms; outdoor pool.*
Rates: *$65–$155, $165–$250 suites. AE, D, DC, MC, V.*
Restrictions: *No pets. 2-night minimum July and Aug. weekends.*

Rookwood Inn

This "painted lady" on a quiet street near the center of Lenox was built in 1885 as a summer "cottage" for a wealthy New York family. Owners Tom and Betsy Sherman have perfectly re-created the Victorian era, with striking period wallpapers, matching linens, chaise longues, and heavy carved couches. In 1992, they added three extra rooms, cleverly incorporating a second turret into the addition, which makes it difficult to spot where the old building ends and the new one begins. Seven of the spacious bedrooms contain working fireplaces, all chambers are furnished with Victorian antiques, and most have brass or four-poster beds. The old turret rooms feature the most interesting shapes, especially the one on the top floor; steps lead into the turret, which contains a daybed and has windows on all sides. The elegant first-floor lounge offers reading material, an open fire, and a screened porch with wicker furniture.

Opening a bed-and-breakfast was a lifelong ambition for Betsy, formerly a nurse in Boston. She has two children and manages the inn with care and quiet efficiency.

Address: *19 Old Stockbridge Rd., Box 1717, Lenox, MA 01240, tel. 413/637–9750.*
Accommodations: *18 double rooms with baths, 1 suite.*
Amenities: *Air-conditioning, breakfast room.*
Rates: *$55–$190; full breakfast and afternoon tea. AE.*
Restrictions: *No smoking, no pets.*

The Turning Point Inn

This 200-year-old inn used to be a stagecoach stop between New York City and Boston. Irv and Shirley Yost have owned it for 16 years, and it is now managed by their daughter Jamie, a musician and natural-foods cook. The Yosts renovated the house completely, turning the upstairs ballroom into guest rooms and converting the barn into a two-bedroom cottage, which contains modern furnishings, a full kitchen, and a screened porch. Despite remodeling, the old building retains its fair share of narrow passageways, twisting staircases, and sloping floors. Guests share a large living room, with two fireplaces and a piano, and a kitchen with a bread oven; chestnut planks from the old walls were used to make the tables. Bedrooms, with uneven, wide-board floors, tend to be small, and several have sloping roofs; they contain eclectic antiques, and some colonial-style beds. The healthy breakfasts include multigrain hot cereals, frittata, and home-baked muffins or cakes. The inn is close to swimming, boating, horseback riding, and skiing.

Address: *RD 2, Box 140, Great Barrington, MA 01230, tel. 413/528–4777.*
Accommodations: *4 double rooms with bath, 2 doubles share 1 bath, 2-bedroom cottage.*
Amenities: *TV in lounge, fans; cross-country ski trail.*
Rates: *$75–$100, full breakfast; cottage $200 (no breakfast). AE, MC, V.*
Restrictions: *No smoking, no pets.*

The Weathervane Inn

The open fireplace and beehive oven in the lounge of this friendly, family-run inn date back to the 1760s, when the original building was constructed. Most of the other additions were made in 1830, although the current innkeepers added new bedrooms downstairs and recently converted the carriage house into three more rooms. The formal parlor next to the lounge features striking reproduction wallpaper, and guest rooms are decorated in a colonial style with stencils, country curtains, wreaths, Norman Rockwell prints, and rocking chairs. The inn has a varied past, and at one period served as a dog kennel—one of the guest bathrooms incorporates an original dog-size bathtub! Dinner is served Friday and Saturday evenings in the formal dining room; breakfast takes place on the sunny porch overlooking the lawn. The Murphy family does most of the cooking and also waits at tables; guests are required to eat some meals at the inn, depending on the season.

Address: *Rte. 23, South Egremont, MA 01258, tel. 413/528–9580.*
Accommodations: *12 double rooms with baths.*
Amenities: *Dining rooms, air-conditioning, TV in lounge; outdoor pool.*
Rates: *$95–$165 ($75–$115 single); full breakfast (MAP [breakfast and dinner] required on weekends). AE, MC, V.*
Restrictions: *No pets. 3-night minimum during Tanglewood and holiday weekends, closed Dec. 20–26.*

The Williamsville Inn

Situated a couple of miles south of West Stockbridge, this inn was purchased in 1990 by Kathleen Ryan and her daughter Gail, from New York. With backgrounds in acting and real estate, they've combined their talents to re-create the atmosphere of a 1790s farmhouse, with extensive vegetable and flower gardens. Guest rooms feature wide-board floors, embroidered chairs, and four-poster and canopy beds, all in the 18th-century Early American style; several chambers also contain working fireplaces, and those beneath the eaves have sloping roofs. Four dining rooms with fireplaces overlook the surrounding woodland.

The restaurant's chef, who was formerly at Yosemite, serves gourmet country cuisine with produce from the garden. The former barn has been turned into spacious guest rooms that have a country look, with brass beds and wood stoves. On the grounds you can play horseshoes, croquet, badminton, and volleyball.

Address: *Rte. 41, Williamsville, MA 01266, tel. 413/274–6118.*
Accommodations: *14 double rooms with baths, 1 suite.*
Amenities: *Restaurant, bar, air-conditioning; pool, tennis.*
Rates: *$100–$145; full breakfast. MC, V.*
Restrictions: *No smoking, no pets in restaurant. 3-night minimum July–Aug. and holiday weekends.*

Windflower Inn

Barbara and Gerald Liebert of Vermont bought this inn in 1980 as a 25th wedding anniversary present to themselves; they still enjoy running the place with the help of their daughter and son-in-law, Claudia and John Ryan.

A comfortable, casual atmosphere prevails, yet the inn is professionally managed. Barbara and Claudia—both former chefs—do all the cooking, and everything is homemade with produce from the inn's organic garden in summer. Specialties include duckling in plum sauce and salmon in citrus butter. Meals are served either in the sunny dining room or on the screened porch. The living room has a big open fireplace, a cloverleaf marble coffee table, and couches. Bedrooms vary in size, but most are spacious; they're furnished with four-poster beds and filled with antiques, including Victorian washing jugs and bowls. Several rooms contain working fireplaces; the most impressive one has a stone surround that takes up an entire wall.

Address: *Rte. 23 (Egremont Star Rte., Box 25), Great Barrington, MA 01230, tel. 413/528–2720 or 800/992–1993.*
Accommodations: *13 double rooms with baths.*
Amenities: *Restaurant, air-conditioning, black-and-white TVs in rooms; piano, pool.*
Rates: *$160–$200; (MAP); full breakfast and dinner Wed.–Sun., Jul.–Oct. No credit cards.*
Restrictions: *Smoking only in living room, no pets. 3-night minimum Tanglewood and holiday weekends.*

Vermont

Vermont

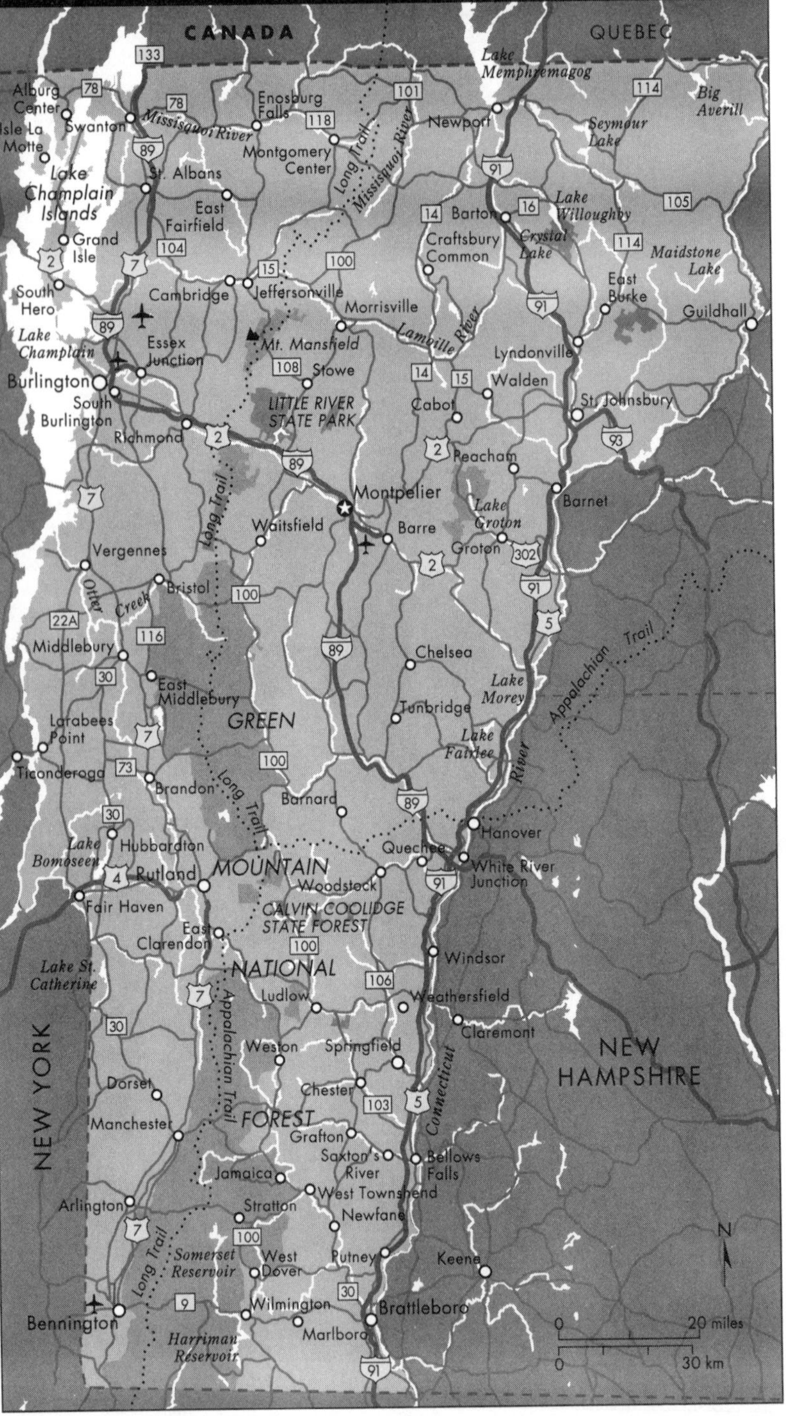
CANADA
QUEBEC
Lake Memphremagog
Big Averill
Seymour Lake
Alburg Center
Swanton
Isle La Motte
Missisquoi River
Enosburg Falls
Montgomery Center
Newport
Long Trail
Missisquoi River
St. Albans
Lake Champlain Islands
East Fairfield
Barton
Lake Willoughby
Crystal Lake
Craftsbury Common
Maidstone Lake
Grand Isle
South Hero
Cambridge
Jeffersonville
Morrisville
East Burke
Guildhall
Lake Champlain
Essex Junction
Mt. Mansfield
Lamoille River
Lyndonville
Burlington
South Burlington
Richmond
Stowe
LITTLE RIVER STATE PARK
Cabot
Walden
St. Johnsbury
Peacham
Montpelier
Barnet
Lake Groton
Waitsfield
Barre
Groton
Long Trail
Vergennes
Otter Creek
Bristol
Middlebury
East Middlebury
Chelsea
Lake Morey
Tunbridge
Appalachian Trail
GREEN
Larabees Point
Ticonderoga
Lake Fairlee
Brandon
River
Long Trail
Barnard
Hanover
Lake Bomoseen
Hubbardton
Quechee
MOUNTAIN
Rutland
White River Junction
Woodstock
Fair Haven
CALVIN COOLIDGE STATE FOREST
East Clarendon
NATIONAL
Windsor
Lake St. Catherine
Appalachian Trail
Ludlow
Weathersfield
Claremont
NEW YORK
Weston
Springfield
Connecticut
NEW HAMPSHIRE
Dorset
Chester
FOREST
Manchester
Grafton
Saxton's River
Bellows Falls
Jamaica
West Townshend
Arlington
Stratton
Newfane
Somerset Reservoir
West Dover
Putney
Keene
Long Trail
Wilmington
Bennington
Brattleboro
Marlboro
Harriman Reservoir
N
0 20 miles
0 30 km

Southeastern Vermont

There are no big cities in southeastern Vermont. On the contrary, this is a region where, even more than the rest of the state, charm is on a small scale. Once you leave I–91, which parallels the Connecticut River along the state's eastern edge, the countryside is a marvelous patchwork of small towns and surrounding farms, each a picture postcard.

What brings visitors back year after year are the varied pleasures of the different seasons. Summer means driving, biking, or hiking along tree-shaded back roads or trails; stopping at a small country store for a cool drink; shopping for handmade crafts both traditional and contemporary; or just sitting on the front porch doing nothin' much. Autumn, with every hill a palette of color, is peak season—the time of year when the region is practically overrun with leaf peepers checking the daily foliage reports and creeping along the highways gasping at every new vista along the road. Winter brings skiers as well as those whose idea of a winter sport is drinking cocoa by a roaring fire. Spring's new shoots of greenery may exhilarate those who have been cooped up all winter and are eager for a drive in the country, but most locals think of it simply as "mud season," when thawing snow turns roads to muck and many businesses close down to make necessary repairs.

But it doesn't really matter during which season you visit: At any time of year southeastern Vermont is an ideal place to escape to for those in search of a quieter way of life, if only for a day or two.

Places to Go, Sights to See

Billings Farm and Museum (Woodstock, tel. 802/457–2355). The exhibits in the reconstructed farmhouse, school, general store, and workshop demonstrate the daily activities and skills of early Vermont settlers. It is financed by the same Rockefeller money that has helped preserve the town of *Woodstock,* 4 miles west of Quechee, with its tree-lined village green, exquisitely preserved Federal houses, and covered bridge in the center of town.

Catamount Brewing Company (58 S. Main St., tel. 802/296–2248). Vermont isn't lagging behind in contributing to the country's new found passion for quality beer: Catamount, in White River Junction, is the state's largest microbrewery. They make a golden ale, a British-style amber, and a dark porter, as well as seasonal specialties like their hearty Christmas Ale. Tours and tastings are available.

Grafton. This picturesque village at the intersection of Routes 35 and 121 got a second lease on life when the Windham Foundation provided funds for the restoration of most of the town's crisp white 18th- and 19th-century houses; it's now one of the best-kept and most charming hamlets in the state. About 12 miles south on Route 30 is Newfane, whose town green also is a perennial favorite; the *Newfane Country Store* (tel. 802/365–7916) has a wonderful selection of quilts and homemade fudge.

Green Mountain Flyer (tel. 802/463–3069). This train takes visitors on a 26-mile round-trip from Bellows Falls (on the Connecticut River about 12 miles east of Grafton) to Chester and Ludlow in cars that date from the golden age of railroads. The journey goes through scenic countryside that includes the Broadway Mills gorge.

The Molly Stark Trail (Route 9). Running from Brattleboro to Bennington, this is the principal east–west highway through southern Vermont. Along the eastern half of the road lies Marlboro, home of the annual summer *Marlboro Music Festival* of classical music, which draws musicians and audiences from around the world, and the *Luman Nelson New England Wildlife Museum* (tel. 802/464–5494), a comprehensive taxidermy display of New England game.

Quechee Gorge. The 165-foot drop to the bottom of the mile-long Quechee Gorge (6 miles west of White River Junction) is an impressive sight, and many visitors picnic nearby or scramble down one of the several descents to get a closer look. Nearby in the village of Quechee, the *Simon Pearce* glassblowing factory (Main St., tel. 802/295–2711) houses a pottery workshop, a retail shop, and a restaurant with a wonderful view of the Ottauquechee River; visitors can watch potters and glassblowers at work.

Vermont Country Store (Rte. 100, tel. 802/824–3184). More a way of life than a retail store, this old-fashioned emporium in Weston still sells such nearly forgotten items from the past as Lilac Vegetal aftershave, Monkey Brand black tooth powder, Flexible Flyer sleds, Vermont Common Crackers, pickles in a barrel, and tiny wax bottles of colored sugar-water.

Restaurants

At **Simon Pierce** (tel. 802/295–1470), in Quechee, the sparkling glassware from the studio downstairs accents Irish specialties inspired by the owner's background. The **Four Columns Inn** (tel. 802/365–7713) in Newfane is well-known for its exquisite, regionally inspired cuisine. Try the **Common Ground** (tel. 802/257–0855), in Brattleboro, for a funkier, down-to-earth vegetarian meal.

Nightlife

The **Weston Playhouse** (tel. 802/824–5288) is a local favorite for a summer night's drama, as is the **Saxtons River Playhouse** (tel. 802/869–2030). Try the **Mole's Eye Cafe** (tel. 802/257–0771) in Brattleboro for live music: Folk on Wednesdays, danceable R&B, blues, or reggae on weekends.

Tourist Information

Mount Snow/Haystack Region Chamber of Commerce (E. Main St., Box 3, Wilmington, VT 05363, tel. 802/464–8092); **Woodstock Area Chamber of Commerce** (4 Central St., Woodstock, VT 05091, tel. 802/457–3555); **Quechee Chamber of Commerce** (Box 106, Quechee, VT 05059, tel. 802/295–7900); **Great Falls Regional Chamber of Commerce** (Box 554, Bellows Falls, VT 05101, tel. 802/463–3537); **Windsor Area Chamber of Commerce** (Box 5, Windsor, VT 05089, tel. 802/672–5910).

Reservations Service

Vermont Bed & Breakfast (Box 1, East Fairfield, VT 05448, tel. 802/827–3827).

Governor's Inn

The atmosphere at this formal little retreat just 10 minutes away from the Okemo Mountain ski area is high Victorian. Everything from the vest-pocket lobby, where afternoon tea is served, to the innkeepers' collection of antique teacups and chocolate pots evokes a turn-of-the-century elegance. As visitors learn during Deedy Marble's orientation tour, the governor in question is Vermont Governor William Wallace Stickney, who in 1890 had the house built as a wedding present for his wife; the bridegroom's portrait still stands on the mantel over the painted slate fireplace in the living room. These romantic beginnings haven't been forgotten by innkeepers Charlie and Deedy Marble, who have created an appealing hideaway for honeymooners and couples celebrating anniversaries. The Marbles' thoughtful attention to detail is evident everywhere: the inn's wide-plank pine floors gleam; puffy lace-trimmed floral chintz duvets on the beds match the sheets; arriving guests find glasses and miniature cordials in their rooms, and the inn's special chocolates appear every evening when the beds are turned down.

The hosts take as much pleasure in entertaining their guests as in providing a restful atmosphere. It was partly because they had become so proficient at orchestrating elaborate dinner parties for friends that they finally left management jobs in 1981 to open an inn. Before welcoming their first guests, however, they decided to hone their skills at Roger Verge's famed cooking school in the south of France. As a result of the Marbles' training (and their flair for presentation), the five- or six-course dinners at the Governor's Inn border on the theatrical. Fresh-faced teenage waitresses in floral skirts, white high-neck blouses, and mob caps announce each course. Guests dine by candlelight with table settings of antique bone china and sterling silver and often linger over meals that might include hot wine broth, Cornish hens with cinnamon glaze and apple and pâté stuffing, and Edwardian cream with raspberry sauce. Charlie is in charge of breakfast, which often includes his signature rum-raisin French toast.

Address: *86 Main St., Ludlow, VT 05149, tel. 802/228–8830 or 800/GOV-ERNOR.*
Accommodations: *8 double rooms with baths.*
Amenities: *Restaurant, air-conditioning, fireplace in public area, games room, afternoon tea.*
Rates: *$190–$220 MAP. MC, V.*
Restrictions: *No smoking, no pets. 2-night minimum on weekends, 3–4-night minimum on holidays and at Christmastime.*

Inn at Long Last

Innkeeper Jack Coleman made national headlines in the 1970s when he took a sabbatical from his post as president of Haverford College in Pennsylvania to work in a variety of blue-collar jobs. In 1986, when he finally decided to leave the world of academia and foundations for good, he moved north and opened this Victorian country inn. The result mirrors the diversity of his interests and his puckish wit. Bookshelves in the large wood-paneled library hold volumes in literature, science, biography, music, history, and labor economics (Coleman's field); one entire shelf is devoted to George Orwell. An army of toy soldiers fills a glass case beside the enormous fieldstone fireplace in the pine-floored lobby, where guests like to gather for after-dinner drinks, lounging on one of the large couches in front of the fire.

Individual rooms are named after people, places, and things important to Coleman and are decorated simply with personal memorabilia; a pamphlet in each room explains the significance of the room names. The Dickens Room, with a high carved headboard, is the most spacious, and the Audubon and Tiffany rooms offer access to the second-story porch. The quietest section of the house is at the back.

The eclectic dinner menu might include Mediterranean fish stew with tomato, saffron, and garlic; shredded pork quesadillas with sour cream and lime; and Shaker lemon pie. The wine list is, surprisingly, less diverse: All the wines are from California. The spectacular mahogany bar with its marble countertop and silver chafing dish gives the dining room a turn-of-the-century opulence that in the candlelight blends beautifully with abstract pastel prints on the walls. Breakfast is served in a sunny room filled with music, a little bit of everything.

The town of Chester is fairly sleepy, necessitating a certain resourcefulness from its visitors. Guests with an interest in history enjoy strolling through the nearby "stone village," a cluster of privately owned Civil War-era stone houses that town legend says may have been part of the Underground Railroad. There are also numerous good bike routes in the area.

Address: *Main St., Box 589, Chester, VT 05143, tel. 802/875–2444.*
Accommodations: *27 double rooms and 3 singles with baths.*
Amenities: *Restaurant, TV in public area; 2 tennis courts.*
Rates: *$170 MAP. MC, V.*
Restrictions: *Smoking in restaurant only, no pets. 2-day minimum on some holidays and foilage weekends; closed Apr., 2 weeks Nov.*

The Inn at Sawmill Farm

Staying at this aristocratic little inn in the Haystack Mountain/Mt. Snow ski region is like being a guest at the country home of a British lord whose family fortune is still intact. The decor here may be country, but it's the kind of country featured in glossy home-and-garden magazines: There's a polished copper milk tank used as a table base, plaid carpet, a brick foyer decorated with a horse collar and farm tools, and chamber music piped into the low-ceilinged reception area. Guests like to congregate around the huge fireplace in the living room in winter with their afternoon tea, or stroll by one of the two ponds when it's warm.

In 1968 architect Rodney Williams and his wife, Ione, an interior designer, bought an old dairy farm that dated back to 1897, but don't expect a rugged rural retreat. The atmosphere is on the formal side—men must wear jackets in the public areas after 6 PM—and the owners cater to a select clientele.

Wallpaper in the guest rooms matches the bedspreads and upholstery; one room might be all soft pastels, another bright with vibrant hues. The carpet is thick enough to swallow high heels. The bed might be decorated with a tiny lace pillow, or a wall might display a framed quilt sample. The 10 cottages have larger rooms with working fireplaces.

The Williams' son Brill presides as chef in the two restaurants, one of which is a formal dining room with six tables, an antique sideboard, Early American portraits, Queen Anne furniture, and a baby grand piano. In the second, a greenhouse-like area, simple whitewashed timber pillars contrast nicely with silver napkin rings. The menu features such entrées as roasted free-range chicken stuffed with shallots and mushrooms, lobster, and baby frogs' legs in Riesling sauce with truffles.

The Inn at Sawmill Farm is comparable to a city sophisticate who has retreated to the country—reserved, perhaps, but with impeccable taste.

Address: *Rte. 100, West Dover, VT 05356, tel. 802/464–8131, fax 802/464–1130.*
Accommodations: *20 double rooms with baths.*
Amenities: *Restaurant, air-conditioning in some rooms, fireplaces in cottages, TV in public area; swimming pool, tennis court, 2 trout ponds.*
Rates: *$290–$310 MAP. No credit cards.*
Restrictions: *No smoking in dining room, no pets. 2-night minimum on weekends.*

Inn at Weathersfield

When Ron and Mary Louise's home in Thornburn, Ohio, was bought as part of a historic preservation project, they decided to move to New England and restore this rambling Colonial farmhouse, originally built in 1795. Visitors are greeted in the entry by dried wildflowers dangling from the low-beamed ceiling and hot apple cider simmering in an iron kettle over an open hearth. On Thanksgiving and Christmas, Mary Louise uses the hearth, its brick beehive oven, and antique utensils to cook dinner for the guests. Her authentic 18th-century recipes are only slightly modified for modern taste. She cooks on ordinary days as well, but then she sticks with more modern appliances; visitors often see her coming out of the kitchen dressed in her chef's whites. A former sales executive turned amateur entertainer, Ron provides dinner music on the dining room's grand piano, singing Cole Porter or Gershwin tunes with enthusiasm.

The 10 rooms and two suites are individually decorated, all with period antiques that complement the Colonial atmosphere. In the Otis Stearns Room, for instance, swaths of lace over the iron bedstead form a canopy anchored by a bouquet of dried flowers. A camelback trunk sits at the foot of a four-poster bed in one room, a stenciled Windsor chair and hardwood floors lend a simple grace to another. A bowl of nuts and apples in each room greets guests; Colonial spareness doesn't preclude such modern comforts as electric blankets and a small aerobics area in the basement. Some bathrooms are on the small side and have 1940s-style fixtures. The best rooms are in the newer section, which includes a suite with skylights and a private deck, reached by a circular staircase.

In the afternoon, a lavish English tea, complete with homemade pastries and hors d'oeuvres served from silver chafing dishes, is only a warmup for Mary Louise's five-course dinner, which might include escargots, farm-raised partridge with sauce chasseur, and lemon-champagne sorbet. At breakfast, guests are often treated to a poetry reading by Harold Groat, an eighth-generation Vermonter.

Address: *Rte. 106, Weathersfield, VT 05151, tel. 802/263–9217 or 800/477–4828, fax 802/263–9219.*
Accommodations: *9 double rooms with baths, 3 suites.*
Amenities: *Restaurant (open Thurs.–Mon.), sauna, exercise equipment, pool table, afternoon tea.*
Rates: *$175–$205 MAP. $5 charge for use of fireplace. AE, D, MC, V.*
Restrictions: *Smoking only in public areas, no pets. 2-night minimum on most weekends, 3-night minimum on holiday weekends.*

Kedron Valley Inn

A strong sense of family strikes visitors as soon as they step into Max and Merrily Comins's inn; in 1985 they moved from New York and began the renovation of what in the 1840s had been the National Hotel, one of the state's oldest hotels. Mannequins in the entry hall wear the antique wedding dresses of Merrily and her grandmother, the couple's collection of family quilts is scattered throughout the inn, and framed antique linens deck the walls.

But the dresses and quilts are not the only reason for the inn's familial flavor. This is one of the rare antiques-filled inns that welcomes children, who are encouraged to build sand castles on the pond's small beach and make friends with Blondie, the dog, or Max and Merrily's 9-year-old son, Drew. Many rooms have either a fireplace or a Franklin stove, and each is decorated with a quilt. Two rooms have private decks, another has a private veranda, and a fourth has a private terrace overlooking the stream that runs through the inn's 15 acres. Families often are housed in one of six units in a one-story log building at the back of the property, where the rooms, lined up ski-lodge style, are more rustic than the rooms in the main inn. They're decorated in similar fashion, with a mix of antiques and reproductions. Refugees from the Big City will find the country charm they're looking for in such features as the hand-stenciled walls, Franklin stoves and working fireplaces with pewter dishes on the mantels, and four-poster canopy beds with white chenille bedspreads and peony-patterned pastel sheets.

The dining room, where Max serves as host in the evenings, specializes in French dishes with a nouvelle twist, such as fillet of Norwegian salmon stuffed with herb seafood mousse, in puff pastry; or shrimp, scallops, and lobster with wild mushrooms, sautéed in shallots and white wine and served with Frangelico cream sauce.

The bustling town of Woodstock is nearby for strolling or shopping as is Kedron Valley Stables—an operation not affiliated with the inn—which offers trail rides and lessons.

Address: *Rte. 106, Woodstock, VT 05071, tel. 802/457–1473, fax 802/457–4469.*
Accommodations: *27 double rooms with baths.*
Amenities: *Restaurant, lounge, cable TV in some rooms; ½-acre swimming/skating pond with sand beach, riding center.*
Rates: *$114–$202, full breakfast, $154–$244 MAP. D, MC, V.*
Restrictions: *2-night minimum on weekends, mid-Sept.–late Oct., and Dec. 24–Jan. 1; 3-night minimum on holiday weekends; closed Apr.*

The Old Tavern at Grafton

The white-columned porches on both stories of the main building wrap around a structure that dates back to 1788 and has been an inn for most of that time. Today's guests can still take a look at the register that bears the signatures of such prominent visitors as Daniel Webster and Nathaniel Hawthorne. Despite its long and distinguished career, the inn hardly shows its age, largely because of the efforts of the Windham Foundation, which in 1963 began buying and restoring historic homes like this one in and around Grafton. Thanks to the foundation, visitors can now enjoy whiling away the hours in a perfectly preserved white-clapboard town that encourages creative idleness: strolling down to the stream that flows through the center of town; spending long mornings on the Old Tavern's porch watching a car go by every half hour or so; taking a horse-drawn carriage tour; or reading the notices posted on the bulletin board in front of the general store.

The main building has 14 rooms, the oldest just above the lobby. Families are usually given rooms in the newer building across the street or in one of the seven rental cottages. The rooms in the main building evoke New England's 18th-century frontier days. Each is decorated with country antiques; some have crocheted canopies or four-poster beds that could easily be as old as the inn itself. The newer rooms are generally sunnier and sport bright pastels. There's a well-stocked library off the lobby, and the old barn in the back houses a comfortable tavern where guests can partake of afternoon tea. Both spots have brick fireplaces that invite guests to linger long after dinner. Two dining rooms—one with Georgian furniture and oil portraits, the other with rustic paneling and low beams—serve traditional, hearty New England dishes, such as venison stew or grilled quail; some offerings feature cheddar cheese made just down the road at the Grafton Village Cheese Factory.

Address: *Rte. 121, Grafton, VT 05146, tel. 802/843–2231, fax 802/843–2245.*
Accommodations: *35 double rooms with baths.*
Amenities: *Restaurant, lounge, games room, TV in public area; swimming pond, platform tennis and tennis courts.*
Rates: *$95–$140; Continental breakfast. AE, MC, V.*
Restrictions: *Pets allowed in some buildings. 2-night minimum during foliage season, 3-night minimum on some holidays, closed Apr., Dec. 24–25.*

The Darling Family Inn

The name isn't a cutesy advertising ploy; the owners really are named Joan and Chapin Darling. After tiring of corporate life in New York and Hartford, they opened the rural inn in 1980. The rooms in this renovated 1830 farmhouse welcome guests with baskets of apples, quilts on the beds, wide-plank floors, and Joan's skilled hand-stenciling on the walls. Two housekeeping cottages behind the main house each have twin beds, and baths with showers. Often used by families, these cottages are not as meticulously furnished as the five rooms in the main house, which are decorated with such elegant American and English antiques as a Federal-style highboy and a sterling silver pitcher on the dresser. Dinner, with complimentary wine, is served to guests who request it a day in advance. Guests often enjoy playing the spinet piano, accompanied by Chapin on guitar. Those who can tear themselves away from sitting under the apple trees and contemplating the surrounding 400 acres of farmland might enjoy visiting Weston's serene Benedictine monastery.

Address: *Rte. 100, Weston, VT 05161, tel. 802/824-3223.*
Accommodations: *5 double rooms with baths, 2 cottages.*
Amenities: *TV/VCR in library, fireplaces in living room and library; swimming pool, cross-country ski trails.*
Rates: *$75–$95; full breakfast and cheese and wine. No credit cards.*
Restrictions: *Pets permitted in cottages only. 2-night minimum on weekends, closed at Christmas.*

Eaglebrook of Grafton

Tired of conventionally charming country decor? Marge and Eli Prouty have somehow managed to combine a historic house and well-preserved antiques with touches of city sophistication. With the collection of abstract art and the cathedral-ceilinged sun room overlooking the Saxtons River, the elegant retreat feels very much like a private home, one that might have been featured in a glossy interior-design magazine.

Of special interest are the pastel watercolor stencils in the hallways, done by an itinerant stenciler in 1840 and restored during the 1950s. Fireplaces with soapstone mantels are everywhere; there are seven in all in the inn's 11 rooms. Blue-checked fabric gives one of the rooms a French provincial air; another leans toward American country; a third has a Victorian flavor. Bathrooms are new and comfortable, and the second-story balcony has a view of Bear Mountain. The lushly landscaped stone terrace is a perfect place to sip sherry on a summer evening or eat the Continental buffet breakfast served from a long Mennonite table. In Eaglebrook's case, small is truly beautiful.

Address: *Main St., Grafton, VT 05146, tel. 802/843-2564.*
Accommodations: *1 double room with bath, 2 doubles share 1 bath.*
Amenities: *TV in public area.*
Rates: *$75–$80; Continental breakfast. MC, V.*
Restrictions: *No smoking in guest rooms, no pets. Closed Apr., Christmas week.*

Four Columns

With its village green surrounded by pristine white buildings, Newfane has often been called the quintessential New England town, and the Four Columns is part of the reason. Erected 150 years ago for a homesick Southern bride, the majestic white columns of this Greek Revival mansion are more intimidating than the Colonial-style rooms inside. Room 1 in the older section has a double Jacuzzi and an enclosed porch overlooking the town common. Pam and Jacques Allembert have decorated all rooms individually, though each has antiques, brass beds, and quilts; some also have fireplaces. The third-floor room in the old section is the most private. The inn's restaurant, decorated with antique tools and copper pots, became famous under the direction of a former White House chef, René Chardain; his successor, Greg Parks, has maintained his high standards.

Address: *West St., Box 278, Newfane, VT 05345, tel. 802/365–7713.*
Accommodations: *15 double rooms with baths.*
Amenities: *Restaurant, tavern, air-conditioning, TV in public area; swimming pool, hiking trails.*
Rates: *$105–$180; full breakfast; $185–$225 MAP mandatory during foliage season. AE, MC, V.*
Restrictions: *No smoking; pets by prior arrangement. 2-night minimum on weekends, 3-night minimum on holiday weekends, closed Apr., late Nov.–early Dec.*

The Hermitage

Staying at this 19th-century inn is a little like visiting an English country estate during the shooting season. Owner Jim McGovern dotes on his English setters and collection of decoys, while various game birds roam the fields near the duck pond (visitors shouldn't get too attached to the birds, however, since they'll probably have one for dinner before they leave). There's also a hunting preserve and shooting range on the property; Haystack Mountain and Mt. Snow ski areas are nearby.

Guest rooms are spread among four buildings: the Carriage House; the Wine House; the Brookbound Inn, with 14 rustic rooms; and the Federal-style main inn. Most of the furnishings are in simple turn-of-the-century New England style: muslin curtains, white shutters, beds with towering oak headboards or four-posters and chenille bedspreads.

Address: *Coldbrook Rd., Box 457, Wilmington, VT 05363, tel. 802/464–3511.*
Accommodations: *25 double rooms with baths, 4 doubles share 2 baths.*
Amenities: *Restaurant, TV in common area, fireplaces or Franklin stoves in 11 bedrooms and 3 common rooms, phones in rooms; sauna, swimming pool, tennis court, cross-country ski center and trails, sporting clays.*
Rates: *$130–$200 MAP. AE, DC, MC, V.*
Restrictions: *No pets. 2-night minimum on most weekends.*

Hickory Ridge House

Innkeepers often have interesting backgrounds, but Steve Anderson's may be one of the most unusual; in his pre-Vermont life, he was both a professor and chimney sweep. He and wife Jacquie Walker have since turned a stately 1808 Federal mansion into a homey bed-and-breakfast in which the unusually spacious rooms reflect the original owner's fortune. Putney was one of the centers of the 1960s back-to-the-land movement, and traces of that ethos are still evident in the vegetarian breakfasts served at Hickory Ridge. Home-baked breads, stuffed pumpkin pancakes, and various soufflés are some of the inn's specialties.

The rooms, which were renovated in 1984, feature country farmhouse decor that is simple yet comfortable. Rag rugs cover pine floors, white lace curtains hang at the windows, and walls are painted in cheerful pastels; rooms in the newer section have low ceilings and are less expensive. Bathrooms have large tubs and are spare but clean.

Address: *Hickory Ridge Rd., RD 3, Box 1410, Putney, VT 05346, tel. 802/387–5709.*
Accommodations: *3 double rooms with baths, 4 doubles share 3 baths.*
Amenities: *TV in public area, fireplaces in 4 rooms.*
Rates: *$45–$85; full breakfast. MC, V.*
Restrictions: *No smoking, no pets. 2-night minimum on holiday weekends.*

Juniper Hill Inn

An expanse of green lawn with Adirondack chairs and a small pond sweeps up to the white-columned portico of this Greek Revival mansion. Built at the turn of the century by William Maxwell Evarts, the grandfather of the distinguished book publisher Maxwell Evarts Perkins, the structure is now a National Landmark. The central living room, once the ballroom, has hardwood floors, oak paneling, Oriental carpets, and wing chairs and sofas. An impressive staircase sweeps up past a large Palladian window to the spacious guest rooms, some of which have fireplaces, marble sinks in the bathrooms, and brass or four-poster beds (one even has a small porch). The rooms are all decorated with authentic Edwardian and Queen Anne furnishings.

Guests can tour Windsor's Old Constitution House, where the document that made Vermont an independent republic was signed, or explore the Windsor–Cornish covered bridge, the longest in New England. Innkeepers Rob and Susanne Pearl also can recommend hiking and cross-country ski trails in the area.

Address: *Juniper Hill Rd., Box 79, Windsor, VT 05089–9703, tel. 802/674–5273.*
Accommodations: *16 double rooms with baths.*
Amenities: *Restaurant, TV in public area, pool, ceiling fans, hiking trails nearby.*
Rates: *$90–$120; full breakfast. MC, V.*
Restrictions: *No smoking; no pets. Closed Apr., 2 weeks in Nov.*

Parker House

Perched along the Quechee River and only minutes from the famous Quechee Gorge, the 1857 Parker House has one of the most picturesque settings in Vermont. The four spacious rooms are furnished in Victorian splendor, with soft peach and blue pastels predominating. From Joseph's Room guests have a sweeping view of the Otaquechee river. Emily's Room boasts a marble fireplace and an iron and brass bed. The matching armoire and dressing table in Rebecca's Room have dyed-rosewood inlays in a delicate floral pattern.

The food is as delectable as the surroundings are posh; the intimate formal dining rooms, furnished in burgundy and cream linens, are all candlelight and classic French cuisine. The terrace, which is used in summer and fall and is more casual, offers a spectacular river view. Guests often like to stroll next door to the Simon Pearce factory, where they can watch glassblowers and potters at work and buy their wares.

Address: *16 Main St., Box 0780, Quechee, VT 05059, tel. 802/295–6077.*
Accommodations: *7 double rooms with baths.*
Amenities: *Restaurant, air-conditioning, TV in public area.*
Rates: *$95–$120; Continental breakfast. MC, V.*
Restrictions: *No pets. 2-night minimum during foliage season, graduation, Christmas, and holidays; closed Mar. and 2 weeks in Nov.*

Village Inn of Woodstock

One of the main advantages of this house is its location within walking distance of Woodstock's popular village green. Guests here can visit it without getting caught in the notoriously heavy summer traffic along Route 4, the town's main drag.

Innkeepers Kevin and Anita Clark have made the most of the Village Inn's exquisite Victorian detailing, such as the pressed tin ceilings, the beveled-glass Palladian window on the staircase landing, and the stained-glass window behind the elaborate bar in the lounge. The country-style decor in the rooms is simple and a bit sparse but neat, with chenille bedspreads, brass headboards, and dried flowers or straw hats decorating the walls.

The dining room mixes Vermont specialties, such as roast turkey, with Italian dishes like mussels marinara and fettuccine. After dinner, guests often like to sit outside on the wide front porch and watch the passing parade, grateful not to be in it.

Address: *41 Pleasant St., Woodstock, VT 05091, tel. 802/457–1255.*
Accommodations: *6 double rooms with baths, 2 doubles share 1 bath.*
Amenities: *Restaurant, air-conditioning, TV in public area, fireplace in dining room.*
Rates: *$70–$110; full breakfast; MAP required on weekends. MC, V.*
Restrictions: *No pets; 2-night minimum on weekends and during foliage season, closed 1 week in Nov. and mid-Apr.*

Whetstone Inn

A favorite of visitors to (and sometimes performers at) the Marlboro Music Festival, the 200-year-old Whetstone looks as a Colonial farmhouse might if it were decorated by Marimekko. This inn's beginnings as a stagecoach tavern are reflected in the pewter mugs that hang over the dining-room mantel, the powder-horn rifle, and hand-hewn roof timbers. But the stenciled curtains, wide-plank floors and Revolutionary War–era antiques are cheek-to-cheek with Scandinavian-style wall hangings and furnishings reminiscent of the '50s.

Innkeepers Harry and Jean Boardman are clearly avid music lovers; the library has an extensive and eclectic record collection, as well as volumes of Thoreau, Tolstoy, Zola, Hugo, and Proust. Rooms added over the centuries have created a rabbit warren upstairs. All the rooms are light and furnished with a combination of antiques and family hand-me-downs. Jean is the breakfast cook; she also serves dinner on weekends and concert nights.

Address: *South Rd., Marlboro, VT 05344, tel. 802/254–2500.*
Accommodations: *8 double rooms with baths, 4 doubles share 1 bath.*
Amenities: *Restaurant, fireplaces in living and dining rooms, kitchenettes in 3 rooms; skating pond.*
Rates: *$55–$95; breakfast extra. No credit cards.*
Restrictions: *No smoking in public areas. 1-week minimum July–Aug. during music festival, 3-night minimum on holiday weekends.*

Windham Hill Inn

If you happen to drive up a winding dirt road in the middle of nowhere on a summer's evening and hear strains of Bach or Vivaldi emanating from an old barn, you'll know you've stumbled upon the Windham Hill Inn. The barn is often used on weekends for small live concerts, which may feature anything from a jazz ensemble to a local chamber group; in winter there's a cross-country ski center on the property.

Ken and Linda Bustede converted this 1825 dairy farm into an inn in the early 1960s. Personal touches abound; for example, Linda's fascination with antique shoes is evident throughout the inn, and the antiques-filled rooms feature such decorative details as christening dresses on the wall and handmade quilts. Two of the five rooms in the barn share an enormous deck that overlooks the West River Valley; rooms in the main building, some of which also have balconies, are slightly more formal.

Address: *Windham Hill Rd., West Townshend, VT 05359, tel. 802/874–4080, fax 802/874–4080.*
Accommodations: *15 double rooms with baths.*
Amenities: *Restaurant, fireplaces in common rooms; skating pond.*
Rates: *$170–$225 MAP. AE, MC, V.*
Restrictions: *No smoking, no pets. Closed Apr.–mid.-May, Nov. 1–Thanksgiving.*

Southwestern Vermont

This is the part of Vermont where the state's tradition of rebellion and independence began. Many towns founded in the early 18th century as frontier outposts or fortifications became important trading centers. The state's second and third largest cities are located here: Rutland is historically tied to the marble industry and Bennington is where the Green Mountain Boys fought off both the British and the claims of land-hungry New Yorkers—a battle some say their descendants are still fighting. As a result of this history of trade and industry, there's a blue-collar tradition beneath the quiet charm—which is not to say that the region is some sort of industrial wasteland. This is, after all, Vermont.

Because the southwest corner is a major gateway to Vermont, parts of the area also have a definite city sophistication: Many of the people who sought to escape New York's hustle and bustle have resettled here and brought with them radicchio, vintage wines, and marketing studies. Most residents, however, are also determined to preserve the quality of life that lured them here, even as they go about giving the image of an unspoiled paradise a certain polished perfection.

Arlington (about 15 miles north of Bennington) prides itself on its association with Norman Rockwell, who lived here for 14 years; many of the models for his portraits of small-town life were his neighbors, so if anyone around town looks familiar, you'll know why. A drive up Route 7A along the eastern edge of the Green Mountain National Forest skirts one of the most beautiful wilderness areas in the country.

Places to Go, Sights to See

Bennington. Here, at the Catamount Tavern, Ethan Allen organized the Green Mountain Boys, who helped capture Fort Ticonderoga in 1775. In 1777

American general John Stark urged his militia to attack the Hessians across the New York border: "There are the Redcoats; they will be ours or tonight Molly Stark sleeps a widow!" Now Vermont's third largest city and the focus of the state's southwest corner, Bennington has retained much of the industrial character it developed in the 19th century, when paper mills, gristmills, and potteries formed the city's economic base.

A Chamber of Commerce brochure describes a self-guided walking tour through *Old Bennington,* a National Register Historic District just west of downtown, where impressive white-columned Greek Revival and sturdy brick Federal houses stand around a village green. In the graveyard of the Old First Church, at the corner of Church Street and Monument Avenue, the tombstone of poet Robert Frost proclaims, "I had a lover's quarrel with the world." *The Bennington Museum* (W. Main St., tel. 802/447–1571) boasts a rich collection of Americana that includes artifacts of rural life piled high in large cases. Devotees of folk art will want to see the exhibit of the work of Grandma Moses, who lived and painted in the area. The museum is also known for its collections of American glass (including some fine Tiffany specimens) and early Bennington pottery. Those in search of more recent examples of Bennington pottery can visit the *Bennington Potters Yard* (324 County St., tel. 802/447–7531), which has a large store of seconds for sale.

Green Mountain National Forest. The 275,000 acres of Vermont's largest single wilderness area extend into the center of the state, providing scenic drives, picnic areas, campsites, lakes, and hiking and cross-country ski trails. The territory includes the 255-mile Massachusetts-to-Canada *Long Trail* (popular with serious hikers). The *Green Mountain Club* (tel. 802/244–7037) is a source of information about good places for day hikes and picnics.

Manchester. This has been a popular summer retreat since the mid-19th century, when Mary Todd Lincoln visited. *Manchester Village*'s tree-shaded marble sidewalks and stately old homes converted to bed-and-breakfasts reflect the luxurious resort lifestyle of a century ago, while *Manchester Center*'s upscale factory-outlet stores, which sell everything from designer fashions and crystal to sporting goods, appeal to the 20th-century's affluent ski crowd drawn by nearby Bromley and Stratton mountains.

Hildene (Rte. 7A, Manchester, tel. 802/362–1788), the summer home of Abraham Lincoln's son Robert, is situated on the 412-acre estate of the former chairman of the board of the Pullman Company. His descendants lived here as recently as 1975. Tours include a walk through the 24-room Georgian Revival mansion and the elaborate formal gardens. The *Southern Vermont Art Center* (West Rd., tel. 802/362–1405) is also worth a visit while you're in Manchester.

Vermont Marble Exhibit (4 mi north of Rutland, tel. 802/459–3311). Here visitors can watch stonemasons at work and see how rough stone is transformed into slabs, blocks, and decorative objects. This is one of the state's most popular tourist attractions.

Restaurants

Those who seek classic French cuisine in Bennington go to **Four Chimneys** (tel. 802/447–3500), while those in search of down-home eats or all-day breakfasts head to the **Blue Ben Diner** (tel. 802/442–8977). The **Arlington Inn** (tel. 802/375–6532) has one of the most repected restaurants in the state, and **Wildflowers** (tel. 802/362–2568), in the Reluctant Panther Inn in Manchester, has long been known for its elegant cuisine. Try **Laney's** (tel. 802/362–4456) in Manchester for a lively, contemporary place that features an open kitchen with a wood-fired brick oven.

Nightlife

The **Dorset Playhouse** (tel. 802/867–2223) hosts a resident professional troupe in the summer months and performances by a community group in winter. The Vermont Symphony Orchestra performs at the **Southern Vermont Art Center** (tel. 802/362–1405) in Manchester in the winter and is also the site of concerts and various performances during the summer. Try the numerous bars and clubs around the Killington and Mt. Snow ski areas for dancing and live music.

Tourist Information

Rutland Region Chamber of Commerce (7 Court Sq., Box 67, Rutland, VT 05701, tel. 802/773–2747); **Bennington Area Chamber of Commerce** (Veterans Memorial Dr., Bennington, VT 05201, tel. 802/447–3311); **Chamber of Commerce–Manchester and the Mountains** (Adams Park Green, Box 928, Manchester, VT 05255, tel. 802/362–2100).

Reservations Services

Bennington Area Chamber of Commerce (Veterans Memorial Dr., Bennington, VT 05201, tel. 802/447–3311); **Chamber of Commerce–Manchester and the Mountains** (Adams Park Green, Box 928, Manchester, VT 05255, tel. 802/362–2100); **Vermont Bed and Breakfast** (Box 1, East Fairfield, VT 05448, tel. 802/827–3827).

1811 House

Parts of this rambling inn date from 1770, and when one walks through the door into the low-ceilinged entryway, the first impression gathered is of entering a typical Colonial building. The experience of staying here, however, is more like visiting an elegant English country home, without having to pay the transatlantic airfare. The inn's genteel air is in keeping with Manchester's traditional role as a summer getaway for the rich, and the innkeepers admit they enjoy catering to an upper-crust clientele. This hostelry has been in operation since 1811 (the only break in service was when it was owned by Abraham Lincoln's granddaughter). Current owners Bruce and Marnie Duff wanted a place where they could spend time on their special interests: cooking, for Marnie, and gardening and wine, for Bruce.

The decor is basically Federal with a relaxed touch. A veritable stable of horse paintings give a distinctly Windsoresque atmosphere to many of the public rooms, and the Waterford crystal, stenciled floral borders along the ceilings, and ornately carved chairs in the dining room all contribute to an inn worthy of the Princess of Wales. The pub-style bar (open only to guests) is suitably dark and cozy, decorated with horse brasses and exposed rafters, and boasts the largest collection of single malt scotches in Vermont.

English floral landscaping, extensive gardens, terraces, and a pond all decorate the 7½ acres surrounding the inn. Both public and guest rooms contain elegant English and American antiques from the family's own collection; six guest rooms have working fireplaces, and many are quite spacious. Bathrooms are a bit old-fashioned but serviceable; the Robinson Room has a marble-enclosed tub, not to mention a terrific view of the lawn from its own porch. The Mary Lincoln Isham Room has a canopy bed covered with white chenille and matching floral wallpaper and drapes.

Breakfast is often in the hearty English tradition, with potatoes, mushrooms, bacon and eggs, and scones.

Address: *Rte. 7A, Manchester, VT 05254, tel. 802/362–1811 or 800/432–1811.*
Accommodations: *14 double rooms with baths.*
Amenities: *Lounge, air-conditioning.*
Rates: *$110–$180; full breakfast. AE, MC, V.*
Restrictions: *Smoking in pub only, no pets. 2-night minimum on weekends and holidays and during foliage season, closed Christmas Day.*

Arlington Inn

The Greek Revival columns at the entrance to this carefully restored railroad magnate's home give the building an imposing presence. The rooms, however, are anything but intimidating. Their cozy charm is created by claw-foot tubs in some bathrooms, linens that coordinate with the Victorian-style wallpaper, and the original moldings and wainscoting. The main section of the inn was built in 1848 by Martin Chester Deming, and rooms here are named after members of his family. The decor features Victorian antiques, massive headboards that tower over sleepers, and etched glass shades on curving bronze Victorian oil lamps. The carriage house, built at the turn of the century and renovated in 1985, blends country French and Queen Anne period furnishings with folk art. The inn is separated from the road by a spacious lawn, so all guest rooms are fairly quiet.

New innkeepers Bob and Sandee Ellis moved from a hectic life in southern California to this quiet New England town in 1991 and were eager to put his experience in construction and her genuine hospitality to work revitalizing the inn. While emphasing the mansion's gracious social and historical significance, they have upgraded the rooms with such modern conveniences as phones and queen- and king-size beds. Their efforts are also commendable in the dining room, where the deft touch of chef Ken Panquin presides. Using local products from Vermont farms whenever possible, Panquin's seasonal menus might include such creations as pan-seared sea scallops on Napa cabbage with ginger tomato and coconut-scented sauce, accompanied by house-cured gravlax and aquavit, maple sauce, and black pepper pasta. Polished hardwood floors, green napkins and walls, candlelight, and soft music complement the elegant food. The Ellis's have received the prestigious Award of Excellence from the Wine Spectator for their extensive collection. Continental breakfast, with fresh fruit, cereal, and home-baked pastries, is served in a solarium at the back of the inn.

Arlington is Norman Rockwell country—the faces in many of his illustrations are those of Arlington townfolk—and the inn is within walking distance of a small exhibit devoted to his work.

Address: *Rte. 7A, Arlington, VT 05250, tel. 802/375–6532.*
Accommodations: *13 double rooms with baths.*
Amenities: *Restaurant, lounge, air-conditioning, TV and VCR in public area, fireplaces in public areas and 2 guest rooms; tennis court.*
Rates: *$75–$160; Continental breakfast. AE, MC, V.*
Restrictions: *No pets. 2-night minimum on weekends in Oct., closed Christmas, New Year's Day.*

Vermont Marble Inn

When insurance broker Bea Taube and her husband, pressman Richie Taube, decided to leave New York City and start a country inn, Bea's best friend, Shirley Stein, decided to come along with them. Together the trio has transformed a deteriorating relic into the hautest of haute Victorian inns. The two ornate Carrara marble living-room fireplaces look and feel as though they were carved from solid cream, and the crystal chandeliers in the dining room, the plush settees, Oriental rugs, and etched-glass front doors are worthy of Lillie Langtry or Diamond Jim Brady at their most extravagant. The individually decorated rooms are named after such authors as Byron, Shakespeare, or Elizabeth Barrett Browning, whose works are set by the appropriate bedside. Furnished with antiques, from Victorian to Art Deco, the rooms have such elegant touches as a canopy bed, a working fireplace, and an antique trunk. Bathrooms are large enough to accommodate people wearing the flowing dresses of 1867, when the inn was built as a private home; eight of the bathrooms have shower stalls only.

Bea and Shirley were attracted to the inn business because they love to entertain; they're the type of motherly women who beg you to put on your coat so you don't catch your death of cold. They do all the baking, including the pastries and cakes for an elaborate afternoon tea served from a sterling silver service. No guest leaves the table hungry after their hearty five-course breakfast.

The nine-table dining room here is intimate enough to allow diners to make new friends over dinner, and guests frequently retire to the living room for long conversations. Anything less than the classical music, the crystal chandelier, the candlelight, and the antique Victorian sideboard would scarcely do justice to the sumptuous meals. These might include veal loin sautéed in saffron oil with sweet peppers and olives in a chive pesto, or braised duckling in port and raspberry sauce with wild rice. All food is prepared to order, so special diets can be accommodated, and there are often such vegetarian offerings as lentil- and vegetable-stuffed zucchini, grilled polenta, and vegetables du jour. The tray of home-baked desserts is worth any amount of extra calories.

Address: *12 West Park Pl., Fair Haven, VT 05743, tel. 802/265–8383 or 800/535–2814.*
Accommodations: *12 double rooms with baths.*
Amenities: *Restaurant, TV in library, public phone.*
Rates: *$145–$195 MAP; afternoon tea. AE, MC, V.*
Restrictions: *No pets.*

West Mountain Inn

Everywhere you turn at the West Mountain Inn are reminders of owners Wes and Mary Ann Carlson's idiosyncratic enthusiasms. Just for starters, take the llama ranch on the property, which started as a hobby. The small African violets in the rooms, which guests are invited to take home with them, come with instructions for care. The white Adirondack chairs on the front lawn are perfect for contemplating a spectacular view of the surrounding countryside, and in winter the sloping lawn practically cries for a sled.

All of which is to say that the Carlsons, both former educators, have created a place that has the feeling of being a world apart; that's part of what lured movie stars Michael J. Fox and Tracy Pollan to get married here (Wes still tells stories about tabloid reporters' efforts to bribe employees). This 1840s farmhouse, restored over the past 13 years, sits on 150 secluded acres where squirrels come up and feed outside guests' windows. Plush carpet, quilted bedspreads, chocolate llamas on the bedside stands, and copies of the books of local author Dorothy Canfield Fisher lend an air of simple, comfortable luxury to the guest rooms. Rooms 2, 3, and 4 in the front of the house afford the same panorama as the front lawn (though there are almost no bad views in the place); the three small nooks of Room 11 resemble railroad sleeper berths and are perfect for children.

At happy hour, guests gather in the library to nibble on complimentary hors d'oeuvres, such as chicken fingers and fruit, and get acquainted before moving into the low-beamed, paneled, candlelighted dining room. The menu offers hearty New England specialties with interesting little twists, such as veal tenderloin topped with sun-dried tomatoes and Asiago cheese. Aunt Min's Swedish rye and other flavorful breads, as well as desserts, are made on the premises. Tables by the windows offer a splendid view of the mountains, which goes a long way to promote inner peace.

Address: *River Rd., off Rte. 313, Arlington, VT 05250, tel. 802/375-6516.*
Accommodations: *13 double rooms with baths.*
Amenities: *Restaurant, library/pub, bar, air-conditioning in dining room, TV and phones in public area, fireplaces in 4 rooms, trail maps in rooms; walking and cross-country ski trails.*
Rates: *\$155–\$180 MAP; full breakfast, hors d'oeuvres, and dinner. AE, D, MC, V.*
Restrictions: *Smoking in pub only, no pets. 2-night minimum on weekends.*

Birch Hill Inn

Up the driveway past the stand of white birches, you'll come to the former horse farm that has been in Pat Lee's family since the early part of the century. You'll spot family photos all over the inn, and even the meals feel like family events; Pat and Jim usually sit down with guests for dinner or breakfast.

The Lees have avoided fussy period antiques; instead, the bright, immaculate, and spacious guest rooms have comfortable furniture, quilts or chenille bedspreads, and such thoughtful extras as stamped envelopes and cassette players and classical music tapes in each room. Rooms on the north side offer spectacular views of Mt. Bromley or the horse pasture. Many guests seem to enjoy lolling in the white wicker furniture of the sun room or, in summer, on the terrace's wrought-iron chairs. The Birch Hill is not far from the Southern Vermont Art Center, which exhibits local and nationally known artists.

Address: *West Rd., Box 346, Manchester, VT 05254, tel. 802/362–2761.*
Accommodations: *5 double rooms with baths, 1 cottage with bath.*
Amenities: *Fireplace in living room and 1 guest room, minifridge; swimming pool, tennis courts.*
Rates: *$96–$106; full breakfast. MC, V.*
Restrictions: *No pets. 2-night minimum on weekends, closed Nov.–Dec., Apr.–Memorial Day.*

Hill Farm Inn

Just off Route 7A, this homey inn still has the feel of the country farmhouse it used to be: The mix of sturdy antiques and hand-me-downs, the spinning wheel in the upstairs hall, the paintings by a family member, the beefalo that roam the 50 acres, the jars of homemade jam that visitors may take away—all convey the relaxed, friendly personalities of the owners, George and Joanne Hardy, former human service workers. An inn since 1905, and one of the first in the area, the Hill Farm's proximity to the Battenkill River has been luring trout enthusiasts for decades. Room 7, the newest, has a cathedral ceiling with beams and a porch with a view of Mt. Equinox; the rooms in the 1790 guest house are private. The cabins are popular with families in summer. With advance notice, Joanne will cook dinner any night except Wednesday. This is the sort of unpretentious, charming place that makes you wish you'd grown up on the farm.

Address: *RR 2, Box 2015, Arlington, VT 05250, tel. 802/375–2269 or 800/882–2545.*
Accommodations: *6 double rooms with baths, 5 doubles share 3 baths, 2 suites, 4 cabins (available in summer only).*
Amenities: *Restaurant, TV in public area, pets allowed in cabins.*
Rates: *$60–$105; full breakfast. AE, D, MC, V.*
Restrictions: *No smoking in guest rooms. 2-night minimum on most weekends; 3-night minimum on holiday weekends.*

Inn at Manchester

Innkeepers Harriet and Stan Rosenberg have given this Victorian home the feeling of Olde Vermont Meets Beaver Cleaver. Guests may relax on the spacious porch overlooking Manchester Village's Main Street, or in a lushly appointed Victorian sitting room with a bay window. Or they can pop a six-pack of beer into the fridge and watch TV in the family room, where a bumper-pool table dominates and a Norman Rockwell print hangs next to a tapestry over Formica and Naugahyde furniture.

The four new guest rooms in the carriage house in the back are closest to the pool; the Sweet William Room has a cathedral ceiling and a loft; and all the rooms have access to a small sitting room. The older rooms in the main building have fireplaces and simple antique furnishings, such as brass and iron beds. The Lavender Room and the Wood Lily Room have handpainted headboards. Art posters and prints decorate the walls.

Address: *Historic Rte. 7A, Box 41, Manchester Village, VT 05254, tel. 802/362–1793.*
Accommodations: *10 double rooms with baths, 6 doubles share 3 baths, 3 suites.*
Amenities: *Air-conditioning in some rooms, TV in public area; swimming pool.*
Rates: *$85–$160; full breakfast. AE, D, MC, V.*
Restrictions: *No smoking in public areas, no pets. 2-night minimum on most weekends.*

Inn at Westview Farm

When Helmut and Dorothy Stein bought the Inn at Westview Farm in 1987, they upgraded the rooms and redecorated according to their own personal tastes. They succeeded in creating a quality inn on an intimate scale, reminiscent of the best of European inns. The delicate paisley stripe wallpaper used in some rooms is a resfreshing change from Vermont country florals, and the new carpeting and bathrooms are a contemporary complement to the period antiques. Crisp white curtains and baskets of flowers give a country ambience. The formal living room, with rag rugs, and the generous sitting room both have fireplaces; guests enjoy looking at the album of before and after photos documenting the inn's renovation. The dining room is lushly green, with handing plants adorning the large bay window. The menu does well by such French-inspired dishes as grilled duck breast with honey and thyme or grilled beef fillet with lemon and ginger sauce. Clancy's Tavern, decorated with stained-glass panels, offers a bistro-style menu.

Address: *Rte. 30, Dorset, VT 05251, tel. 802/867–5715.*
Accommodations: *9 double rooms with baths, 1 suite.*
Amenities: *Restaurant, tavern, air-conditioning, TV in public area and suite, Rumford fireplace; terrace.*
Rates: *$96–$120 with full breakfast; $156–$180 MAP. MC, V.*
Restrictions: *No pets. 2-night minimum on holiday weekends, closed late Mar.–late April, late Oct.–mid-Nov.*

Molly Stark Inn

This gem of a B&B will make you so comfortable you'll feel like you're visiting an old friend. Innkeeper Reed Fendler prides himself on the relaxed atmosphere he has created by combining the building's exposed brick archways and gleaming hardwood floors with such generous allowances as an open kitchen where guests may prepare their own tea or coffee and grab a home-baked brownie or two before settling into one of the wing-backed chairs in front of the wood-burning stove. The attic suite is the most spacious of the relatively small quarters of this Queen Anne–style Victorian home, but the antique quilts, claw-foot tubs, and thoughtfully placed country furnishings make each room reminiscent of one you might have slept in had you grown up in New England a few generations ago. Reed's genuine hospitality and quirky charisma delight guests as do his full country breakfasts. His specialties include cinnamon-apple cheddar cheese quiche and puffed apple pancakes.

Address: *1067 E. Main St., Bennington, VT 05201, tel. 802/442–9631 or 800/356–3076.*
Accommodations: *2 rooms with baths, 4 rooms share 2 baths.*
Amenities: *Wood-burning stove and TV in public area; air-conditioning in some rooms, ceiling fans in all rooms.*
Rates: *$65–$85, full breakfast; AE, D, MC, V.*
Restrictions: *No smoking, no pets. 2-night minimum on weekends June–Oct. and holidays.*

Reluctant Panther

Such luxurious touches as goose-down duvets, complimentary wine, and Pierre Deux linens are the norm here. The new innkeepers, Maye and Robert Bachofen, have redecorated in soft grays and peach, but the lounge still has its leaf-pattern wallpaper made from real leaves! The building dates to the 1850s, but renovation has given all the rooms private baths, and furnishings are an eclectic mix of antique and contemporary. Ten rooms have fireplaces—the Mary Porter and Mark Skinner suites even have two, one in each of the bathrooms. Suites have whirlpools, one with a double Jacuzzi. The best views are from Rooms B and D, while Room J has windows on three sides.

The inn's restaurant, Wildflowers, has long been known for its elegant cuisine. Robert, former director of food and beverage at New York's Plaza Hotel, is upholding that tradition magnificently. A huge fieldstone fireplace dominates the larger of the two dining rooms; the other is in a small greenhouse with five tables.

Address: *West Rd., Box 678, Manchester, VT 05254, tel. 802/362–2568 or 800/822–2331, fax 802/362–2586.*
Accommodations: *16 double rooms with baths.*
Amenities: *Restaurant; lounge, air-conditioning, phones, and cable TV in rooms.*
Rates: *$175–$250 MAP; AE, MC, V.*
Restrictions: *Smoking in lounge only, no pets.*

South Shire Inn

Don't be discouraged when you drive through a rather mundane residential area to get here. Canopy beds in thickly carpeted rooms, ornate plaster molding, leaded glass bookcases, 10-foot ceilings, and a carved-wood fireplace in the library create turn-of-the-century grandeur. This magnificent Victorian estate in a quiet neighborhood exhibits the same kind of craftsmanship evident in the grandiose summer homes of Newport.

Furnishings are antique except for reproduction beds that provide contemporary comfort. Innkeepers Kristina and Timothy Mast have placed a small journal by each bedside so visitors can record memories of their stay. The full breakfast, which might include fresh fruit, homemade muffins, and the innkeepers' choice of eggs Benedict, stuffed French toast, or pancakes, is served in the peach-and-white wedding cake of a dining room. It's only a short drive from the inn to Old Bennington and within walking distance of the bus depot and downtown stores.

Address: *124 Elm St., Bennington, VT 05201, tel. 802/447–3839.*
Accommodations: *9 double rooms with baths.*
Amenities: *Air-conditioning, TV in public area, fireplaces in some rooms, whirlpools in some rooms.*
Rates: *$95–$145; full breakfast. AE, MC, V.*
Restrictions: *No smoking, no pets. 2-night minimum on most weekends.*

Wilburton Inn

This stone Tudor mansion could be the setting for one of those murder mysteries in which the detective names the killer as lightning flashes and thunder pounds outside. The estate sits atop 20 acres of rolling manicured lawn, and the dining room and the outdoor terrace overlook the Battenkill Valley. Rooms are spacious, and the chenille-covered beds date to the conversion in 1946, though rooms in the six cottages are a bit newer, dating to the early 1960s. The public areas—with an ornately carved mantel, mahogany paneling, a stained-glass dining-room door, a sweeping stone staircase to the lawn, and Oriental rugs on hardwood floors—are as elaborate as a railroad magnate's fortune would permit. Owners Albert and Georgette Levis, who also own the Wilburton Art Gallery, have placed contemporary sculpture on the grounds.

The menu has such offerings as Vermont pheasant braised in orange-scented wine served with cranberry chutney.

Address: *River Rd., Manchester, VT 05254, tel. 802/362–2500 or 800/648–4944.*
Accommodations: *34 double rooms with baths.*
Amenities: *Restaurant, air-conditioning in some rooms, TV in lobby; pool, 3 tennis courts.*
Rates: *$95–$155; full breakfast and afternoon tea. AE, MC, V.*
Restrictions: *No pets. 2-night minimum on holidays.*

Northern Vermont

Northern Vermont, where much of the state's logging and dairy farms can be found, is a land of contrasts: It has both the state's largest city and the state capital, some of New England's most rural areas, and many rare species of wildlife. Its recorded history dates from 1609, when Samuel de Champlain explored the lake now named after him. A strong Canadian influence can be felt here: Montréal is only an hour from the border, and Canadian currency and accents are encountered often.

In the Northeast Kingdom, as former U.S. Senator George Aiken dubbed the northeastern section of the state, you'll find many areas that have more cows than people and a Yankee accent so thick it's almost unintelligible to a flatlander (which may be part of the point). Those who wander through the forested hills and farmland often feel as though they've stepped into the Vermont of 100 years ago; harsh winters and geographic isolation have kept major development away—so far.

Burlington has the cultural sophistication one would expect of a larger city in a more densely inhabited part of the country, an appealing quality due in part to the large student population, but also attributable to the many culture-addicted "city people" who've moved up here in droves and want the best of both worlds. For years it had the nation's only Socialist mayor (who is now the nation's only Independent congressman).

Places to Go, Sights to See

Ben and Jerry's Ice Cream Factory. (Rte. 100, Waterbury, tel. 802/244-5641). Ben and Jerry began selling homemade ice cream from a bus in the 1970s; today their Waterbury headquarters, which gives tours of the factory and explains the ice cream–making process, has become one of the state's most popular tourist attractions.

Burlington. Its pedestrian mall, waterfront parks, restaurants with eclectic cuisines, and high level of artistic activity make the state's largest city appealing to nearly everyone. The *Flynn Theatre* (153 Main St., tel. 802/864–8778) is the city's cultural heart and schedules various music, dance, and theater productions. Stroll down *Church Street* to soak up the local color and stop by one of the several cafés with outdoor tables.

Lake Champlain. Formerly the focus of a shipping industry, this area has become a major center for outdoor recreation. The Lake Champlain islands are replete with beaches and water-sports facilities. North of Burlington, the scenic drive through the islands on Route 2 begins at I–89 and travels north through South Hero, Grand Isle, and Isle La Moote to Alburg Center.

Montpelier. The impressive gold dome and massive granite columns of the *Vermont State House* (State St., tel. 802/828–2228) belie the intimate scale of the legislative chambers within. Visitors can tour the House chamber and the even smaller Senate Chamber, which looks like a rather grand committee room. Next door is the *Vermont Museum* (109 State St., tel. 802/828–2291), which contains exhibits about early Vermont life.

Mt. Mansfield. The highest elevation in the state can be reached by car, hiking trail, or gondola; the mountain resembles the profile of a man lying on his back. *Smugglers' Notch,* a spectacular but somewhat harrowing narrow pass over the mountain, is said to have sheltered 18th-century outlaws and their booty in caves, a few of which can be seen from the road. The area is worth exploring and a good spot for a picnic.

Shelburne Farms (Rte. 7, tel. 802/985–8686). Founded in the 1880s as a private estate, the 1,000-acre property just south of Burlington is now an educational center devoted to the responsible stewardship of agricultural and natural resources. Visitors can tour a working dairy farm, listen to nature lectures, or simply stroll on the grounds, landscaped by Frederick Law Olmstead, the creator of New York's Central Park and Boston's Emerald Necklace.

Shelburne Museum (Rte. 7, tel. 802/985–3346). The 35-building complex has one of the country's finest collections of Americana, including early houses and furniture, fine and folk art, farm tools, Audubon prints, and even a private railroad car from the days of steam.

Restaurants

Cafe Chatillion (tel. 802/388–1040) in Frog Hollow in Middlebury features an eclectic regional cuisine and outdoor tables that overlook the Otter Creek falls. **The Daily Planet** (tel. 802/862–9647) and **Deja Vu** (tel. 802/864–7917), both near the bustling pedestrian mall in Burlington, feature globally influenced fare. Situated in an 1860s barn with soaring hand-hewn rafters, **The Common Man** (tel. 802/583–2800), at Sugarbush ski area near Waitsfield, offers fine, European-style dining and seasonal game specialties.

Miguel's Stow-Away (tel. 802/583–3858 at Sugarbush or 802/253–7574 at Stowe) makes its own chips and salsa and boasts innovative Mexican food that's especially satisfying après-ski.

Nightlife

Catamount Center for the Arts (tel. 802/748–2600) in St. Johnsbury offers a vast array of theater, dance, and musical performances. The **Flynn Theater** (tel. 802/864–8778), a grandiose old structure, is the cultural heart of Burlington and includes in its scheduling the Vermont Symphony Orchestra. Try the **Vermont Pub and Brewery** (tel. 802/865–0500) or **Papa's Blues Cellar** (tel. 802/860–7272) for the jazz, blues, and folk offerings around town or **K.D. Churchill's** (tel. 802/860–1226) and **Club Metronome** (tel. 802/865–4563) for dancing.

Tourist Information

Vermont Travel Division (134 State St., Montpelier, VT 05602, tel. 802/828–3326); **Vermont Chamber of Commerce** (Department of Travel and Tourism, Box 37, Montpelier, VT 05602, tel. 802/223–3443); **Addison County Chamber of Commerce** (2 Court St., Middlebury, VT 05753, tel. 802/388–7951); **Lake Champlain Regional Chamber of Commerce** (209 Battery St., Box 453, Burlington, VT 05402, tel. 802/863–3489); **Greater Newport Area Chamber of Commerce** (The Causeway, Newport, VT 05855, tel. 802/334–7782); **Stowe Area Association** (Box 1230, Stowe, VT 05672, tel. 802/253–7321); **Central Vermont Chamber of Commerce** (Box 336, Barre, VT 05641, tel. 802/229–5711); **Smugglers' Notch Area Chamber of Commerce** (Box 364, Jeffersonville, VT 05464, tel. 802/644–5195).

Reservations Services

Vermont Bed and Breakfast (Box 1, East Fairfield, VT 05448, tel. 802/827–3827); **Stowe Area Association** (Box 1230, Stowe, VT 05672, tel. 802/253–7321).

Inn at Montpelier

Until 1988, if you had wanted to stay in the state capital, you had your choice of large chain hotels or small motels. But then came Maureen and Bill Russell, who decided to renovate a spacious yellow Federal brick house only a short walk from the center of town. The inn, built in 1828, was designed with the business traveler in mind, but the architectural details, the antique four-poster beds and Windsor chairs, and the piped-in classical music also attract visitors whose most pressing business in town is deciding how late to sleep. The formal sitting room, with a large marble fireplace, cream-colored woodwork, and stately tapestry-upholstered wing chairs, has an elegant Federal feel to it, as though the original owners were about to glide down the polished staircase in rustling taffeta and black knee breeches. The wide wrap-around Colonial Revival porch, with it's octagonal corner section, is especially conducive to relaxing, and is one of the inn's most notable features.

The guest rooms in the frame building across the driveway are just as elegant as the ones in the main inn, and there are small pantries in each building where guests can prepare coffee, store food, and find snacks for late-night nibbling. The smallest rooms are in the main inn. All the rooms are done in a mix of antique and reproduction furniture, with rich floral decorator fabrics. Maureen's Room has a private sun deck, others have separate sitting rooms, and many of the walls are hung with original art.

As a destination, Montpelier has much to recommend it; it's centrally located for exploring the state's rural northern section. Guests of the inn can walk the few short blocks to the state capitol with its vest pocket-size legislative chambers or the Vermont Museum next door, which contains artifacts of early Vermont life. Despite the inn's proximity to town—it's in Montpelier's National Historic District—it is nestled on a quiet street and is quite tranquil. The moral of the story: This inn is a relatively undiscovered gem.

Address: *47 Main St., Montpelier, VT 05602, tel. 802/223–2727, fax 802/223–0722.*
Accommodations: *19 double rooms with baths.*
Amenities: *Restaurant, air-conditioning, TV and phones in bedrooms, fireplaces in 6 bedrooms, 2 shared kitchenette areas, 2 large and 2 small meeting rooms.*
Rates: *$93–$135; Continental breakfast. AE, MC, V.*
Restrictions: *No pets.*

The Inn at the Round Barn Farm

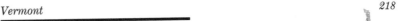

Wedding parties have replaced cows in the big round barn here, but the Shaker-style building still dominates the farm's 85 acres of quiet countryside. As Jack and Doreen Simko's picture albums attest, the process of restoring the 1910 12-sided barn involved jacking up the entire structure and putting in a new foundation. The result is one of the 12 remaining round (at least dodecagonal) barns in the state; it's used for summer concerts, weddings, and parties and is on the National Register of Historic Places.

It was the barn that first attracted the Simkos' attention; they had owned a ski house in the Mad River valley for 15 years and had driven past the barn frequently. Looking for a place to retire from the family floral business, they bought the property in 1986 within 24 hours of learning it was for sale. Their daughter, AnneMarie, left her job as an events coordinator for Harvard University and joined them halfway through the 18-month renovation.

The inn's ten rooms are not in the barn but in the 1806 farmhouse, where books line the walls of the cream-colored library, and breakfast is served in a cheerful solarium that overlooks a small landscaped pond and rolling acreage. The florist's touch is evident in the abundance of fresh flowers scattered throughout the inn, and the collection of pig memorabilia. The rooms have an elegant country style, with eyelet-trimmed sheets, new quilts on four-poster beds, brass wall lamps for easy bedtime reading, and floral drapes that match the wallpaper. Two of the larger rooms have whirlpool tubs and the three most recently renovated rooms in the north wing of the house have fireplaces, but many guests ask for the Palmer Room, which has a bed with a carved headboard of burled mahogany, a marble-top nightstand, and a spectacular view. Chocolate-chip cookies served on a small antique china plate mysteriously appear at the bedside while guests are at dinner; Anne Marie does the cooking at breakfast—her favorites appear to be French toast or cottage-cheese pancakes with a maple-raspberry sauce.

The inn is only a short drive to either Waitsfield or Warren, towns oriented to the nearby Sugarbush ski area.

Address: *E. Warren Rd., RR 1, Box 247, Waitsfield, VT 05673, tel. 802/496–2276.*
Accommodations: *10 double rooms with baths.*
Amenities: *TV in public area, fireplaces and whirlpools in some rooms; swimming pool.*
Rates: *$95–$165; full breakfast. AE, MC, V.*
Restrictions: *No smoking, no pets. 2-night minimum on weekends preferred.*

Inn on the Common

If you're looking for a serious getaway, you can't get much farther away than Vermont's Northeast Kingdom. The rolling farmland has an out-of-time quality that gives a glimpse of the way most of the state used to be: The area's sheer distance from civilization and its rugged weather have kept most of the state's development farther south. When Penny and Michael Schmitt decided in 1973 to leave New York's Fifth Avenue and investment banking behind to renovate the early 19th-century Federal building, they spared no expense; that means that behind the white picket fence are Scalamandré reproductions of historic wallpapers, Crabtree and Evelyn toiletries, thick plush carpets, and a 250-label collection of vintage wines.

One of the inn's three white clapboard buildings is directly on the common; the other two, the main building and the south annex, are just off it. Each building has no more than six rooms, so the feeling is intimate. Families often are housed in the south annex, which has a kitchenette with a microwave and refrigerator and a VCR with a large selection of films. Though each room is different (some are on the small side), all are beautifully detailed, with quilts on the beds, swag draperies with trim that coordinates with the wallpaper, bathrobes in the closets, and flowered champagne glasses at the ready. Dinner is served only to inn guests at communal tables, and Penny and Michael greet guests beforehand for hors d'oeuvres and cocktails.

Breakfast, which might include bacon, muffins, pancakes, and French toast, is served overlooking the rose garden in summer. Afterward, guests may visit the 140-acre Craftsbury sports center nearby, where, in addition to facilities for cross-country skiing in winter and water sports in summer, they find a staff of naturalists eager to offer information on local wildlife.

This is one of the most highly regarded inns in the state, and may be booked as much as a year in advance for peak seasons. But if you can get there and get a room, it's well worth it.

Address: *Rte. 14, Craftsbury Common, VT 05827, tel. 802/586-9619 or 800/521-2233, fax 802/586-2249.*
Accommodations: *16 double rooms with baths; 1 suite.*
Amenities: *TV/VCR and fireplace in living room, fireplace or wood stove in 5 bedrooms; swimming pool, tennis court.*
Rates: *$240–$260 MAP; $15 charge per pet. MC, V.*
Restrictions: *No smoking in dining room. 2-day minimum on holiday weekends, 3-day minimum Christmas–New Year season.*

Rabbit Hill Inn

When the door swings open and you are welcomed—often by name—into a warmth that will melt away even the most stressful of journeys, you'll know you've found the place. The Rabbit Hill Inn, situated on 15 wooded acres, has been receiving guests since its days as a stagecoach stop on the route between Montreal and Portland, Maine, nearly 200 years ago, and innkeepers John and Maureen Magee are dedicated to upholding its long-standing tradition of gracious hospitality. Maureen's knack for details and talent for bestowing just the right amount of attention on her guests somehow enables her to lure people into refocusing their priorities—at least for the time being.

The Magee's obvious fondness for the gentility of days past is expressed in the formal, Federal-period parlor where mulled cider from the fireplace crane is served on chilly afternoons. The low wooden beams and cozy warmth of the Irish-style pub right next door, where John tends bar and shares his knowledge of the area, create a comfortable contrast that is carried throughout the rest of the inn. The individually decorated rooms are as stylistically different as they are consistently indulgent: The Loft, with its 8-foot Palladian window, king canopy bed, double Jacuzzi, and corner fireplace, is one of the most requested; the abundant windows, Victrola, and working pump organ with period sheet music make the Music Chamber another favorite. Rooms toward the front of the inn get views of the Connecticut River and the White Mountains in New Hampshire. Rooms in the Carriage House, although more private, tend to be smaller and less lush—particularly the downstairs section.

In the elegant dining room chef Russell Stannard prepares an eclectic, regional cuisine that might include grilled sausage of Vermont pheasant with pistachios, or smoked chicken and red lentil dumplings nestled in red pepper linguine. The bountiful country breakfast begins with a buffet overflowing with home-baked coffee cakes and muffins, quiches, and fresh fruits.

Address: *Rte. 18, Lower Waterford, VT 05848, tel. 802/748–5168 or 800/76–BUNNY.*
Accommodations: *6 double rooms with baths, 7 suites.*
Amenities: *Restaurant, pub, TV in public area, whirlpools in some rooms, fireplaces in many rooms; walking/cross-country ski trails on property, canoes.*
Rates: *$150–$220 MAP; MC, V.*
Restrictions: *No smoking, no pets. 3-night minimum stay Christmastime and holiday weekends; closed Apr. and first 3 weeks in Nov.*

Swift House Inn

Andrea and John Nelson didn't exactly intend to open an inn when they did; they were looking at inns with the idea of buying something in 10 years, after John retired from IBM's finance department. But on the way to the airport to go home to New Jersey one day in 1985, they stopped by the big white Federal home set atop a sweeping expanse of lawn, and their decision was made. Since then they've made the Swift House Inn one of the most elegant in the state—the kind of place that gives new meaning to the line about having a silver spoon in one's mouth.

The patrician air here is no coincidence; the inn was the private home of two of Middlebury's most prominent families: the Swifts, who built the oldest section of the house in 1814, and the Stewarts, one of whom married the grandson of the original owner and lived in the home until 1943. As a result of the long private ownership, elegant Gilded Age detailing has been well preserved. The richly ornamented cherry paneling and trim glow in the dining room, where the bright purple and green grape—clustered wallpaper is an exact reproduction of the pattern installed in 1905. Rooms have the same luxurious feel. The Emma Willard Swift Room not only has a private porch but also retains the built-in brass wall phone Mrs. Swift installed so she could listen to church services. White eyelet-trimmed sheets, gathered lace curtains at the windows, floral chintz draperies that match a wing chair, a fresh carnation in a bedside bud vase—the attention to detail gives the impression that this is still an affluent family's private home.

The carriage house was converted in 1990 and is recommended for families, although the more-than-spacious rooms and the enormous new bathrooms with whirlpool baths would lure any guest looking for luxury. One of the rooms has French doors that open onto its own patio. Rooms in the gate house are closer to the road and therefore a bit noisier. In the dining room, an attentive staff serves an adventurous menu that might include angel-hair pasta with imported mushrooms in macadamia pesto sauce, or smoked pheasant salad with vinaigrette.

Address: *25 Stewart La., Middlebury, VT 05753, tel. 802/388–9925, fax 802/388–9927.*
Accommodations: *21 double rooms with baths.*
Amenities: *Restaurant, air-conditioning, TV in public area, phones in rooms, fireplaces in common areas and in some rooms; sauna, steam room, conference room.*
Rates: *$90–$150, full breakfast; MAP available. AE, MC, V.*
Restrictions: *No pets. Restaurant closed Tues.–Wed.*

Black Lantern

When you drive to within 6 miles of the Canadian border to a town so small you can pass through it in one minute, you don't expect to find yourself sitting down to a candlelight dinner of shrimp étouffée or filet mignon with mushrooms and onions. But Rita and Allan Kalsmith have created a tiny gem in this quiet town not far from the Jay Peak ski area. Though the feeling is country, little touches of sophistication abound. The beige and navy wallpaper in the dining room is a Provençal print; the suites in the newly renovated building next door are painted with a subtle rag-rolled finish; and a bedspread is a soft pastel plaid instead of a cliché floral. And yet a bowl of potpourri on an antique nightstand, the weathered wood used in renovation, and the marble-top table in a sitting room all keep the Black Lantern charming without screaming "Quaint! Quaint! Quaint!" This is a true getaway—and there's always the surrounding countryside to explore.

Address: *Rte. 118, Montgomery Village, VT 05470, tel. 802/326–4507.*
Accommodations: *10 double rooms with baths, 6 suites.*
Amenities: *Restaurant, TV and VCRs in some rooms, fireplaces in 5 suites, whirlpools in suites.*
Rates: *$75–$100, full breakfast; MAP available. AE, MC, V.*
Restrictions: *No pets.*

Edson Hill Manor

Fans of the movie *The Four Seasons* will enjoy the Edson Hill, where the winter scenes were filmed. This 1939 mansion, built in the style of a grand English country estate on 200 acres, has the feel of a family compound owned by a rather horsey uncle. Bookshelves line the spacious pine-paneled living room, which has an exquisitely tiled fireplace and a view of the sweeping lawn. Rooms in the main building are Colonial style, with turned head-boards, pine paneling, and oil landscapes. The newer rooms in the carriage houses in the back are decorated similarly but have newer plumbing and a bit more privacy. But most guests spend a lot of time outdoors on the 40 miles of bridle paths; the riding center on the premises becomes a cross-country skiing center in winter. Innkeepers Eric and Jane Lande made their living as maple sugar makers before they bought the inn in 1991. Guests select from a breakfast menu that includes such traditional favorites as pancakes, French toast, and bacon and eggs.

Address: *Edson Hill Rd., Stowe, VT 05672, tel. 802/253–7371 or 800/621–0284.*
Accommodations: *26 double rooms with baths.*
Amenities: *Restaurant, fireplaces in 23 rooms; pool, stables, pond.*
Rates: *$195–$225 MAP. AE, D, MC, V.*
Restrictions: *No pets. 5-night minimum at Christmastime, 3-night minimum Presidents' Day weekend, closed mid-Nov. and late Apr.*

Fox Hall Inn

Moose are a passionate subject of debate in Vermont these days, and innkeepers Sherry and Ken Pyden have responded by creating a sort of sanctum to the re-emergence in the state of this previously scarce animal. Throughout this 1890 Cottage Revival, which is listed on the Register of Historic Places, furnishings are embellished by many a moose miscellany, including a child's moose rocker and of course a moose head above the fireplace mantel. The generous wrap-around veranda that overlooks fjord-like Lake Willoughby is well-appointed with swinging seats and comfortable chairs, perfect for a summer evening spent listening to the loons. The two corner turret rooms are the most distinctive and spacious, and have the most expansive views of the lake.

Nearby Mt. Pisgah and Mt. Hor provide opportunities for hiking, and the nearby lake is perfect for canoeing, swimming, and fishing in summer and cross-country skiing and skating in winter.

Address: *Rte. 16, Barton, VT 05822, tel. 802/525–6930.*
Accommodations: *4 double rooms with baths, 5 double rooms share 3 baths.*
Amenities: *2 fireplaces in public areas; hiking and cross-country ski trails, canoes.*
Rates: *$60–$90; full breakfast, afternoon snacks; MC, V.*
Restrictions: *No smoking, no pets. 2-night minimum during fall foliage.*

The Gables Inn

This Federal farmhouse, built in the mid-1800s, grew over time, with an addition here and a stairway there, to form a rabbit warren of charming rooms filled with American country antiques. Bedrooms have four-poster beds with white lace canopies, rag rugs on wide-plank floors, and little touches added by owners Sol, Lynn, and Josh Baumrind. The tiny sun room filled with plants and wicker is perfect for morning coffee; a wood-burning stove gives a warm glow on winter evenings.

Rooms in the carriage house, renovated in 1989, have cathedral ceilings, fireplaces, and whirlpools. Lynn's generous breakfasts are served until noon; summer guests enjoy it outdoors. It might include sautéed chicken livers with onions and scrambled eggs or French toast stuffed with cream cheese, walnuts, and molasses.

Address: *1457 Mountain Rd., Stowe, VT 05672, tel. 802/253–7730 or 800/422–5371.*
Accommodations: *17 double rooms with baths.*
Amenities: *Restaurant, air-conditioning and TV in some rooms, TV in public area, fireplace in living room; pool, hot tub.*
Rates: *$55–$110 mid-Apr.–mid.-Dec. $140–$180 MAP in winter. AE, MC, V.*
Restrictions: *No smoking in bedrooms or dining area, no pets.*

Queen City Inn

Incongruously located in the middle of a strip of commercial development, this inn begs to be surrounded by acres of lawn instead of malls. The 1881 mansard-roofed, red-brick Victorian house is meticulously restored and the minute a guest steps inside the heavy entrance doors and looks up at the massive mahogany staircase, the cars outside might as well be horsedrawn carriages. The architectural detailing is spectacular—polished oak arches that frame bay window alcoves in two rooms; a marble, brass, and tile fireplace; polished wainscoting—and what isn't original matches so well that it's hard to tell the difference. Rooms at the rear get virtually no road noise.

With an arty reputation (this is the home of the University of Vermont) and its Lake Champlain waterfront, Burlington is a lively destination, but charming inns aren't abundant here. The Queen City Inn is a welcome addition, and there's also a 13-room motel on the property.

Address: *428 Shelburne Rd., South Burlington, VT 05403, tel. 802/864–4220.*
Accommodations: *12 double rooms with baths.*
Amenities: *Air-conditioning, phones and cable TV in rooms.*
Rates: *$60–$120; Continental breakfast buffet. MC, V.*
Restrictions: *No smoking, no pets.*

10 Acres Lodge

Only minutes from the center of Stowe, this small and red clapboard inn, built in the 1840s, has a very country feel, although owners Cathy and Curt Dann have made sure to give it touches of city sophistication, too. The large, sunny rooms in the new building high on the hill have contemporary furnishings as well as private decks, fireplaces, and convenient access to the inn's outdoor hot tub. The eight rooms in the main inn have more of a country feel with such details as pine paneling and blue-checked bed canopies. The floral swag curtains and contemporary art on the walls make clear, however, that this is the country decor of posh home-and-garden magazines. The bay windows, mauve-colored walls, and barn-board wainscoting in the dining room are as casually elegant as the breakfast buffet table, which usually offers fruit, home-baked breads, homemade granola, and quiche.

Address: *14 Barrows Rd., Stowe, VT 05672, tel. 802/253–7638 or 800/327–7357.*
Accommodations: *16 double rooms with baths, 2 housekeeping cottages.*
Amenities: *Restaurant, air-conditioning, TV in some rooms, phones in rooms; swimming pool, hot tub, tennis court.*
Rates: *$85–$275; full breakfast and après-ski snacks. AE, MC, V.*
Restrictions: *Pets in cottages only. 5-night minimum at Christmas and New Year, 3-night minimum on Columbus Day and Presidents' Day weekends.*

Waybury Inn

The Waybury Inn has been offering food and lodging since 1810—long before TV producers made it the Stratford Inn on the *Newhart* show. This former stagecoach stop shows its age in places—the plumbing is a bit geriatric and the floors and walls don't always meet at right angles—but innkeepers Marcia and Marty Schuppert have given it a comfortable, down-home feel. Hand-hewn beams in the low-ceilinged entry, the covered porch in front, the painted wainscoting, and the squashy upholstered furniture in the sitting room all make for a relaxed country charm. The inn pub, which sports a copper-top bar, farm implements, baskets, and an antique sled, is a real charmer. East Middlebury is Robert Frost country; the poet lived in the area, and the inn is not far from a wooded nature trail that has Frost quotations posted at strategic points along the way. It's also close to the site of the Breadloaf Writers' Conference, which is held each summer, and you might see a favorite novelist strolling through the woods.

Address: *Rte. 125, East Middlebury, VT 05640, tel. 802/388–4015.*
Accommodations: *14 double rooms with baths.*
Amenities: *Restaurant, pub; TV in public area, ceiling fans.*
Rates: *$80–$115; full breakfast. AE, D, MC, V.*

Ye Olde England Inn

From the outside, it would be easy to think that someone had merely slapped an English veneer on this inn. Not so: Owners Chris and Lyn Francis *are* British and have fitted the inn out in a style worthy of royalty. Regal golden lions guard the entrance, and a red London call box stands outside the door. Royal portraits in the lobby, signs that say, "To the Loo," and hunting prints throughout the inn make one want to stand up and sing "God Save the Queen." The rooms, which are on the small side, have delicate pastel Laura Ashley furnishings, deep-pile carpet, brass headboards, and wicker baskets—all of which adds up to a feeling of luxury. Chris is a polo fanatic—his local team has been known to play matches in the snow—and Pickwick's Polo Pub doubles as the inn's trophy room. It's fun to view the team photos and polo regalia on the walls while sampling the outstanding selection of single-malt Scotches. The dining room can provide Welsh rarebit for breakfast as well as standard American fare.

Address: *433 Mountain Rd., Stowe, VT 05672, tel. 802/253–7558, fax 802/253–8944.*
Accommodations: *17 double rooms with baths, 3 cottages.*
Amenities: *Restaurant, pub, air-conditioning; TVs, fireplaces, and whirlpools in some rooms; swimming pool.*
Rates: *$115–$158, cottages $150–$205; full breakfast. AE, MC, V.*
Restrictions: *Pets by prior arrangement. 2-night minimum on weekends.*

New Hampshire

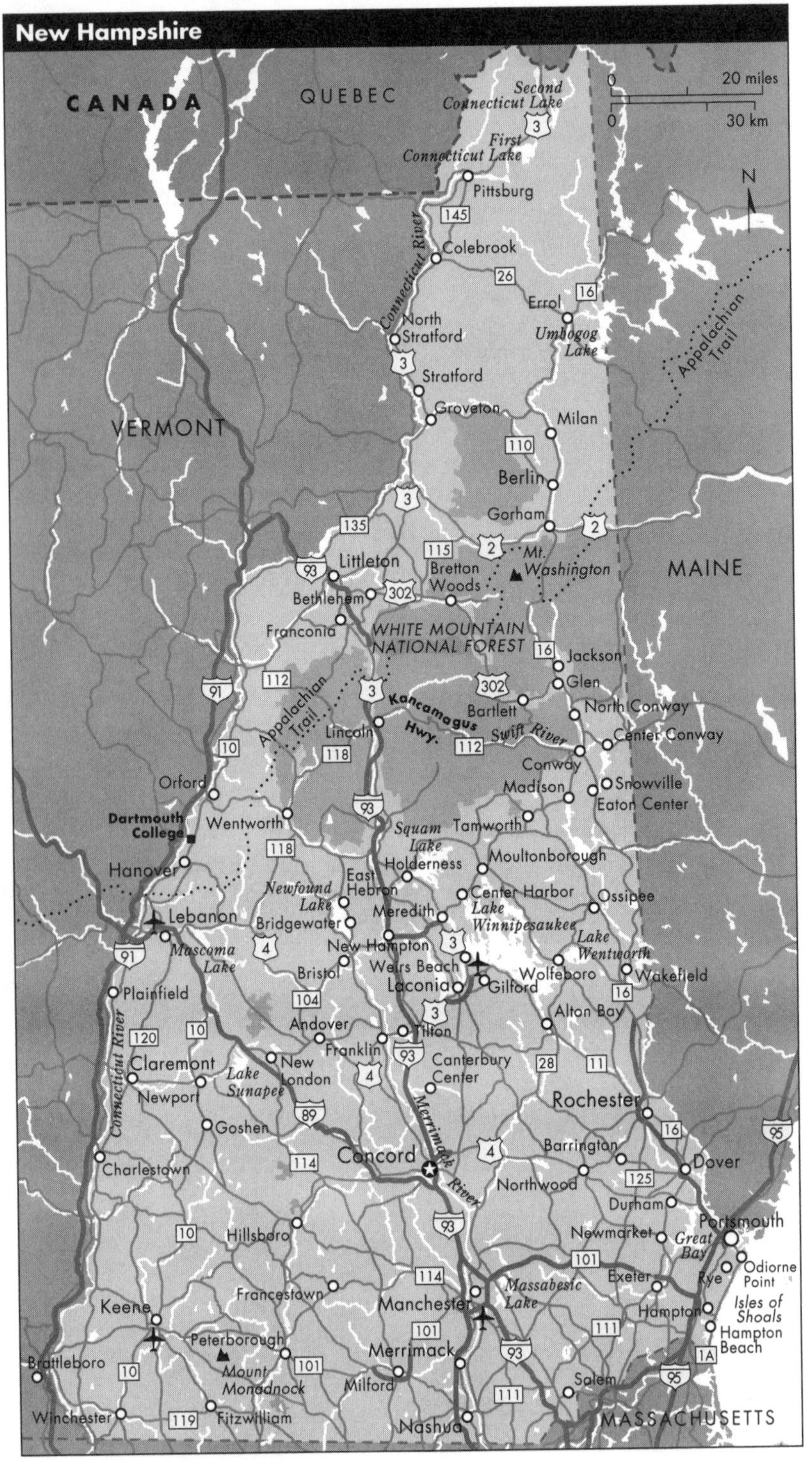
New Hampshire
CANADA
QUEBEC
VERMONT
MAINE
MASSACHUSETTS
20 miles
30 km
N
Second Connecticut Lake
First Connecticut Lake
Pittsburg
Connecticut River
Colebrook
Errol
Umbagog Lake
North Stratford
Stratford
Groveton
Milan
Berlin
Gorham
Appalachian Trail
Littleton
Bretton Woods
Mt. Washington
Bethlehem
Franconia
WHITE MOUNTAIN NATIONAL FOREST
Jackson
Glen
Bartlett
North Conway
Center Conway
Kancamagus Hwy.
Swift River
Lincoln
Conway
Snowville
Madison
Eaton Center
Orford
Dartmouth College
Wentworth
Tamworth
Squam Lake
Holderness
Moultonborough
Hanover
Newfound Lake
East Hebron
Center Harbor
Ossipee
Lebanon
Bridgewater
Meredith
Lake Winnipesaukee
Mascoma Lake
New Hampton
Lake Wentworth
Weirs Beach
Wolfeboro
Wakefield
Bristol
Laconia
Gilford
Plainfield
Alton Bay
Andover
Tilton
Franklin
Claremont
New London
Canterbury Center
Lake Sunapee
Newport
Rochester
Goshen
Merrimack River
Barrington
Charlestown
Concord
Dover
Northwood
Durham
Portsmouth
Hillsboro
Newmarket
Great Bay
Odiorne Point
Rye
Exeter
Massabesic Lake
Francestown
Manchester
Isles of Shoals
Hampton
Keene
Hampton Beach
Peterborough
Merrimack
Brattleboro
Mount Monadnock
Milford
Salem
Winchester
Fitzwilliam
Nashua
3
145
26
16
110
2
135
115
93
302
112
91
10
118
4
104
120
28
11
89
114
125
95
101
111
1A
119

The Seacoast

Tucked between the long Atlantic frontiers of Maine and Massachusetts, New Hampshire's shore, only 18 miles long, is a microcosm of pleasure. This relatively brief span contains beaches for swimming and exploring and a quintessential boardwalk. In addition, there are ideal spots for surf and deep-sea fishing, whale-watching, boating, and water sports. Go inland a few miles and you find Colonial villages, farms, and orchards. The region's very compactness makes it an ideal vacation spot—you can stay wherever you like and always be within a half hour of any attraction. Though many of the best restaurants are near the waterfront in Portsmouth, a bed-and-breakfast on the ocean, in town, or in country, as you prefer, is also convenient for dining out.

The history of our nation is linked with this craggy shore. Scottish fishermen created a settlement at Odiorne in 1623. Captain Kidd, Miles Standish, and Captain John Smith were early visitors to the Isles of Shoals. When Portsmouth—a Colonial city with a royal governor in residence—stood Tory at the time of the Revolution, Exeter wholeheartedly supported the patriot cause and became for 30-odd years capital of New Hampshire. Both Portsmouth and Exeter have well-preserved historic houses. In Portsmouth you can visit the boardinghouse of John Paul Jones, among others, on the Portsmouth Trail walking tour. In Exeter, you will see the place where residents came for safety from Indian attack as well as to plot the overthrow of British rule.

Portsmouth has a warren of curious streets for shopping and exploring near the harbor, as well as all-year theater, and at Prescott Park, a nearly continuous round of concerts, fairs, and special events attracts the visitor. Turn inland and you will find pick-your-own apple orchards and berry patches, along with open farmland. Route 4, Portsmouth to Durham, is a worthy antiques strip, with shops and barns overflowing with dusty treasures.

Typical of the state, the seacoast region appeals to and welcomes all ages. You will see three generations dancing at the Casino on Hampton Beach. Because the area is easily reached and only little more than an hour from Boston, people drive up for dinner and summer theater or jazz in the park or a day at the beach. As everywhere in this family-oriented state, traveling with children is considered the only logical way to go.

Places to Go, Sights to See

Great Bay. This tidal sea, nearly 5 miles long and more than 3 miles wide, is just out of sight of the tourist coast. It is a nature preserve kept for migrating waterfowl and animals, a place to go early in the morning with your camera and a supply of insect repellent. There is no major entry point, though you can ask for directions in Newmarket, Stratham, or Durham. Footpaths are marked to tell you which birds to watch for, and there is a picnic area.

Hampton Beach Casino (Hampton Beach, Rte. 1A, tel. 603/926–4541; open mid-Apr.–Oct.). Seven acres of multigenerational entertainment—from shooting galleries and video games to concerts by name artists—and four water slides make up this old-fashioned beachside complex. Snacks and food spots fill the holes, but you may want to go elsewhere for dinner.

Harbor, Island, and Whale-Watch Cruises. Narrated boat trips are offered at *Rye Harbor State Marina* (tel. 603/964–5545 or 603/382–6743) from May to September. The 6 mile sail from Portsmouth Harbor to the nine Isles of Shoals has a picnic stop, and you can buy snacks and sandwiches on board.

Nature Center at Odiorne Point (tel. 603/862–3460). Tide pools and nature walks at the mouth of Portsmouth harbor are even better after a stop at the Nature Center, sponsored by the Audubon Society and the University of New Hampshire. Picnic areas invite you to bring your own lunch. There are many special programs, so you may want to call first just to see what is on for the day.

Strawbery Banke (Marcy St., tel. 603/433–1100). Costumed interpreters staff 42 historic houses at this waterfront outdoor museum in Portsmouth, and give demonstrations in crafts from broom-tieing to spinning. Also on the grounds are gardens, a gift shop, and an eatery.

Restaurants

French cuisine that falls somewhere between light and classic is on the menu at **L'Auberge** (tel. 603/436–2377), on Bridge Street, Portsmouth. Watch the sunset as you try the bouillabaise at **The Oar House** (tel. 603/436–4025), also in Portsmouth. For the classically informal, **Newick's Lobster House** (tel. 603/742–3205) is a mostly outdoor, always crowded fresh-seafood place on Dover Point Road, Dover. True Italian cookery at a moderate price is the attained goal of small, friendly **Guido's Trattoria** (tel. 603/431–2989) in the harbor district of Portsmouth.

Beaches

The town of Hampton, on Route 1A, encompasses several sandy beaches: One is opposite and one south of the resort's high life. Seashell is a band amphitheater where you can catch a lot of '40s music. There's a public dock and fishing, too. **North Beach** and **North Hampton Beach,** as you continue on 1A, are good for swimming.

Jenness Beach, in Rye, is less frantic than Hampton, and good for those who want to swim rather than party. **Wallis Sands Beach,** also in Rye, is 700 feet long and 150 feet wide at high tide, and offers good swimming close to Portsmouth.

Tourist Information

Seacoast Council on Tourism (1000 Market St., Portsmouth, NH 03801, tel. 603/436–7678 and, outside NH, 800/221–5623).

Moody Parsonage Bed and Breakfast

Moody Parsonage, built in 1730 for John Moody, the first minister of Newmarket, is the oldest and perhaps most welcoming residence–turned–bed-and-breakfast in New Hampshire. Today's world and worries seem far away in a red clapboard house where a spinning wheel sits on the landing, and you can still see the original paneling, staircases, and wide pine floors. Five fireplaces—one is always going in the dining room on chilly mornings—are cozy reminders of days when even the seacoast was on the edge of the wilderness.

Owner Deborah Reed grew up in the Parsonage, returning to it after 35 years of marriage and residences that spanned the globe, from Germany to Washington State. A retired registered nurse, she eased into innkeeping by first opening her house to University of New Hampshire students. Now she says she has "discovered that a B&B is definitely in the care-giving category."

One bedroom and bath are on the first floor. The other three rooms are upstairs and share a bath, making a good arrangement for a family. Though one of these is comparatively small, the other bedrooms are very large and have working fireplaces. The house is decorated with family portraits and furnished with family antiques, rushseat and wing chairs, electrified oil lamps, iron-bound wood footlockers, and copper kettles. A fluffy white down comforter covers a queen-size canopy bed.

Fresh flowers are everywhere. "With 2 acres to care for, I guess you could say my hobby is gardening, and I enjoy every minute of it," Deborah says. She also refinishes furniture when time permits.

Great Bay, the magnificent estuary and wildlife sanctuary for migrating waterfowl, is within 2 miles, and across the road is a golf course. You can sit on the Parsonage lawn and watch the golfers tee off. Other options include a shopping mall or two, a great Sunday flea market, the facilities of the Great Bay Athletic Club, and a ballroom that plays Big Band music. You are only a 15-minute drive from the museums and restaurants of Durham, Exeter, and Portsmouth, or the beaches and boardwalk of Rye and Hampton; Newmarket itself is only 2 miles south.

Address: *15 Ash Swamp Rd., Newmarket, NH 03857, tel. 603/659–6675.*
Accommodations: *1 double room with bath, 3 doubles share 1 bath.*
Amenities: *Air-conditioning, fireplaces in bedrooms.*
Rates: *$50–$60; Continental breakfast. No credit cards.*
Restrictions: *No smoking indoors, no pets.*

Rock Ledge Manor

Rock Ledge Manor was built between 1840 and 1880 as part of a major seaside resort colony so the style is pure Victorian gingerbread. The white mansard gambrel-roofed house, replete with the black shutters and wraparound porch, overlooks the Atlantic at Concord Point just south of Rye State Beach. The islands you see in the distance are the Isles of Shoals.

The owners, Norman and Janice Marineau, turned their oceanfront home into a bed-and-breakfast in 1982. Norman had been in catering, which may be why breakfast here is such a major event. It could be crepes, or Belgian waffles, or omelets and homemade sweet rolls.

The meal is served in a breakfast room with a view of the sea. The table is set formally with china and linens, the way breakfast was served a century ago. Off the breakfast room, a delightfully old-fashioned sun room full of plants is just the place to retire to with the morning papers. Or you might prefer to let the breeze ruffle your pages on the wide porch.

Two bedrooms are on the ground floor and two on the second, all with sea views. Marble-top sinks and dressers are part of the authentic Victoriana, as are the brass-and-iron beds and the languidly turning paddles of the ceiling fans.

You may have to reserve well in advance in summer, when many returning guests come for a week or more, but Rock Ledge Manor is open year-round, and the seacoast is gloriously uncrowded in the spring and fall. You are only 5 miles from historic Portsmouth with its museums, galleries, restaurants, and all-year schedule of special events. From May to October, cruises to the off-shore islands and whale-watching trips leave from Rye Harbor. A few miles south in North Hampton is the Factory Outlet Center, where you can shop seven days a week at more than 35 stores, tax free.

The two Seacoast State Parks are both in Rye. Rye Harbor Park has picnic areas and saltwater fishing. Odiorne Point was the site of the first European settlement in New Hampshire (1623) and has an Interpretive Center with programs offered by the Audubon Society and University of New Hampshire. Its tide pools are wonderful.

Address: *1413 Ocean Blvd. (Rte. 1A), Rye, NH 03870, tel. 603/431–1413.*
Accommodations: *2 double rooms with baths, 2 doubles with half baths, shared shower.*
Rates: *$75–$85; full breakfast. No credit cards.*
Restrictions: *No smoking, no pets. 2-night minimum on weekends June 15–Oct. 15.*

Exeter Inn

The Exeter Inn is enough to make you wish you were a preppy—or had a preppy to visit. The redbrick Georgian-style inn is owned by and only slightly removed from prestigious Phillips Exeter Academy. You are within the historic district of the Colonial town (Exeter was the capital of New Hampshire during the American Revolution) and just about midway between Newburyport, Massachusetts, and Portsmouth, New Hampshire.

This could be a fusty place, but it is not, thanks largely to innkeeper John Hodgins, a hotel professional who was a student at Exeter years ago. It is a very well-managed and dignified small hotel with large, traditional rooms furnished with proper period furniture like pineapple-carved pencil-post beds. The award-winning restaurant has a fig tree growing in the center and a notable Sunday brunch.

Address: *90 Front St., Exeter, NH 03833, tel. 603/772–5901 or 800/782–8444, fax 603/778–8757.*
Accommodations: *49 double rooms with baths, 1 suite with fireplace.*
Amenities: *Restaurant; air-conditioning, cable TV, and phones in rooms, fitness room with sauna, meeting and reception rooms.*
Rates: *$75–$105, suite $165. AE, D, DC, MC, V.*
Restrictions: *2-night minimum on Parents' Weekend.*

Governor's House Bed and Breakfast

For thirty years this handsome Georgian Colonial was the private home of New Hampshire governor Charles M. Dale; nowadays it is owned by Nancy and John Grossman, who opened the mansion as a bed-and-breakfast in 1992 after extensive renovation that included installing artist Nancy's unique tiles in the bathrooms, part of the Grossman theory that such a formal house needs a balancing casual ambience.

In addition to the working fireplaces in the parlor and dining room, the homey feeling is enhanced by a library full of good books, a brimful cookie jar, and a guest-friendly baby grand piano. The house itself is on a quiet side street and is insulated from city sounds by a garden, old pines and cedars as well as by solid walls.

On winter mornings Nancy likes to prepare a New England breakfast in front of the fire for her guests. It's a full meal, too, and may well include hot popovers. After that, old Portsmouth can be taken in stride.

Address: *32 Miller Ave., Portsmouth NH 03801, tel. 603/431–6546, fax 603/427–0803.*
Accommodations: *4 double rooms with baths.*
Amenities: *Cable TV in library, ceiling fans; tennis court; off-street parking.*
Rates: *$70–$140; full breakfast. MC, V.*
Restrictions: *No smoking, no pets (kennel nearby).*

The Governor's Inn

Once the residence of former Governor Huntley Spaulding, this beautifully restored mansion is now operated as a bed-and-breakfast inn by the Ejarque family. The ambience is impressive but not imposing: You may still climb an elliptical staircase to a grand bedroom and eat your breakfast crepes looking through French windows on the sun porch, but the rooms are casually furnished in white wicker, and the flowered wallpapers are light and bright. Badminton, horseshoes, and croquet share the back lawn with a gazebo and a tennis court.

The inn restaurant—an end in itself—is open to the public by reservation only. The fixed menu may include curried butternut soup with apple, medallions of beef tenderloin served with salsa and guacamole or sautéed tuna Maltaise followed by coconut cake with Grand Marnier oranges.

The inn is roughly halfway between Portsmouth and Lake Winnipesaukee. The White Mountains are only 45 minutes away by car.

Address: *78 Wakefield St., Rochester, NH 03867, tel. and fax 603/332–0107.*
Accommodations: *Five double rooms with baths.*
Amenities: *Restaurant; air-conditioning; cable TV; wide-screen cable TV and VCR in recreation room; tennis court, lawn sports; conference room in Carriage House.*
Rates: *$45–$95; full breakfast. AE, MC, V.*
Restrictions: *No smoking, no pets.*

Highland Farm Bed and Breakfast

You may find yourself humming the score from *Brigadoon* during your stay at Highland Farm. The three-story bed-and-breakfast, housed in a pre-1850 farmhouse, has a thistle for a logo, and Bobby Burns is quoted on the flier. Scones for breakfast? You bet. You can have them in the dining room or, in warm weather, on the porch overlooking the rose garden and plum trees.

Noreen and Andy Bowers decided to open their four-chimney redbrick Victorian to guests because they had so enjoyed staying in B&Bs during their own travels.

It's a formal sort of house, with a parlor, a library, and, in back, a sun room facing south toward the river. The bedrooms are quite large (two will sleep an extra person), with hooked rugs and antique beds. In winter, you can cross-country ski and, in summer, hike on trails along the river.

Highland Farm is quiet and rural, but it is only 2 miles to historic Dover and a tad farther to the food and entertainments of Portsmouth.

Address: *148 County Farm Rd., Dover, NH 03820, tel. 603/743–3399.*
Accommodations: *4 double rooms share 2 baths.*
Amenities: *Cable TV/VCR in library.*
Rates: *$60; full breakfast. MC, V.*
Restrictions: *No smoking indoors, no pets.*

Inn at Christian Shore

The owners, former antiques dealers and house restorers, say buying the broken-down old place that has become the Inn at Christian Shore "seemed like a good idea." They will show you photographs of the restoration and readily admit that the off-white Federal house (circa 1800) is a wonderful place to display their private collections and acquisitions, some of which are for sale. They will also point out that not every piece is an original.

To say "hearty breakfast" is understating the full morning meal. It is served in the dining room, which has a fireplace, a trestle table with Windsor chairs, and small tables for two with pairs of wing chairs. The assumption is you need solid food—like steak or pork tenderloin, home fries, and veggies—to fuel you through your trips to the sights and shops of historic Portsmouth. Whoever of your three hosts is at hand, he is sure to be a gold mine of information on local restaurants and historic Portsmouth, as well as on the regional antiques scene.

Address: *335 Maplewood Ave., Portsmouth, NH 03801, tel. 603/431–6770.*
Accommodations: *3 double rooms with baths, 1 double room with half-bath, 1 double and 1 single with shared bath.*
Amenities: *Air-conditioning and cable TV in all rooms.*
Rates: *$75; full breakfast. No credit cards.*
Restrictions: *Smoking in common rooms only, no pets.*

The Inn at Elmwood Corners

It was built by a retired sea captain and named after a long-gone elm of legendary size. The wicker-furnished porch that wraps around the big white house gives it a circa-1870 family look.

A home and a family business are the goals of owners John and Mary Hornberger, who now juggle outside jobs along with caring for two young sons and operating their bed-and-breakfast. John is cook, innkeeper, handyman, and gardener; Mary does the baking, bookkeeping, wall-stenciling, and quilt-making. Mary's handmade baskets hang from the rafters, and you just might catch John tying flies as he prepares to take his boys fishing.

The inn is a mile from the ocean and an easy walk to the village. You are located conveniently for the movies, Hampton Summer Theater (which presents children's matinees), restaurants, and shops. Golf and tennis are nearby, too.

Address: *252 Winnacunnet Rd., Hampton, NH 03842, tel. 603/929–0443 or 800/253–5691.*
Accommodations: *5 double rooms share 3 baths, 2 housekeeping suites.*
Amenities: *TV, books, games in library, playpen available.*
Rates: *$65–$90; full breakfast. MC, V.*
Restrictions: *No smoking in bedrooms, no pets. 2-night minimum on holidays May–Oct.*

Martin Hill Inn

The yellow Martin Hill Inn was built in downtown Portsmouth in 1820 and its Guest House in 1850, so it is no wonder that guests feel at home visiting the Colonial houses and historic waterfront of the charming old city.

It was on their second visit to the inn that Paul and Jane Harden found it was for sale. Within the week they resigned their managerial jobs and became innkeepers. "Gardening has become the only hobby we have time for," Paul says.

The two houses are now connected by a flower-lined brick walk and patio. Both have bedrooms large enough to contain a sofa and are rather formal in feeling, with Oriental rugs and fine Colonial antiques, including canopy and four-poster pineapple beds. In the Guest House, three suites have been decorated in country Victorian style with flowered chintzes and spindle or brass-and-iron beds. The Greenhouse Suite has a solarium area and private entrance. The inn is on a major street that quiets down at night.

Address: *404 Islington St., Portsmouth, NH 03801, tel. 603/436–2287 or 800/445–2286.*
Accommodations: *4 double rooms with baths, 3 suites.*
Amenities: *Air-conditioning; off-street parking.*
Rates: *$80–$105; full breakfast. MC, V.*
Restrictions: *No smoking, no pets.*

The Oceanside

The Oceanside is a small hotel just on the edge of action-oriented Hampton Beach. Nightly fireworks and concerts, and the total boardwalk ambience of cotton candy and street performers, make for a lively July and August. If you want to people-watch without having to dodge the crowds, head for the inn's second-floor veranda.

Owners Debbie and Skip Windemiller also recommend the off-season (June, September, October), when the beach is quiet and the Oceanside is about the only thing still open. Then there might even be a fire burning in the breakfast-café or the living room/library, and Skip will have time to talk about his past adventures as a free-style ski instructor. Despite the Oceanside's quintessentially commercial location, Debbie has done the rooms individually, using a deft hand with her own eclectic collectibles to retain the turn-of-the-century private-home character of the classic beach-front structure.

Address: *365 Ocean Blvd., Hampton Beach, NH 03842, tel. and fax 603/926–3542.*
Accommodations: *9 double rooms with baths.*
Amenities: *Air-conditioning; guest refrigerator; beach chairs and towels.*
Rates: *$80–$103; breakfast extra. AE, DC, MC, V.*
Restrictions: *No smoking, no pets. 3-night minimum, closed Nov.–mid-May.*

Sise Inn

This elegant Queen Anne bed-and-breakfast inn has the amenities of a complete hotel, including being in the heart of town. It is three blocks to the waterfront; shops and restaurants are nearer still; and you can walk to Strawbery Banke.

Formally decorated with antiques and fine period reproductions to recapture the 1880s when the house was built by a prosperous merchant, the handsome bedrooms and suites have been featured in countless home and design magazines. Every room is different, though all have tables, desks, and luxury touches, such as professionally done fresh-flower arrangements.

The inn is one of a handful geared for disabled visitors: All three floors are serviced by an elevator and some of the bathrooms are equipped with railings.

Address: *40 Court St., Portsmouth, NH 03801, tel. 603/433–1200 or 800/267–0525 (reservations only); fax 603/433–1200, ext 505.*
Accommodations: *25 double rooms with baths, 9 suites.*
Amenities: *Air-conditioning; cable TV/VCR and phones in rooms; some rooms with whirlpool baths, fireplaces, stereos; 3 meeting rooms; off-street parking.*
Rates: *$99–$125, suites $150–$175; Continental breakfast, AE, DC, MC, V.*
Restrictions: *No cigar smoking, no pets.*

The Victoria Inn

Romantic Victorian is an obvious understatement for this 1875 carriage house, now a luxurious bed-and-breakfast inn. A gazebo beckons from the garden, and that sun room just over the front door belongs to a honeymoon suite done all in white (lots of lace and a brass king-size bed complete the picture). The Lilac Room and Peach Suite are done in the colors Victorians loved best. The formal mauve and cream of the Victoria Room sets off its dark woods. Franklin Pierce, 14th president of the United States, had a summer home next door and is remembered in The Pierce Room.

Innkeepers Linda and Leo Lamson make sure breakfasts are memorable. For example, Saturday's hearty "Logger's Breakfast" brings to mind the days of sail when New Hampshire provided the masts for the king of England's ships and includes New England's traditional baked beans and brown bread. Sunday there's sure to be strudel and maybe "Eggs Leon" (Leo's version of eggs Benedict) or a turkey sausage bake.

Address: *430 High St., Hampton, NH 03842, tel. 603/929–1437.*
Accommodations: *3 double rooms with private baths; 3 doubles share 1 hall bath.*
Amenities: *Cable TV in 3 bedrooms; air-conditioning; off-street parking; public beach nearby.*
Rates: *$65–$95 private bath; $55–$80 shared bath; full breakfast. MC, V.*
Restrictions: *No smoking; no pets (kennel nearby).*

The Lakes Region

When glaciers retreated from New Hampshire, they left behind a gift of fresh water: more than 1,300 lakes and ponds and 1,000 miles of streams. Although lakes are scattered throughout the state, the concentration of 273 parcels of water in the center—including 72-square-mile Lake Winnipesaukee—has been singled out as the Lakes Region.

Winnipesaukee means Smile of the Great Spirit, a name as appropriate today as when it was an abundant fishing ground for Native Americans. Its shores and those of its satellite lakes hold such vacation delights as bustling boardwalks and utter isolation, the nation's first summer resort at Wolfeboro, and one of its oldest summer theaters. Nearly all the region's 42 towns touch water, and boating can mean a canoe, a cruise ship, and all manner of craft in between.

The Lakes Region covers a big area, and each section has its advocates. If you follow the Connecticut River north through countryside made familiar by Maxfield Parrish, you'll come to Hanover, home of Dartmouth College. Wolfeboro is a "been coming here forever" place with an all-ages crowd meeting old friends for Sunday brunch at the inn or making the rounds at the antiques shows. The west side of Lake Winnipesaukee has honky-tonk Weirs Beach, where teenagers can hang out while their elders browse through the art galleries and crafts shops in Meredith and Moultonboro. Squam Lake perhaps is best remembered for the movie On Golden Pond, which was filmed here on the lakeshore.

Near pristine Lake Sunapee, the League of New Hampshire Craftsmen holds the oldest (and possibly the best) crafts show in the nation for a week every August. In September, when the explosive colors of autumn start south from the Canadian border and move through New Hampshire, the lakes are blue mirrors reflecting the reds and golds of the season. Winter is the time for ice fishing and ice boating on Lake Winnipesaukee and for skiing at Gunstock.

Places to Go, Sights to See

Castle-in-the-Clouds. The estate of eccentric millionaire Thomas Gustave Plant in the Ossipee Mountains is a special place to ride horseback or hike in the woods. You can take a paddleboat on the pond and visit the mansion, too. *Rte. 171, Moultonboro, tel. 603/476–2352. Open mid-May–mid-Oct.*

Canterbury Shaker Village (southwest of Lake Winnipesaukee off Rte. 106 at 288 Shaker Rd., tel. 603/783–9511). Now an educational and historic site, the Canterbury community established in 1792 has been preserved as a living museum of Shaker life. You can lunch on Shaker food in *The Creamery* restaurant and take escorted tours through many of the 22 buildings. There are candlelight dinner tours of the village as well, by reservation.

Gilford/Gunstock. The largest public beach on Lake Winnipesaukee is the waterfront of Gilford town, and if you take Route 11A to *Gunstock Recreation Area* (tel. 603/293–4341), you will have a choice of outdoor playgrounds, an Olympic-size swimming pool, fishing, paddleboats, horseback riding, and special events. Gunstock also has a family campground with 300 tent and trailer sites, where pets can be unleashed.

Madison Boulder. This granite boulder, 37 feet high and 83 feet long, is one of the world's largest glacial erratics and a National Natural Landmark. Look for signs east of Madison on Route 113.

Science Center of New Hampshire (tel. 603/968–7194). Live, indigenous beasts from bears and bobcats to reptiles and bald eagles enrich the static natural-science displays. The center and its 2-mile nature trail on Route 113 at Holderness are a year-round favorite of all ages. There are daily programs in July and August and on weekends in May, June, September, and October.

Weirs Beach. Fun and games by the hundreds, bowling lanes by the dozens, four water slides, and all the cotton candy and pizza you can eat make this a natural target for the teens. On summer evenings, music blares, and skyrockets zoom. Lake cruises are offered by *Mt. Washington Cruises* (tel. 603/366–5531).

Restaurants

Hickory Stick Farm (tel. 603/524–3333), in the woods near Laconia, specializes in roast duckling with sherry-orange sauce. The **Woodshed** (tel. 603/476–2311), in Moultonborough, features prime ribs in a converted barn. **Le Chalet Rouge** (tel. 603/286–4035), on the west side of Tilton not far from the toe of Silver Lake, is a modest dining room serving simple but authentic country French food. **The Sweetwater Inn** (tel. 603/476–5079), in Moultonborough, is known for its freshly made pasta, all-herbs-and-spices seasoning (no salt), and Spanish paellas. Look to The **Tamworth Inn** (tel. 603/323–7721) for New American cuisine and to **The Pasquaney Inn on Newfound Lake** (tel. 603/744–9111; *see* review, below) for exceptional French-Belgian cuisine.

Nightlife

Barnstormers (tel. 603/323–8500), the Equity summer theater in Tamworth, has an eight-week season, mid-July–Labor Day. **The Tamworth Inn** (tel. 603/323–7721) across the street offers dinner-theater packages. Moonlight dinner/dance cruises are offered by the **M/S *Mount Washington*** (tel. 603/366–2628.) Meredith Station (tel. 603/279–7777) is an 1849 railroad station-cum-pub with deejay dancing overlooking the lake.

Tourist Information

Lakes Region Association (Box 154502 Center Harbor, NH 03226, tel. 603/253–8555); **New Hampshire Office of Vacation Travel** (Box 856, Concord, NH 03301, tel. 603/271–2666 or 800/944–1117); **New Hampshire Division of Parks and Recreation** (Box 856, Concord, NH 03301–0856, tel. 603/271–3254 or 224–4666).

Reservations Services

New Hampshire B&B (329 Lake Drive, Guildford CT 06437, tel. 603/279–8348); **Lake Sunapee Business Assoc.** (Box 400, Sunapee, NH 03782, tel. 603/763–2495 or 800/258–3530).

The Nutmeg Inn

All the rooms are named after spices and decorated accordingly. The walls of Sage, for example, are just *that* shade of green, and should you wonder how the innkeepers, Shirley and Bo Lawrence, managed to find a shower curtain to match the squares of the quilt, the answer is Shirley (and her daughter-in-law) made both. In fact, Shirley's handicrafts are displayed throughout the inn.

The Cape-style house was built in 1763 by a sea captain who dismantled his ship to get the timber for the beams and paneled what is now a dining room with illegal "king's boards," those extra-wide cuts reserved for royal needs. An 18th-century ox yoke, said to have been used during the original construction, is bolted to the wall over a walk in–size fireplace, and the wide-board floors are also original.

The Nutmeg has been a stagecoach tavern, working farm, and, in the recent past, a private school. By the time the Lawrences found it, it was the quintessential fixer-upper. Son Daryl was in the construction business and Shirley was a registered nurse, but they dropped all that and began the renovation and restoration, doing most of the work themselves.

The Nutmeg is located on a rural side street off Route 104, the main road that runs between I-93 and Lake Winnipesaukee. Annalee's Doll Museum and showroom are nearby. Two miles away is Meredith village, where there are galleries, shops, and the dock for lake cruise ships. Gunstock ski and recreation area is about 10 miles away, and there is easy access to the White Mountains as well. However, the Nutmeg has a 20-by-40-foot swimming pool and more than 7 acres of lawn and gardens. You might just want to stay right here and take it easy.

Address: *Pease Rd., RFD 2, Meredith, NH 03253, tel. 603/279–8811.*
Accommodations: *7 double rooms with baths, 2 doubles share 1 bath, 1 suite.*
Amenities: *Air-conditioning, some rooms with working fireplaces; swimming pool, 3 rooms for private parties and meetings.*
Rates: *$65–$85; full breakfast. AE, D, MC, V.*
Restrictions: *No smoking, no pets. 2-night minimum on weekends and holidays.*

The Pasquaney Inn on Newfound Lake

The cream-colored 150-year-old inn and guest house facing Newfound Lake began its new life when Bud and Barbara Edrick left Manhattan to pursue the peaceful lifestyle of New Hampshire innkeeping. In 1992 they were joined by Paul and June Johnson. Bud, a onetime advertising man who always loved to cook, had trained at the French Culinary Institute and practiced at Flamand Restaurant in New York. He was ready to make his second-career dream come true, and now his French-Belgian cuisine rates cheers not only from the public, but also from drop-in newspaper and magazine food critics. His weekend cooking classes, begun to enliven the slow season, are booked a year in advance.

The rooms are small but bright, with some Victorian antiques, some four-poster and canopy beds, and claw-foot tubs in the old-fashioned baths. Pastels and the recurring motif of cozy, comfortable cats set the tone. Barbara Edrick is ready to talk cats any time, though the three resident cats stay in the owners' quarters.

All the inn folks share an enthusiasm for spring-fed Newfound Lake, acclaimed as the third cleanest lake in the world. All front rooms at the Pasquaney have lake views, but you can also watch the reflected sunset from the dining rooms and front porch. The inn's 26-foot cabin cruiser leaves from its own dock to take guests on one-hour cruises in summer. Boats are for rent at the north shore marina. The inn has its own beach.

While the White Mountains and Lake Winnipesaukee are easy to reach on day trips, and there are antiques and handcrafts to be found in nearby Plymouth, there is little after-hours entertainment in the neighborhood. On a rainy afternoon, the indoor shuffleboard and basketball hoop in the barn get a workout, and the old piano is kept in tune.

Address: *Star Rte. 1, Box 1066, Bridgewater, NH 03222, tel. 603/744–9111.*
Accommodations: *Main inn, 6 double rooms with baths, 4 doubles with private hall baths, 8 doubles share 4 baths; in Lilac House (open May–Oct.) 8 doubles with baths (4 can be made into suites).*
Amenities: *Restaurant, cooking school; badminton, croquet, recreation room in barn.*
Rates: *$86–$120; suites, $155; full breakfast (Continental breakfast in Jan.). AE, D, MC, V.*
Restrictions: *No smoking in large dining room, no pets. 2-night minimum on weekends June–Oct., restaurant closed Jan.*

Six Chimneys

Six Chimneys (count them) sits on a knoll at the northeast corner of Newfound Lake, midway between Bristol and Plymouth, as convenient now for visitors to the lakes and White Mountains as when the building was a tavern 200 years ago and the room rate was 10¢ a night.

Go through the red door of the olive green Colonial today, and you find a bed-and-breakfast that bridges the centuries. There are, for example, three cozy common rooms on the first floor warmed in winter by wood stoves or fireplaces. One is a quiet back parlor, and two have their own cable TV and VCRs, with more than 200 tapes stored in an English monk's bench. Owners Peter and Lee Fortescue have a special interest in old movies. Peter's mother was Priscilla Fortescue, a celebrity interviewer on Boston radio in the '40s and '50s.

Lee and Peter lived in Europe during his career as an Air Force officer, so all the antiques you see are not Early American. Lee, a former school-teacher, says she planned on having only old pieces throughout the house, but became so intrigued with the high quality of handcrafts now being made in the area that she began to acquire them, too. She can tell you where to find present-day quilts and such collectibles as the mouse dolls you see on the bedroom highboy.

The old wide-board floors tilt a bit, and there are gun-stock corner posts and pine wainscoting in several of the bedrooms. An upstairs sitting room furnished with Oriental rugs and old pine and cherry furniture has been created under the sloping roof. In space once reserved for drovers, a family can have a suite by combining the twin and single bedrooms (which share a bath) with the sitting ell.

Bountiful country breakfasts (fruit compote, French toast, sausage, and raspberry muffins, for example) are cooked on a 125-year-old "Dairy Household" wood-burning range, then served in a dining room where the exposed original beams and pegs complement the rush-seat chairs. Jams, jellies, and maple syrup are all local products, and the just-laid eggs come from the Fortescue's own chickens.

Address: *Star Rte. 114, East Hebron, NH 03232, tel. 603/744-2029.*
Accommodation: *2 double rooms with baths, 3 doubles and 1 single share 2 baths.*
Amenities: *Cable TV/VCRs in 2 common rooms; lake beach.*
Rates: *$50–$60; full breakfast. MC, V.*
Restrictions: *Smoking only in downstairs den, no pets. 2-night minimum on some weekends, closed late Mar.–early Apr.*

The Tamworth Inn

Tamworth village is synonymous with The Barnstormers Playhouse, summer-night entertainment no one—visitor or resident—would think of missing. Just down the street, the tower of the venerable Tamworth Inn is nearly as well-known.

Phil and Kathy Bender, who bought the rambling 1830s Victorian a few years ago, have achieved a rare balance. This haven for rest and refreshment since stagecoach days is now where townspeople come for a wedding in the gazebo, New American cuisine in the dining room, or a casual evening in the pub.

Behind the inn, gardens and lawn taper to Swift River. Here Kathy has put her former profession of landscape architect to work, making the most of the romantic gazebo setting with plants and flowers indigenous to New England. Phil, a former banker, manages and co-hosts the inn.

The Benders have reduced the total number of rooms in favor of all private baths and four suites. Some rooms are large enough for a third person, and all are furnished with a mixture of 19th-century country antiques and 20th-century pieces.

In winter, fires crackle on the hearths of the dining room, library, and living room, and pots of potpourri in water sit over warming candles. In the pub, there's time for conversation around the Franklin stove as cross-country skiers drop in, and regulars swap ice-fishing stories.

In summer, diners sit in the main dining room and in the screened porch, and the 20-by-40-foot outdoor swimming pool becomes the center for relaxation as well as a hangout for the theater cast and crew. You can also carry a good book down to the hammock by the river and just forget the world completely.

Morning coffee will be brought to your bedroom, if you like. When you amble at leisure to the cheery corner breakfast room you can help yourself to juice, cereal, home-baked breads and muffins, Kathy's special eggs or French toast.

Address: *Box 189, Main St., Tamworth, NH 03886, tel. 603/323-7721 or 800/642-7352.*
Accommodations: *11 double rooms with baths, 4 suites.*
Amenities: *Restaurant, partial air-conditioning, TV/VCR (with movie collection); swimming pool, fly fishing in stream.*
Rates: *$80–$130; full breakfast; $110–$160 MAP for two. MC, V.*
Restrictions: *No smoking. 2-night minimum on holidays.*

The Wakefield Inn

When you turn off Route 16 and drive east to the historic district of Wakefield Corner, time and traffic vanish. A New England miracle? Well, no, but the Wakefield Inn is listed on the National Register of Historic Places for good reason. It is a gem of Federal architecture, as square and substantial as a fully rigged ship, which is precisely what its seagoing builder demanded. He also insisted it be an unconventional three stories high, so he could have the tallest house in the village, and he originally built two houses side by side. Soon the two were joined as one, and later on, a wraparound porch was added.

All this and more you learn from Harry Sisson, who shares innkeeping and ownership with his wife, Lou. The Sissons came to New Hampshire from Connecticut. "We moved in, and the first thing I had to do was cater a wedding reception," Lou recalls. Wedding receptions are numerous here (the village church is across the street). Two doors away is the Museum of Childhood. Inn guests receive free passes.

Inside the inn there are surprises: a three-sided fireplace in the dining room; the free-standing spiral staircase (no supporting center pole) is one of the few in the United States. Indian shutters and wide pine floors are typical of the late-Colonial era. Upstairs, the guest rooms are named after important 19th-century visitors, such as John Greenleaf Whittier. Throughout the inn are framed tintypes of unsmiling New Englanders. Some pictures the Sissons found in the attic; some are the gifts of inn guests. Many of the subjects are unknown, the "instant ancestors" of the flea market.

All the bedrooms are large—several have an extra bed, ideal for a family—with views of the mountains and countryside or of the historic village. Forget your toothbrush? No matter. Baskets of "most likely to be forgotten" items sit on hall stands inviting you to help yourself.

Lou's handmade quilts provide the decorative center for the bedrooms. She also holds special "quilting weekends" at the inn, assuring guests they will return home with completed (or nearly so) quilts of their own.

Address: *Rte. 1, Box 2185, Mountain Laurel Road, Wakefield, NH 03872, tel. 603/522–8272, or 800/245–0841.*
Accommodations: *7 double rooms with baths.*
Amenities: *Guests-only restaurants; crafts shop.*
Rates: *$65–$70; full breakfast. Many special-rate packages. AE, MC, V.*
Restrictions: *No smoking in bedrooms, no pets. 2-night minimum on holidays.*

The Wolfeboro Inn

A landmark lakeside inn with the amenities of a complete resort and the warmth of a bed-and-breakfast, the Wolfeboro is one block from town and a stroll from the galleries, shops, and sights of the historic village. The original white clapboard house with green shutters faces Main Street, but extensions overlook Wolfeboro Bay.

The rooms and suites are furnished in well-polished cherry and pine, flowered chintzes, with no kitsch whatsoever. The baths have heating lamps, and TVs are mostly tucked out of sight in armoires. Some rooms have quilts and folk art, but the general feeling is one of controlled elegance: blue, mauve, and maroon are the principal colors.

Structural additions have been made since the inn's beginnings in the 1800s: Rooms in the newest wing are a tad brighter than the older ones, and many have balconies or decks. The oldest part of the inn includes some original (1812) bedrooms with fireplaces, as well as the venerable Wolfe's Tavern. The main dining room has Windsor chairs, a working fireplace, and paneling from the 1760s.

Things get a bit more rustic in the old tavern, where there is an oven fireplace, and the serving staff can offer 40 brands of beer from all over the world. On the menu of hearty hot and cold specialties is Montcalm's Revenge, a sandwich big enough for six hungry people.

Guests at the inn are multigenerational and many are lake regulars (and remember coming here as children) as well as first-timers and honeymooners. It would be a shame to come just for overnight and not take advantage of the full span of facilities. Everything is available for a prolonged lake holiday, from the inn's two excursion boats (no charge to guests for boat trips or any other amenity) to many other sports facilities. Tennis and golf are nearby.

In winter you can try skiing, skating, ice fishing, and ice boating while taking advantage of low off-season package rates. The tavern is handy for hot mulled cider between events.

Address: *44 N. Main St., Box 1270, Wolfeboro, NH 03894, tel. 603/569–3016 or 800/451–2389, fax 603/569–5375.*
Accommodations: *38 double rooms with baths, 5 suites.*
Amenities: *Restaurant and tavern, air-conditioning, cable TV and phones in rooms, elevator, room service noon–10; private lake beach, 2 excursion boats, fishing, wind-surfing, canoes, bicycles, conference facilities in inn or on boat.*
Rates: *$99–$121, suites $155–$207; Continental breakfast buffet. AE, D, MC, V.*
Restrictions: *No pets.*

The Inn on Golden Pond

Ever since *On Golden Pond* was filmed at Squam Lake in 1984, its reputation as the "best-kept secret in New Hampshire" has been in jeopardy. The lake is the state's second largest, but it's too shallow for big boats, and the summer places along the shore are passed down through families instead of appearing on the real-estate market. About the closest you can get is The Inn on Golden Pond.

Bill Webb, who came to innkeeping from publishing, quickly got involved in environmental issues and is president of the Science Center of New Hampshire at Holderness. He can tell you where to take an early morning nature walk, and if you want the ultimate in quiet—except for the occasional call of a loon—he suggests a third-floor room in the back.

Braided rugs and country curtains hold to the period when the house was built—in 1879. The most recent addition was a new wing in 1988; it is white clapboard, of course, like the rest of the inn.

Address: *Rte. 3, Holderness, NH 03245, tel. 603/968–7269.*
Accommodations: *7 double rooms with baths, 2 suites.*
Amenities: *Cable TV in common room.*
Rates: *$95–$135; full breakfast. MC, V.*
Restrictions: *No smoking, no pets.*

Kona Mansion Inn

Following the signs from Route 25 along country roads to the inn builds a certain tension, but then the Tudor mansion high on a hill reassuringly comes into focus. The red tile roof has neo-Oriental corners; the first floor is built of granite stones rounded by ancient glaciers and running water; the second is half-timber. Even a knight in armor would feel at home in Valhalla, the baronial dining room.

Kona Mansion, built in 1900 as a country estate for merchant magnate Herbert Dumaresq, was for years a working farm. Now whittled to 130 acres, it still has its own beach and boat dock on Lake Winnipesaukee, lots of room to ramble, and such diversions as a nine-hole golf course and two tennis courts. In the main house, accommodations vary from Room 1, a big front master bedroom with two double beds and one twin bed, to minuscule Room 5, a bargain with one double bed. There are also six housekeeping efficiency cottages on the lake to rent by the week.

Address: *Moultonboro Neck Rd., Moultonboro, Box 458, Center Harbor, NH 03226, tel. 603/253–4900.*
Accommodations: *9 double rooms with baths, 4 housekeeping cottages, 2 3-bedroom chalets.*
Amenities: *Restaurant, TVs in rooms, air-conditioning in main building, 3 meeting rooms; swimming, golf, tennis free to guests.*
Rates: *$60–$140; breakfast extra. MC, V.*
Restrictions: *No pets in main building. Closed Nov.–Apr.*

Red Hill Inn

An amiable clutter of memorabilia from the first half of the 20th century makes this red-brick mansion on Overlook Hill an unusual country inn. A high school yearbook from the '40s; puzzles and board games from the '30s; mysterious gewgaws and whatnots from the '20s are what a fortunate houseguest in an old movie might discover. When Rick Miller and Don Leavitt found Red Hill, it was a complex of vandalized buildings on the 60-acre campus of a defunct college. Happily they did not heed the advice to tear it down, but began the salvation and restoration of the main house, farmhouse, and stone cottage, which had, in 1904, been a grand summer estate and working farm. Outdoor porches were converted into bathrooms and sitting rooms, the latter with sweeping views of meadows, mountains, and Squam Lake. Period furniture and even books popular when the inn was a private house were acquired and set in place. If you ever wondered what happened to that old Philco radio, look in the Chocorua Suite. Surprise!

Address: *RFD 1, Box 99M, Center Harbor, NH 03226, tel. 603/279–7001.*
Accommodations: *16 double rooms with baths, 5 suites.*
Amenities: *Restaurant, TV/VCR and phones in rooms, many Franklin stoves, some whirlpool baths; tennis courts nearby.*
Rates: *$65–$145; full breakfast. AE, D, DC, MC, V.*
Restrictions: *No pets. 2-night minimum on weekends.*

The Tuc' Me Inn

Country Victorian ambience are some of the reasons young and old find this village bed-and-breakfast so appealing. Rooms at the Tuc' Me Inn vary in size, the furnishings are eclectic, and the name is corny. But though the front bedroom can be noisy, it is also big, bright, and popular with return guests; two rooms share a large enclosed porch as well as a bath, making a nice arrangement for a family or two congenial couples. Authentic family pieces from the last century and a 1909 wind-up Victrola complete with the old records round out the inn's comfortable, homey feel.

This white clapboard inn, built in the mid-1800s, is located two blocks from the town center, near the beach and the dock of the M/S *Mt. Washington.* Drive or hike up the road and you will reach Wolfeboro Falls and the Libby Museum of local artifacts. Go down the road and you can visit the three buildings maintained by the Wolfeboro Historical Society. Antiques stores are thick throughout the area, and in summer and fall you are never far from a flea market or multidealer show.

Address: *68 N. Main St., Wolfeboro, NH 03874, tel. 603/569–5702.*
Accommodations: *3 double rooms with baths, 4 with shared baths.*
Amenities: *Cable TV in parlor, air-conditioning in bedrooms.*
Rates: *$57–$73; full breakfast. MC, V.*
Restrictions: *No smoking, no pets.*

The White Mountains

The White Mountains, highest in the Northeast, are a rugged range where rock-climbers and alpine skiers feel right at home. Still, though 80% of this northern region is encompassed by the White Mountain National Forest, those vigorous pursuits are not all there is.

Villages founded in the 1700s came to full bloom in the late 19th century, when the elite of Boston, New York, and Philadelphia hied themselves north in private trains to Bethlehem and Bretton Woods. Today Bostonians are joined by visitors who come from all over the world to Mt. Washington valley for weekend shopping sprees at the designer-outlet boutiques of North Conway and to enjoy the serenity of country inns. The variety of regional architecture is astounding: English Tudor-style mansions, Colonial farmhouses, gingerbread-trimmed public buildings, and dairy barns and carriage houses converted into shops and lodgings.

Story Land and Santa's Village theme parks and the living-history museum of Heritage–New Hampshire are pleasant diversions for families. The subtle sophistication of Jackson Village begins at the red covered bridge that is its gateway; the town offers infinite possibilities for romantic retreats.

In July and August, a gigantic tent pitched at Settlers' Green, North Conway, provides concerts, dance, and circus acts under the aegis of the local Arts Jubilee. The Eastern Slope Playhouse, also in North Conway, is an archetypical summer theater, with a professional company doing Broadway musicals. Galleries and antiques cooperatives are concentrated here, too.

The spectacular scenery of the Presidential Range and its gorges makes simple sightseeing an end in itself. The area is vast enough to absorb the hordes of summer visitors and still leave isolation for those who seek it, particularly in the tranquil mountain, valley, and lakeside villages between Route 16 and the Maine border.

Though summer is the busiest season for the region, the first and second weekends of October are dense with foliage-viewers. Do not be so cavalier as to try for these dates without reservations, and six months ahead is not too early to book a special inn. Foliage season is followed by a lull before the first snows bring skiers. Then, among seasonal special events, there is a 60-kilometer inn-to-inn Hot Chocolate Run for the cross-country set in Jackson; sleigh rides, slaloms, and snowmobiling. For alpine skiers, the lifts and runs of Waterville Valley, Loon Mountain, Cannon Mountain, Wildcat, Black Mountain, and Mt. Cranmore are household words.

Places to Go, Sights to See

Kankamagus Highway. Route 112 stretches 33 miles from Lincoln to Conway with only one exit, Bear Notch Road to Bartlett. It is considered the prime foliage-viewing road in New England, but at any time of year it is a beauty. You can take self-guided trails to overlooks.

Mount Washington. The weather station on top of the highest mountain in the northeast (6,288 feet) has recorded a world's record in wind velocity (231 mph) and temperatures that rival the Antarctic. You can reach the summit via the *Mt. Washington Auto Road* (call tel. 603/466–3988 or 603/466–2222 for road conditions) from Route 16, Pinkham Notch, or via *Mt. Washington Cog Railway* (tel. 603/846–5404 or 800/922–8825) from Bretton Woods, mid-April–October, weather permitting. You can also walk.

The Old Man of the Mountains. The symbol of New Hampshire is a 40-foot-high outcrop of rock (actually five separate ledges) bearing an acute resemblance to a human profile, 1,200 feet above Profile Lake in Franconia Notch. This is the Great Stone Face of Nathaniel Hawthorne's famous short story, and there are several designated viewpoints from which to gaze at it. Other sights of the glacier-carved notch are *The Basin,* a 20-foot pothole at the base of a waterfall; *The Flume,* a granite chasm nearly 800 feet long with a stunning series of waterfalls and pools; and *Echo Lake,* where you can try the acoustics over a picnic lunch. *Cannon Mountain Aerial Tramway* (tel. 603/823–5563) operates from Memorial Day to late October. You ascend 2,022 feet in five minutes to the Summit Observation Platform, then follow trails to other outlooks. The *New England Ski Museum* (tel. 603/828–7177) is at the foot of the tramway.

The White Mountain National Forest. More than 1,300 miles of trails make this spectacular combination of rugged mountains and wooded valleys heaven for hikers and mountain climbers. More than 300 species of animals and birds live here, while an additional 120 species pass through on a regular basis. In winter you can ski, snowshoe, or try ice climbing; in summer, swim, canoe, fish, and camp; any time of year, enjoy the quality of life in a protected wilderness covering nearly 758,000 acres. The *Appalachian Mountain Club* (tel. 603/466–2727) has its home base at Pinkham Notch.

Restaurants

Reservations are imperative at country inns where the lodger comes first, but well worth the effort. New England contemporary cuisine is served at the **Inn at Thorn Hill** (tel. 603/383–4242), in Jackson; **The 1785 Inn** (tel. 603/356–9025), in North Conway; and **Darby Hill Country Inn & Restaurant** (tel. 603/447–2181), in Conway. **The Scottish Lion** (tel. 603/356–6381), in North Conway, serves oatcakes with every meal.

Tourist Information

White Mountains Attractions (Box 10, North Woodstock, NH 03262, tel. 603/745–8720 or 800/346–3687); **Mt. Washington Valley Chamber of Commerce and Visitors Bureau** (Box 2300, North Conway, NH 03860, tel. 603/356–3171 or 800/367–3364); **White Mountain National Forest** (Box 638, Laconia, NH 03247, tel. 603/528–8721).

Reservations Services

Reservation Service of the Country Inns in the White Mountains (tel. 603/356–9460 or 800/562–1300); **Mt. Washington Valley Chamber of Commerce** (*see* above, tel. 603/356–5701 or 800/367–3364). **Jackson Resort Association** (tel. 800/866–3334); **Mt. Washington Valley Central Reservation Service** (tel. 800/367–3364). For referrals (not direct reservations) in communities around Berlin, contact the **Northern White Mountains Chamber of Commerce** (tel. 800/992–7480).

The Bells

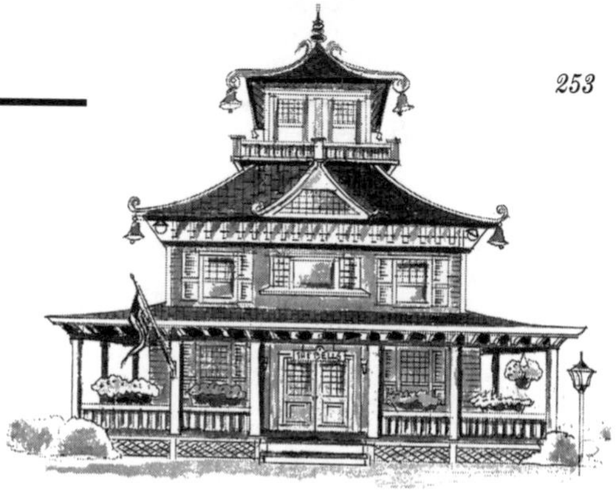

The Bells would stand out anywhere, but in a region known for Colonial farmhouses and stone mansions, a bed-and-breakfast inn shaped like a pagoda is eye-grabbing. The pagoda also has bells dangling from each turned-up point and flower baskets suspended over the window boxes of its porch.

Louise and Bill Sims, who owned an antiques shop for many years, surround their guests with treasures: there's a collection of beaded evening bags on the wall of the vestibule, a series of iron doorstops on the stairs, an 1886 music box, and a dress form garbed in black and named Mrs. Danvers to greet guests.

At the top of the house, a white room in the cupola is a favorite of honeymooners. The Red Suite has an unusual cannonball trundle bed in the bedroom, and in its sitting room, magazines are held in a doll bed made during the Civil War by Louise's great-grandfather. Behind the pagoda, the Simses' original antiques shop has become The Summer House, a guest cottage furnished entirely in 1920s style.

The Bells sits on a quiet residential side street off Route 302 in Bethlehem, at the western end of the White Mountains. At the turn of the century, when The Bells was built, the town's fame as a pollen-free environment was spreading (The National Hay Fever Relief Association was founded here in the 1920s), and it boasted 30 resort hotels. Trains from New York and Boston made two stops a day to unload vacationers. More architectural styles are supposed to be represented in Bethlehem than in any other town in New England.

Bill, a retired engineer, and Louise, who was a grants-application writer, are still researching their house. After trying 15 different color combinations on the once-brown exterior, Louise settled on a cream with blue-green trim, only to find, under the layers, that the original color was almost exactly the same. The Simses know The Bells was built in 1892 by a minister from Connecticut, but have yet to fathom its pagoda connection. They have uncovered a hand-painted sign with a drawing of Mount Fuji and something like "Welcome to Our Happy Home Under the Mountain" written in pseudo-Japanese.

Address: *Strawberry Hill St., Bethlehem, NH 03574, tel. 603/869–2647.*
Accommodations: *1 double room with bath, 2 suites, 1 cottage suite.*
Amenities: *TV in living room and in suites; ceiling fans.*
Rates: *$60–$90; full breakfast. AE, MC, V.*
Restrictions: *No pets. 2-night minimum Sept. 15–Oct. 15.*

Inn at Thorn Hill

Romantic is a word you hear a lot at Thorn Hill, the mansion designed by Stanford White, the Gilded Age's most famous architect. Staying here, you are within walking distance of shops, galleries, and sports, but still in your own special place, and the view of Mount Washington from here is superb.

Jim and Ibby Cooper, owners and proprietors, came to Thorn Hill from hospitality and education careers in California, Texas, and Florida. Their older children—excited to be involved—fit right in with a lifestyle that seems less a business than a constant round of entertaining good friends. Yet the elegant past is never far away. In the drawing room you are greeted by two mannequins wearing 1870s wedding and wedding reception dresses. In one bedroom, a blue velvet fainting couch is an invitation to swoon; spectacular Oriental rugs and electrified Victorian oil lamps are everywhere.

While the main house is unabashedly romantic-traditional, the carriage house has been done in the country style of the same period. Here the open fireplace and overstuffed sofas of the Great Room suggest you can sprawl, and the Steinway baby grand piano of the main house drawing room is balanced with the Carriage House's outdoor hot tub. Three cottages—beloved by honeymooners—are done in an eclectic blend best described as, well, romantic.

Thorn Hill is a year-round retreat. In spring, summer, and autumn, there are wildflowers and pine forests, swimming, hiking, fishing, and the like. In winter, you can step directly from the inn's waxing room onto the 150-kilometer Jackson Ski-Touring cross-country trail network or ski downhill at five major areas nearby. You can toboggan on the property, and a horse-drawn sleigh will pick you up at the door.

Thorn Hill's dining room is becoming known throughout the valley for its contemporary New England cuisine and its wine list—as well as the candlelight.

Address: *Thorn Hill Rd., Jackson, NH 03846, tel. 603/383–4242 or 800/289–8990, fax 603/383–8082.*
Accommodations: *13 double rooms with baths, 3 suites, 3 cottages.*
Amenities: *Restaurant, pub, air-conditioning in main house and cottages, cable TV/VCR in parlor; swimming pool, badminton, shuffle-board, croquet, horseshoes, cross-country ski trails, tobogganing, small meeting room in carriage house.*
Rates: *\$100–\$182, full breakfast; \$130–\$212 MAP. AE, MC, V.*
Restrictions: *No smoking, no pets. 2-night minimum on foliage, Christmas, and holiday weekends; closed Apr.*

Notchland Inn

In the barn of Notchland Inn there are llamas and pygmy goats, Russian karakul lambs, not to mention Hillaby, the Barbados black-bellied sheep who thinks he is a person. Yet rare animals are only part of the surprises of this highland estate overlooking the Saco River Valley at the entrance to Crawford Notch.

The mountain lodge, built of locally quarried granite and native timbers, is equally unexpected. It was constructed in 1852 by Samuel Bemis, a Boston dentist. The lifetime bachelor bequeathed it to his loyal caretaker, whose children began to take in summer guests. Notchland became a year-round inn after John and Pat Bernardin, the present owners, decided to change their urban lifestyle and move from Massachusetts in 1983.

Now there is a new wing with a gourmet restaurant, and a gazebo by the duck pond. An old schoolhouse has become a two-suite guesthouse, with working fireplaces and early photographs of the mountains on the walls.

The main house has not changed much since the 19th century. The bedrooms have armoires, wing chairs, and afghans as well as fireplaces. Guests gather in the Map Room for apéritifs before dinner. The accessories are as predictable as dried flowers and as unusual as the slate grave marker that reads "1788. Nancy Barton died in a snowstorm in pursuit of her faithless lover."

The seasons unfold from this mountainside vantage point. You can try white-water canoeing in springtime, hiking and trout fishing in summer. There is ice skating on the inn pond in winter and miles of trails for cross-country skiing.

The recent acquisition of a pair of draft horses now means hayrides in autumn and sleigh rides in winter. Notchland is surrounded by a National Forest, and while there is much to do outdoors at Hart's Location, it's an early-to-bed sort of place.

Address: *Rte. 302, Hart's Location, Bartlett, NH 03812, tel. 603/374–6131 or 800/866–6131.*
Accommodations: *9 double rooms with baths, 9 suites.*
Amenities: *Fireplaces in bedrooms; outdoor hot tub, river swimming, hiking and cross-country ski trails, 2 meeting rooms.*
Rates: *$95–$115; full breakfast. MAP mandatory on weekends. AE, D, MC, V.*
Restrictions: *No smoking indoors, no pets. 2-night minimum on weekends except Apr.–June.*

Snowvillage Inn

From 1,000 feet up on the side of Mt. Foss, the span of the Presidential Range at sunset appears hand colored. No wonder Frank and Trudi Cutrone find it ideal for their own country inn. For hikers, skiers, readers, and environmentalists as well as lovers of good food, Snowvillage was, and is, irresistible.

The guest rooms (including one with 12 windows) are in the main house, in an old carriage barn/library, and in a new lodge, where every room has a working fireplace. Each has been named for a writer or literary genre and contains appropriate bedside reading. Although many of the fascinating pictures and accessories are Tyrolean, the architecture is New England farmhouse, and the buildings are a cheerful cranberry red with white trim.

Rag rugs, wing chairs, good reading lights, knotty pine paneling, and welcoming homemade chocolate chip cookies will make you feel not only cared for, but right at home. Breakfast includes a high-energy fitness minimenu as well as fruit pancakes, omelets, and the like. Sunday's special is eggs Benedict served with champagne. Packed lunches and special guided hikes with gourmet food can be arranged, right down to a 5-course champagne lunch packed in by the Snowvillage Inn's own llamas. Steve Raichlen's famous cooking classes are held at the inn three times a year: spring, fall, and winter.

In winter, there's professional instruction in cross-country skiing, and at any time of year Frank is ready to point out a trail through the blueberry barrens or map out the way to the area's numerous antiques and discount-shopping meccas. Guests have resident beach privileges at Crystal Lake, minutes away.

It's impossible to talk about Snowvillage Inn without mentioning Boris and Natasha, the beautiful, friendly Samoyeds who have posed for innumerable photographers and have their own picture book. Even if Snowvillage weren't the perfect weekend getaway—and it is—Boris and Natasha would be worth a special trip.

Address: *Stuart Rd., Snowville, NH 03849, tel. 603/447–2818 or 800/447–4345.*
Accommodations: *18 double rooms with baths.*
Amenities: *Restaurant; resident privileges at lake, tennis court, volleyball, horseshoes, cross-country skiing (equipment rental, lessons), hiking trails, sauna, cooking school, 4 small conference rooms.*
Rates: *$90–$130; full breakfast; MAP also available. AE, MC, V.*
Restrictions: *No smoking in bedrooms or dining room, no pets. Closed Apr.*

The Franconia Inn

The Franconia Inn is a white clapboard rambler built as an inn in 1934 when the original 18th-century farm homestead was destroyed by fire. Just across the road are its glider field and tennis courts.

Alec and Richard Morris, brothers who are third-generation innkeepers, bought the property a decade ago and began to turn it into the complete resort it is today. Do you want to swim? Ride? Fly? Hike? Ski? Relax? Want a king-size Jacuzzi tub in your suite? Everything is right here on 107 scenic acres in Easton Valley.

Rooms are decorated in designer country chintzes, and many have canopy beds. The Inn Suite comes with a fireplace and a wet bar; family suites have connecting bedrooms. This is an inn for all seasons and ages.

Address: *Easton Rd., Franconia, NH 03580, tel. 603/823–5542.*
Accommodations: *31 double rooms with baths, 3 suites.*
Amenities: *Restaurant, cable TV in lounge, movie room, games room, hot tub; swimming pool, 4 tennis courts, sleigh rides, cross-country skiing, bicycles, croquet, riding stable (8 horses), soaring center, golf privileges at nearby 9-hole course.*
Rates: *$75–$113; full breakfast. AE, MC, V.*
Restrictions: *No pets. closed Apr. 1–Mother's Day.*

The Horse & Hound Inn

This 1838 farmhouse, on a back road near Franconia Notch and Cannon Mountain, was expanded in 1946 by an Englishman who envisioned living the sporting life of a country gentleman and operating a traditional country-house hotel on the side.

Today's owners, Jim Cantlon and Bill Steele, both formerly professional hoteliers in Virginia, are comfortable with that image. "It also seemed a good place to spread out all the things we had collected over the years," Jim says. "We both enjoy cooking and gardening generally, and Bill makes great desserts."

Dogwood-patterned china sets the tables of the paneled dining room, with its working fireplace and windows looking out on the terrace and lawn. The cuisine is Continental with a French emphasis, and there are English grills on the menu, too. Upstairs, the bedrooms are named for their respective artwork: Audubon; Currier & Ives; and The Garden Room.

Address: *Wells Rd., Franconia, NH 03580, tel. 603/823–5501.*
Accommodations: *8 double rooms with baths, 2 double suites.*
Amenities: *Restaurant, cable TV in lounge; cross-country ski trail.*
Rates: *$60–$80, suites $110–$120; full breakfast. AE, DC, MC, V.*
Restrictions: *No pets. Closed Apr.*

Inn at Crystal Lake

Where does a geologist go to retire? The Inn at Crystal Lake, of course. Although Walter and Jacqueline Spink did move far away from Ryder College, New Jersey, they brought with them rocks and geodes enough to decorate the tables in the dining room and make fascinating arrangements throughout the inn (along with Walter's metal sculptures). Still, you can't take the educator out of the man, so when the bedrooms were named and color-coded for gems, each was given an illustrated information sheet about the stone as well. Ruby is a real beauty, with its 1850 Honduras mahogany canopy bed and hand-crocheted spread in the Irish Rose pattern. Even the foyer's marble floor has fossils in it. The yellow 19th-century inn with its green shutters, hanging baskets, and white wicker porch furniture is set in a quiet village, looking like a page from a calendar. Not for those seeking lively entertainment perhaps, but just right for families. A room just off the TV/den sleeps up to eight, and there's a resident cat.

Address: *Rte. 153, Box 12, Eaton Center, NH 03832, tel. 603/447–2120 or 800/343–7336.*
Accommodations: *11 double rooms with baths.*
Amenities: *Restaurant (reservations required); canoes, lake swimming.*
Rates: *$83–$99; full breakfast, MAP also available. AE, D, MC, V.*
Restrictions: *Smoking only in lounge, no pets. 2-night minimum on holidays.*

The Lavender Flower Inn

The outside of this 1850s farmhouse turned bed-and-breakfast is done in five shades of lavender, and if you time your visit for mid-June, you will see beds of blue and white iris at their full glory. The iris motif is repeated inside, from wallpaper and prints to shower curtains. Gardening is one of the shared hobbies Ray and Noreen Berthiaume enjoy to the fullest now that they have left the corporate world for innkeeping and small-town life. Ray also restores antique furniture. Notice, in particular, the old Turkish fainting couch and the Victorian mahogany and cherry tables and beds. From Center Conway you can go shopping or skiing in the Mt. Washington valley one day, down to the lakes the next. Portland, Maine, is only an hour away. In winter, you can snowmobile or cross-country ski right here.

Address: *Box 328, Main St., Center Conway, NH 03813, tel. 603/447–3794 or 800/729–0106.*
Accommodations: *3 double rooms with baths, 4 doubles share 2 baths.*
Amenities: *Cable TV in living room.*
Rates: *$50–$85; full breakfast and snacks. AE, D, MC, V.*
Restrictions: *No smoking, no pets. 2-night minimum on holiday weekends.*

The Mulburn Inn

The 1913 Tudor-style mansion with its circular driveway, stone porticos, and 3 acres of grounds stands at the eastern end of Bethlehem. It was once a summer cottage known as Ivie Estate, built for a branch of the Woolworth family, and has such notable architectural details as imported tile around the fireplaces, stained-glass windows, and ornate mantels.

It is large enough to provide third-floor living space for the growing families of the two young couples—Cheryl and Bob Burns and Linda and Moe Mulkigian—who now own it, and still have seven large, airy bedrooms for guests on the second. The rooms are named after peaks in the Presidential Mountain Range. Each is distinctive: The Monroe has its closet in a disused elevator; the Madison has its pineapple-post bed set in the round of a turret; the Adams has a 7-foot tub in the bathroom; the Pierce sleeps up to five. Year-round sports and all the sights of Franconia and the White Mountains are close at hand.

Address: *Main St., Bethlehem, NH 03574, tel. 603/869–3389.*
Accommodations: *7 double rooms with baths.*
Amenities: *TV in common room, 2 18-hole golf courses nearby.*
Rates: *$55–$65; full breakfast and afternoon tea. AE, D, MC, V.*
Restrictions: *No smoking indoors, no pets. 2-night minimum on holiday weekends.*

The 1785 Inn

This pretty white Colonial with blue trim is one of the oldest structures in Mt. Washington Valley. It was a Publick House right from the start and so popular the roof had to be raised—literally—to accommodate more guests. Becky and Charlie Mallar restored the inn completely when they exchanged their careers in education for innkeeping. Their restaurant and its wine cellar continue to win prizes. In fact, the only thing debatable about the inn is which window has the best view of the mountains and the spectacular autumn color. Each room is different, not only in its coordinated colors, but in the varied Colonial-to-Victorian antiques and country-style furnishings. Rooms on the back are quietest, and No. 5, with a king-size bed, has a wonderful view.

Address: *Box 1785, Rte. 16, North Conway, NH 03860, tel. 603/356–9025 or 800/421–1785.*
Accommodations: *12 double rooms with baths, 5 doubles share 2 baths, 1 suite.*
Amenities: *Restaurant and bar, air-conditioning, cable TV in bar and suite, cable TV/VCR in guest living room, 4 fireplaces in public rooms, room service; swimming pool, cross-country ski and hiking trails, volleyball, shuffleboard, tennis.*
Rates: *$60–$145; full breakfast. AE, D, DC, MC, V.*
Restrictions: *No smoking in main dining room or in bedrooms, no pets. 2-night minimum during foliage season.*

Sugar Hill Inn

The late film star Bette Davis used to visit old friends in this house before she bought her own Butternut Farm nearby, so it is logical that the largest bedroom with the best view is called the Davis Room. Each of the rooms in this 18th-century white-clapboard inn has charm (note the original sugar-maple floors; the oak-and-maple dresser in Grandma's Room), and the setting on the side of Sugar Hill is bucolic.

Jim and Barbara Quinn, former Rhode Islanders, own the inn now. Jim cooks the bountiful country breakfasts, bakes all the breads, and makes dinner for inn guests as well. Barb handles reservations and decorating, right down to her own stencils on the walls. "It's a wonderful life," she says.

The Quinns are also involved in the Franconia community, especially the Sugar Hill Museum, where there is Bette Davis memorabilia on display, along with the work of local artists.

Address: *Sugar Hill Rd., Franconia, NH 03580, tel. 603/823–5621 or 800/548–4748.*
Accommodations: *10 double rooms with baths in main house, 6 doubles with baths in 3 cottages.*
Amenities: *Restaurant; air-conditioning in dining room.*
Rates: *$80–$105; full breakfast and afternoon tea. MC, V.*
Restrictions: *No smoking, no pets. 2-night minimum in foliage season, closed Apr., Christmas week.*

Whitneys' Inn

In 1992, Robert and Barbara Bowman bought Whitneys' Inn, a casual country retreat at the foot of Black Mountain and set about making it better than ever. In winter you can walk to the ski lifts; the rest of the year you can enjoy other regional attractions such as Story Land and the Heritage–New Hampshire theme museum.

The 1842 farmhouse has grown a deluxe wing and added a chalet, and two cottages, all furnished appropriately with prints and pine. The 200-year-old brown barn is used for large functions and as a summer games room for teens. It houses an original shovel handle used on the mountain's first overhead-tow lift, plus a collection of historic ski photos. Upstairs is an après-ski bar.

It adds up to an ideal place for active people of any age and is especially great for families.

Address: *Rte. 16B, Jackson, NH 03846, tel. 603/383–6886 or 800/677–5737.*
Accommodations: *20 double rooms with baths, 8 suites, 2 2-bedroom cottages.*
Amenities: *Air-conditioned restaurant; cable TV in lounge, pub, and games room; fireplaces in cottages; swimming pond, tennis, 3 meeting rooms with catering.*
Rates: *$48–$98; breakfast; MAP also available. AE, DC, MC, V.*
Restrictions: *No smoking. 2-night minimum on holidays and on weekends, Jan.–Mar., July–Aug., mid-Sept.–mid-Oct.*

Off the Beaten Track

Amos A. Parker House

"Oh, what's this?" are words Freda Haupt hears a lot from her guests. Great bunches of her own dried flowers hang in the barn sitting room of the Amos A. Parker house, only one of the hobbies of the creative and energetic owner. An eye-stopping garden slopes to the river behind the house, and on the roadside, a genuine liberty pole attests to its history as a meeting place for Revolutionaries. Today's kitchen and Great Room were the original cabin in 1700, but by 1780, the shelter had grown to a family home requiring six (still working) fireplaces.

You stroll downhill to the Fitzwilliam Green with its ring of 18th-century houses and overflowing antiques stores. Minutes away are Rhododendron State Park and the all-faith outdoor Cathedral of the Pines.

Address: *Rte. 119, Box 202, Fitzwilliam, NH 03447, tel. 603/585–6540.*
Accommodations: *3 double rooms with baths, 2 double rooms share 1 bath, 1 housekeeping suite.*
Amenities: *Tennis courts and cross-country trails nearby.*
Rates: *$55–$80; full breakfast. No credit cards.*
Restrictions: *No smoking, no pets. 2-night minimum on holidays and college weekends.*

The English House

When you see the steaming cup of tea on the sign outside the green Edwardian house next door to Proctor Academy, you know you are in the right place. The English House is a bed-and-breakfast for Anglophiles, a slightly aloof country house in the center of a prep-school village between Lakes Sunapee and Winnipesaukee. Inside you will find it replete with polished maple paneling and flowered chintz, with a sunny sitting room just for guests. The original watercolors throughout the house are the work of Gillian Smith's mother and uncle, both artists well known in the United Kingdom. Gillian, herself a professional needle-woman whose quilted fashions are shown and sold in shops of the League of New Hampshire Craftsmen, is also a masterly cook. In addition to the baked goods served at afternoon tea and the English breakfast, even the yogurt and granola are homemade. Ken Smith, a retired British Army officer who once coached his country's Olympic cross-country ski team, makes the inn's jams and marmalades.

Address: *Box 162, Rtes. 4 & 11, Andover, NH 03216, tel. 603/735–5987.*
Accommodations: *7 double rooms with baths.*
Amenities: *Air-conditioning, cable TV in guest sitting room; cross-country skiing.*
Rates: *$75; full breakfast and afternoon tea. MC, V.*
Restrictions: *No pets. 2-night minimum stay on holiday and school weekends.*

Hannah Davis House

The fragrance of baking bread sets the mood for this 1820 Federal house only steps from the Monadnock village green. Kaye Terpstra occasionally helps out her neighbor at the Amos Parker House. In Kaye's kitchen-hearth room, the old beehive oven no longer functions, but elsewhere in the house, four fireplaces all work, and the oversize bathrooms have tubs with cat's-paw feet and brass fittings. The enormous hanging scale in the kitchen is a memory of the country store the Terpstras owned elsewhere before deciding to open their bed-and-breakfast. Kaye, a former social worker, and Mike, who was an engineer, now pursue cooking and carpentry. Kaye describes her mouth-watering breakfasts: omelet stuffed with bacon, cream cheese, tomato, and herbs; crepes with parsley sauce; homemade granola, applesauce, and breads. In returning the house to its original form, Mike has managed to save much of the old glass as well as the T-over-T doors and chair-rail wainscoting. And he has thoughtfully added a deck so guests can enjoy Fitzwilliam's picture-book spires and rooftops just beyond the trees.

Address: *186 Depot Rd., Fitzwilliam, NH 03447, tel. 603/585–3344.*
Accommodations: *3 double rooms with baths, 2 suites.*
Amenities: *Cable TV/VCR in common area.*
Rates: *$55–$80; full breakfast. No credit cards.*
Restrictions: *No smoking in bedrooms, no pets.*

Home Hill Country Inn & French Restaurant

If a slice of French countryside could be magically set down on 22 acres in rural New Hampshire, you might call it Home Hill. Brittany native Roger Nicolas felt that way when he saw the white brick Federal mansion—then a private home—and promptly sold his San Francisco restaurant to move to this bucolic spot on the Connecticut River. Just across the river in Vermont, Mt. Ascutney offers convenient downhill skiing. Although Paul Dionne is now in charge of the kitchen, Roger still has a deft hand at the stove, and his good taste shows also in the tasteful toile wallpaper in the three dining rooms and the high brass bedsteads and French country antiques of the upstairs bedrooms and suites. A newly renovated carriage house contains two rooms and a luxurious suite, and a guest house overlooks the swimming pool.

Address: *River Rd., Plainfield, NH 03781 (mailing address: RR 3, Box 235, Cornish, NH 03745), tel. 603/675–6165.*
Accommodations: *6 double rooms with baths, 3 suites.*
Amenities: *Restaurant; swimming pool, tennis court, cross-country ski trails.*
Rates: *$85–$120; Continental breakfast. MC, V.*
Restrictions: *No pets. 2-night minimum stay on holiday weekends and in foliage season.*

Maine

Maine

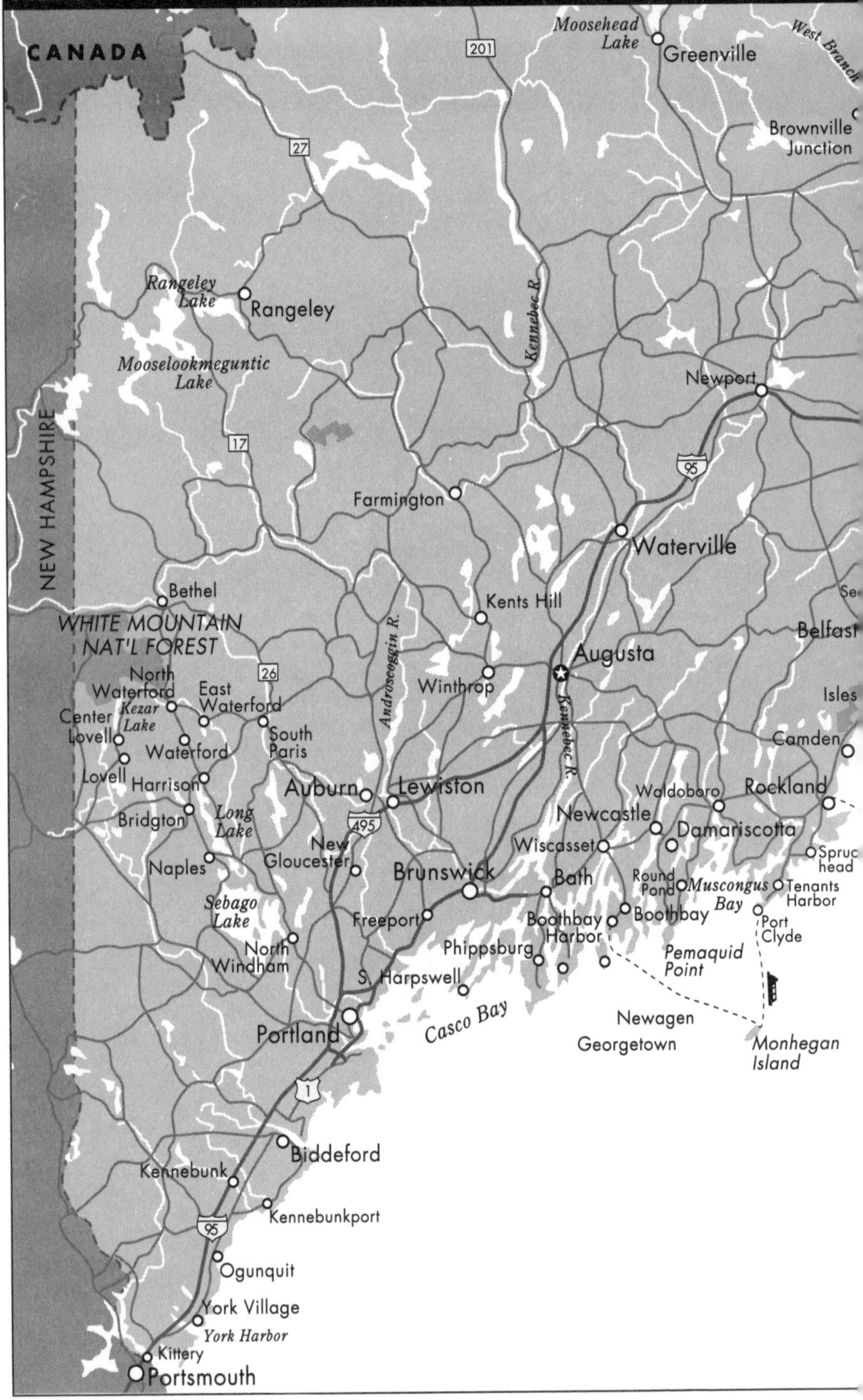
CANADA
NEW HAMPSHIRE
Moosehead Lake
Greenville
West Branch
201
27
Brownville Junction
Rangeley Lake
Rangeley
Mooselookmeguntic Lake
Kennebec R.
Newport
17
95
Farmington
Waterville
Bethel
Kents Hill
WHITE MOUNTAIN NAT'L FOREST
Belfast
Augusta
26
North Waterford
East Waterford
Winthrop
Isles
Androscoggin R.
Center Lovell
Kezar Lake
South Paris
Waterford
Camden
Lovell
Harrison
Auburn
Lewiston
Waldoboro
Rockland
Bridgton
Long Lake
495
Newcastle
Damariscotta
New Gloucester
Wiscasset
Naples
Brunswick
Bath
Round Pond
Muscongus Bay
Tenants Harbor
Sebago Lake
Freeport
Boothbay
Boothbay Harbor
Port Clyde
North Windham
Phippsburg
Pemaquid Point
S. Harpswell
Casco Bay
Newagen
Georgetown
Portland
Monhegan Island
1
Biddeford
Kennebunk
Kennebunkport
95
Ogunquit
York Village
York Harbor
Kittery
Portsmouth

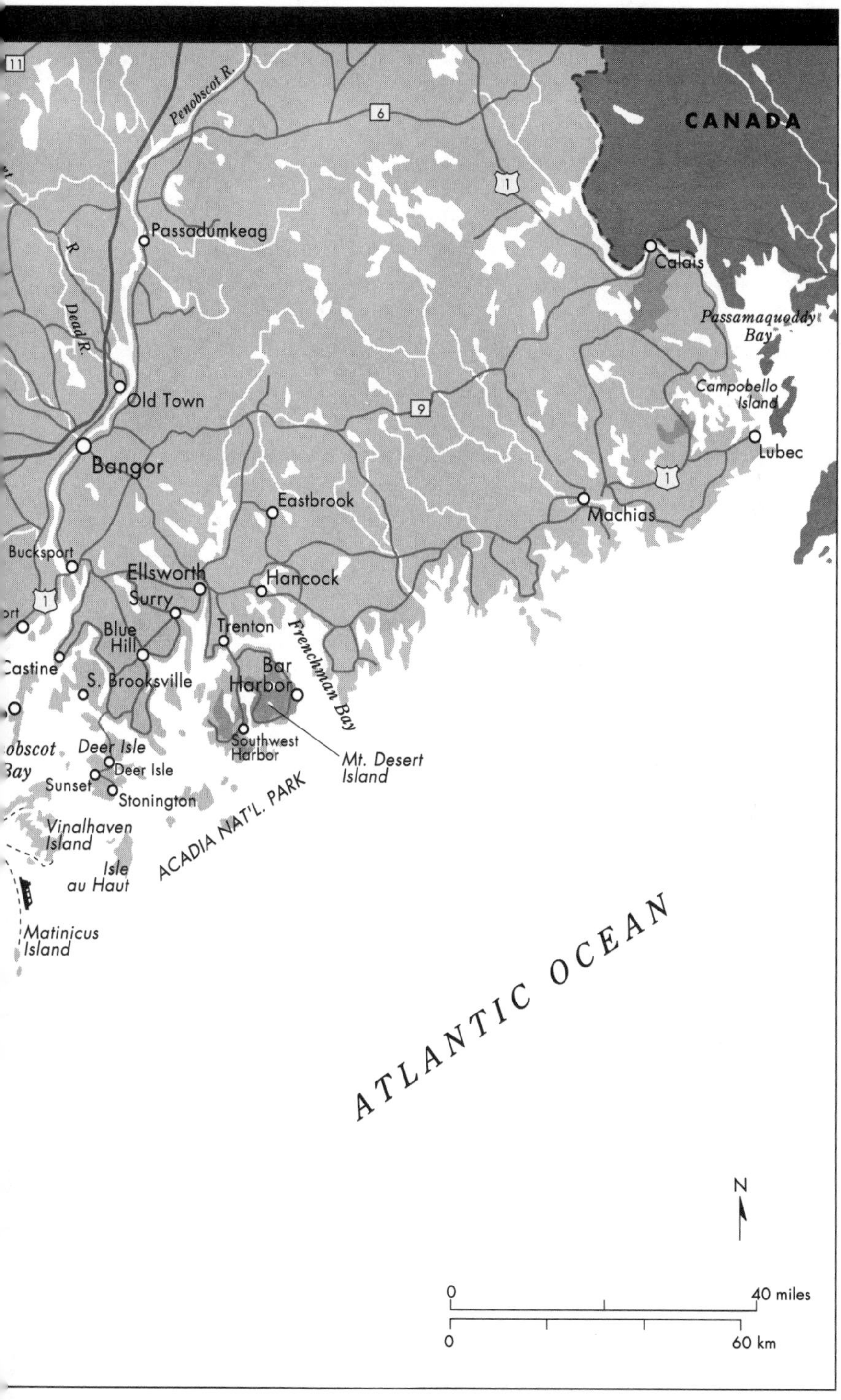
CANADA
Penobscot R.
Passadumkeag
Dead R.
Old Town
Bangor
Eastbrook
Bucksport
Ellsworth
Hancock
Surry
Trenton
Blue Hill
Castine
S. Brooksville
Bar Harbor
Frenchman Bay
Southwest Harbor
Mt. Desert Island
Deer Isle
Deer Isle
Sunset
Stonington
Vinalhaven Island
Isle au Haut
ACADIA NAT'L. PARK
Matinicus Island
Calais
Passamaquoddy Bay
Campobello Island
Lubec
Machias
ATLANTIC OCEAN
N
0
40 miles
0
60 km

The Southern Coast
Kittery to Portland

Maine's southern coast is no secret to visitors. Within easy striking distance of the big cities, with the biggest sand beaches in Maine and the warmest water (hardly tropical, but less frigid than points north and east), the southern coast towns fairly swarm with tourists in summer. York Beach, Ogunquit, and Wells Beach are summer colonies whose raison d'être is sand. Right behind the beaches, crowding as close to the water's edge as possible, come nearly unbroken ranks of beach cottages, motels, oceanfront restaurants, and ice-cream stands.

But ticky-tack has by no means overspread the entire landscape. Farther inland, along Route 1, the highway that runs the length of the Maine coast from Kittery to Machias, are older and more dignified villages: York, which has a historic district on the National Register, and serene, dignified Kennebunkport, the retreat of former president George Bush and site of the area's finest inns, most gracious old homes, and a number of varied shops.

If you've come for bargains, head down to Kittery, where you'll find a host of factory outlets. Wells also has a smattering of outlets along Route 1 as well as flea markets, antiques stores, and barns crammed with old books.

Crowning the region is Portland, perhaps the best-kept secret in New England, an extremely manageable small city with a good art museum, an impressive selection of restaurants and shops, and a tastefully restored downtown waterside district known as the Old Port Exchange. Portland is very much a port city, and you can hop on a boat for cruises of the harbor or take a ferry out to one of the Calendar Islands (so called because British mariners thought there were 365 of them).

The southern coast may lack the lonely, wind-bitten starkness of points down east, but it compensates with a fine overlay of civilized amenities—museums, galleries, restaurants, restored old homes—and, of course, those long sand beaches.

Places to Go, Sights to See

Kennebunkport Historic District. Kennebunkport has the prettiest sea captains' homes in the region—nobly proportioned Federal and Greek Revival houses on Spring, Maine, Pearl, and Green streets, with fanlights, hip roofs, columns, and high windows. *Walking tours* (tel. 207/967–2751) depart from the Nott House on Maine Street on Tuesday and Friday mornings during July and August.

Marginal Way. You can walk along Ogunquit's oceanfront on the mile-long public path, viewing the townscape behind you and the rolling surf in front.

Old Port Exchange is Portland's restored waterfront district of old brick warehouses converted to trendy shops and restaurants. The Old Port is best explored on foot. Leave yourself a couple of hours to wander down Market, Exchange, Middle, and Fore streets. On *Custom House Wharf* you can soak up some of the older, rougher waterfront atmosphere.

Perkins Cove. This neck of land connected to the Ogunquit mainland by a pedestrian drawbridge contains a jumble of sea-beaten fishhouses that the tide of tourism has transformed into shops and galleries.

Portland Museum of Art (7 Congress Sq., tel. 207/775–6148). This is one of the finest art museums in New England, with a strong collection of Maine landscapes and seascapes by such masters as Winslow Homer, John Marin, Andrew Wyeth, and Marsden Hartley. Winslow Homer's *Pulling the Dory* and *Weatherbeaten,* two quintessential Maine-coast images, are both here. The striking modern Charles Shipman Payson wing with huge arched windows was designed by I. M. Pei & Partners in 1983. Also part of the museum complex is the *McLellan Sweat House* at 111 High Street, a fine example of the Federal style with a semicircular front portico and open-work balustrade around the roof.

Whale-Watching. The *Nautilus* sails daily from the Arundel boatyard, from the end of May through Columbus Day, on a 5½-hour narrated whale-watching cruise (tel. 207/967–0707 or 207/967–5595).

York Historic District includes a number of 18th- and 19th-century buildings clustered along York Street and Lindsay Road. You can purchase tickets to enter all the buildings at **Jefferds Tavern** (corner of Rte. 1A and Lindsay Rd., tel. 207/363–4974), a late 18th-century inn that has been restored.

Restaurants

Kennebunkport's **Cape Arundel Inn** (Ocean Ave., tel. 207/967–2125) has superb seafood served in an airy, water-view dining room. **Raphael's** (36 Market St., tel. 207/773–4500) offers some of Portland's most sophisticated dining—delicate Northern Italian cooking in a suave, stylish, airy dining room. For funkier atmosphere and New American cooking, trying **Alberta's** (21 Pleasant St., Portland, tel. 207/774–0016) or **Katahdin** (106 High St, tel. 207/774–1740).

Beaches

York's **Long Sands Beach** has the most ticky-tack. The sand is a bit lighter and finer at Ogunquit (a jump north) and Wells Beach (another jump north). **Drake's Island Beach,** in Wells, adjoins a stretch of salt marsh protected by the Rachel Carson National Wildlife Refuge. In the Kennebunk area, **Goose Rocks Beach** is the biggest and favorite of families with young children. **Gooch's** and **Middle Beach** attract a lot of teens. **Kennebunk Beach** has a small playground and thus a crowd of tots and moms. **Old Orchard Beach** has a an amusement park and pier. **Scarborough Beach** and **Crescent Beach State parks** are popular with greater Portland residents; the latter is a good choice for families with toddlers.

Tourist Information

Kittery Chamber of Commerce (Box 526, , ME 03904, tel. 207/439–7545); **Kittery Tourist Information Center** (Rte. 1 and I–95, Box 396, Kittery, ME 03904, tel. 207/439–1319); **Ogunquit Chamber of Commerce** (Box 2289, Ogunquit, ME 03907, tel. 207/646–2939); **Wells Chamber of Commerce** (Box 241, Wells, ME 04090, tel. 207/646–2451); **The Yorks Chamber of Commerce** (Box 417, York, ME 03909, tel. 207/363–4422); **Kennebunk-Kennebunkport Chamber of Commerce** (Cooper's Corner, Rtes. 9 and 35, Box 740, Kennebunk, ME 04043, tel. 207/967–0857); **Convention and Visitors Bureau of Greater Portland** (305 Commercial St, Portland, ME 04101, tel. 207/772–4994).

Reservations Services

B&B Down East, Ltd. (Box 547, Macomber Mill Rd., Eastbrook, ME 04634, tel. 207/565–3517, fax 207/565–2076); **Peg Tierney B&B of Maine** (16 Florence St., Portland, ME 04103, tel. 207/775–7808).

The Captain Jefferds Inn

If you have a taste for the exquisite, and if your idea of beauty is heaps of precious, delicately crafted objects, then this is the inn of your dreams. (Those who find this style fussy and cluttered would be happier at the more stately and formal Captain Lord Mansion across the street.) Innkeeper Warren Fitzsimmons and his partner, Don Kelly, are avid collectors and antiquarians who once owned antiques shops in the posh Long Island resort of Southampton. They have put their passions to work in renovating and decorating the 1804 Captain Jefferds Inn and its carriage house. The white-clapboard black-shuttered sea captain's home, with its collections of majolica, American art pottery, and Sienese pottery, is clearly a labor of love, the realization of Fitzsimmons's dream of "serving people in gracious settings."

Public rooms include the exuberantly colorful parlor, where the extensive majolica collection resides, and the solarium, furnished with Art Deco rattan and copies of Della Robbia reliefs. Breakfast, served beneath the formal dining room's Venetian glass chandelier, is as fancy as the decor, with frittatas, eggs Benedict, and blueberry crepes commonly on the menu.

Most of the rooms are done in Laura Ashley fabrics and wallpapers, with the addition of prize antiques: English curly maple chests, marble-top chests, old books (in all, the inn houses 10,000 volumes), and oil paintings and watercolors that would not look out of place in the Portland art museum. Among the bigger and better rooms are No. 2, with an English pine armoire and a downstairs corner location, and No. 12, which has its own little balcony, white wicker furniture, and an airy, contemporary feel. Number 8 at the top of the house gives you lots of room, privacy, quiet, and a taste of the old-fashioned Maine look, with rag rugs and chenille bedspreads. One pleasant surprise: The resident Lhasa apso and "Disney dog" welcome visiting pets.

Address: *Pearl St., Box 691, Kennebunkport, ME 04046, tel. 207/967–2311.*
Accommodations: *12 double rooms with baths, 3 carriage-house suites.*
Amenities: *Cable TV in parlor, huge record library; croquet.*
Rates: *$85–$155; full breakfast. MC, V.*
Restrictions: *No smoking in dining room, pets welcome (with advance notice). 2-day minimum July–Oct., closed early Dec.–Apr.*

The Captain Lord Mansion

Of the mansions in Kennebunkport's Historic District that have been tastefully converted to inns, the 1812 vintage Captain Lord Mansion is hands-down the most stately and sumptuously appointed. The three-story pale yellow house sits in the middle of a manicured lawn across the street from the Captain Jefferds Inn, from which it differs considerably in decor. While the Captain Jefferds hums, even riots, with color and clutter, the Captain Lord keeps an air of formal—but never stiff—propriety, seen to best advantage in the refined Gathering Room, which looks like a period room (Chippendale) in a museum, except for the guests lounging before the hearth.

Innkeepers Bev Davis and Rick Litchfield, former advertising executives in search of a career change, are far more laid-back in style than the house they meticulously restored. They chat and joke with guests over family-style breakfasts served informally at the two harvest tables in the cheery country kitchen. Bev and Rick rescued the Captain Lord Mansion from its Victorian gloom and refurbished it with crisp, authentic Federal decor.

Guest rooms, which are named after old clipper ships, are large and stately, though the formality relaxes as one ascends the elliptical staircase. The soberly elegant Brig Merchant, a desirable corner room on the ground floor, has a bed with a fishnet canopy, dark mahogany period furniture, and a maroon rug. Ship Lincoln, to many minds the finest room in the house, with a step-up four-poster bed and damask-covered walls, is also the room in which the inn's benign resident ghost appears (only women have ever seen her). Bark Hesper, on the third floor, is a whimsical, country-style room, quainter and smaller than the downstairs rooms, with green dot-and-flower wallpaper and leafy views out the windows.

Bev and Rick have succeeded admirably in creating a pleasing base from which to venture forth on forays to Kennebunkport's architectural treasures, the shops of Dock Square, or the sand beaches lining the chill Atlantic.

Address: *Box 800, Kennebunkport, ME 04046, tel. 207/967–3141.*
Accommodations: *16 double rooms with baths.*
Amenities: *11 rooms with fireplaces, gift shop, TV room.*
Rates: *$149–$199; full breakfast and afternoon tea. D, MC, V.*
Restrictions: *No smoking in public areas, no pets. 2-night minimum on weekends, 3-night minimum on holiday weekends.*

Dockside Guest Quarters

With the water views, seclusion, and quiet of its private 8-acre island in the middle of York Harbor, the Dockside has the best location of any small hotel in the Yorks. The Maine House, the oldest building on the site, is a classic New England turn-of-the-century clapboard house, kept in impeccable condition and set off with wide lawns and gardens. The four modern multiunit cottages tucked away behind lush trees have less character, but they feature sliding glass doors on the water and private decks; many come with kitchenettes.

David and Harriette Lusty have owned the place since 1953, and they have filled it with their personal warmth, colorful conversation; and their collection of nautical charts, ship models, and pictures. David, who has a background in the Navy, loves to sail, to take guests out on harbor tours, and to arrange charterboat trips out to the Isles of Shoals. The Lustys' sons have since come aboard. Eric, a licensed merchant marine officer, keeps the tradition going as assistant manager.

Rooms in the Maine House are furnished with Early American antiques, some with white wicker and painted floors, and the ever-present marine motif. The effect is rather simple, spare, and airy. Cottage units are a logical choice for families and for those who insist on being right on the water. The inn's wraparound porch catches the ocean breeze, and a grandfather clock ticks sedately in the snug sitting room overlooking the ocean.

Loyal guests tend to settle in at the Dockside and stay put, spending their days strolling around Harris Island and down the dock, observing the parade of yachts on the harbor, and reading and lounging in the garden. You can walk to York's historic district, and the Kittery outlet shops beckon just a few miles to the south. The dining room, open to the public for dinner, is one of the finest in the area.

Address: *Box 205, York, ME 03909, tel. 207/363–2868.*
Accommodations: *3 double rooms in the Maine House and 10 cottage doubles, all with baths, 2 doubles share 1 bath, 7 apartment suites.*
Amenities: *Restaurant, TV in most rooms; private dock, motorboat and canoes for rent, croquet, badminton, shuffleboard, horseshoes, fishing.*
Rates: *$58–$138; breakfast extra. MC, V.*
Restrictions: *6 bedrooms reserved for nonsmokers, no pets. 2-day minimum July–early Oct., weekends, and holidays; closed late Oct.–Apr.*

Old Fort Inn

This inn at the crest of a hill on a quiet road off Ocean Avenue has a secluded, countryish feel and the welcome sense of being just a touch above the Kennebunkport action. Not that there is anything snooty about the Old Fort Inn. Innkeepers Sheila and David Aldrich, refugees from California, had jobs with an airline and in an antiques shop (she) and with an oil company (he). They have brought relaxed hospitality and clever interior design ideas to their new occupation, and Sheila's love of antiques shows up everywhere.

The front half of the former barn is now an antiques shop (specializing in Early American pieces); the rest of the barn is the reception area and a large parlor decorated with grandfather clocks, antique tools, and funny old canes. Here the Aldriches serve their guests a breakfast of homemade croissants and breads, granola, yogurt, and melon and berries.

To get to the guest rooms, you cross a lawn, skirt the bright flower beds that set off the ample pool (a rarity at an inn), and enter the long, low fieldstone and stucco carriage house that has been artfully converted to lodgings. Guest rooms vary in size and their decor reflects the Aldriches' witty and creative way with design and antiques: There are quilts on the four-poster beds; wreaths, primitive portraits, and framed antique bodices hang on the walls; the loveseats are richly upholstered, some with blue-and-white ticking. Some rooms have hand stenciling, and several of the beds have fishnet canopies. Numbers 2 and 12 have choice corner locations. Number 1 is one of the smaller rooms.

During the day, when inn guests scatter to bike on Kennebunkport's shaded lanes, bask on the beaches, or drive up the coast to shop at L. L. Bean, the Old Fort's pool is an oasis of blissful solitude.

David remembers saying to himself, the first time he drove over the drawbridge into Kennebunkport, "This is where I want to be." More than a decade later, the enthusiasm that the Aldriches bring to living in Kennebunkport and running the Old Fort Inn are as apparent as ever.

Address: *Box M, Kennebunkport, ME 04046, tel. 207/967–5353 or 800/828–3678, fax 207/967–4547.*
Accommodations: *14 double rooms with baths, 2 suites.*
Amenities: *Phones, cable TV, and wet bars in rooms, laundry facilities; pool, 1 tennis court, bikes for rent.*
Rates: *$125–$240; buffet breakfast, cookies and candies in rooms. AE, D, MC, V.*
Restrictions: *No pipes or cigars in guest rooms, smoking limited, no pets. 2-night minimum July–Labor Day, 3-night minimum on holiday weekends, closed mid-Dec.–mid-Apr.*

Bufflehead Cove

When Harriet Gott's children grew up and she found herself with some time and some bedrooms on her hands, she thought that her gambrel-roof house at the end of a dirt road on 6 acres of land on the Kennebunk River would make a perfect bed-and-breakfast. She was right.

Bufflehead Cove offers the serenity and space of a country location (fields, apple trees, waterfowl) just five minutes from Dock Square. The turn-of-the-century house has the warm feel of a home that has always been loved, cared for, and comfortably lived in.

Guest rooms are as pretty as a dollhouse (and a touch small), with white wicker and flowers painted on the walls. The Balcony Room, with a mahogany double armoire and a small balcony on the river, is the favorite of honeymooners.

Address: *Box 499, Kennebunkport, ME 04046, tel. 207/967–3879.*
Accommodations: *3 double rooms with baths, 2 suites.*
Amenities: *Private dock for views and bird-watching.*
Rates: *$85–$130; full breakfast and evening wine and cheese. AE, MC, V.*
Restrictions: *No smoking, no pets. 2-night minimum on weekends June–Sept., closed Jan.–Mar.*

The Green Heron

It's not fancy or dramatically situated, but the Green Heron on Ocean Avenue offers plain, comfortable accommodations. Rarest of all in Kennebunkport, it is excellent value for your money. Charlie and Elizabeth Reid bought the inn and small housekeeping cottage from his brother in 1988, and Denise Coppenrath, originally from the south shore of Massachusetts, manages it for them with youthful informality. The Reids have retained the homey atmosphere while sprucing the place up, inside and out.

Many of the rooms face tidal Fairfield Creek (Nos. 48 and 50 have the best views), as does the cheerful, small breakfast room. In the evening, guests gather in the comfortable living room to swap sightseeing tips.

Don't miss the sumptuous breakfast, one of the best on the Maine coast, which may include fresh berries with cream, waffles, raspberry crepes, muffins, pancakes, and homemade applesauce.

Address: *Box 2578, Kennebunkport, ME 04046, tel. 207/967–3315.*
Accommodations: *10 double rooms with private baths, cottage sleeps 4.*
Amenities: *Air-conditioning and TV in bedrooms, common TV/VCR.*
Rates: *$68–$86; full breakfast. No credit cards.*
Restrictions: *No pets on 2nd floor. Closed Jan.*

The Inn at Harbor Head

Cape Porpoise, a peninsula just north of Kennebunkport, is worth a detour for its working harbor dotted with lobster boats, its gray rock shores, and its soft wooded landscape. Cape Porpoise is worth a longer stay for this exquisite, artfully converted 100-year-old shingled farmhouse right on the harbor. Joan Sutter, who runs the inn with her husband, Dave, is an artist whose taste is apparent throughout the house: in the delicately harmonious color schemes, the choice of antiques—an old Chinese screen with cloth hinges, an English pine armoire, an heirloom pewter collection—and most of all in the nautical and floral murals she has painted in the guest rooms.

The Harbor Suite upstairs, with canopy bed and fireplace, has the best view, and its murals echo the water and townscape out the window. The Greenery downstairs has a whirlpool tub, hand-painted furniture, and garden view. In fine weather you can take your breakfast of fruit, omelet, and bread outside to eat beside the wild roses.

Address: *RR 2, Box 1180, Kennebunkport, ME 04046, tel. 207/967–5564.*
Accommodations: *3 double rooms with baths, 2 suites.*
Amenities: *Fresh flowers in rooms; private dock; beach passes and towels; robes.*
Rates: *$95–$195; full breakfast and afternoon refreshments. MC, V.*
Restrictions: *No smoking, no pets. 2-night minimum on weekends.*

The Maine Stay Inn and Cottages

Located on a quiet residential street, a short walk from Dock Square, is the Maine Stay Inn, its circa 1860 square block Italianate main house listed on the National Register of Historic Places. Additions over the years have included a cupola, wraparound porch, a pair of sunburst crystal glass windows, detailed interior moldings, and a magnificent flying staircase. Innkeepers Lindsay and Carol Copeland bought the inn in 1989, leaving banking careers in Seattle to bring their young family to New England.

Although somewhat small, room No. 14, in the rear of the house and overlooking the garden, offers quiet and a private entrance and patio. Suite No. 12 is bright and airy, with plenty of windows to let in the early morning sun, plus a fireplace and a stained-glass window in the bathroom. Families often prefer the cottages, which have kitchens and offer a bit more privacy. Cottage guests can choose to have their breakfast delivered to them.

Address: *34 Maine St., Box 500A, Kennebunkport, ME 04046, tel. 207/967–2117 or 800/950–2117, fax 207/967–8757.*
Accommodations: *4 double rooms with baths, 2 suites, 11 cottages.*
Amenities: *4 cottages and 1 suite have fireplaces; cable TV and clock-radios in rooms; guest courtesy telephone; jungle gym; croquet.*
Rates: *$125–$190; full breakfast and afternoon tea. AE, MC, V.*
Restrictions: *No pets. 2-night minimum on weekends.*

The Pomegranate Inn

Alan and Isabel Smiles, who bring to innkeeping their experience with antiques, interior design, and importing Irish linen, have put a witty sensibility to work in transforming this gray stucco house into the city's most stylish bed-and-breakfast. Clever touches like the *faux marbre* moldings, mustard colored rag-rolling on the hall walls, and the eclectic blend of antiques (Regency to Italian Art Deco) and modern art give the place a postmodern air. In the Victorian Western Promenade neighborhood, just a 10-minute walk from downtown, the inn is both quiet and convenient.

Most of the guest rooms are big and bright, with murals on floral themes. No. 7, in the carriage house, is done in a bright pastel floral motif and has a private patio. If you find the eggplant tones of No. 3 a bit jarring, request the more serene No. 2, with a grape arbor painted in muted tones. Full breakfasts of quiche, croissants, French toast, or eggs will fuel you through a morning at Portland's art museum or a boat ride out on Casco Bay.

Address: *49 Neal St., Portland, ME 04102, tel. 207/772–1006 or 800/356–0408, fax 207/773–4426.*
Accommodations: *6 double rooms with baths in main house; 1 double room with bath, 1 suite in carriage house.*
Amenities: *Cable TV and phones in all rooms.*
Rates: *$95–$165; full breakfast. AE, D, MC, V.*
Restrictions: *No smoking in guest rooms, no pets.*

The White Barn Inn

A five-minute walk from Kennebunkport Beach and the shops of Dock Square, the White Barn offers accommodations in the main house, carriage house, and cottages. Laurie Cameron runs the inn, while her husband, Laurie Bongiorno, runs the formal but rustic dining room.

The living room is decorated in deep reds and blues and has Oriental rugs and a leather sofa; afternoon tea is served in the adjacent sitting room, which has an embroidered sofa and TV.

Although small, room No. 10 in the main house is sweet, with a brass bed, lace curtains, and a claw-foot tub. The Red Suite in the carriage house has a king-size four-poster bed, private porch, fireplace, and a huge bath with a Jacuzzi tub and glassed-in shower.

Address: *Box 560 C, Beach St., Kennebunkport, ME 04046, tel. 207/967–2321, fax 207/967–1100.*
Accommodations: *13 double rooms with baths in main inn, 4 double rooms in "gatehouse" cottages, 6 suites in carriage house, 1 cottage.*
Amenities: *Fresh fruit, robes, and phones in rooms; fireplaces and Jacuzzis in some rooms; restaurant, lounge with piano bar, cable TV.*
Rates: *$110–$275; Continental breakfast and afternoon tea. AE, MC, V.*
Restrictions: *Smoking limited. 2-night minimum on holidays and weekends.*

York Harbor Inn

On Route 1A directly across from the ocean, the rambling white clapboard York Harbor Inn has sprouted various wings and a carriage house over the course of three centuries, but somehow they all come together. At the inn's heart is a mid-17th-century fishing cabin, with venerable dark timbers and a fieldstone fireplace. The cabin was brought over from the Isles of Shoals on a barge, and now serves as the inn's parlor.

Two brothers from New Jersey, Gary and Joe Dominguez, and their wives, Nancy and Jean, own and run the inn. Their interest and researches in local history and design have helped in harmonizing the decor of the various sections. Room 15, in the carriage house, has a fireplace, pumpkin-pine floors, and a bed with an oak headboard. Ask for a room in the newest wing, where you won't hear the traffic.

Address: *Box 573, York Harbor, ME 03911, tel. 800/343-3869, fax 207/363-3545, ext. 295.*
Accommodations: *20 double rooms with baths, 4 doubles share 2 baths in inn; 7 doubles with baths, 1 suite in carriage house.*
Amenities: *Restaurant, pub, air-conditioning in bedrooms, 3 non-smoking rooms, 2 fireplaces in carriage house, gift shop in lobby.*
Rates: *$65–$134; Continental breakfast. AE, D, MC, V.*
Restrictions: *No pets.*

Mid-Coast
Freeport to Port Clyde

North of Portland, the long, smooth arcs of sandy beaches all but vanish, and the shoreline takes on the jagged, rocky, deeply indented aspect that we think of as quintessential Maine. Long bony fingers of land point south into the ocean, with great rivers—the Kennebec, the Sheepscot, the Damariscotta—flowing alongside them, their upper reaches draining and filling with the tides. To the fingertips cling the scenic lobstering villages and resorts of South Harpswell, Newagen, Pemaquid Point, and Port Clyde.

The larger towns of the mid-coast are looped together by Route 1. Freeport, less than half an hour north of Portland, is an entity unto itself, a town made famous by a store: L. L. Bean, which began with a pair of waterproof boots, has become a shopping mecca for the entire world. In the wake of L. L. Bean's success, scores of upscale factory outlets have opened.

Brunswick, a good-size city with some 27,000 people, is best known for Bowdoin, its fine liberal arts college. Bath, 12 miles up the 150-mile Kennebec River, has been a shipbuilding center since 1607. The Bath Iron Works continues the tradition, and the Maine Maritime Museum preserves its history.

Wiscasset bills itself as the prettiest town in Maine and lives up to its advertising. Well situated on the Sheepscot River, it brims with antiques shops, old white clapboard houses, and historic churches.

The Boothbays, consisting of coastal Boothbay Harbor, East Boothbay, Linekin Neck, and Southport Island, and the inland town of Boothbay, are the most visited mid-coast towns, attracting hordes of vacationing families and flotillas of pleasure craft. Boothbay Harbor was an old fishing and boatbuilding town that now calls itself the Boating Capital of New England. Tourism peaks during the Windjammer Days in late June when vessels of all sorts glide into the harbor in full sail.

When you need a blast of pure ocean air, head down the Pemaquid Peninsula to its terminus—an immense, striated shelf of granite angled into the sea. Here rises the Pemaquid Point Light (1824), one of the most photographed and painted (and visited) structures in Maine. A jump east will take you to the St. George Peninsula, where the small towns of Tenants Harbor and Port Clyde preserve the spirit of old Maine: harbors filled with lobster boats and green-black spruces framing views of the outer islands. Port Clyde is the major port of departure for trips to Monhegan Island, where lobstermen coexist peacefully with artists.

Places to Go, Sights to See

The Bath Maine Maritime Museum (243 Washington St., tel. 207/443–1316) will fascinate all who have a taste for things nautical. The museum's collection includes ship models, journals, photographs, and other artifacts relating to Maine's three centuries of shipbuilding.

Boothbay Harbor is the region's boating and yachting center, with numerous boat tours and deep-sea fishing trips departing from the town's piers off Commercial Street.

Bowdoin College Museum of Art (Walker Art Bldg., tel. 207/725–8731) has a fine collection of Dutch and Italian Old Masters, Gilbert Stuart portraits, and Winslow Homer paintings.

Colonial Pemaquid Restoration (Rte. 1, tel. 207/677–2423). On the way to Pemaquid Point, stop at this important archaeological site dating to the mid-17th century. Excavations at Pemaquid Beach starting in the mid-1960s have turned up thousands of artifacts from the Colonial settlement and from even earlier Native American settlements, as well as the foundations and remains of an old customshouse, tavern, jail, forge, and houses.

L. L. Bean (Rte. 1, Freeport, tel. 800/341–4341). The store that Leon Leonwood Bean started in 1912 has grown into a retail empire, attracting some 3.5 million shoppers a year. Across the street from the main store, Bean has opened a factory outlet for second-quality and discontinued merchandise.

Montsweag Flea Market (tel. 207/443–2809). Between Bath and Wiscasset on Route 1 is a wonderful flea market that's open on weekends from mid-May to the end of October, and also on Wednesday and Friday from mid-July to mid-September, which sells antiques and collectibles—and kitchen sinks as well.

The Pemaquid Point Light (1824) stands atop a dramatic chunk of striated granite and commands a stunning view of the sea and islands. Although the coastal rock formations are less dramatic at the *Marshall Point* lighthouse near Port Clyde, the views are just as fine as at Pemaquid Point and the crowds far thinner.

Popham Beach State Park (Phippsburg, tel. 207/389–1335), at the end of Route 209 south of Bath, is one of the larger beaches in the mid-coast region, with 1½ miles of sand divided into three stretches. In addition to its sandy ocean beaches, the park has salt marshes, where wading birds congregate; extensive dunes; and a picnic area.

Reid State Park (Georgetown, tel. 207/371–2303), on Georgetown Island off Route 127, has a stretch of sand beach as well as tidal pools, rocky outcrops, a nature area, and picnic tables.

Restaurants

The Osprey (Robinhood Marina, Georgetown, tel. 207/371–2530) offers well-prepared new American fare on its glassed-in porch overlooking the marina. In South Freeport, the **Harraseeket Lunch** (Main St., tel. 207/865–4888) is a bare-bones lobster pound next to the town landing, serving lobsters and fried seafood.

Tourist Information

Bath Area Chamber of Commerce (45 Front St., Bath, ME 04530, tel. 207/443–9751); **Damariscotta Region Chamber of Commerce** (Box 13, Damariscotta, ME 04543, tel. 207/563–8340); **Brunswick Area Chamber of Commerce** (59 Pleasant St., Brunswick, ME 04011, tel. 207/725–8797); **Freeport Merchants Association** (Box 452, Freeport, ME 04032, tel. 207/865–1212); **Boothbay Harbor Region Chamber of Commerce** (Box 356, Boothbay Harbor, ME 04538, tel. 207/633–2353).

Reservations Services

B&B Down East, Ltd. (Box 547, Macomber Mill Rd., Eastbrook, ME 04634, tel. 207/565–3517); **Peg Tierney B&B of Maine** (16 Florence St., Portland, ME 04103, tel. 207/775–7808); **Pineapple Hospitality** (Box F821, New Bedford, MA 02742, tel. 508/990–1696).

The Craignair Inn

The Craignair is a place for those who love the bold, rough, unpretentious spirit of the Maine coast—those to whom Maine means invigorating blasts of salt spray rather than sleeping on Ralph Lauren sheets. Built in the 1930s as a boardinghouse for stonecutters and converted to an inn a decade later, the Craignair, like the East Wind Inn (*see* below), commands a quintessential Maine coast view of rocky shore and sheltered water worked by lobster boats, but its setting is even quieter and farther off the beaten track.

Innkeepers Terry and Norman Smith bought the three-story, gambrel-roof building in 1978 and happily traded the traffic and pollution of New York's Long Island for the freedom and beauty of Maine. They haven't looked back. "After all these years, I still smile when I step outside and look at this view," Terry notes with characteristic bubbliness.

She is an energetic grandmother, and the inn's decor reflects her passions for collecting, with lots of country clutter and books, with cut glass on display in the parlor, and with braided rugs, brass beds, and some rather dowdy old dressers in the bedrooms. It's a far cry from Camden's plush Norumbega or Kennebunkport's Captain Jefferds, which is just what its loyal guests like about the place. The sitting room on the second floor is a quiet spot for reading or for parents to relax while their children sleep down the hall.

In 1986 the Smiths converted an 1890s church into an annex, with eight rooms that are larger and more modern in feel than those in the main inn, but whose water views are more limited. Three of the upstairs church rooms have sliding glass doors opening onto decks; No. 28 is the choice room.

Guests take breakfast in the sunny, waterside dining room, decorated with Delft and Staffordshire plates. Fancy dinners (rabbit, duck, and seafood) are also served here.

Inn guests have the use of a small sandy beach down the road. Miles of quiet back roads are ideal for biking, and Monhegan Island beckons offshore for a long day trip out of nearby Port Clyde. Small pets are welcome.

Address: *Clark Island Rd., Spruce Head, ME 04859, tel. 207/594-7644.*
Accommodations: *13 double rooms and 2 singles in the inn share 6 baths; 8 double rooms with private baths in the annex.*
Amenities: *Restaurant.*
Rates: *\$65–\$90; full breakfast. AE, MC, V.*
Restrictions: *Closed Feb.*

The East Wind Inn & Meeting House

If you've read *The Country of the Pointed Firs,* Sarah Orne Jewett's charming sketches of coastal Maine, you may have an eerie sense of déjà vu as you drive the 10 miles down Route 131 into Tenants Harbor. The neat little white clapboard houses set in tangles of tall grass and beach roses, the narrow harbor from which the nearly black evergreens rise like sawteeth, the distant glimpse of islands and open water: All this is pretty much unchanged since Jewett wrote here at the turn of the century.

In the course of its 130 years set on a little knob of land overlooking the harbor and islands, the three-story white clapboard East Wind Inn has served as a sail loft and mason's hall. Today it's hard to imagine it as anything other than the perfect rustic inn, complete with wraparound porch. Innkeeper Tim Watts gave up his work as an accountant to buy the East Wind in 1974, and in his year-long renovation, he was careful to leave its innocence and simplicity very much intact.

Guests lodge either in the inn or the Meeting House, a converted ship captain's house, just up the hill. The inn is a bit closer to the water, and its front rooms command a view of sunrise over the islands. The bedrooms are furnished with a hodgepodge of simple Early American-style brass bedsteads and pine chests; oak and mahogany furnishings give the rooms of the Meeting House more of a Victorian air. All the rooms are appealingly plain, as is the inn's living room, with its baby grand piano, nautical charts, and comfortable, well-worn sofas.

From the East Wind, you can drive (or bike) to Port Clyde for a picnic at the Marshall Point lighthouse or a day trip to Monhegan, or head up to Rockland for an afternoon with the Wyeths at the Farnsworth art museum.

Address: *Box 149, Tenants Harbor, ME 04860, tel. 207/372–6366, fax 207/372–6320.*
Accommodations: *Inn: 1 double room with bath, 14 doubles share 4 baths, 1 suite; Meeting House: 8 double rooms with baths, 2 suites, 1 apartment.*
Amenities: *Restaurant, telephones in rooms, TV in suites, apartment, and living room, conference room; sailboat cruises and sailing seminars based at the premises.*
Rates: *$70–$130; Continental breakfast. AE, MC, V.*
Restrictions: *No pets.*

The Newcastle Inn

"The first time we stayed at an inn, we loved it," reminisces Chris Sprague (an office manager turned innkeeper) amid the family photos, Oriental rugs, plush red velvet, and brass ornaments of The Newcastle Inn's sunny parlor. "We both love to cook, and Ted [a former high school chemistry teacher] loves to putter and garden, so we thought we'd like to try having an inn of our own."

Six years later, the Spragues love what they do more than ever, and it really shows in the way they have transformed this small, mid-19th-century white clapboard house into one of Maine's friendliest, most impeccably run inns. Born hosts, the Spragues seem always to be around when you need to chat, get directions, or ask advice about sightseeing, yet they vanish discreetly when you prefer solitude. They also bring a certain creative flair to their new career, organizing bird-watching expeditions, canoe trips, and excursions to Monhegan Island for inn guests.

Guest rooms, though not large, are decorated carefully with old spool beds, toys, and sofas; the effect is of minimum clutter and maximum light and river views. On the second floor, No. 6, with midnight blue floral paper, is at the back of the house, which means both quiet and a generous river view.

The Spragues go all out for breakfast (a full meal that might include scrambled eggs with caviar in puff pastry, ricotta cheese pie, or a frittata), and the five-course prix fixe dinner (open to the public by reservation) makes a stay rewarding even if it rains the whole time.

Newcastle is a town with more charm than action; but the inn, set just off a picturesque winding road on a lawn that slopes down to the Damariscotta River, makes a convenient base for forays to Boothbay Harbor or Pemaquid Point, or a quiet afternoon of canoeing on the river. In the summer months, the inn's sun porch, with white wicker furniture and ice-cream-parlor chairs, makes a particularly appealing spot to contemplate the Damariscotta River and congratulate yourself for having found such a special place.

Address: *River Rd., Newcastle, ME 04553, tel. 207/563–5685.*
Accommodations: *15 double rooms with baths.*
Amenities: *Restaurant.*
Rates: *$100–$130; full breakfast, MAP available. MC, V.*
Restrictions: *No smoking, no pets.*

The Squire Tarbox Inn

As you drive the 8½ miles from Route 1, down Route 144, onto Westport Island, you may wonder if you made a wrong turn, for the signs of civilization peter out into lush rolling hills, woods, and a sprinkling of farmhouses. Then the reassuring champagne-yellow clapboard front of the Squire Tarbox looms into view, and you know just where you are: deep in the country at one of Maine's most serene inns.

"This is a really nourishing place," says innkeeper Karen Mitman with a soft smile, as she sits in a rocking chair, next to the fireplace, beside the grandfather clock. "People come here to reflect, to walk in the woods, to look at the birds." They also come to watch Karen and her husband, Bill, milk their goats and to sample their delicious goat cheese, served each night. For the Squire Tarbox is not only an inn, and on the National Register of Historic Places, but is a working farm, with a small herd of 16 goats, a horse, and a few donkeys.

Karen and Bill had hotel experience in Boston, but none as goat farmers, when they bought the inn in 1981. Yet somehow they seem to have been in the rambling Federal house forever. Some of it dates from 1763 and some from 1820, and among the downstairs public rooms are a rustic dining room, where dinner is served beneath old ships' beams, and a music room with a player piano.

Of the bedrooms, No. 1 in the main part of the house is choice—a huge room with king-size bed, braided rugs on pumpkin-pine floors, and an antique footlocker. The attached barn has four rooms, more rustic in feel and smaller than the inn rooms, but also more private. Number 11 is the best for privacy, with gray-green woodwork, more space than the other barn rooms, and a view over the pasture.

When you tire of strolling around the property and bird-watching from the deck, ask the Mitmans to direct you to the shops of Wiscasset, the Maritime Museum at Bath, the lobster pier and scenic backroads of Five Islands (good for biking), and the beach at Reid State Park.

Address: *Rte. 144 (RR 2, Box 620), Wiscasset, ME 04578, tel. 207/882–7693.*
Accommodations: *11 double rooms with baths.*
Amenities: *Restaurant, fireplaces in 4 rooms; rowboat, farm animals.*
Rates: *$70–$150; Continental breakfast, goat cheese in evening, MAP available. AE, D, MC, V.*
Restrictions: *Smoking only in barn sitting room, no cigars, no pets. Closed late Oct.–mid-May.*

The Bradley Inn

Within walking distance of the Pemaquid Point lighthouse and beach, the 1900 Bradley Inn began as a rooming house for summer rusticators and alternated between abandonment and operation as a B&B until its complete renovation in the early 1990s. Chuck and Merry Robinson purchased the inn in 1992, after managing a corporate retreat in Vermont; their golden retriever, Barney, has been greeting guests enthusiastically ever since.

Rooms are comfortable and uncluttered; ask for one of the cathedral-ceilinged, waterside rooms on the third floor, which offer breathtaking views of the sun setting over the water. Downstairs, the public spaces—a living room with a baby grand piano and a TV, pub, and dining room—are furnished with a mixture of antiques, country furniture, Oriental rugs, and nautical artifacts. In fine weather, you can eat on the large wraparound deck overlooking the gardens at the back of the inn.

Address: *Route 130, HC 61, 361 Pemaquid Point, New Harbor, ME 04454, tel. 207/677–2105, fax 207/677–3367.*
Accommodations: *12 double rooms with baths, 1 cottage.*
Amenities: *Restaurant, pub, cable TV and phones in rooms, croquet, bicycles, entertainment on weekends.*
Rates: *$95–$135; Continental breakfast. AE, MC, V.*
Restrictions: *Smoking permitted on first floor only.*

Brannon-Bunker Inn

A 5-mile drive south of Damariscotta down a pleasant country road brings you to the Brannon-Bunker. This true country inn occupies a taupe 1820s Cape Cod house, an attached barn, and a carriage house. The Hovances, who came from New Jersey with their three children in the mid-1980s, are antiques buffs who collect World War I memorabilia and Heisey glassware and gladly share their knowledge of the local shops. They have an antiques shop in the barn.

The guest rooms vary in size and are furnished to reflect different periods—Victorian, Empire, Colonial. Number 4, the nicest inn room, has a bird's-eye maple bed, braided rugs on green-painted floors, four big windows open to the surrounding greenery, and a glimpse of the Damariscotta River. The carriage house next door contains a three-room suite with a kitchen. Cribs are available. Pemaquid Point is an easy 10-mile bike ride away.

Address: *HCR 64, No. 045, Damariscotta, ME 04543, tel. 207/563–5941.*
Accommodations: *2 double rooms with baths, 3 doubles share 1 bath, 1 3-room housekeeping suite.*
Amenities: *TV in parlor, antiques shop.*
Rates: *$50–$75; Continental breakfast. AE, MC, V.*
Restrictions: *No smoking, no pets.*

The Briar Rose

Fred and Anita Palsgrove ran an antiques business outside Washington, DC before moving to Maine in 1986. The Briar Rose was an impulse buy they've never regretted. "We were meant to live here," Anita declares. It's easy to see why they fell in love with the place: The 3-story, mansard-roofed Briar Rose overlooks the harbor and village of Round Pond, a sleepy enclave of artists, craftspeople, fishermen, and shipbuilders, a short drive or bike ride from Pemaquid Point.

Two large guest rooms and one suite, each with a view of the harbor, are light and airy, decorated with period antiques and country collectibles, braided and rag rugs, and floral wallpaper. Added touches include Anita's display boxes of women's sewing whimsies, Dutch whimsies, and Easter things, as well as a framed lace collection. An old-fashioned country breakfast is served in the dining room, which also overlooks the harbor.

Address: *Box 27, Route 32, Round Pond, ME 04564, tel. 207/529–5478.*
Accommodations: *2 double rooms share bath, 1 suite.*
Amenities: *Clock-radios in rooms; antiques and country collectibles shop.*
Rates: *$58–$70; full breakfast. No credit cards.*
Restrictions: *No smoking; no pets. By reservation only in winter.*

Broad Bay Inn and Gallery

Waldoboro, about midway between Damariscotta and Rockland on the Medomak River, is decidedly off the main tourist routes, which means that its Main Street remains serenely sleepy all summer long. If you decide to make the detour, you might want to spend the night at this snug little bed-and-breakfast in a fine white clapboard house with pale gray shutters and pine trees on the lawn.

Jim and Libby Hopkins are commercial artists from Princeton, New Jersey, who vacationed in Maine, liked it, and decided to move here year-round when they retired. They have done a fine job of furnishing the inn with antiques but have kept the feel simple and uncluttered. They sell watercolors, prints, and local pottery and crafts in the gallery in the barn, and hold exhibits and seminars in summer. Sarah's Canopy Room is the best in the house, a corner room with four windows, a huge French armoire, a canopy bed with a white bedspread, gauzy swag curtains, and a deep-rose color scheme. The gourmet breakfast features baked eggs, eggs Benedict, and fruit compote.

Address: *Main St., Waldoboro, ME 04572, tel. 207/832–6668.*
Accommodations: *5 double rooms share 3 baths.*
Amenities: *Cable TV in common room, terry bathrobes.*
Rates: *$45–$70; full breakfast, tea, and sherry. MC, V.*
Restrictions: *No smoking indoors, no pets. 2-night minimum in Aug.*

Fairhaven Inn

A cedar-shingled 1790 house set on 27 acres of rolling meadows, white-pine and birch woods, and lawns sloping down to the Kennebec River, the Fairhaven would be special for its location alone. Sallie and George Pollard fell in love with the inn when they came here as guests in 1987, and they did not hesitate when they learned it was for sale.

The handsome guest rooms are furnished with handmade quilts and mahogany pineapple four-poster beds, and a horsehair sofa, old photos, and new watercolors decorate the parlor. The Cherry and Apple rooms face the river and get the most light. The Pollards serve a 3-course breakfast consisting of hot cereal, fruit, and such entrées as pear soup with blintzes or oatmeal pancakes with cranberry sauce.

In winter you can cross-country ski out the inn's door, and the lawns are pleasant for strolling in summer. The Bath Country Club is nearby, the Swan Island State Park Wildlife Area a short drive away, and the towns of Freeport and Bath are within easy striking distance. The Fairhaven offers excellent value.

Address: *N. Bath Rd., Bath, ME 04530, tel. 207/443–4391.*
Accommodations: *5 double rooms with baths, 2 doubles share 1 bath.*
Amenities: *Tavern; badminton, cross-country ski trail.*
Rates: *$60–$80; full breakfast. MC, V.*
Restrictions: *No smoking.*

The Isaac Randall House

Freeport, dominated by the L. L. Bean empire and scores of upscale outlets, is a surprising place to find country inns. The Isaac Randall was the first and remains the most inviting.

Situated on a pleasant 5-acre lot just outside town, the circa-1829 inn has classic details of hip roof and twin chimneys. Inside you'll find a country kitchen, where breakfast is served family style (blueberry pancakes and banana-lemon bread stand out), and bedrooms with quilts, pumpkin-pine floors, and a mix of Victorian antiques and country pieces. The Rose Room, with a brass bed, fan quilt, and ornate mirror, has a superior corner location, as does the Iris Room, off the kitchen.

Nova Scotians Shannon and Cynba Ryan purchased the inn in 1991, and they bring to innkeeping a quiet, warm welcome, which extends even to pets.

Address: *Independence Dr., Freeport, ME 04032, tel. 207/865–9295.*
Accommodations: *6 double rooms with baths, 2 doubles share 1 bath.*
Amenities: *Air-conditioning, small kitchen and fridge for use of guests, cable TV in sitting room.*
Rates: *$80–$115; full breakfast. MC, V.*
Restrictions: *No smoking.*

Mill Pond Inn

On a residential street in Damariscotta Mills, young innkeepers Sherry and Bobby Whear greet you enthusiastically at the Mill Pond Inn. Sherry, the romantic, reminisces about their wedding, amid lilacs on the inn's deck, just before they opened the inn. Bobby, the boating and birding enthusiast, presses a pair of binoculars on you, to see the loons, and dashes off for photos of the bald eagles that nest nearby. Clearly, this couple is mad for Maine, for their rambling gray-shingled house, and for the mill pond and birds at their back door.

Sherry's penchant for the romantic shows up in the softly feminine decor, with quilts, lots of fluffy pillows, floral-stripe wallpapers, and fresh flowers in all the rooms. The Eagle's Nest, on the third floor, has the best water view, dark wood furniture, original beams, and a rather low ceiling. If you're game, Bobby will take you fishing at dawn in his restored 53-year-old Lyman Lapstrake.

Address: *RFD 1, Box 245, Newcastle, ME 04553, tel. 207/563-8014.*
Accommodations: *7 double rooms with baths.*
Amenities: *Cable TV/VCR in games room; private beach, boats, canoes, bicycles, horseshoes, skating on pond.*
Rates: *$55–$65; full breakfast. No credit cards.*
Restrictions: *Smoking on ground floor only, no pets.*

181 Main Street

Partners Ed Hassett and David Cates left New York City in 1987 to try their hand at innkeeping. They brought their skills in design, furniture refinishing, and gardening to the enormous task of converting a derelict 1840s Greek Revival cape house into this snug and inviting inn, a few blocks down Main Street from L. L. Bean.

The cozy parlors, on either side of the delicately wrought central staircase, are equipped with games and books, and furnished with a Chippendale love seat, American primitive portraits, and a collection of Anderson pottery. The bedrooms, some of which are a bit small, have a pleasingly uncluttered mix of Victorian, country, and Empire pieces, including tiger-maple bedsteads, marble-top dressers, and some beds with fishnet canopies.

The rooms are quiet, despite the urban location, and the large backyard and pool are a delight after a hot day of shopping. Ed and David are on hand in the evening to chat with guests and help them plan activities, ranging from whale-watching cruises to a day at Popham Beach.

Address: *181 Main St., Freeport, ME 04032, tel. 207/865-1226.*
Accommodations: *7 double rooms with baths.*
Amenities: *Cable TV in parlor; swimming pool.*
Rates: *$95; full breakfast. MC, V.*
Restrictions: *No smoking, no pets.*

Around the Penobscot Bay
Rockland to Blue Hill

To purists, the Maine coast begins at Penobscot Bay: Everything to the south and west is part of "vacationland," where fishhouses have been converted to T-shirt shops and sand beaches invite un-Maine-like lounging and easy entry into water that is warm enough to swim in. But at Penobscot Bay, Maine's largest and, to many minds, most beautiful bay, land and seascape change. The vistas over the water are wider and bluer. The shore is a chaos of broken granite boulders, cobblestones, and gravel, punctuated by so-called pocket sand beaches, which look small enough to scoop up in a child's shovel. The water is numbingly, inexorably cold. Presiding over the bay are the rounded eminences of the Camden Hills, looming green over Camden's fashionable waterfront and turning gradually bluer and fainter as one moves farther away.

Chic, sleek Camden is the most popular destination on Penobscot Bay, and it also offers the most amenities: inns ranging from bucolic to sumptuous, musical and theatrical entertainment, scores of gift shops, skiing in winter, and in summer, of course, the world-famous fleet of windjammers, whose comings and goings send ripples of excitement through the harbor. Less frivolous, but perhaps more representative of the hard-working spirit of the bay, is Belfast, a jump up the coast, which has a couple of blocks of handsome brick buildings downtown and back streets sprinkled with some very fine Greek Revival houses.

Searsport, another jump northeast, bills itself as the antiques capital of Maine. Bargains may be hard to come by in the shops that line Route 1 in Searsport, but in the summer months, vast flea markets spring up, with merchandise ranging from old china to new hardware.

Route 1, which follows the west side of the bay, can get a little frenzied during the summer. Far more serene are the back roads that wind through the juts and jags of land on the bay's east side. Routes 175 and 166 take you through gently wooded landscape with increasingly stunning water views, until the roads terminate at historic Castine, a gem of a small town. Here you should give yourself a few hours (or days) to wander amid the white clapboard houses and perfect churches, to soak up the atmosphere at the picturesque harbor, or to wander down to Dyce's Head lighthouse for vistas out to islands, water, and back to the Camden Hills. Blue Hill, about 15 miles east of Castine, is another splendid coastal town made for leisurely strolls, and it also has the region's greatest concentration of pottery workshops, art galleries, and craft galleries. The back roads between Brooklin and Blue Hill offer some of the best biking in coastal Maine.

Though Penobscot Bay itself may be too painfully cold to plunge into, it is wonderfully soothing to gaze out upon from the villages, woods, and rock peninsulas beside it.

Places to Go, Sights to See

Camden Harbor. If you turn around, you'll see the famous Camden Hills rising right over the town. If you face forward, you'll have a terrific view of Penobscot Bay, the islands, and the windjammers that put this town on the nautical map. If you wish to hike in the hills, drive north on Route 1 to the Camden Hills State Park (tel. 207/236–3109).

Castine and Blue Hill. These are quintessential small New England towns of white clapboard houses, white steepled churches, ancient elms and maples, and dreamy water views. Blue Hill has more crafts shops (pottery is a local specialty); Castine has a greater range of architectural styles (Main and Perkins streets have the finest houses), a prettier harbor, and an astoundingly long, bloody, and varied history, with painted signs posted around town recounting most of it.

Maine State Ferry Terminal. Hop a ferry at the Rockland Terminal on Route 1 for a day trip or longer sojourn to the islands of Vinalhaven, North Haven, or the tiny outer island of Matinicus.

The Owl's Head Transportation Museum (Rte. 3, Owl's Head, tel. 207/594–4418) has an extensive collection of antique aircraft, cars, and engines. On weekends, some of the planes are flown by volunteers, and beginning in May biweekly events are held: car auctions, rallies, air shows, and fly-ins.

Penobscot Marine Museum (Church St., Searsport, tel. 207/548–2529). The seven buildings display sea captains' portraits, lots of scrimshaw, navigational instruments, and treasures from the China trade. Save it for a rainy or foggy day.

William A. Farnsworth Library and Art Museum (19 Elm St., tel. 207/596–6457). The rather grimy commercial town of Rockland has one of the finest art museums in Maine, with a strong collection of landscapes and portraits by Andrew, Jamie, and N. C. Wyeth; Winslow Homer; Rockwell Kent; and Louise Nevelson (who was born in Rockland).

Beaches

Lincolnville Beach, north of Camden, has a small strip of sand on Penobscot Bay and, unfortunately, right on Route 1 as well. **Laite Memorial Park and Beach** offers bay swimming off Camden's upper Bayview Street. Castine has a small sandy beach on Penobscot Bay, about ¼ mile west of the junction of Routes 166 and 166A.

Restaurants

Jonathan's (Main St., tel. 207/374–5226), in Blue Hill, is a romantic, rustic place with a nautical touch that serves imaginative American cuisine—ask for the chicken breast in fennel sauce with peppers, garlic, rosemary, and shallots. In Rockport, the **Sail Loft** (tel. 207/236–2330), with unsurpassed views of the town's quaint harbor, offers a varied menu emphasizing seafood and is a popular Sunday brunch spot.

Tourist Information

Rockland Area Chamber of Commerce (Public Landing, Box 508, Rockland, ME 04841, tel. 207/596–0376); **Rockport–Camden–Lincolnville Chamber of Commerce** (Box 919, Camden, ME 04843, tel. 207/236–4404); **Searsport Chamber of Commerce** (Searsport, ME 04974, tel. 207/548–6510); **Blue Hill Chamber of Commerce** (Box 520, Blue Hill, ME 04614, no phone); **Castine Town Office** (tel. 207/326–4502).

Reservations Services

B&B Down East, Ltd. (Box 547, Macomber Mill Rd., Eastbrook, ME 04634, tel. 207/565–3517); **Peg Tierney B&B of Maine** (16 Florence St., Portland, ME 04103, tel. 207/775–7808).

The Castine Inn

We're the keepers of the flame," says Mark Hodesh of his role as innkeeper of the Castine Inn, a historic inn in a historic (and literary) seacoast town. The late Mary McCarthy, who summered up the street, used to drop in for dinner. The poet Philip Booth, McCarthy's next-door neighbor, told the Hodeshes that his grandfather stayed at the Castine Inn the night before he was married. Old Castine society wanted the inn to maintain the right style and tone—"Not high antique," as Mark puts it, "but comfortable, traditional Maine." He and his wife, the artist Margaret Parker, who come to Castine via Ann Arbor and New York City, have succeeded admirably.

The stately yellow-clapboard, 100-year-old inn mixes Victorian antiques, sturdily traditional new furniture, and paintings done by Margaret. The sitting room, in crimson velvet and old leather with well-worn Oriental rugs and books, is the kind of place in which you can let out a huge sigh and relax. Off the lobby there is a snug little pub, the perfect spot for an evening rendezvous.

Newer touches include Margaret's impressive mural of the town and harbor—which wraps around the spacious dining room—the big porch added to the east side of the inn, and the formal garden Margaret designed, with its arched bridge, roses, benches, gravel path, and arbor, where concerts are held in the summer.

Your rooms might have a dark-wood pineapple four-poster bed, white upholstered easy chairs, and oil paintings. Spacious Room 1 on the second floor offers a glimpse of the harbor and has a superior corner location. The third-floor rooms are the biggest and command the finest views. From one side you see the harbor over the back garden, from the other you see the town's picturesque Main Street.

Castine is a perfect New England small town that invites you to linger, stroll along Main Street down to the harbor, or out along Perkins Street, past Federal, Greek Revival, and shingle-style houses to the lighthouse. The sea air and exercise will make the return to the Castine Inn and its hearty dinners all the more welcome.

Address: *Main St., Castine, ME 04421, tel. 207/326-4365.*
Accommodations: *17 double rooms with private baths, 3 suites.*
Amenities: *Restaurant, pub.*
Rates: *$75–$110; full breakfast. MC, V.*
Restrictions: *No smoking in dining room, no pets. 2-night minimum in July and Aug., closed Nov.–Apr.*

The John Peters Inn

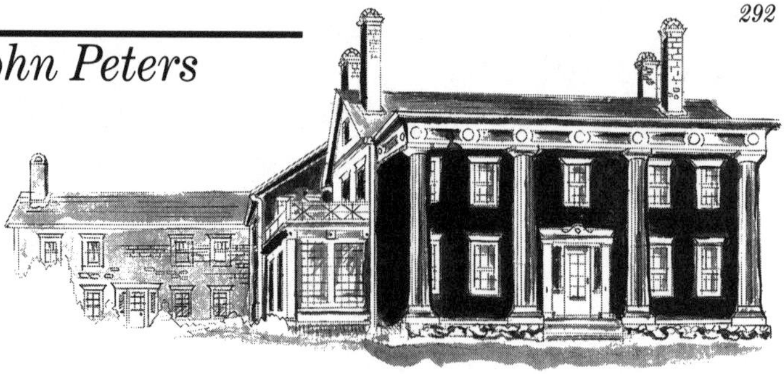

When you turn down the narrow lane and catch your first glimpse of this country inn, you may wonder whether your car has slipped into some bizarre wrinkle in the space–time continuum—for the John Peters, with its four colossal Doric pillars and open views over green fields to the head of Blue Hill Bay, looks like something out of Tidewater Virginia.

On closer inspection, you will see that it is actually a classic brick Federal mansion to which the columned porch was added in the 1930s. No matter. The John Peters is unsurpassed for the privacy of its location, the good taste in the decor of its guest rooms, and the whimsical informality of innkeepers Barbara and Rick Seeger. Rick gladly left an engineering job in Massachusetts for what the Seegers describe as their "fantasy utopia" just outside the town of Blue Hill.

More often than not, you will be greeted excitedly by the resident Welsh terrier, DOC (for disobedient canine), before Barbara or Rick escorts you into the living room with its two fireplaces, books and games, baby grand piano, and Empire furniture. Oriental rugs, which the Seegers collect, are everywhere. Huge breakfasts in the light and airy dining rooms include the famous lobster omelet, served complete with lobster-claw shells as decoration. After breakfast, you can lope down the hill to your boat or stroll into Blue Hill for a morning of browsing in the pottery and crafts shops.

The Surry Room, one of the best rooms (all are nice), has a king-size bed, a fireplace, curly-maple chest, gilt mirror, and six windows with delicate lace curtains. The Honeymoon Suite is immense, with wet bar and minifridge, white furniture, deck, and a view of Blue Hill Bay. If you choose, you can have breakfast served to you in bed in this room. The large rooms in the carriage house, a stone's throw down the hill from the inn, have been completely renovated, with dining areas, cherry floors and woodwork, wicker and brass accents, and a modern feel. Four have decks, kitchens, and fireplaces, a real plus here. But nothing at the John Peters is a minus, except having to say goodbye.

Address: *Peters Point, Box 916, Blue Hill, ME 04614, tel. 207/374–2116.*
Accommodations: *7 double rooms with baths, 1 suite in inn; 6 doubles with baths in carriage house.*
Amenities: *Phones in 4 carriage-house rooms, fireplaces in 9 bedrooms; swimming pool, canoe, sailboats, pond, 2 moorings.*
Rates: *$85–$135; full breakfast. MC, V.*
Restrictions: *No pets. Closed Nov.–Apr.*

Norumbega

This sumptuous century-old turreted stone castle looks as if it blew in from some craggy corner of Bavaria. Though you may find the style a touch bogus and overpowering amid Camden's elegant clapboard houses, you may not be able to argue with the superb views of the bay and the luxurious splendor (for a price, of course) of the accommodations.

Designed and built in 1886 by Joseph B. Stearns, the inventor of duplex telegraphy, Norumbega was obviously the fulfillment of a deep-seated imperial fantasy. Current owner Murray Keatinge, who bought the inn in 1987, has updated the fantasy to a kind of Ralph Laurenesque environment of infinite leisure and seemingly old wealth. Kathleen Keefe manages the inn for Mr. Keatinge, who lives in California.

The public rooms have gleaming parquet floors, oak and mahogany paneling, richly carved wood mantels over the four first-floor fireplaces, gilt mirrors, and Empire furnishings. You feel as if you should dress in white linen or silk and languish in elegant repose over afternoon wine and cheese.

Sandringham (the rooms are named, appropriately, after castles and palaces), the former master bedroom, is in the turret and, though it lacks a water view, it is huge, airy, and ducal, with dark green wallpaper, a fireplace, and polished hardwood floors. At the back of the house, several decks and balconies overlook the garden, the gazebo, and the bay. The views from rear-facing rooms keep getting better as you ascend: The penthouse suite, with a small deck, fireplace, private bar, fabrics in tropical motifs, and a skylight in the bedroom, is nothing short of celestial.

Such little touches as wine and cheese in the afternoon, a small breakfast served in the guest rooms (or full breakfast served family style in the formal dining room), and beds turned down in the evening complete the luxury of staying here.

Address: *61 High St., Camden, ME 04843, tel. 207/236–4646.*
Accommodations: *10 rooms with baths, 2 suites.*
Amenities: *Air-conditioning in penthouse, cable TV and pool table in games room, phones in rooms, 4 rooms with fireplaces, cable TV in some rooms; croquet, tennis privileges, murder mystery weekends Feb.–Mar.*
Rates: *$195–$325, penthouse $425; full breakfast and afternoon tea. AE, MC, V.*
Restrictions: *No pets.*

Whitehall Inn

Camden's best-known inn started life in 1834 as a ship captain's home and sprouted another wing around the turn of the century when it began receiving guests. You will certainly feel the long history of civilized comfort as you cross the wide, flower-bright porch and walk through the decorous lobby on the soft, time-faded Oriental rugs. Penobscot Bay opens up across the road, and the inn's location midway between the shops, restaurants, and windjammers of Camden and the trails of Camden Hills State Park is ideal.

The Whitehall is dear to the hearts of literary folk, for it was here that Edna St. Vincent Millay, a Rockland girl, came in the summer of 1912 to recite her poem "Renascence" and launch her literary career. The Millay Room, just off the main lobby, contains Millay memorabilia.

Ed Dewing, a former Boston advertising executive, and Jean, his late wife, fell in love with the Whitehall in 1971; since then the inn has been very much a family affair, with son J.C. and his wife Wendy, brother Chip, sister Heidi and her husband Dane, and uncle Don Chambers all active in the day-to-day management of the inn.

The inn's loyal adherents cherish its high-toned, literary aura and the fact that everything looks the same year after year, down to the old-fashioned phones connected to an ancient switchboard with plugs, but newcomers may be a bit disappointed with the smallish, sparsely furnished rooms, with their old dark-wood bedsteads, Currier and Ives prints, clawfoot bathtubs, and not much else in the way of style.

Though the Whitehall has a countrified stateliness, you'll hear the traffic on Route 1 unless you get a garden-facing room in the rear wing. The rooms in the Victorian annexes, the Maine and the Wicker house across Route 1, offer more seclusion and king-size beds, and their quiet back rooms face the water. The dining room is open for dinner and breakfast.

Address: *Box 558, Camden, ME 04843, tel. 207/236–3391.*
Accommodations: *35 double rooms with baths, 4 doubles share 2 baths, 5 singles with baths.*
Amenities: *Restaurant; phones in bedrooms; cable TV in public room, 2 large and 4 small meeting rooms; 1 all-weather tennis court, shuffleboard, golf privileges.*
Rates: *$135–$170; full breakfast and dinner (B&B rates available). AE, MC, V.*
Restrictions: *No pets. Closed mid-Oct.–mid-May.*

Blue Hill Inn

Situated on Union Street amid other old white clapboard buildings, this dignified, time-burnished Federal inn is perfectly in keeping with the spirit of its location: subdued, refined, but not overly fussy.

Owners Mary and Don Hartley are a soft-spoken, youngish couple who decided to give innkeeping a try after working as psychologists in Ohio. They have carefully kept intact the inn's pumpkin-pine and painted floors and its fireplaces, and have furnished the guest rooms with a hodgepodge of Empire and early Victorian pieces, including marbletop walnut dressers, Oriental rugs, and wing chairs. The house provides hors d'oeuvres at a nightly reception in the parlor or in the perennial garden during fine weather, and guests are served elaborate six-course dinners in the rather plain dining room.

Address: *Box 403, Blue Hill, ME 04614, tel. 207/374–2844.*
Accommodations: *11 double rooms with baths.*
Amenities: *Air-conditioning on third floor, fireplaces in 5 rooms.*
Rates: *$140–$160; full breakfast and hors d'oeuvres, MAP also available. AE, MC, V.*
Restrictions: *No smoking, no pets. 2-night minimum on weekends July–Oct.*

The Camden Maine Stay

The Greek Revival Camden Maine Stay (no relation to the Maine Stay in Kennebunkport) sits among other National Historic Register homes, just a few minutes' walk from the center of Camden.

Native Mainer Captain Peter Smith, an ex–U.S. Navy pilot, his wife, Donny, and her twin sister, Diana Robson, have furnished the house with antiques, collectibles, and Oriental rugs, many acquired during Peter's 15 years overseas. The quietest rooms are at the back of the house, away from Route 1. Spacious No. 8 has a private patio, a wood stove, and a large window seat; the deep-blue wallpaper in Room No. 5 on the second floor sets off the white wicker chairs and the white eyelet comforter on the bed.

Peter's attention to detail includes providing guests with complete information—itineraries, mapped-out routes, and dining and lodging recommendations—on what to do in the Camden area, throughout the state, and New England.

Address: *22 High St. (U.S. Route 1), Camden, ME 04843, tel. 207/236–9636.*
Accommodations: *3 double rooms with baths, 5 doubles share 4 baths.*
Amenities: *Cable TV and VCR with movies in common room, portable telephone.*
Rates: *$80–$110; full breakfast. MC, V.*
Restrictions: *No smoking, no pets.*

Breezemere Farm

South Brooksville is really the sticks, a place of country roads, spruce woods, wildflowers, berries, and glimpses of the water. Breezemere Farm, a 60-acre property on Orcutt Harbor, gives you the chance to experience this out-of-the-way serenity in simple comfort.

Innkeepers Joe and Linda Forest acquired the farm and the circa-1850 farmhouse inn in 1990, after selling their vineyard in Sonoma, California. Linda brings her experience in renovating old houses to Breezemere, where she has done over the rooms, keeping the country-antique decor but adding carpets and sprucing up the wallpapers. Seven rustic cottages dating from the 1930s and '40s are scattered around the grounds. They each have one or two bedrooms, Franklin fireplaces, kitchen, and porches. Meals are served in the lodge, which has a stone fireplace and a screened porch.

Address: *Box 290, South Brooksville, ME 04617, tel. 207/326–8628 or 800/448–4700.*
Accommodations: *2 double rooms with baths, 5 doubles share 4 baths, 7 housekeeping cottages.*
Amenities: *Lodge with piano and fireplace; hiking trails, bikes, badminton, rowboats.*
Rates: *$75–$95; full breakfast. MC, V.*
Restrictions: *No smoking in the inn, no pets. Closed mid-Oct.–mid-May.*

Edgecombe-Coles House

The Edgecombe-Coles is a plush, beautifully decorated bed-and-breakfast on the residential northern edge of Camden. The advantage here is that the rambling white clapboard house (whose various sections span the late 18th to the late 19th century) is set well back from Route 1 at the top of an open grassy rise, with views of Penobscot Bay.

Terry and Louise Price, who hail from San Francisco, bought the house in 1984 after vacationing in Maine one bright, crisp autumn. Their passion for antiques is evident in the velvet sofa and oil paintings in the living room, and their excellent design sense is shown to best advantage in the superb Sea Star room, with blue patterned bedding, a cream rug, a picture window looking out on the bay, and a fireplace. Breakfast is served on the front porch when weather permits.

Address: *64 High St., HCR 60, Box 3010, Camden, ME 04843, tel. 207/236–2336.*
Accommodations: *6 double rooms with baths.*
Amenities: *Cable TV in den (in-room TV available); cross-country ski trails.*
Rates: *$110–$170; full breakfast. AE, D, MC, V.*
Restrictions: *No smoking in public rooms, no pets. 2-day minimum July–Aug.*

Homeport Inn

Searsport is one of the antiques centers of Maine, and the Homeport Inn provides an opulent Victorian environment that puts you in the mood to rummage through beautiful old things. Route 1 traffic roars by just beyond the front garden (complete with pseudo-classical statuary), but the inn is so solid and stately it won't bother you.

This 1861 ship captain's house is the home of Dr. and Mrs. George Johnson (and their intriguing cat Casper and dog Tina), a house filled with family heirlooms and an air of privacy and formality. Ceilings are immensely high, the public rooms sparkle with polished hardwood, crystal candelabra, and gilt, and the guest rooms are large, some with canopy beds and fleur-de-lis wallpaper. The back rooms downstairs have private decks, good light, and views of the bay. The breakfast, served on the inviting glass porch, will give you a good start for a morning at local shops, flea markets, or the Penobscot Maine Museum, just half a mile away.

Address: *Rte. 1, E. Main St., Searsport, ME 04974, tel. 207/548–2259.*
Accommodations: *6 double rooms with baths, 4 doubles share 1 bath.*
Amenities: *Cable TV in living room, 3 rooms open to deck; croquet, badminton.*
Rates: *$55–$75; full breakfast. AE, D, MC, V.*
Restrictions: *Smoking limited, no pets.*

Londonderry Inn

Tourists and second-home owners who have wearied of the crowds and high prices of Camden are starting to discover Belfast, with its graceful brick Victorian buildings downtown and Greek Revival ship captains' homes tucked away on back streets. The Londonderry Inn, a mile out of Belfast in a country setting of fields and woods, is within easy striking distance of both Camden and Searsport.

The Westbrook family purchased the inn in 1991, choosing to relocate from Indonesia, after visiting the area on a holiday. Debbie runs the inn with the help of her daughter Mandy.

The restored 1803 white Georgian farmhouse, with a bright herb garden out front, offers homey, spotless accommodations at reasonable prices. The public rooms include a games room with a piano and a sitting room with a TV, and the large, airy bedrooms have wide-plank pine floors and eclectic country-farmhouse furniture.

Address: *Star Rte. 80, Box 3, Belfast, ME 04915, tel. 207/338–3988.*
Accommodations: *5 double rooms share 2 baths.*
Amenities: *TV in parlor.*
Rates: *$45–$50; full breakfast. MC, V.*
Restrictions: *Smoking limited, no pets.*

The Lookout

This old-fashioned inn and restaurant has been in the hands of the Flye family for more than 100 years, and you can see why they held onto it: The high, stately white clapboard building sits all by itself at the end of a country road in a huge field at the tip of Flye Point, with a superb view of the water and the mountains of Mount Desert Island rising in the distance.

Rooms are homey and rustic, furnished with Maine country antiques original to the house and newer matching pieces. The floors do have a tendency to slope, and a century of damp has left a certain mustiness behind.

On the property also are six house-keeping cottages of various sizes, from one room with a loft to four bedrooms, all with ocean views, kitchenettes, and wood stoves.

The dining room, which overlooks an organic garden and meadows rolling down to the sea, is a romantic spot for dinner, and there's a lobster cookout every Wednesday.

Address: *North Brooklin, ME 04661, tel. 207/359–2188.*
Accommodations: *6 double rooms share 2 baths, 6 housekeeping cottages.*
Amenities: *Restaurant.*
Rates: *$70–$90, cottages $390–$800 per week; full breakfast. MC, V.*
Restrictions: *No pets in inn. Cottages rented by the week, closed mid-Oct.–Memorial Day.*

The Pentagoet

The pale yellow Pentagoet nods at the Castine Inn across Main Street, the former embracing more of the soft Victorian frills that complement its rambling, turreted exterior, the latter a bit more restrained and traditionally down east in its decor. When Lindsey and Virginia Miller, Arkansas natives who had worked as a doctor and nurse, bought the Pentagoet in 1985, they embarked on an extensive renovation program, and now all the rooms have private baths, the dining room is bigger, and the porch wraps around three sides of the inn.

The guest rooms have hooked rugs, lace curtains, and a mix of antiques, in keeping with the Pentagoet's Victorian character. The turret rooms are the most romantic. The Millers also own the 18th-century house next door at 10 Perkins Street, whose six additional rooms have colonial decor. Each night at a reception before the elaborate formal dinners, the house provides soft drinks and hors d'oeuvres.

Address: *Main St. at Perkins St., Castine, ME 04421, tel. 207/326–8616.*
Accommodations: *15 double rooms with baths, 1 suite.*
Amenities: *Restaurant, fireplace in suite.*
Rates: *$154–$174; full breakfast and dinner. MC, V.*
Restrictions: *No smoking, no pets. 2-night minimum holiday and event weekends; closed Nov.–Apr.*

Windward House

Camden has a slew of bed-and-breakfasts lining Route 1 just east of town, but this one is choice. Situated on a large plot and shaded by an ancient birch tree, the 1854 Greek Revival shipbuilder's house has good-size bedrooms furnished with canopy beds, cherry highboys, and curly-maple bedsteads, and such up-to-date touches as carpeted bathrooms and lamps placed perfectly for reading in bed. Mary and Jon Davis moved here from New Jersey in the mid-1980s—she had been a nurse; he had just retired from an executive position with AT&T—and they are clearly having a ball keeping the Windward House trimmed, upholstered, and polished.

The Rose Room, on the second floor, is the prize bedroom, with a soft, feminine feel imparted by the rosy curtains and Queen Anne claw-foot dresser. The Mount Battie Room, on the third floor, has a spool bed, patchwork quilt, and mountain view. If you get up early, you can take morning coffee in the inviting wicker room while you wait for the full gourmet breakfast (quiches, apple puff pancakes, peaches-and-cream French toast).

Address: *6 High St., Camden, ME 04843, tel. 207/236–9656.*
Accommodations: *7 double rooms with baths, 1 suite apt.*
Amenities: *TV in the library.*
Rates: *$85–$125; full breakfast. AE, MC, V.*
Restrictions: *Smoking only on deck, no pets.*

Down East
Deer Isle and Mount Desert Island

Deer Isle and Mount Desert Island, Maine's two largest islands, are a study in contrasts. Separated by only a little more than 10 miles of chilly water, they seem like worlds apart both in their basic geology and in the experiences they offer visitors. The slow rolling terrain typical of Deer Isle—and much of the Maine seaboard—makes an abrupt rise on Mount Desert into hump-backed peaks, with Cadillac Mountain the highest spot on the East Coast.

Deer Isle's relative isolation from the main flow of tourist traffic along Route 1 has kept the island fairly pristine: Stonington, its largest settlement, remains very much a rough-around-the-edges fishing village, and, away from the rocky shore, the island's gentle landscape is dotted with old farmhouses, hayfields growing up in spruce, and a few low-key crafts shops and galleries.

Mount Desert has been repeatedly and ecstatically discovered by tourists. Its spectacular landforms, dramatic coastline (including the only fjord on the East Coast), and deep-water harbors attracted wealthy summer visitors as far back as the mid-19th century. Early in the 20th century, much of the finest land and coast on the island was enshrined as Acadia National Park, and today the 33,000-acre park lures some 4.3 million visitors annually, making it the nation's second most popular.

Not surprisingly, the hordes of tourists have left their mark on the landscape. Bar Harbor, the upper-class 19th-century resort turned 20th-century tourist town, which services the national park, fairly swarms with motels, gift shops, restaurants, and places to buy upscale sportswear.

However, with a little extra effort, one can still enjoy the granite headlands, freshwater lakes, hiking trails, and wildflower-choked meadows of Acadia in relative peace. On the quieter west side of the island, in the villages of Somesville, Southwest Harbor, and Bass Harbor, the working boats of lobstermen bob alongside yachts. The offshore islands, including Swans Island and the Cranberries, preserve environments where traffic jams are unknown and where the silence of a summer day is interrupted only by the putt-putt of a lobster boat. And even the island's east side, where the Park Loop Road hugs the shore, empties considerably in the off-season. Natives claim that October is the best month of all to visit.

But on Deer Isle, with its country lanes, three-shop villages with such names as Sunshine and Sunset, pink granite shore, and tidal coves, it always feels like off-season.

Places to Go, Sights to See

Acadia National Park. For a quick introduction to the park, stop off at the Hulls Cove visitor center for brochures and maps, and then take the Park Loop Road. You'll pass the immense piles of granite rubble on the east shore; dramatic Otter Cliffs, with ocean views to the horizon; Jordan Pond, ringed by mountains; and the entrance to the road up 1,530-foot Cadillac Mountain. Consuming popovers on the lawn of the Jordan Pond House restaurant is an island tradition.

Haystack Mountain School of Crafts (Deer Isle, tel. 207/348–2306). A short drive from Deer Isle Village brings you to this renowned crafts school in a striking modern building on the shore designed by Edward Larrabee Barnes. The school's extensive grounds include a long stretch of pink granite coastline, where you can pick your way among the boulders for a contemplative hike or birding expedition.

Isle au Haut. From Stonington, you can take a passenger ferry for Isle au Haut (for information, tel. 207/367–5193), more than half of which is part of Acadia National Park. Far less developed and more remote than the main section of the park on Mount Desert, Isle au Haut offers a true escape into the wilds of cobble beaches, hushed birch and spruce woods, and 17½ miles of trails that clamber over the island's high central spine. Camping, by advance reservation (write Acadia National Park, Box 177, Bar Harbor, ME 04609), is available in lean-tos at Duck Harbor. The island's sole inn is about halfway between the park and the small village of Isle au Haut.

Somes Sound. The only fjord on the East Coast takes a long, deep bite out of Mount Desert Island, with mountains rising on either side. Somesville, at the head of the sound, is a perfect white clapboard village. Northeast Harbor, on the east side of the sound's entrance, is a posh yachting center. You can hop a ferry here for the Cranberry Isles, which command superb views of the mountains and harbor small villages of fishermen and summer communities of artists and academics. Southwest Harbor, on the west side of Somes Sound, makes a good base for exploring nearby mountains and lakes.

Stonington. Stonington, at the southern tip of Deer Isle, is a working fishing village of weathered houses clinging to a rocky hill. Main Street has a scattering of gift shops and galleries, which look a bit incongruous in this rough port town. The real draw of Stonington is its working waterfront, a jumble of piers, lobster co-ops, warehouses, and views of the archipelago of tiny, spruce-clad islands known as Merchants Row.

Beaches

The **Sand Beach** off the Park Loop Road on Mount Desert Island has mountains rising behind it and hiking trails departing from its east end. The crowds on hot summer days can be forbidding. **Echo Lake,** near Southwest Harbor, offers freshwater swimming.

Tourist Information

Acadia National Park (Box 177, Bar Harbor, ME 04609, tel. 207/288–3338 or 207/288–4932); **Bar Harbor Chamber of Commerce** (Box BC, Cottage St., Bar Harbor, ME 04609, tel. 207/288–5103, mid-May–mid-Oct. tel. 207/288–3393); **Mount Desert Chamber of Commerce** (Box 675, Northeast Harbor, ME 04662, tel. 207/276–5040); **Deer Isle-Stonington Chamber of Commerce** (Box 268, Stonington, ME 04681, tel. 207/348–6124).

Reservations Services

B&B Down East, Ltd. (Box 547, Macomber Mill Rd., Eastbrook, ME 04634, tel. 207/565–3517); **Peg Tierney, Bed & Breakfast of Maine** (16 Florence St., Portland, ME 04103, tel. 207/775–7808).

Claremont Hotel

Built in 1884 and continuously operated as an inn since then, the Claremont conjures up the atmosphere of the long, slow vacations of days gone by. The imposing yellow four-story clapboard inn, with its satellite guest houses and cottages, commands a spectacular view of Somes Sound, and there is croquet on the lawn (the August tournament is a highlight of the year) and cocktails at the boathouse from mid-July to the end of August. The Claremont's location at the end of a quiet road affords seclusion, though the busy harbor is a short stroll away.

Public rooms may look underfurnished to those whose taste in inns runs to the plush Victorian style of Bar Harbor's Cleftstone Manor or Holbrook House; but the stone fireplaces, wicker, straight-back chairs, and piano in the Claremont's library and sitting room feel just right for Southwest Harbor, which has retained some of the rugged character of a fishing village. John Madeira, Jr., has managed the inn for years for the McCue family, and a large, youthful staff joins him in the summer months.

Guest rooms in the inn are bright, white, and extremely plain. The 12 housekeeping cottages and two guest houses tucked away on the grounds have a more rustic feel. For water views, the inn rooms are unbeatable, and the sight of Somes Sound at dawn turning pale silver through the Claremont's gauzy white curtains is something to remember forever.

The large, rather formal airy dining room (open to the public for dinner), awash in sea light streaming through the picture windows, makes a fine setting in which to plan your day of hikes in the national park, bike rides on the network of carriage paths, sailing on Somes Sound, simply reading on the inn's cool lawn, or meditating on croquet. Modified American Plan (breakfast and dinner included) is required from mid-June through mid-September.

Address: *Box 137, Southwest Harbor, ME 04679, tel. 207/244–5036.*
Accommodations: *17 double rooms with baths, 3 double rooms with hall baths, 3 suites, 12 housekeeping cottages, 2 guest houses.*
Amenities: *Restaurant, library, cable TV in parlor; 1 clay tennis court, croquet, bikes, private dock, 3 rowboats, 10 moorings.*
Rates: *$120–$155; full breakfast. No credit cards.*
Restrictions: *No smoking in guest rooms, no pets. Hotel and dining room closed mid-Sept.–mid-June, cottages closed late Oct.–mid-May.*

Cleftstone Manor

Attention, lovers of Victoriana! This inn was made in high Victorian heaven expressly for you. Ignore the fact that it is set amid sterile motels just off Route 3, the road along which traffic roars into Bar Harbor. Do not be put off by the unpromising, rambling, black-shuttered exterior. Inside, a deeply plush, mahogany and lace world of Victorian splendor awaits you.

An ornately framed portrait of Queen Victoria greets you as you enter the mansion, the former summer home of the Blair family (for whom Washington's Blair House is named). The parlor is cool and richly furnished with red velvet and brocade sofas trimmed with white doilies, grandfather and mantel clocks, and oil paintings hanging on powder-blue walls. In the imposingly formal dining room, Joseph Pulitzer's library table seemingly extends for miles beneath a crystal chandelier.

Of the guest rooms, the prize chamber (especially for honeymooners) is the immense Romeo and Juliet, once a section of the ballroom, which now has a pillow-decked sofa; blue velvet Victorian chairs; a lace-canopy bed; a massive, ornately carved Irish buffet that takes up most of one wall; and a handsome, dark-wood fireplace. There's more light in Hampton Court, a suite, with wicker furniture in its sitting room, a four-poster bed, and a working fireplace. Smaller and simpler is the inappropriately named Oscar Wilde, with a brass and white-iron bed and green and rose wallpaper.

Innkeepers Pattie and Don Reynolds are far more youthful and far less formal than their surroundings. Don, originally from Louisiana, is an Air National Guard pilot. When the Reynoldses moved to Bangor in 1974, Don and Pattie had a great time renovating old homes, so getting involved with the Cleftstone seemed a logical next step.

The inn is convenient to Bar Harbor, 2 miles down the road, and to all the hiking, boating, biking, and beaching opportunities afforded by Acadia National Park.

Address: *Rte. 3, Eden St., Bar Harbor, ME 04609, tel. 207/288–4951 or 800/962–9762.*
Accommodations: *14 double rooms with baths, 2 suites.*
Amenities: *3 rooms with fireplaces.*
Rates: *$98–$185; full breakfast, afternoon tea, evening wine and cheese. D, MC, V.*
Restrictions: *No smoking, no pets. 2-night minimum in summer; closed Nov.–Apr.*

Holbrook House

The Holbrook House offers a far more restrained (and more authentic) approach to Victorian interior design than the Cleftstone Manor. Jean and Jack Ochtera, corporate refugees from Massachusetts, bought the house in 1990 and became innkeepers in order to spend more time with each other.

Built in 1876 as a boardinghouse with a wraparound porch for rocking and big shuttered windows to catch the breeze, the lemon-yellow Holbrook House sits right on Mount Desert Street, the main access route through Bar Harbor. In 1876 it was no doubt pleasant to listen to the horses clip-clop past, but today, the traffic noise can be annoying, especially from the porch.

The downstairs public rooms include a lovely, formal sitting room with bright, summery chintz on chairs and windows, a Duncan Phyfe sofa upholstered in white silk damask, and an antique Victorian organ. China, crystal, and crisp linen add an elegant touch to the sunny, glassed-in porch, where a full breakfast is served.

The guest rooms are furnished with lovingly handled family pieces in the same refined taste as the public rooms. Room 6, on the second floor, has a corner location with four big windows, a four-poster bed, and oil paintings. Though smaller, Room 11, with its Laura Ashley fabrics, is the quietest room, and has a snug, country feel.

Right in town, Holbrook House is a short walk to the shops and restaurants of Bar Harbor, with the wonders of Acadia and the sea spread out all around. A stay at the Holbrook House is like a visit with your most proper (but by no means stuffy) relatives, the ones who inherited all the best furniture and have kept it in impeccable condition.

Address: *74 Mt. Desert St., Bar Harbor, ME 04609, tel. 207/288–4970.*
Accommodations: *10 double rooms with baths in inn, 2 doubles share 1 bath and living room in Lupine cottage, 2 doubles share 1 bath and living room in Fern Cottage.*
Amenities: *Cable TV in library and in cottages; croquet.*
Rates: *$110–$175; full breakfast and afternoon tea. MC, V.*
Restrictions: *No smoking, no pets. 2-night minimum, closed mid-Oct.–Apr.*

Pilgrim's Inn

The pleasures of Deer Isle—back roads and tidal coves, pink granite and dark green spruce, sleepy villages and unspoiled fishing harbors—sink in slowly, and so does the special charm of the Pilgrim's Inn. The place looks pleasant enough at first sight—a barn-red, four-story, gambrel-roofed house, circa 1793, set just a few feet from the road, with a millpond out back and the harbor across the way. But a stay at the Pilgrim's Inn is more than pleasant. Its specialness has to do with the sweet aroma of bread and cakes baking that greets you at the door, with the way the light reflects off the water, with the simplicity and appropriateness of the furnishings, with the bright splashes of flower beds set in green lawns, and, of course, with its hospitable owners.

Innkeepers Jean and Dud Hendrick have lots of experience working with people. Dud was the lacrosse coach at Dartmouth for 13 years, and Jean has a background both in counseling and in working with food. When they got married they wanted a job they could do together, and they found it here. They have brought a spirit of ease, warmth, and unerring good taste to the Pilgrim's Inn.

The inn's formal parlor, just off the front entrance, is cool and stylish, with beige Oriental rugs and pale sofas, but guests tend to congregate downstairs in the rustic taproom with huge fireplaces, pine furniture, braided rugs, parson's benches, and a bay window overlooking the pond.

The water is visible from nearly all the guest rooms, which have English fabrics and generous proportions. Favorites include No. 8 on the second floor, with country pine furniture, a tall headboard, and three bright windows, and No. 5, with a cherry four-poster bed, cherry chest of drawers, and burgundy-and-white color scheme.

The attached barn has been converted to a dining room, a big open space that succeeds in being rustic and romantic at the same time, with original barn-wood walls, farm implements on display, and tiny windows overlooking the pond. Repeat guests to the inn are rewarded with a complimentary gift package of locally produced jellies, but one hardly needs that incentive to return.

Address: *Deer Isle, ME 04627, tel. 207/348-6615.*
Accommodations: *8 double rooms with baths, 4 doubles and 1 single share 2 baths, 1 housekeeping cottage.*
Amenities: *Restaurant.*
Rates: *$136–$190; full breakfast and dinner. No credit cards.*
Restrictions: *No smoking in bedrooms, no pets. Closed mid-Oct.–mid-May.*

Eggemoggin Inn

Though the guest rooms with their hooked rugs and odds and ends of yard-sale furniture are a bit dowdy and the public rooms have the look of a 1955 farmhouse, the secluded location on Little Deer Isle in a knobby clearing overlooking Eggemoggin Reach is ample compensation. The Pumpkin Island lighthouse, the seabirds, and the yachts cruising the Reach are your nearest neighbors. The wide-porched house was built as a private estate at the turn of the century, and Sophie Broadhead has run it as an inn since 1964.

The finest room is on the second floor, a spacious retreat with a single bed, a double bed, and a sun deck. Children are welcome, and a crib is available. The inn makes a good base for long biking rambles around Deer Isle or jaunts down to the shops and galleries of Stonington and Deer Isle Village. Here you'll find a little pocket of old-time hospitality in a place where Laura Ashley still fears to tread.

Address: *Little Deer Isle, ME 04627, tel. 207/348–2540.*
Accommodations: *2 double rooms with baths, 8 rooms share bath.*
Amenities: *Fridge for use of guests.*
Rates: *$45–$65; Continental breakfast. No credit cards.*
Restrictions: *No pets. Closed late Oct.–Memorial Day.*

Inn at Canoe Point

Those in search of seclusion, intimacy, and privacy will find it at this snug, 1889 Tudor-style house in a superb location, pinned between rocky shore and woods at Hulls Cove, only 2 miles from Bar Harbor. Innkeeper Don Johnson fell in love with Mount Desert Island when he worked here one summer while in college, and he vowed to return for good someday. He fulfilled his vow a decade ago with an inn at Southwest Harbor, and then five years ago he acquired the property of his dreams on Hulls Cove.

The Master Suite, a large room with a fireplace, is the favorite of most guests, for its size and its French doors opening onto a waterside deck. The Garden Room, though smaller, has windows on three sides, with both water and woods views, and a private entrance. The inn's large living room has huge windows looking out on the water, a fieldstone fireplace, and, just outside, a deck that hangs out over the water.

Address: *Hulls Cove (Box 216, Rte. 3, Bar Harbor, ME 04609), tel. 207/288–9511.*
Accommodations: *3 double rooms with baths, 2 suites.*
Amenities: *Cable TV in common room, guest phone; private beach.*
Rates: *$150–$250; full breakfast and decanters of port or sherry in guest rooms. No credit cards.*
Restrictions: *No smoking preferred, no pets.*

The Inn at Southwest

Grandest of the three Main Street inns, the gray, mansard-roofed, three-story Inn at Southwest is a genuine Victorian relic, complete with gingerbread touches on the porch, high ceilings, and solid-to-the-core construction. Innkeepers Kathy and Ted Combs, who hail from Westport, Connecticut, and careers in real estate (hers) and microbiology (his), have preserved the old-time aura of the downstairs with lace curtains and a mahogany baby grand piano, while enlivening the bedrooms with such up-to-date touches as Impressionist museum posters.

The atmosphere here is a touch relaxed and comfy. Guest rooms are done in cheerful flowered prints. The beds have good brass reading lamps, and the superior rooms, such as No. 3, are large and bright and contain amusing objects, such as antique bird cages and old dollhouses. Rooms 8 and 9 on the third floor have chapel windows lit by the afternoon sun.

Address: *Box 593, Southwest Harbor, ME 04679, tel. 207/244–3835.*
Accommodations: *9 double rooms with baths.*
Amenities: *Cable TV in living room, communal fridge.*
Rates: *$70–$105; full breakfast and afternoon tea. AE, D, MC, V.*
Restrictions: *No smoking, no pets. 2-night minimum on holiday weekends; closed Nov.–Easter.*

The Island House

Ann Gill, certainly one of the sweetest and most tactful people in the bed-and-breakfast business, makes the Island House in Southwest Harbor a truly special place to stay. Sitting in her snug living room with its wide-plank pumpkin-pine floor and Oriental rugs, Ann loves to recount the history of how her white clapboard house near the harbor was once a grand inn, the first on the island, and how it shrank over the years. She moved in back in 1969 and began taking in guests 15 years later.

The simple, pretty bedrooms are full of air and light, with such plain, old-fashioned Maine touches as white-painted furniture and gauzy white curtains. The carriage house is great for honeymooners, with a loft bed, skylight, serene treetop view, and new kitchenette.

Address: *Box 1006, Southwest Harbor, ME 04679, tel. 207/244–5180.*
Accommodations: *4 double rooms share 3 baths, 1 carriage-house suite.*
Amenities: *Cable TV in parlor and in carriage house.*
Rates: *$60–$95; full breakfast. No credit cards.*
Restrictions: *No smoking; no pets.*

The Kingsleigh Inn

Of Southwest Harbor's three Main Street inns, the bright, cheerful, immaculately kept Kingsleigh has the best harbor views. In the Turret Suite you can recline on a wicker love seat and gaze down on the yachts and lobster boats below (the room is even equipped with a telescope). From softly feminine Room 5, you can glimpse the harbor from bed, but the bedrooms on the street side are darker and lack the view.

Even without the view, this would be a superior inn for its lack of clutter and for the tasteful country decor, with wrought-iron bedsteads, wreaths, and comforters.

Innkeepers Nancy and Tom Cervelli were refugees in 1990 from the New York rat race who wanted to be near the mountains and harbors of Acadia. They are clearly delighted with their change of gears and of locale.

Address: *100 Main St., Box 1426, Southwest Harbor, ME 04679, tel. 207/244–5302.*
Accommodations: *7 double rooms with baths, 1 suite.*
Amenities: *Cable TV in suite.*
Rates: *$85–$155; full breakfast and afternoon refreshments. AE, D, MC, V.*
Restrictions: *No smoking, no pets.*

Manor House Inn

The rambling, yellow Manor House Inn (circa 1887) sits well back from shaded, residential West Street, a quieter location than most of the other Bar Harbor inns, yet only a stone's throw from the harbor and the town's shops and restaurants.

Malcolm Noyes and James Dennison bought the inn in 1989, and their renovations have brought it back to its turn of the century splendor. The double parlor fairly gleams, with its polished wood floor, Oriental rugs, baby grand piano, and dappled light. Suite A in the renovated chauffeur's cottage, behind the inn, is the best room, with a king-size bed and swag curtains. Number 5 in the inn is very large, with a marble-top dresser, wicker furniture, and an ornately carved headboard. Two rustic housekeeping cottages lack the inn's old-fashioned decor.

Address: *West St., Bar Harbor, ME 04609, tel. 207/288–3759 or 800/437–0088.*
Accommodations: *9 rooms with baths in inn, 3 suites in chauffeur's cottage, 2 housekeeping cottages each sleep 3.*
Amenities: *TV in common room, fireplace or wood stove in 4 rooms, cable TV in housekeeping cottages.*
Rates: *$85–$175; full breakfast. AE, MC, V.*
Restrictions: *No smoking, pets restricted. 2-night minimum July–Aug., closed mid-Nov.–Mar.*

Mira Monte

Built as a private summer home in 1864, the Mira Monte has all the trappings of Victorian leisure, including columned verandas and spacious grounds. Marian Burns, one of the very few native innkeepers in Bar Harbor, knows Acadia intimately, having spent a lifetime hiking in the park and helping to establish the Wild Gardens of Acadia. Her own knack for gardening shows up in the lush flower beds, formal and informal, that surround the inn.

Guest rooms have four-poster beds, gilt mirrors, and velvet fainting couches, but the decor comes off as rather a hodgepodge, lacking the refinement of the Holbrook House or the stateliness of the Cleftstone. Advantages here include private balconies (in many rooms), double-pane windows to cut down on road noise, some fireplaces, and fresh flowers in rooms.

Address: *69 Mt. Desert St., Bar Harbor, ME 04609, tel. 207/288–4263 or 800/553–5109, fax 207/288–3115.*
Accommodations: *11 double rooms with baths.*
Amenities: *Air-conditioning, VCR in library, cable TV and phones in rooms, working fireplaces in 8 rooms, balconies in 7.*
Rates: *$90–$140; full buffet breakfast and afternoon refreshments.*
Restrictions: *Smoking limited. 2-night minimum, closed late Oct.–early May.*

Moorings Inn

Manset, on the quiet, western side of Mount Desert Island, is a boatyard, a restaurant, a little collection of summer homes, and this inn, all situated on a bumpy road that runs along one of the most spectacular stretches of waterfront in Maine. The view of Somes Sound and the mountains of Acadia is reason enough to stay here; the total absence of bustle or commercialism is another.

Leslie and Betty King have owned the Moorings for a quarter-century now, and they bring not only a wealth of hotel experience (Leslie's family has been running inns for four generations), but also a wealth of treasures from local auctions. They are also keen bird-watchers.

The Moorings is really a mix of accommodations—country-style rooms in the main house (four have balconies), housekeeping cottages, and a small motel wing. Nothing is fancy except the view.

Address: *Shore Rd., Box 744, Southwest Harbor, ME 04679, tel. 207/244–5523.*
Accommodations: *2 single rooms with baths, 3 double rooms with baths, and 4 double suites in inn, 3 motel rooms, 3 cottages (including 1 with 3 units).*
Amenities: *TV in living room and in cottages, kitchenettes in motel rooms, fireplaces in cottages; bikes, canoes, pier, outdoor gas grills.*
Rates: *$45–$90; coffee, orange juice, and doughnuts. No credit cards.*
Restrictions: *No smoking, no pets. Closed Nov.–mid-May.*

Penury Hall Bed 'n Breakfast

Of the cluster of bed-and-breakfasts that sit together on Southwest Harbor's Main Street, Penury Hall is the smallest and the homiest. Gretchen and Toby Strong, the owners, are an older couple who have lived and worked in places ranging from Vermont to Missouri, in jobs ranging from garbage collection to a college dean of students. Gretchen gardens, collects art, and serves as the town manager for the town of Tremont. Toby loves to sail.

The Strongs' philosophy is that guests become honorary members of their family, and they really make them feel like long-lost relatives. The house has a lived-in and not too tidy feel, with carved birds on the mantel, minimal decor in the bedrooms, and Patches, a large Maine coon cat, in evidence. Loyal adherents reserve two months in advance and come for the good company, the huge breakfasts, and the copious advice on hiking, biking, canoeing, boat rental, beaches, and lighthouses, on the quiet side of Mount Desert. The small sauna is great in winter.

Address: *Box 68, Southwest Harbor, ME 04679, tel. 207/244–7102.*
Accommodations: *3 double rooms share 2 baths.*
Amenities: *TV in living room, washer and dryer; sauna, canoe, sailboat.*
Rates: *$60; full breakfast. MC, V accepted; personal checks preferred.*
Restrictions: *Smoking limited. 2-night minimum June–Sept.*

Around Sebago Lake

The first sign of Maine's lake country appears less than half an hour from Portland: peacock blue mountains ascending at the end of a long, gleaming runway of water; the soft, graceful boughs of white pines interlaced along the shore; a lone canoe leaving its wake across the reflections of cumulus clouds. Because Maine tapers to a point at its south end, the Sebago–Long Lake region is just 40 miles northwest of Portland, and the Oxford Hills area an additional dozen miles to the north. Though the lakes and hills seem a world away from the coast, you can, in fact, dip into them on a day trip.

Summer, of course, is the prime season for the region, when the morning cries of the loons are quickly drowned out by the buzz of motorboats and waterskiers, and boats line up to pass through Songo Lock, connecting Long Lake with Sebago Lake, creating a 42-mile inland waterway. Fisherfolk crowd the lake shores in pursuit of trout and salmon, and highways thicken with traffic, particularly on July and August weekends when parents visit their children at the many local camps.

Winter is a more contemplative time of year here. Downhill skiers have their choice of Shawnee Peak, just 6 miles west of Bridgton, or the larger Sunday River Ski Resort near Bethel, at the northern fringe of the region. Cross-country skiers can head off just about anywhere—across frozen lakes or onto the fields fringing the perfect small town of Waterford, a National Historic District where white clapboards and green shutters are mandatory. Though Waterford and its sister towns of North, South, and East Waterford don't offer much to do aside from basking on small lake beaches in summer, gazing at hillsides ablaze with foliage in fall, cross-country skiing in winter, and swatting blackflies in spring, it really doesn't matter. One comes here, as to the Cotswolds in England, for the serenity of being in picturesque surroundings in which one can relax without mad dashes to cathedrals or to four-star views.

As you meander west and north, the Oxford Hills give way to the mightier and loftier White Mountains, which reach their apex across the border in New Hampshire's Presidential Range. The Maine side, however, may well command the finest view, especially just around sunset. When the sun descends into the jagged mountaintops, it doesn't matter what season it is. You can congratulate yourself year-round on having found a very special corner of Maine.

Places to Go, Sights to See

Bridgton. Though not a very appealing town in its own right, Bridgton is the antiques center of the region, with a number of shops on Main Street and on the fringes of town.

Center Lovell. Less than 10 miles due west of Waterford is the town of Center Lovell, which perches above the dark water of Kezar Lake. Though you won't see much of the lake from Route 5, the main road through town, you will be rewarded with a magnificent view of the White Mountains.

Kezar Lake, tucked away in a fold of the White Mountains, has long been a hideaway of the rich and exclusive; more recently a couple of inns have opened this unspoiled scenery to visitors. The lake is the backyard of Westways, a former executive retreat where you can dine or spend the night (*see* below).

Sabbathday Lake Shaker Museum (Rte. 26, New Gloucester, tel. 207/926–4597). Though a bit off the beaten track, the museum is worth a detour for its displays of Shaker architecture and design, including the 1794 meeting house, tools, farm implements, furniture, and crafts in tin, textile, and wood. The Shaker Community at Sabbathday Lake is one of the oldest and most active remaining in the United States and the last one in Maine. Members continue to raise vegetables and culinary and medicinal herbs.

Songo Lock. Near Naples, the Songo Lock (tel. 207/693–6231), 2½ miles south of Route 302 on Songo Locks Road, permits passage from Sebago Lake to Long Lake by way of the Songo River and the Brandy Pond. It is the only surviving lock of the Cumberland-Oxford Canal.

Waterford is a National Historic District and the most picturesque of the collection of villages known as the Waterfords. It's so small you can stroll all around town in no time—from the Congregational Church, past the general store, to the small sand beach on Keoka Lake.

Beaches

Sebago Lake State Park (tel. 207/693–6613 June 20–Labor Day, tel. 207/693–6231 Labor Day–June 19), on the north shore of Sebago Lake, attracts anglers. It has a large sand beach and a separate camping area, as well as boat ramps.

Restaurants

The Lake House (Waterford, tel. 207/583–4182) features creative American cuisine.

Tourist Information

Bethel Area Chamber of Commerce (Box 121, Bethel, ME 04217, tel. 207/824–2282); **Bridgton–Lakes Region Chamber of Commerce** (Box 236, Bridgton, ME 04009, tel. 207/647–3472); **Naples Business Association** (Box 412, Naples, ME 04055, tel. 207/693–3285).

Reservations Services

B&B Down East, Ltd. (Box 547, Macomber Mill Rd., Eastbrook, ME 04634, tel. 207/565–3517); **Peg Tierney B&B of Maine** (16 Florence St., Portland, ME 04103, tel. 207/775–7808); **Bethel Area Chamber of Commerce** (Box 121, Bethel, ME 04217, tel. 207/824–2282).

The Noble House

Set on a hill crest amid massive white pines, looking across Highland Lake to the White Mountains, this grand but utterly unpretentious house was built on a quiet residential street near town by a Maine state senator in 1903 and occupied for 40 years by the town dentist. In 1984 the Starets family, who had roots in Maine, left California to buy the place and convert it into one of the most refined, welcoming bed-and-breakfasts in the region.

Jane Starets runs the inn with her husband, Dick (when he isn't at work as a commercial pilot), and the summertime help of their four children. She is a soft-spoken woman whose good sense and good taste show up in the subdued, rather simple decor. You cross the wide porch to enter a simply appointed parlor with a comfortable sofa and wing chairs, dominated by a grand piano. Behind it is the dining room, where abundant breakfasts (fruit, eggs, blueberry pancakes, waffles, muffins, and breads) are served family style on china and linen, with the family's silver on the sideboard.

The guest rooms don't quite measure up to the elegance of the public rooms: Most are small and a bit spartan in their furnishings, with floral bedspreads, some quilts, and such corny touches as crossed skis hanging on the walls. The Honeymoon Room, however, has a good lake view, a whirlpool bath (as do three other rooms), white wicker furniture, and fresh flowers. The Staples Suite on the third floor offers the most space, privacy, and quiet, with white wicker furniture and fabrics in greens and browns.

A real asset of The Noble House is the dock across the street on Highland Lake, with chairs and a hammock and the view of Mount Washington and the Presidential Range rising in the distance. "There is a certain magic about being on a lake," comments Jane, "and we've grown very partial to ours." Noble House is a fine place to develop your own partiality for Highland Lake and a good base for exploring the antiques shops of Bridgton and for day trips to Sebago or Long Lake, the nearby Oxford Hills, or even up to the White Mountain National Forest.

Address: *Box 180, Bridgton, ME 04009, tel. 207/647–3733.*
Accommodations: *6 double rooms with baths, 3 doubles share 1 bath.*
Amenities: *TV in lounge; floating dock for swimming, croquet, canoe, paddleboat.*
Rates: *$70–$115; full breakfast. AE, V.*
Restrictions: *No pets. 2-night minimum on weekends, open only with advance reservations mid-Oct.–mid-June.*

The Waterford Inne

The tiny white-clapboard and green-shuttered villages known as the Waterfords boast a fine collection of country inns, but the Waterford Inne stands out for its breezy hilltop location and for its warmly convivial owners, Barbara and Rosalie Vanderzanden, a mother-and-daughter innkeeping team.

Back in the mid-1970s Barbara and Rosalie were schoolteachers in New Jersey and avid world travelers when they decided they wanted a change of lifestyle and geography. As Barbara tells it, they had been looking all over Maine, when a real-estate agent showed them what was to become the Waterford Inne. They made an offer on the spot. "It was the feeling of the house that settled it," Barbara reminisces.

The property had been a dairy farm back in the 1820s, and 40 years later a prominent lumber family bought it. With open fields all around the house, huge pine trees fringing the fields, an orchard out back, and a big red barn off to the side, the place retains vestiges of its farming heritage and its decades serving as a wealthy family's hideaway.

Barbara and Rosalie have done a superb job of renovating the gold-painted, curry-trimmed house. The sitting room is cozy, with dried flowers hanging from exposed beams, a sofa facing the fireplace, and barnwood walls. In the more formal parlor they display china and antiques and a collection of Quimper plates.

The bedrooms, each furnished on a different theme, have lots of nooks and crannies. Nicest are the Nantucket Room with whale wallpaper and a harpoon, and the Chesapeake Room, with a private porch, fireplace, pumpkin-pine floors, a king-size bed, and ducks, ducks, ducks. A converted wood shed has five additional rooms, and though they have slightly less character than the inn rooms, four of them have the compensation of sunny decks.

The Vanderzandens enjoy trading travel tips with their guests and directing them to local lakes, ski trails, and antiques shops. They will prepare elaborate dinners by prior arrangement. Pets are welcome, but there is an extra charge.

Address: *Box 149, Waterford, ME 04088, tel. 207/583–4037.*
Accommodations: *6 double rooms with baths, 3 doubles share 1 bath, 1 suite.*
Amenities: *TV in common room; apple picking in orchard, antiques shop in barn, cross-country ski trails, ice-skating pond, badminton.*
Rates: *$60–$90; breakfast extra. AE.*
Restrictions: *No smoking in dining room.*

Westways

Built in the 1920s as a corporate retreat for the president and executives of the Diamond Match Company, Westways on Kezar Lake was opened to the public as a sumptuous, secluded hotel in 1975. A stay here today is like a visit with relatives everyone hopes for—rich, discreet, and very generous.

Kezar Lake, the secret of a small set of exclusive summer people, brims literally at the back door of the gray-shingled main lodge (10 privately owned cottages, rented by the week through the inn, are tucked away on the densely wooded grounds). The rustic splendor continues inside in a palatial living room with massive stone fireplace, wood floors, and overstuffed easy chairs. The inn is suffused with a dim, silvery light reflected off the lake and filtered through the surrounding pines. It is restful in the height of summer, though it can be a touch somber for those who prefer bright sunshine.

The Horses Room, a large, masculine room decorated with fox-hunt prints and maple furniture, has the best lake view. The Maple Room, in the southwest corner, is another choice room, with Italian Renaissance prints, floral bedspreads, and water views from all windows. The East Wing rooms, once the servants' quarters, are smaller (but by no means cramped), more spartan in their furniture, and less expensive.

The dining room (open to the public for dinner by reservation) is a glassed-in porch facing the lake, where hearty meals are served on china and linen. Aside from enjoying water sports at your back door, you can also go on hikes in the surrounding White Mountains, antiquing forays down to Bridgton, and even rafting trips on the Saco River.

Address: *Box 175, Center Lovell, ME 04016, tel. 207/928–2663.*
Accommodations: *3 double rooms with baths, 4 doubles share 3 hall baths, 10 cottages with 3, 4, or 7 bedrooms.*
Amenities: *1 clay tennis court; lake swimming and boating; recreation hall with bowling, ping-pong, billiards; softball field; fives court; 2 canoes.*
Rates: *$99–$159, cottages $800–$1650 per week; Continental breakfast. MC, V.*
Restrictions: *No pets in inn. Closed Nov and Mar.–Apr.*

Inn at Long Lake

From the outside, the Inn at Long Lake has an old-fashioned air. The three-story grayish beige and burgundy-trimmed building, built as an inn in 1900, sits on a hillside just off Route 302, the main route through the lake town of Naples. Inside, the old-fashioned feel has been tempered somewhat by plush carpeting throughout, air-conditioning, uncluttered bedrooms, and soda and ice machines.

Irene and Maynard Hincks lived in Pittsfield, Massachusetts, for 25 years and have returned to their home state to become innkeepers. They were delighted to find that the Inn at Long Lake needed very little renovation. The guest rooms, all named after barges, include the superior Freeport, which has views of the lake and a birch four-poster bed, and the softly romantic Sebago Room, with gray and pink wallpaper and white wicker furniture.

The inn's location off the main road ensures quiet, and you are within walking distance of the busy Naples Causeway for boating trips on Long Lake and through the Songo Lock.

Address: *Lake House Rd., Box 806, Naples, ME 04055, tel. 207/693–6226 or 800/437–0328.*
Accommodations: *14 double rooms with baths, 2 suites.*
Amenities: *Air-conditioning and TV in all rooms.*
Rates: *$75–$110; Continental breakfast. AE, D, MC, V.*
Restrictions: *No smoking in bedrooms, no pets.*

Kedarburn Inn

The Kedarburn is about as close as you can get to experiencing a real English bed-and-breakfast without crossing the Atlantic. Margaret and Derek Gibson used to run an inn in Bournemouth, and when they bought the rambling white clapboard house in 1988, they did it over with cheery floral wallpapers, bright quilts and pillows (made by Margaret), bowls of potpourri, and knickknacks in abundance. The Balcony Room is popular with families, and cribs are available.

With a colorful flower garden outside, a small deck, Kedar Brook gurgling past, two dogs (your own pets are welcome, too), and a town location near Lake Keoka, the Kedarburn Inn scores very high indeed on genteel comfort.

Two bits of England especially dear to guests are the high teas, complete with biscuits and tea sandwiches, and the English pub, complete with darts.

Address: *Rte. 35, Box 61, Waterford, ME 04088, tel. 207/583–6182.*
Accommodations: *5 double rooms with baths, 2 doubles share 2 baths, 1 suite.*
Amenities: *Pub, TV in parlor, crafts shop.*
Rates: *$69–$80; full breakfast. MC, V.*
Restrictions: *No smoking.*

Lake House

Though not actually on a lake, the Lake House is near several (Keoka Lake is a stone's throw away and Long Lake is 5 miles south) and it's right in the middle of the tiny, postcard-pretty town of Waterford. The most Victorian in style of the area inns, the Lake House has a carpenter-gothic front with a pleasant screened porch and guest rooms that some may find a touch cluttered.

The oddest, but also the finest, room in the house for space and light is the Grand Ballroom Suite, with a four-poster bed, stained pine floor, and bathtub open to the room. The Waterford Flat Suite has a gray-painted floor and small sitting area with lots of books.

Suzanne and Michael Uhl-Myers moved to Maine from Massachusetts in 1976, right out of college. They wanted careers that would give them time together and a chance to putter around the house. The Lake House suits their needs perfectly. The restaurant, open to the public for dinner, serves creative fare in a romantic setting.

Address: *Rtes. 35 and 37, Waterford, ME 04088, tel. 207/583–4182 or 800/223–4182.*
Accommodations: *4 double rooms with baths, 1 cottage.*
Amenities: *Restaurant, fireplace in sitting room, coffeemakers in guest rooms.*
Rates: *$79–$129; full breakfast; MAP available. MC, V.*
Restrictions: *No smoking, no pets.*

Sebago Lake Lodge & Cottages

This is an old-fashioned, unpretentious inn with a superb location right on Sebago Lake, only 18 miles from Portland. It's the kind of place fathers bring their sons to for fishing trips and where families hold reunions and cookouts.

Chip and Debra Lougee, originally from Portland, bought the lodge in the early 1980s. Though they had no previous experience in innkeeping, they brought a relaxed, easygoing style, a love of the lake, and considerable boating know-how. Inn rooms are plain and simple, with pine or maple furniture, white curtains, and lake views. Nine cottages, rented by the week, have screened porches and sit even closer to the shore. Pets are welcome in the cottages at an extra charge.

Address: *White's Bridge Rd., North Windham, ME 04062, tel. 207/892–2698.*
Accommodations: *8 double rooms with baths, 4 doubles share 2 baths, 9 1- and 2-bedroom housekeeping cottages.*
Amenities: *Wood stoves and fireplaces in cottages, kitchenettes in 10 rooms in inn, TV in 8 rooms; private dock, waterskiing, free use of canoes and rowboats, gift and tackle shop.*
Rates: *$48–$95, cottages $385–$600 per week; Continental breakfast. AE, MC, V.*
Restrictions: *2-night minimum on weekends July–Labor Day.*

Off the Beaten Track

Country Club Inn

If you play golf or ski, you'll be in heaven here; this 1920s retreat was built by a millionaire sportsman on a hilltop next to the Mingo Springs Golf Course, overlooking Rangeley Lake and the mountains. The inn has a rustic, baronial splendor, most apparent in the living room with its cathedral ceiling and fieldstone fireplaces.

Sue and the late Robert Crory, originally from Michigan, had always dreamed of having their own inn, and they lucked into this one in the mid-1970s. Sue now runs the inn with the help of her daughter and son-in-law, Margie and Steve Jamison. The spotless, sparsely decorated guest rooms all face the lake and the mountains. Those downstairs in the main building are more desirable than those in the separate motel-style wing. The light and airy dining room is open to the public for dinner. Pets are allowed (at extra charge).

Address: *Box 680, Mingo Loop Rd., Rangeley, ME 04970, tel. 207/864–3831.*
Accommodations: *19 double rooms with baths.*
Amenities: *Restaurant, TV in lobby, lounge; pool, public golf course next door.*
Rates: *$98; full breakfast, MAP available. AE, MC, V.*
Restrictions: *Closed mid-Oct.–Dec. 26, Apr.–mid-May.*

The Crocker House Inn

Once one of 70 inns in the thriving summer community of Hancock Point, this century-old, shingle-style cottage amid tall fir trees sat abandoned for 20 years before Richard Malaby rescued it in 1980, and, he's been restoring it ever since. The living room has a nice country feel to it, although the furniture is worn. Guest rooms in the main inn are simply decorated with a mix of country furniture, oak and iron beds, oak washstands, white tie-back curtains, Martha Washington bedspreads, and stenciling. The carriage house has two additional rooms which have a more modern feel, as well as a TV room, small library, and large Jacuzzi. The inn's dining room serves up a full breakfast and is also open for dinner.

The Crocker House is a good jumping off point for excursions to Acadia's Schoodic Point and spots further up the coast.

Address: *Hancock Point Rd., Hancock, ME 04640, tel. 207/422–6806.*
Accommodations: *9 double rooms with baths in main house, 2 doubles with baths in carriage house.*
Amenities: *Restaurant, TV room, Jacuzzi.*
Rates: *$80–$95; full breakfast; MAP available. AE, D, MC, V.*
Restrictions: *Closed Jan.–Apr., part time Nov.–Dec.*

Le Domaine

Nine miles east of Ellsworth, standing on an otherwise rural stretch of Route 1, you will find a little slice of French sophistication that is as welcome as it is improbable. Although Le Domaine is known primarily for its restaurant, the French country-style rooms, done in chintz and wicker, with simple desks and sofas near the windows, are inviting.

Nicole L. Purslow, owner and chef, trained at the Cordon Bleu and apprenticed in Switzerland. Here in the Maine countryside she whips up classic haute cuisine dishes, the perfect accompaniments to which are bound to be hiding amid the more than 6,000 bottles in the inn's wine cellar. Meals are served in an elegant dining room.

Though guest rooms are on the small side, the inn owns 100 acres with paths, and there's badminton on the lawn. Four rooms have balconies or porches over the gardens. The inn is situated halfway between Mount Desert Island and Schoodic Point, another part of Acadia National Park.

Address: *Box 496, Hancock, ME 04640, tel. 207/422–3395.*
Accommodations: *7 double rooms with private baths.*
Amenities: *Restaurant, radios and fruit in rooms.*
Rates: *$200 MAP (dinner and Continental breakfast; 20% reduction for B&B). AE, D, MC, V.*
Restrictions: *No pets. Closed Nov.–Apr.*

Directory 1: *Alphabetical*

G

H

I

J

K

L

M

V

W

Y

Directory 2: *Geographical*

New Hampshire

Rhode Island

Vermont